EXCAVATIONS AT SANTO DOMINGO TOMALTEPEC: EVOLUTION OF A FORMATIVE COMMUNITY IN THE VALLEY OF OAXACA, MEXICO

Frontispiece. The Rio Tomaltepec flows through the piedmont of the northern Tlacolula valley. The site of Tomaltepec appears in the black rectangle at center.

MEMOIRS OF THE MUSEUM OF ANTHROPOLOGY
UNIVERSITY OF MICHIGAN
NUMBER 12

PREHISTORY AND HUMAN ECOLOGY
OF THE VALLEY OF OAXACA

Kent V. Flannery and Richard E. Blanton
General Editors

Volume 6

EXCAVATIONS AT SANTO DOMINGO TOMALTEPEC:
EVOLUTION OF A FORMATIVE COMMUNITY IN THE
VALLEY OF OAXACA, MEXICO

by

MICHAEL E. WHALEN

ANN ARBOR
1981

© 1981 Regents of The University of Michigan
The Museum of Anthropology
All rights reserved

Printed in the
United States of America

ISBN 0-932206-86-7

AN INTRODUCTION TO VOLUME 6 OF THE SERIES

By Kent V. Flannery

This *Memoir* is the sixth in our series of final volumes on the University of Michigan Museum of Anthropology project, "The Prehistory and Human Ecology of the Valley of Oaxaca." It is also the second volume in our series to include an archaeological site report. In it, Michael E. Whalen describes the developmental history of the Formative site of Santo Domingo Tomaltepec.

Tomaltepec was the first Early Formativae site to be discovered in the tributary canyon of the piedmont zone in the Valley of Oaxaca, away from the major river floodplain setting in which we had previously found all our early village sites. Because of its different location, Tomaltepec piqued our curiosity. It was tested by Henry T. Wright and Susan H. Lees in 1969, and again by Wright in 1972. Finally, we decided the site deserved more extensive excavation, and this was accomplished by Whalen during 1974. Whalen had previously worked with Robert D. Drennan at Fábrica San José (see Volume 4 of this series) and was ready to take on a village of his own.

Since Whalen's 1974 excavations, a settlement pattern survey of the Tlacolula region directed by Stephen A. Kowalewski (unpublished) has made it clear that the piedmont location chosen by Tomaltepec was one of the two principal settlement choices made by Early Formative villagers in that section of the Valley of Oaxaca. This makes us all the happier that Tomaltepec has been excavated, since it gives us an in-depth look at one representative of an important settlement type.

Tomaltepec is important for other reasons. It produced an abundance of carbonized plant remains which, thanks to a careful study by Judith Smith (Appendix IX), give us a glimpse of the crops grown in the piedmont. These remains include the tepary bean (*Phaseolus acutifolius*), a species recovered from 3000 B.C. levels in the Tehuacán caves, but not previously recorded for Early Formative Oaxaca.

Tomaltepec also greatly increases our sample of Early and Middle Formative houses and the features associated with them. In Appendix X, Charles Spencer examines the best-preserved of these houses in sufficient detail to extend our knowledge of the activity areas within residences.

A unique result of the Tomaltepec work was Whalen's discovery of a large Early Formative cemetery on the outskirts of the village. Included were burials with stone, shell, and magnetite ornaments, as well as ceramics with stylized "Olmec" motifs. Thanks to the collaboration of Richard Wilkinson, the age and sex of every reasonably well-preserved skeleton is now known, making the Tomaltepec cemetery one of the very few for which the reader can obtain a full catalogue of burial information (age, sex, orientation, offerings, etc.). It is perhaps sobering to consider, however, that this cemetery occurred outside the "limits" of the Early Formative site as defined by surface ceramics; one wonders how many others have been missed for that reason.

Tomaltepec is also important because, in contrast to some of the villages previously excavated by our project, it lies outside the immediate sphere of influence of the Early and Middle Formative civic-ceremonial center at San José Mogote. Tomaltepec had its own public buildings, which show both similarities to and differences from the contemporary public buildings at San José Mogote. Evidently Tomaltepec served the western Tlacolula subvalley as a small civic-ceremonial center, in somewhat the same way that Huitzo served the extreme northern Etla subvalley.

In contrast to Huitzo and San José Mogote, however, Tomaltepec did not lose importance after the founding of Monte Albán. Rather, it reached its apogee during Monte Albán Ic, with a complex of public buildings, elite residences, and at least one important tomb. It also may have functioned as a regional center for the production of fine gray pottery, as suggested by a series of what appear to be two-chambered reduced-firing kilns. Tomaltepec lost some political importance in Monte Albán II, but still remained a tertiary or "third-order" civic-ceremonial center with a single two-room temple. The remains of this temple were investigated by

Jane Sallade (Appendix XI), a promising young archaeologist whose recent premature death was a great loss to the field.

In his summary and conclusions, Whalen argues that some of the Late Formative changes at Tomaltepec can only be understood in the light of evolutionary processes which affect at least the whole Tlacolula subvalley, and perhaps the whole of the Valley of Oaxaca and its hinterland. In a sense, therefore, the final chapter of the Tomaltepec story cannot be written until Kowalewski's settlement pattern study of the Tlacolula subvalley has been published, and the regional context for the Tomaltepec civic-ceremonial center placed in sharper focus.

Ann Arbor, Michigan
April 1, 1981

Excavations at Santo Domingo Tomaltepec

TABLE OF CONTENTS

LIST OF TABLES ix

LIST OF FIGURES x

LIST OF PLATES xi

LIST OF APPENDICES xii

ACKNOWLEDGMENTS xiii

CHAPTER
- I. INTRODUCTION 1
  1. The Analytical Perspective and Objectives of the Study 1
  2. The Cultural Setting: The Formative Period in Mesoamerica 3
  3. The Physical Setting: Oaxaca and the Site of Tomaltepec 9
  4. Excavations at Tomaltepec 15

- II. EARLY FORMATIVE OCCUPATION AT TOMALTEPEC: THE TIERRAS LARGAS PHASE 27
  1. The Tierras Largas Phase, *ca.* 1400 B.C.–1150 B.C. 27
  2. Composition of the Community 27
  3. Social Differentiation 31
  4. Subsistence Activities 31
  5. Craft and Exchange Activities 32
  6. Summary 32

- III. EARLY FORMATIVE OCCUPATION AT TOMALTEPEC: THE SAN JOSÉ PHASE 34
  1. The San José Phase, *ca.* 1150 B.C.–850 B.C. 34
  2. Composition of the Community 34
  3. Social Differentiation 58
  4. Subsistence Activities 59
  5. Craft and Exchange Activities 60
  6. Summary and Discussion of the Early Formative Evidence 61

- IV. MIDDLE FORMATIVE OCCUPATION AT TOMALTEPEC: THE ROSARIO PHASE 64
  1. The Rosario Phase 64
  2. Composition of the Community 64

      3. Social Differentiation 73
      4. Subsistence Activities 73
      5. Craft and Exchange Activities 74
      6. Summary 74

  V. MIDDLE FORMATIVE OCCUPATION AT TOMALTEPEC:
     THE MONTE ALBÁN IA PHASE 75
      1. The Monte Albán Ia Phase, *ca.* 450 B.C.–300 B.C. 75
      2. Composition of the Community 75
      3. Social Differentiation 85
      4. Subsistence Activities 87
      5. Craft and Exchange Activities 87
      6. Summary and Discussion of the Middle Formative Evidence 87

  VI. LATE FORMATIVE OCCUPATION AT TOMALTEPEC:
      THE MONTE ALBÁN IC PHASE 87
      1. The Monte Albán Ic Phase, *ca.* 300 B.C.–100 B.C. 88
      2. Composition of the Community 88
      3. Social Differentiation 102
      4. Subsistence Activities 103
      5. Craft and Exchange Activities 103
      6. Summary and Discussion of the Late Formative Evidence 104

  VII. TERMINAL FORMATIVE ABANDONMENT OF TOMALTEPEC:
       THE MONTE ALBÁN II PHASE 106
       1. The Monte Albán II Phase, *ca.* 100 B.C.–A.D. 200 106
       2. Composition of the Community 106
       3. Social Differentiation 108
       4. Subsistence Activities 108
       5. Craft and Exchange Activities 108
       6. Summary and Discussion of the Terminal Formative Evidence 111

  VIII. FORMATIVE PERIOD DEVELOPMENT WITHIN THE VALLEY OF
        OAXACA: A REGIONAL PERSPECTIVE 112
        1. The Early Formative 112
        2. The Middle Formative 112
        3. The Late Formative 113
        4. The Terminal Formative 114
        5. Conclusions 114

APPENDICES 115

REFERENCES 218

Resumen en Español 222

LIST OF TABLES

1. Artifacts Associated with Possible Units TL-1 and TL-2 30
2. Artifact Counts and Distributions Among Known and Possible Early San José Household Units 36
3. Ages and Sexes of Primary Tomaltepec Cemetery Burials 50
4. Age, Sex, and Association of Secondary Burials from the Tomaltepec Cemetery 57
5. Artifact Counts and Distributions Among Known and Possible Rosario Household Units 66
6. Artifact Counts and Distributions Among Known and Possible Monte Albán Ia Household Units 75
7. Artifact Counts and Distributions Among Known and Possible Monte Albán Ic Household Units 90
8. Feature Descriptions 115
9. House and Structure Descriptions 117
10. Distribution and Frequency of Early Formative Wares 119
11. Distribution and Frequency of Early Formative Decorative Techniques 119
12. Distribution and Frequency of Early Formative Vessel Forms 120
13. Variables Used in Figurine Descriptions 155
14. Attributes of Formative Figurines 156
15. Bone from Early Formative Proveniences 169
16. Bone from Middle Formative Proveniences 169
17. Bone from Late Formative Proveniences 170
18. Bone from Terminal Formative Proveniences 170
19. Shell from Tomaltepec 171
20. Ground Stone from Formative Proveniences 175
21. Stone Tools from Early Formative Proveniences 183
22. Charcoal Identifications 187
23. Percentages of Charcoal Species by Phase 188
24. Carbonized *Zea* Remains 188
25. Counts of Carbonized Seeds 189
26. Measurements of Avocado Seeds and Beans 194
27. Least Squares Regression Analysis of Variance of Inter-Category Average Nearest-Neighbor Distance 201
28. Descriptive Measures of Epicenter-To-Item Distances 202
29. Least Squares Regression, House 4: Analysis of Variance of Inter-Category Average Nearest-Neighbor Distance 203
30. Eighteen Categories of Material from Structure 14, Tomaltepec 205
31. Materials Larger Than One Cubic Centimeter and Variable Labels: Densities per 1/20th Cubic Meter 206
32. Materials Smaller Than One Cubic Centimeter and Variable Labels: Densities per 1/20th Cubic Meter 206
33. Western Floor—Seriation of Correlations (Nine Cases, Eighteen Variables) 208
34. Eastern Floor—Seriation of Correlations (Nine Cases, Eighteen Variables) 208
35. Western Floor—Seriation of Rank Orders (Nine Cases, Eleven Selected Variables) 208
36. Eastern Floor—Seriation of Rank Orders (Nine Cases, Eleven Selected Variables) 209
37. Western Floor—Seriation of Rank Orders (Nine Cases, Five Variables) 209
38. Eastern Floor—Seriation of Rank Orders (Nine Cases, Five Variables) 209

LIST OF FIGURES

1. The Valley of Oaxaca, showing archaeological sites mentioned in the text 10
2. Chronology of the Formative period in Oaxaca 11
3. The Santo Domingo Tomaltepec site, showing Mounds 1-4 12
4. The Santo Domingo Tomaltepec site, showing test pits and major excavated areas 22
5. The Mound 1 construction sequence 26
6. Late Tierras Largas phase occupation at Tomaltepec 28
7. Late Tierras Largas phase features 29
8. Early San José phase occupation at Tomaltepec 35
9. Components of Hosuehold Unit ESJ-1 36
10. Structure 11 (southern limit of structure poorly defined) 39
11. House 4, a part of Household Unit ESJ-2 44
12. Components of Possible Household Unit ESJ-3 47
13. The San José phase cemetery at Tomaltepec 49
14. Numbers and percentages of dead by age group within the Tomaltepec cemetery 51
15. Key diagram of attributes of burials, Tomaltepec cemetery 53
16. Rosario phase occupation at Tomaltepec 65
17. Feature 50, Possible Household Unit R-2 71
18. Monte Albán Ia occupation at Tomaltepec 76
19. Construction of House 3 floor 78
20. Components of Household Unit Ia-1 79
21. Components of Possible Household Unit Ia-2 82
22. Feature 79, Possible Household Unit Ia-3 85
23. Feature 74 of Household Unit Ia-4, as revealed in a test pit 86
24. Monte Albán Ic occupation at Tomaltepec 89
25. Components of Household Unit Ic-1 92
26. Components of Area Ic-2 96
27. Components of Possible Household Unit Ic-3 100
28. Adobe-walled pits from Monte Albán Ic areas 101
29. Monte Albán II occupation at Tomaltepec 107
30. Components of Household Unit II-I 109
31. Flexed burials from the San José phase cemetery 125
32. Extended burials from the San José phase cemetery, I 126
33. Extended burials from the San José phase cemetery, II 127
34. Extended burials from the San José phase cemetery, III 128
35. Burial goods from the San José phase cemetery, I 129
36. Burial goods from the San José phase cemetery, II 130
37. Burial goods from the San José phase cemetery, III 131
38. Burial goods from the San José phase cemetery, IV 132
39. Burial goods from the San José phase cemetery, V 133
40. Burial goods from the San José phase cemetery, VI 134
41. Burial goods from the San José phase cemetery, VII 135
42. Burials with Guadalupe phase affiliations, all located atop Structure 12 136
43. Burial goods from burials with Guadalupe phase affiliations 137
44. Monte Albán Ia burials 138
45. Rosario phase and Monte Albán Ia burial goods, I 139
46. Rosario phase and Monte Albán Ia burial goods, II 140
47. Monte Albán Ic burials 141
48. Details of tomb associated with Burial 5, a Monte Albán Ic interment found inside Structure 9 of Household Unit Ic-1 142
49. Vessels accompanying Burial 5, I 143
50. Vessels accompanying Burial 5, II 144
51. Vessels accompanying Burial 5, III 145
52. Vessel 12 from Burial 5, an elaborate Monte Albán Ic bridge-spout jar 146
53. House 4, Floor E, contour map of charcoal density 198

54. House 4, Floor E, SSA-I configuration based on inter-category average nearest neighbor distances 201
55. House 4, Floor E, SSA-I configuration based on residualized matrix 202
56. House 4, Floor E, SSA-I configuration based on average distance from items to epicenter of charcoal density 203
57. Monte Albán V occupation at Tomaltepec 216
58. Components of Household Unit V-1 217

LIST OF PLATES

1. Two views of Mound 1, Tomaltepec 13
2. Views of Mounds 2 and 4 14
3. Artifact-bearing strata exposed by the Colonial/modern road through the site 16
4. View of the Tomaltepec site from the south side of the Río Tomaltepec canyon 17
5. Early Formative features in the north road cut 18
6. Adobe brick floor construction of Middle Formative House 2, as first discovered 19
7. The 1972 shaft into Mound 1 20
8. The Terminal Formative (Monte Albán II) stucco floor atop Mound 1 21
9. Excavation in progress on the north and south road cuts (Areas B and D) 23
10. The extent of excavations in Area B, 1974 24
11. Beginning work on the depression in the northeast corner of Mount 1 25
12. A portion of the Mound 1 construction sequence 25
13. Components of Household Unit ESJ-1 37
14. Examples of the stone balls occasionally found in Early Formative contexts 38
15. Lateral view of Structure 11 40
16. Bone awls and awl tips from Early Formative proveniences 41
17. Ground stone tools from Structure 11 42
18. Partially-drilled shell ornament from Structure 11 43
19. The House 4 surface, looking west 45
20. A typical extended, face-down burial from the San José phase cemetery 52
21. A flexed burial from the San José phase cemetery 54
22. Bowl with excised decoration which accompanied the burial shown in Plate 21 55
23. A flexed burial from the San José cemetery, covered with irregular stones 55
24. Grave goods from the San José phase cemetery 56
25. Magnetite "U-motif" which accompanied Burial 24, Individual 1 57
26. Structures 12 and 13 (superimposed) 66
27. Burials discovered beneath the upper surface of Structure 12 68
28. Views of Household Unit R-1 69
29. Feature 44a, a large roasting pit associated with Houses 5 and 7 of Unit R-1 70
30. Infant burial associated with Household Unit R-1 71
31. Upper surface of floor, House 2, Household Unit Ia-1 77
32. Features from Household Unit Ia-1 80
33. Burials from Household Unit Ia-1 81
34. Burial from Household Unit Ia-2 83
35. Feature 107 from Household Unit Ia-2 84
36. Construction details of Structure 13 91
37. Structures 9 and 10 93
38. The Burial 5 tomb before opening 94
39. Ceramic offerings found with the Burial 5 tomb 95
40. Feature 44b of Unit Ic-2 97
41. Burials found in the Household Unit Ic-3 98
42. Features of Household Unit Ic-3 99
43. Infant burials probably associated with Household Unit II-1 110
44. Vessels of the San José phase, I 120
45. Vessels of the San José phase, II 121
46. Vessels of the San José phase, III 122
47. Vessels of the San José phase, IV 123
48. Figurines from Early Formative proveniences at Tomaltepec, I 159

49. Figurines from Early Formative proveniences at Tomaltepec, II 160
50. Figurines from Middle Formative proveniences at Tomaltepec, I 161
51. Figurines from Middle Formative proveniences at Tomaltepec, II 162
52. Figurines from Late Formative proveniences at Tomaltepec, I 163
53. Figurines from Late Formative proveniences at Tompaltepec, II 164
54. Figurines from Late Formative proveniences at Tomaltepec, III 165
55. Figurines from Late Formative proveniences at Tomaltepec, IV 166
56. Figurines from Late Formative proveniences at Tomaltepec, V 167
57. Shell objects from Formative proveniences at Tomaltepec, I 172
58. Shell objects from Formative proveniences at Tomaltepec, II 173
59. Type 1 manos 176
60. Type 2 manos 177
61. Pestle 178
62. Type 1 metate 178
63. Type 2 metate 179
64. Type 3 metate 179
65. Ground stone axes 180
66. Sample of teosinte caryopses from Feature 7, a Tierras Largas phase bell-shaped pit 190
67. Middle Formative corn cob fragments showing no introgression with teosinte (from Feature 50, a Rosario phase rosing pit) 191
68. Carbonized avocado seeds 191
69. Carbonized *Phaseolus* 192
70. Floor E of House 4, gridded for artifact plotting 196
71. Stone foundation of House 1, Household Unit Monte Albán V-1 213
72. Large roasting pits associated with Unit V-1 214
73. Two views of Burial 48, a 14-15 yr. old girl associated with Unit V-1 215

LIST OF APPENDICES

I. Provenience Descriptions 115
II. Early Formative Ceramics and the Early San José Occupational Sequence at Tomaltepec 118
III. Human Burials From Tomaltepec 124
IV. Formative Figurines From Tomaltepec 155
V. Modified and Unmodified Bone 168
VI. Shell and Marine Objects 171
VII. Ground Stone Artifacts 174
VIII. Early Formative Chipped Stone Tools (by J. W. Rick) 181
IX. Formative Botanical Remains at Tomaltepec (by J. Smith) 186
X. Spatial Organization of an Early Formative Household (by C. S. Spencer) 195
XI. Excavation and Analysis of Structure 14 (by J. K. Sallade) 204
XII. Postclassic Occupation at Tomaltepec 212

Acknowledgments

The excavations which form the basis of this study were carried out as part of the project "Prehistory and Human Ecology of the Valley of Oaxaca," under the general direction of Dr. Kent V. Flannery of the University of Michigan Museum of Anthropology. It is fair to say that without Dr. Flannery's encouragement and assistance at many points this study could never have been begun, much less completed.

The National Science Foundation supported the field work and laboratory analysis in Oaxaca through Doctoral Dissertation Improvement Grant GS-40325, made to the University of Michigan Museum of Anthropology. Travel and living expenses for some of the participants were provided by an Undergraduate Research Participation grant from the National Science Foundation to the University of Michigan, and by a Ford Foundation grant made to the University of Michigan Department of Anthropology.

The field work was carried out under the auspices of the Instituto Nacional de Antropología e Historia (I.N.A.H.) through *Concesión arqueológica* 16/71. The help and cooperation of a number of officials of I.N.A.H. were entirely indispensable to the success of the project. I extend my appreciation to Dr. Ignacio Bernal, then Director of the National Museum of Anthropology and the first archaeologist to record and describe the site of Tomaltepec; José Luis Lorenzo and Lorena Mirambell of the Prehistory Department; and Ignacio Marquina and Eduardo Matos M. of the Prehispanic Monuments Department. On the local level, Manuel Esparza, Director of the Centro Regional de Oaxaca (I.N.A.H.) and Dr. Marcus C. Winter, Staff Archaeologist for the Centro Regional, facilitated the work in every conceivable way and were instrumental in its completion.

Specialized analyses were carried out on the Tomaltepec material by a number of individuals from different institutions. Dr. Richard G. Wilkinson of the State University of New York at Albany analyzed human remains, and Dr. Kent V. Flannery of the University of Michigan Museum of Anthropology identified non-human bones; the many carbonized plant remains were studied by Dr. Richard I. Ford and Judith Smith, also of the Univeristy of Michigan Museum of Anthropology, and by Dr. C. Earle Smith of the University of Alabama; Dr. Lawrence H. Feldman of the Museum of Anthropology of the University of Missouri identified marine and freshwater shell; and John W. Rick, Charles S. Spencer, and Jane K. Sallade, all of the University of Michigan Museum of Anthropology, respectively carried out specialized studies of stone tools, of an Early Formative house floor, and of a Late Formative public building. Some of these contributions are included as appendices to this study, and all were of the utmost utility in understanding cultural development at Tomaltepec. Many of the Tomaltepec artifacts were carefully drawn in Oaxaca by Lois J. Martin, Valerie McKnight, Nancy Whalen, and Javier Méndez B. Karen Way and F. E. Smiley drafted the illustrations used in this volume.

Charles S. Spencer of the University of Michigan Museum of Anthropology and Elsa Redmond of Yale University were field assistants during the actual excavations, and successful completion of the fieldwork was due in no small part to their unfailing capability, diligence, accuracy, and good spirits.

Upon my return from Oaxaca, facilities and office space at the University of Michigan Museum of Anthropology were made available by Dr. James B. Griffin, then its Director, and by Dr. Richard I. Ford, then its Assistant Director and now Director. The University of Michigan Computer Center and Department of Anthropology made funds available for data processing. David Victor edited the manuscript.

As dissertation committee members, Drs. Kent V. Flannery, Richard I. Ford, Charles Gibson, Jeffrey R. Parsons, and Henry T. Wright III reviewed the thesis and made numerous helpful suggestions. Also extremely beneficial were conversations with Dr. Marcus C. Winter and other past and present members of the Oaxaca Human Ecology Project. None of these individuals is necessarily in complete agreement with the interpretations suggested here, but all of their comments and criticisms were much appreciated.

Finally, no preface of this sort could be concluded without gratefully acknowledging the cooperation of the municipal authorities and citizens of the town of Santo Domingo Tomaltepec. Many of the men of the town were employed on the excavation crews and laboratory staff, and their friendliness and hard work constituted a major and vital contribution to the project.

Chapter I

Introduction

The Analytical Perspective and Objectives of the Study

The theoretical motivation for this research is an interest in the development of more complex societies from simpler antecedents. How any such study proceeds is necessarily a product of the investigator's perception of culture and processes of cultural change. If, for example, culture is seen as a social pattern or value system which can be transmitted unilineally or in a few major lines, then evolutionary studies might reflect exclusive concern with universal stages and classification. Evolution itself, in this case, is essentially automatic, with each culture, race, or society rising to the limit of its capacity. Morgan's (1877) Savagery-Barbarism-Civilization continuum exemplifies this sort of approach. Much of the archaeological work done in the twentieth century, on the other hand, has been characterized by so-called "normative" perceptions of culture. For the normative thinker, 'culture' was composed of a series of normative concepts, or mental templates, which were shared by all of the members of a given culture. Reconstruction of these norms became the object of the archaeologist. As a number of writers have remarked, such an approach quickly led to definitions of culture in terms of objects: typical artifacts, typical sites, etc. The "Basketmaker" culture was defined in this tradition (e.g. Kidder 1924). Developmental studies in these cases were concerned with diffusion of particular normative concepts in the form of styles, ideas, and techniques. Explanation of culture change most often referred to migrations of populations bearing the traits in question. Definition of culture in terms of objects, in other words, necessarily resulted in definition of culture change as shifting artifact inventories, usually attributable to non-local "influence". However, neither of the approaches just discussed has contributed much to our understanding of stimuli and processes of change in prehistoric cultures.

An alternative viewpoint, and the one to be employed in this study, sees culture in adaptive terms. From this perspective, cultures are taken as sets of relationships and responses by which any society maintains itself in a particular physical and social environment, and cultural change is seen as adaptive change in the extent and sophistication of these relationships and responses. Concomitant with this position is an increasing reliance on concepts and models adapted from General Systems Theory.

Systems approaches represent both a body of theory and a type of modeling, together comprising a method for selecting and organizing variables for description, interpretation, prediction of new patterns, etc. General Systems Theory is not simply an analogy but is based on the premise that there exist relations and patterns of operation so basic as to be discernible in entities as diverse as cats and computers. In support of this position, Buckley argues:

> To say physiological, psychological, and sociocultural processes of control all involve (basic systemic principles) is no more of a mere analogy than to say that the trajectories of a falling apple, an artificial satellite, or a planet all involve the basic principle of gravitational attraction. (1968:509)

General Systems Theory has grown and diversified enormously since its development in the mid-twentieth century, and this writer cannot attempt to summarize the field here. Systems concepts are introduced at some length in Walter Buckley's (1968) edited volume, and summaries of systems concepts are available in Watson, LeBlanc, and Redman (1971), and Plog (1976), among others.

Systemic concepts and models have been profitably utilized in diverse types of anthropological studies. Rappaport (1971) uses systemic modeling to consider regulation of environmental relations and maintenance of continuity in an extant human society, while Flannery (1968b; 1972c) applies systemic concepts to analyses of change in extinct societies. As all of these studies demonstrate, the greatest utility of systems theory in anthropology is in providing behavioral models and sets of theoretical expectations within which relevant variables may be selected, organized, and interpreted. Such theoretical constructs transcend simple ethnographic analogy, and writers such as Clarke (1968) maintain that the major paradigms and interpretive frameworks of modern archaeological research must be developed within systemic perspectives.

Arguing within this tradition, Flannery (1972c) maintains that a heuristically useful method of organizing variables in archaeological studies is to conceive of cultures as one class of living system. Living systems are characterized as open, adaptive systems; i.e., open in that they exchange energy and information among their components and with their surroundings, and adaptive in that they are capable of changing their structures in order to maintain a steady state of operation within the occasionally fluctuating limits of their physical and social environments. Within this perspective, cultures can be assumed to experience all of the standard problems of system operation, which include regulating components, regulating environmental relations, processing information, making and transmitting decisions, integrating components, maintaining coherence, etc. Such an approach provides a standardized framework within which to evaluate the mode of operation of any cultural system by asking how and to what extent each of the above functions is carried out. This sort of approach clearly facilitates comparative evaluation of cultures or time periods by providing a concise and workable measure of operational complexity. More complex societies, it is suggested, have the following characteristics relative to their less complex counterparts: 1) greater size and number of components; 2) a higher degree of specialization and differentiation of components, termed "segregation" by Flannery (1972c); and 3) a higher level of integration of components into a coherent whole, termed "centralization" by Flannery, op cit. Study of the development of a more complex society from a simpler one, then, involves consideration of increasing size, increasing levels of segregation, and increasing levels of centralization.

To complete an explanation of complex social evolution, however, one must ultimately progress beyond analysis of mode of operation and identification of processes of change. The final ingredient of explanation is, of course, specification of the stimuli which underlie evolutionary processes. Unfortunately, all of these lines of investigation cannot always be pursued on the same level and in the same detail. It seems, for instance, that the difficulties of adequately specifying the pressures acting on any particular subsystem or lower order system increase in direct proportion to the complexity of the higher order system which encompasses the original unit of observation. Specifically, if we envision a small community existing within the framework of a larger regional system, we might suggest that at lower levels of development significant stimuli for change are more likely to be local in nature. At higher levels of complexity, on the other hand, larger-scale sociopolitical complications also become extremely significant. Furthermore, it is these wider sociopolitical pressures which may not be at all precisely definable from the small community perspective.

The preceding discussion is not intended to imply that evolutionary perspectives are out of place on the small community level. If we maintain that we can most adequately specify ultimate causes of change at the regional rather than local level in complex societies, it also seems reasonable to suggest that specific processes of change from one level of complexity to another are best understood at the community level.

In other words, studies at the individual small community level seem most useful in building concepts of community structure and processes of change, rather than as bases for generating meaningful hypotheses relevant to causes of change in entire cultural systems. Such hypotheses must ultimately be formulated and tested if we are ever to offer successful explanations of cases of cultural evolution, but it is suggested that well-developed regional perspectives based on understandings of component communities are essential to this end.

The Aims of this Study

The specific objective of this study is to consider evolutionary processes in a small community during a crucial period in Mesoamerican cultural development. To this end, the study seeks to monitor changes in 1) the numbers of parts of the community (i.e., individuals, households, and other social groups); 2) levels of differentiation among these parts; 3) specialized functions ascribable to these parts; 4) the extent to which the parts are integrated into a whole; and 5) the means of integration of the whole. It will of course be necessary to take into account both the physical and social surroundings of the community, as well as changes in these surroundings.

To put this plan into effect, the archaeological data will be interpreted under four major headings: 1) community composition, or the nature and patterning of the physical components of the community; 2) status differentiation within the community; 3) subsistence activities, and, by implication, physical environmental relations; and 4) craft and exchange activities, here including much of the community's relation to its social environment.

Our ultimate interests, of course, should be in the evolution of Formative Mesoamerican cultures on regional rather than simply local bases. What would seem to be required, however, is some modicum of understanding of local evolutionary processes, building up to the regional level through analysis and comparison of individuals, households, and communities, as this study attempts to do in Chapters II–VIII. Furthermore, the study seeks to extend these data to comparisons of and conclusions about regional Formative developments in Chapter XIII. Ultimately, it is hoped that the questions thus formed can be applied to general considerations of Mesoamerican Formative developmental processes.

This section has been concerned with establishing a perspective on cultural complexity and cultural evolution. The succeeding sections of this chapter seek to complete the introduction to the study by discussing the cultural and physical environment of the Tomaltepec community, as well as describing both the site itself and the excavations carried out there.

The Cultural Setting: The Formative Period in Mesoamerica

The setting for this study is the southern Mesoamerican Valley of Oaxaca during the period from about 1500 B.C. to A.D. 100. This block of time, designated the Formative Period, is generally divided into Early, Middle, and Late segments.

The latter period is often further subdivided into a Late and a Terminal Formative period, especially in Central Mexico. The Formative Period has been characterized by a number of writers (e.g. Coe and Flannery, 1967; Ford, 1969; Coe, 1962; Sanders and Price, 1968; and Weaver, 1972), and although interpretations differ on many points, there is general agreement that the Formative was a period of enormous changes in every dimension of Mesoamerican culture. In fact, the thousand years between 1300 B.C. and 300 B.C. probably saw more rapid and more profound changes than any other comparable period in the Mesoamerican developmental sequence, beginning with semi-agricultural tribes and ending with the formation of states.

Furthermore, it seems that during the Formative period many of the bases were laid for the impressive developments of later periods. Technology, architecture, ceremonialism, social differentiation, agriculture, irrigation, commerce, writing, and calendrics all seem to have appeared at least in their basic forms prior to the Formative/Classic transition in Mesoamerica at about A.D. 200. One may assert, in fact, that many of the characteristic directions of Mesoamerican cultural development were determined during the Formative period. Many later developments, then, while undeniably impressive in their own right, should be seen as elaborations and variations on established processual directions.

As this study is concerned only with Formative developmental processes, later variations will not be considered beyond the simple recognition of their Formative antecedents. For the purposes of this study, however, the following generalizations on the major subdivisions of the Formative period are offered. Many of the specifics of the discussion are known almost exclusively from Oaxacan data where the Formative developmental stage is being studied in detail by Flannery and his associates. Much of the ensuing discussion is sufficiently general, however, to be broadly applicable to many parts of Mesoamerica.

The Early Formative Period (ca. 1600–850 B.C.)

The most important characteristic of the initial part of the Early Formative period would seem to be the appearance of sedentary villages. Some writers have causally linked this transition to the development of fully efficient agricultural systems (e.g. Coe, 1962; and Sanders and Price, 1968), but Flannery (1972a) argues convincingly that fully efficient agriculture is not a necessary condition for settled life. Collection of marine estuary resources as a supplement to developing agriculture during the Early Formative period on the Guatemalan coast have been explored at some length by Coe and Flannery (1967), and there is certainly no reason to believe that similar farming/collecting strategies could not have been operative in other areas of Mesoamerica. This is particularly the case when Kirkby's (1973) study of ancient and modern maize agriculture in the Valley of Oaxaca is taken into account. Kirkby argues that reliance on maize cultivation as a major staple is not practical unless some 200 kg/ha can be harvested. Flannery (1972a) suggests that such a yield would be difficult to consistently obtain even on the best soils with the races of maize known to have been cultivated prior to 1500 B.C. Thus, while the sedentary villages which characterize the Early Formative are indisputably agricultural, it is probably not inaccurate to suggest that hunting and gathering provided an important element of the subsistence pattern.

When one looks at the settlement pattern data for the Early Formative Valley of Oaxaca, he sees only two rough size classes of sites: small (more than a dozen sites in the 1-3 ha range) and very large (one site, San José Mogote, reached 20 ha late in the Early Formative). This pattern of a single "monster" site, separated from all its contemporary communities by an enormous size difference, can be found elsewhere in Formative Mesoamerica (Marcus 1976a:89), usually in areas which were on the verge of displaying rapid sociopolitical evolution. However, it is evidently the case that Early Formative Oaxaca was not yet characterized by the multi-stage settlement hierarchies which are commonly found in later periods; or stated differently, the center-hinterland relationship which was so significant in later times in Mesoamerica was still not well developed.

Recent excavations at the large center of San José Mogote (Flannery and Marcus 1976a) have produced remains of a plastered building from an initial stage of the Early Formative period (Tierras Largas phase, ca. 1400-1150 B.C.). This structure stands in marked contrast to the simple wattle-and-daub structures which characterized other excavated contemporary villages, and it sets the site apart from its contemporaries from the very beginning of the Early Formative period.

By the latter part of the Early Formative (San José phase, 1150-850 B.C.), the community at San José Mogote covered more than 20 ha, had a population of many hundreds, evidenced some social differentiation, engaged in production of ornaments of shell and magnetite on a larger scale than any other known contemporary community in the region, and maintained trade relations with other areas of Mesoamerica. The community appears to have served as an important ceremonial-civic center, both in its own arm of the Valley of Oaxaca and most probably in the remainder of the area as well.

Another evidently precocious Early Formative community was San Lorenzo, located in southern Veracruz in the basin of the Coatzacoalcos River. Of particular interest are the Early Formative Ojochi, Bajío, Chicharras, and San Lorenzo phases, spanning the period from 1500 to 900 B.C. (Coe, 1970), the latter phase being the Olmec period at San Lorenzo. Work at San Lorenzo indicates that a regional center of considerable complexity existed there, especially during the San Lorenzo phase (ca. 1150-900 B.C., Coe, 1968), contemporary with the San José phase in Oaxaca. A population of about one thousand is estimated for San Lorenzo near the end of the San Lorenzo phase (Ibid.), and if this figure is even approximately correct, we can perhaps infer a population of hundreds of pre-San Lorenzo phase times. Some of the construction at the site, including a small, stepped sand and clay pyramid is also pre-San Lorenzo phase (Ibid.). Obsidian, magnetite, and ilmenite tools and ornaments recovered at San Lorenzo imply that the community participated in a far-flung exchange network.

In several areas of Mesoamerica, then, both in the highlands and in the lowlands, sizable centers are known to have existed and to have maintained external trade relations. Nor is it implied that San José Mogote and San Lorenzo were the only two sizable centers existing in Early Formative Mesoamerica; they are, however, two of the best known, and so were selected for this discussion, which is intended to illustrate types rather than to describe variety.

The majority of Early Formative villages, however, appear to have been of a much simpler sort. Based on a literature survey of reported early

INTRODUCTION

village size, Marcus (1976a) suggests that as many as 90 percent were small hamlets of 10-12 households. Most such hamlets appear to fall into the 1-5 ha size category. Early Formative houses in Oaxaca and Tehuacán were small, wattle-and-daub structures which appear to have been nuclear family residences (Flannery et al., 1970; Winter, 1972; and MacNeish and Peterson 1972). Flannery (1972a) argues that there is evidence in Mesoamerica of a long tradition of the nuclear family as the basic unit of residence, food procurement, and storage, and Winter (1976a) originally proposed the term "household cluster" to define the basic building blocks of early villages in Oaxaca. "Household clusters" were defined as the archeological remains of one household, usually consisting of a rectangular nuclear family wattle-and-daub structure with associated bell-shaped food storage pits, ovens, work areas, and other food and object preparation areas, trash middens, and human burials. While the specifics of this description are drawn from Oaxacan data, the Tehuacán materials tentatively suggest a similar situation (MacNeish and Peterson, op cit.). There is thus sufficient evidence to suggest that the small village composed of nuclear family households characterized much of Early Formative Mesoamerica.

More recently, Flannery (in press) has concluded that so many problems have arisen with the term "household cluster" that it now needs to be abandoned before it gets too imbedded in the literature. According to Flannery,

> .... a number of colleagues hastened to point out to us that several Mesoamericanists have already used the term "household cluster" to refer, not to a cluster of archaeological features surrounding one household, but to a cluster of households (i.e., a "hamlet" or "village" in settlement pattern terms). For example, Borhegyi (1965) applied the terms "cluster", "minor aggregate cluster", and "major aggregate cluster" to hamlets and villages of highland Guatemala. In his northeast Petén survey, Bullard (1960) used the term "Cluster" to refer to one of his three main levels of settlement organization, "clusters of about five to twelve [houses] within an area roughly 200 to 300 meters square". There is therefore an immediate danger of confusion between our use of the term and that of Borhegyi, Bullard, and others.
>
> Second, some problems have arisen with the original definition of the term. Based on his excavations at the hamlet of Tierras Largas, Winter (1976a:25) concluded that "pits, burials, and other features generally occur outside but within a few meters of the house structures" and that therefore the household cluster concept could "provide a context in which pits, burials, house remains, and other features can be understood not simply as isolated cultural features, but as manifestations of a specific segment of society." This worked reasonably well for the "actual" household clusters, such as Cluster No. 1 of the Late Tierras Largas phase at the type site, which contained a series of postmolds, 8 bell-shaped pits, and 3 burials (Winter 1976a: Fig. 2.8 and p. 31). It became shakier when "probable" or "possible" clusters were identified on the basis of a single burial, a single oven, or a single bell-shaped pit (Winter 1976b: Figs. 8.3-8.5). While many of these features probably do indicate that a house is nearby, others do not.
>
> In particular, burials would seem to be a poor indicator of the presence of a "household cluster," because it is now known that isolated burial areas or cemeteries were present in some Formative villages. These might vary from small "*barrio* cemeteries" of 8-15 individuals (such as in Area C at San José Mogote) to larger cemeteries of 60-80 individuals such as the one at Tomaltepec. Drennan (1976:132) was the first to make this problem explicit at Fábrica San José when, after identifying two possible "household clusters" on the basis of burials, he took a hard look at the data and concluded that "one, and possibly two, of the household clusters of the Rosario phase seem not to have been the sites of households at all ... Clusters R-9 and perhaps R-10 were used as a cemetery". In short, the variety of contexts in which burials, pits, ovens, and other features occur is much greater than was originally thought (Flannery, in press).

On the basis of these observations, Flannery (op. cit.) proposed the following changes at the analytical level of the Early Formative household, which will be followed in subsequent volumes in the Oaxaca series.

1. The term "household cluster" should be dropped, being too easily confused with the "cluster of households" already entered in the literature by Borhegyi, Willey, Bullard, and others. It should be replaced by the term "household unit," which expressed unambiguously the fact that a single household is referred to.

2. The term "household unit" should be used to refer to the complex of structures and features resulting from a typical Early Formative household—usually a wattle-and-daub house, its associated storage pits, ovens, middens, activity areas, and any sheds, lean-to's, or burials occurring with it.

3. The presence of a burial, an isolated bell-shaped pit, or any other feature should *not* be taken as proof for a household unit. Only if it can be shown that a house is present—in the form of postmolds, masses of burnt daub, or both—can the term be used with any confidence.

4. The term "household unit" should be used *only* to refer to the aforementioned 300 m² area of a wattle-and-daub house and its associated features and activity areas. It should *not* be extended to large adobe residences, houses with courtyards, or palaces. Such residential units had different modes of storage, different sets of activities, and different personnel, and these differences are only obscured by overextension of the term.

Mortuary data constitute another line of evidence about the nature of Early Formative society. Just as household construction techniques and artifact distributions suggest very little in the way of social differentiation during the Tierras Largas phase, mortuary data also indicate that, at least within the smaller Oaxacan communities, there was little ranking of one individual above another at the beginning of the Early Formative. Such evidence as is available suggests that existing distinctions were achieved, ephemeral ones. However, it should be noted that this situation was apparently shifting by the middle of the Early Formative in Oaxaca (ca. 1000 B.C.). Burials of children accompanied by especially finely made funerary vessels with Olmec motifs (Flannery et al., 1970:72) seem to attest to increasing formalization of status differentiation.

Another important diagnostic characteristic of Early Formative period in Mesoamerica is the interregional flows of exotic goods and status-communicating symbols just referred to. This exchange apparently linked the Gulf Coast Olmec area and Central Mexico, Puebla, Morelos, Oaxaca, and Chiapas. One may thus argue that what were once treated as regional developments of Olmec culture most probably represent a number of distinct Early Formative traditions crosscut by an interaction sphere which manifested itself in restricted areas (i.e., ritual and organizational) of each culture.

Pires-Ferreira (1975) argues for four levels of exchange in Early Formative Mesoamerica, including:

1) Reciprocal exchanges of utilitarian commodities, probably obtained on an individual basis and apparently involving every household. Based on neutron activation analysis characterization of obsidians, it is argued that this material moved largely in this fashion during the Early Formative (see Pires-Ferreira, *ibid.*, Chapter II for details).

2) Pooling of utilitarian goods for distribution by a central figure (or figures) to other community members. This sort of distribution of prismatic obsidian blades apparently began at San José Mogote at about 1000 B.C., although it is *not* in evidence at this time at the smaller sites. More formalized leadership would seem to be implied by this sort of arrangement.

3) Exchanges of unworked, non-utilitarian material (sea shell, for instance) for ornament production by part-time specialists.

4) Interregional exchanges of exotic and status communicating goods and symbols between elites at major centers (such as San José Mogote and San Lorenzo).

In all probability, all of these classes of goods did not move within a single sphere of conveyence. In fact, the numbers of people and communities participating to any significant extent in the exotic goods exchange was by all indications quite limited. Ornamental mirrors of polished magnetite, for example, appear to have been a major Oaxacan contribution to the exotic item exchange networks. Moreover, the mirrors were evidently exclusively manufactured at San José Mogote. No evidence of mirror production has yet been found at any other Oaxacan site (although mirrors themselves do appear in minute quantities at smaller Valley of Oaxaca communities). Thus, only the larger communities and more important families may have been stimulated or eligible—either socially or financially—to participate in the exchange. Participation would, in turn, allow such communities or families to become still larger and more significant in their respective areas, as maintained by Flannery (1968a), in his study of Olmec motifs in the Valley of Oaxaca. Larger communities, according to this conceptualization, would interact with each other and with other smaller villages in their vicinities on an individual, one-to-one basis, while the smaller sites would thus be seen as carrying on limited small-scale trade largely among themselves. This set of assumptions is based largely on the archaeological record in Oaxaca, where smaller sites have yielded some of the exotic and status-communicating goods and symbols referred to earlier, but always in small quantity. This is in marked contrast to San José Mogote itself, where the scale of possession of these items and symbols seems to have reached an entirely different order of magnitude.

In the terminology introduced in the preceding chapter, Early Formative Mesoamerica was characterized by relatively low levels of segregation and centralization, both within and between communities. Archaeological data from all over Mesoamerica suggest that most Early Formative societies were not composed of many different kinds of parts, either in terms of individuals and groups, or in terms of community types. Likewise, what evidence we have suggests that levels of specialization and differentiation were low among individuals, groups, and communities. Notable exceptions, of course, are communities such as San Lorenzo, on the Gulf Coast, and San José Mogote, in Oaxaca. Nevertheless, the *general* structure of Early Formative societies throughout Mesoamerica appears to have been characterized by a relatively high level of homogeneity and repetition.

Evidence currently in hand also implies that there was general informality of regional structure throughout Mesoamerica. Again, a notable exception to this statement may be San Lorenzo. As will be seen presently, it was not until Middle Formative times that Mesoamerican societies seem to have begun to effectively consolidate regional polities. It may also be suggested that a major focus of interaction for the most developed community in Oaxaca (i.e., San José Mogote) was outside of its own area, that is, with San Lorenzo and other communities at comparable levels of sophistication in other parts of Mesoamerica. These interaction spheres were doubtless quite useful in stimulating already extant trends toward increasing social differentiation in Oaxaca and other regions, as Flannery (1968a) first argued.

**The Middle Formative Period
(ca. 850–300 B.C.)**

In its initial phase, the Middle Formative period in Oaxaca and in Mesoamerica in general appears to have carried on and elaborated some of the basic trends of the Early Formative, although fundamental changes also characterize the period. The succeeding Middle Formative period saw the decline of the level of extra-regional trade in exotic materials, constant elaboration and differentiation of society, and the beginnings of consolidation of regional polities.

Drennan (1975:4) observes that during the Middle Formative the absolute number of communities in the Valley of Oaxaca increased more rapidly than in any previous or succeeding period. He also notes that a wider range of environmental zones was more intensely occupied than ever before. During the Guadalupe phase in Oaxaca (ca. 850–700 B.C.), a period defined by a ceramic complex now thought to be largely restricted to the Etla arm of the valley, the previously-noted three-tiered site-size hierarchy continued. By the latter part of the Middle Formative, it was an even more widespread phenomenon. Parsons' Valley of Mexico survey data show a similar pattern emerging during the Middle Formative in Central Mexico. Surveys in the Chalco region of the southern Valley of Mexico revealed sites of three size categories: hamlets, villages, and regional centers (Parsons, 1971b:41, Table 14), while no substantial Early Formative occupation was recorded in the area.

Excavation of Middle Formative components of several Oaxacan sites reveals a similar pattern. Communities investigated included hamlets such as Fábrica San José (Drennan, 1975); middle-range communities with public buildings such as Huitzo (Flannery et al., 1970); and a regional center with massive public architecture, large mounds, and a substantial population at San José Mogote (Flannery et al., 1970; and personal communication).

Throughout such changes in population distribution, the nuclear family seems to have remained the basic unit of production, consumption, and residence. Work on Oaxaca at Tierras Largas (Winter, 1972), Fábrica San José (Drennan, 1975) and Santo Domingo Tomaltepec (Whalen, 1974 and this volume) has confirmed the household unit (defined previously) as the basic building block of the Middle Formative community.

Nevertheless, substantially increased personal differentiation is evident in Middle Formative times. Mortuary data, architectural evidence, and general artifact distributions all suggest such a conclusion (see Drennan, 1975, Chapter IV, for instance). As noted in the discussion of Early Formative times, it is likely that the ascription of status at birth began to appear in the San José phase and was carried forward and elaborated during the Middle Formative. At this time, mortuary data suggest that increased status differentiation apparently existed even in the smaller communities. At the Middle Formative village of Fábrica San José some adults were buried with large mouthfuls of jade beads (up to 55), while others lacked even ceramic offerings (Drennan, 1975). Indeed, by the end of the Middle Formative period at about 300 B.C., a highly differentiated society existed in Oaxaca and in other comparably developed areas of Mesoamerica.

Predictably increasing formalization of leadership on all levels seems to have accompanied the increasing social differentiation referred to earlier. Pires-Ferreira (1975:26) notes that the pooling and redistribution of prismatic obsidian blades during the Early Formative was evident only at the most highly developed Early Formative community. By contrast, her data show that obsidian pooling was even practiced at smaller sites during the Middle Formative. It might be suggested, in other words, that by Middle Formative times the entire Valley of Oaxaca had reached the developmental level which characterized only the most precocious community during the later stages of the Early Formative.

The interregional exchange networks described for the Early Formative continued to some extent into the Middle Formative. On the Gulf Coast, the site of La Venta, while occupied during the Early Formative, would seem to have reached its apogee in Middle Formative times (see C14 dates provided by Coe, 1968:61, Figure 14). Moreover Olmecoid symbols and stylistic elements continued to be widely distributed over Mesoamerica in the initial part of the Middle Formative period.

However, the Middle Formative also witnessed the decline of some of the large, interregional exchange networks. Winter (1972:196), for example, reports that in the Middle Formative community at Tierras Largas, Oaxaca, a much narrower range of exotic and imported goods were found, compared to the Early Formative. No objects definitely identifiable as from the Gulf Coast were found, and neutron activation analysis characterization of obsidian recovered at Tierras Largas indicated that fewer obsidian sources were used in Middle Formative than in Early Formative times. A substantial portion of the obsidian, in fact, may be from a source near the Valley of Oaxaca (Pires-Ferreira, 1975). The quantity of marine shell at Tierras Largas also reaches an all-time high in the latter part of the Early Formative period, declining drastically thereafter. All such lines of evidence tend to indicate a smaller, more localized resource derivation area in Middle Formative times, relative to the Early Formative. This probably reflects a breakdown of some of the interregional exchange networks and the beginning of more intensive local exploitation of sources. Tolstoy and Paradis (1970) in Central Mexico and Heizer (1961) on the Gulf Coast also note similar trends in contemporary communities.

The earliest part of the Middle Formative, then, can be seen as an extension and elaboration of some of the basic orientations and processual directions established in the Early Formative, but with expanding numbers of cultural components and increasing specialization and differentiation of these. By the latter part of the period, however, there were more and more kinds of communities, more differentiation between these, and considerable social differentiation within all communities. The level of segregation of the parts of society, in other words, is definitely on the rise. One can also point to increasing centralization during the Middle Formative period. We have seen above that leadership and rank differences seem to have become more formalized, implying promotion of individuals, groups, and communities to higher levels. More complex linkages also appear to have existed between communities (see Drennan, 1975 for a discussion of Middle Formative community interaction within the Etla arm of the Valley of Oaxaca). The stresses which produced these changes in the area are doubtless many and intricately interrelated, and will not be dealt with here. The final chapter of this study will devote some attention to the problem.

The groundwork for the familiar Mesoamerican administrative hierarchy of sites (as opposed to a purely size-based hierarchy) was also probably laid during this period, but equally probably it cannot be readily recognized in its characteristic form of primary center–secondary center–tertiary settlement until later. In a word, the groundwork was laid for consolidation of the strong regional polity which developed in the succeeding Late Formative period.

**The Late Formative Period
ca. 300 B.C.–100 B.C.**

The Late Formative period saw continued development in a number of the important areas in Mesoamerica. In Late Formative times the Valley of Mexico and the adjacent central highlands emerged as an important area of Mesoamerica. Much of these highlands had remained marginally developed relative to the Gulf Coast and the southern highlands, but this situation appears to have begun to reverse itself by 300 B.C. From

Terminal Formative/Early Classic times to the present day, the central highlands have been the seat of major power centers of the highest population densities in Mexico (Parsons, 1971a).

The Valley of Oaxaca in the south also evidently underwent considerable development during this period. By about 200 B.C., MacNeish (1964) notes, sources of influence on the Tehuacán Valley shift from the Gulf Coast to Monte Albán, in Oaxaca. Furthermore, Flannery et al. (1967) note that techniques of pottery design in Tehuacán and adjacent regions during the Late Formative as well as in subsequent periods featured provincial imitations of Valley of Oaxaca styles.

By Late Formative times, the Valley of Oaxaca contained hundreds of villages including several large sites reaching 100 ha (Blanton: personal communication). Recent surveys by Varner (1974) and Kowalewski (1976) have added greatly to this total. Also present were ceremonial-civic centers, probably with administrative functions, which were constructed on hill and ridge tops overlooking long stretches of prime agricultural land (Flannery and Schoenwetter, 1970).

The mountaintop center of Monte Albán was in its early building stages in the Late Formative, with monumental architecture, calendrics, and hieroglyphic writing already in evidence (Blanton, 1978). Flannery and Schoenwetter (1970) suggest that this area of "massed power" rapidly drew surrounding valleys into its sphere of influence, although not always peacefully, as so-called "conquest glyphs" (believed by Caso [1965] to represent captured towns) show. This hypothesis has since received confirmation through recent work by Marcus (1976b), which names and locates several of the subject areas by study of the inscriptions on Building J at Monte Albán.

As Sanders and Price (1968) have observed, the Late Formative period in Mesoamerica saw the basic dichotomy between "center" and "hinterland" widespread and intensified as never before. In the Valley of Oaxaca, it is suggested that four classes of communities existed: a central place (Monte Albán itself); secondary centers located in each of the three sub-valleys (San José Mogote in the Etla sub-valley, Dainzú in the Tlacolula sub-valley, and Zaachila in the Zaachila sub-valley are three examples); and tertiary communities, often with small public building complexes of their own. Tomaltepec seems to have been one of these tertiary settlements. There probably also existed a fourth widespread class of settlement as well: small villages or hamlets which had no public structures of their own.

As with this distinction between communities, differentiation between individuals was also unparalleled. Archaeological data from all over the Valley of Oaxaca indicates that while some individuals lived in simple adobe structures and were buried in simple pit graves, others occupied elaborate lime-plastered buildings and went to their masonry tombs lavishly accompanied by ceramic and non-ceramic offerings of many sorts. Such buildings and tombs are found even at some of the smaller communities in the area. One Monte Albán Ic tomb at Tomaltepec, described further in Chapter VI, contained a ceramic offering equaled or surpassed by only three Ic tombs from Monte Albán itself. Caso, Bernal, and Acosta (1967) provide a more detailed discussion of the Monte Albán tombs. Such tombs may well suggest an emergent professional ruling stratum of society. We may, in fact, regard the Late Formative period as the culmination of the processes of increasing segregation and centralization which we have traced through the Early and Middle Formative periods. It seems accurate to suggest that by the Late Formative period, the social basis was effectively laid for larger developments in Mesoamerica.

**The Physical Setting:
Oaxaca and the Site of Tomaltepec**

As the major analytical focus of this study is to be Formative Oaxaca, some special consideration should be given to its particular features and problems. Much of the specific information in the previous section was from Oaxacan sources and need not be repeated here. Rather, this section will concentrate on 1) consideration of issues which led to the choice of the Tomaltepec site for intensive excavation, and 2) description of the site and its surroundings.

No detailed description of the Valley of Oaxaca is required, as several have already been published. Flannery et al (1967:446) offer a concise resume as follows:

> The Valley of Oaxaca lies in the southern highlands of Mexico between 16°40′–17°20′N and 96°15′–96°55′W. It is drained by two rivers: the upper Rio Atoyac, which flows

from north to south, and its tributary, the Rio Salado or Tlacolula, which flows westward to join the Atoyac near the present city of Oaxaca. The valley is shaped like a Y or three pointed star, whose center is Oaxaca City and whose southern limit is defined by the Ayoquesco Gorge, where the Atoyac River leaves the valley on its way to the Pacific Ocean. The climate is semiarid, with 500 to 700 mm of annual rainfall, confined largely to the summer months. The valley floor elevation averages 1550 m.

Situated in the mountainous central part of the state of Oaxaca, the region is surrounded by valleys with steep sides, narrow floors, and perennially flowing streams. In contrast, the Valley of Oaxaca is a wide, open plain with abundant flat land and streams which are dry most of the year. Yet it was this valley, where moisture is scarce and man must devise means to control it, which became the most powerful nuclear area in the southern highlands. It is generally believed that this development was the work of the Zapotec Indians, who now inhabit the valley and whose history can be traced back many thousands of years in that region.

A typical cross section of the valley shows four distinct physiographic zones: (i) the "low alluvium," or present river flood plain; (ii) a zone of "high alluvium," which is mainly an abandoned flood plain of Pleistocene-to-Recent age, formed by the Atoyac River and its tributaries when they flowed at a higher elevation; (iii) a piedmont zone flanking the high alluvium; and (iv) the surrounding mountains.

Figure 1 shows the Valley of Oaxaca.

Since 1966, research conducted by the University of Michigan Human Ecology Project and its offshoots, under the general direction of Michigan, in collaboration with Hunter College and Purdue University, has broadened our understanding of Formative Oaxaca. Proceeding from preliminary site surveys and definition and clarification of the chronological sequence (Fig. 2) attention shifted to questions of site specialization and

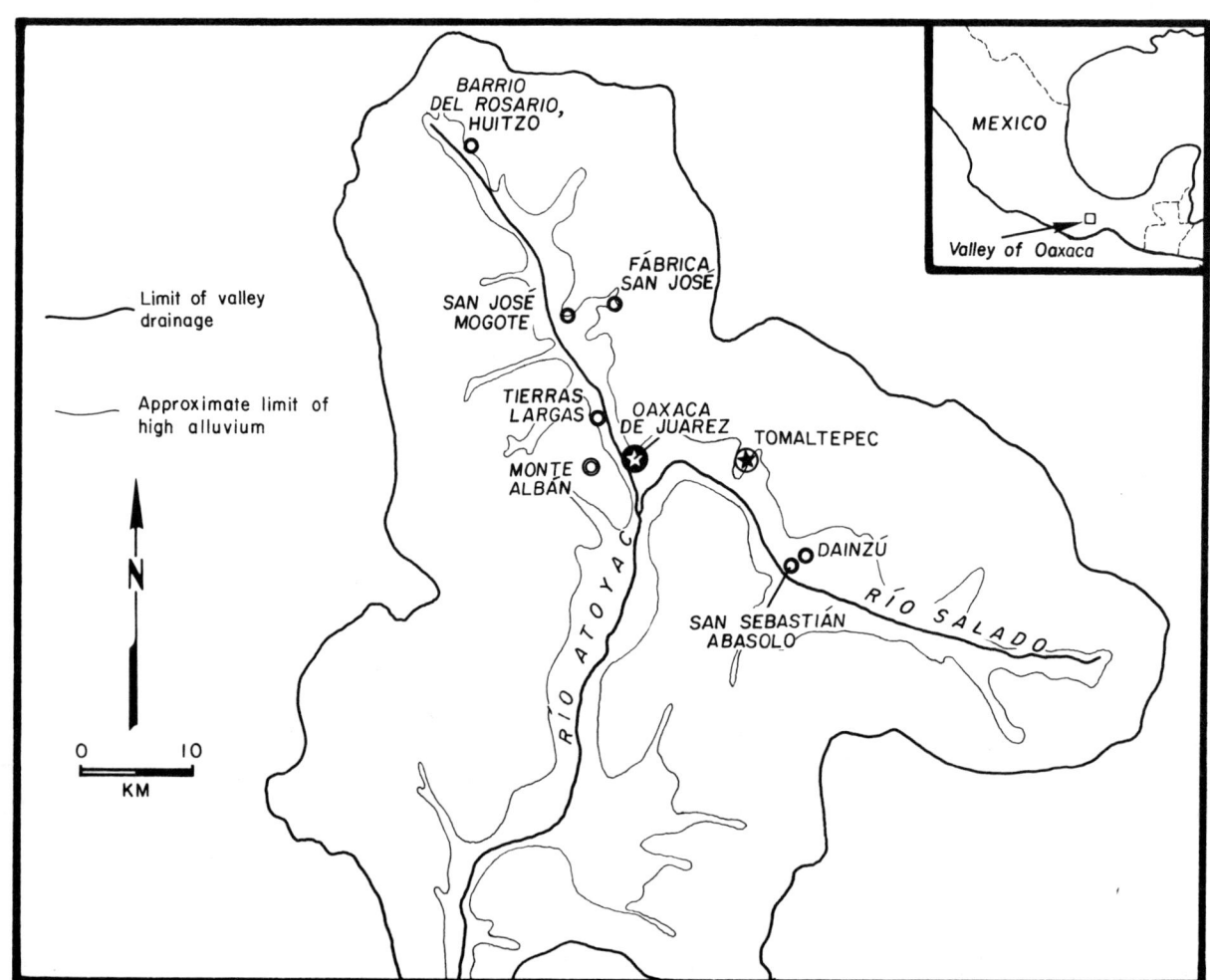

FIGURE 1. The Valley of Oaxaca, showing archaeological sites mentioned in the text.

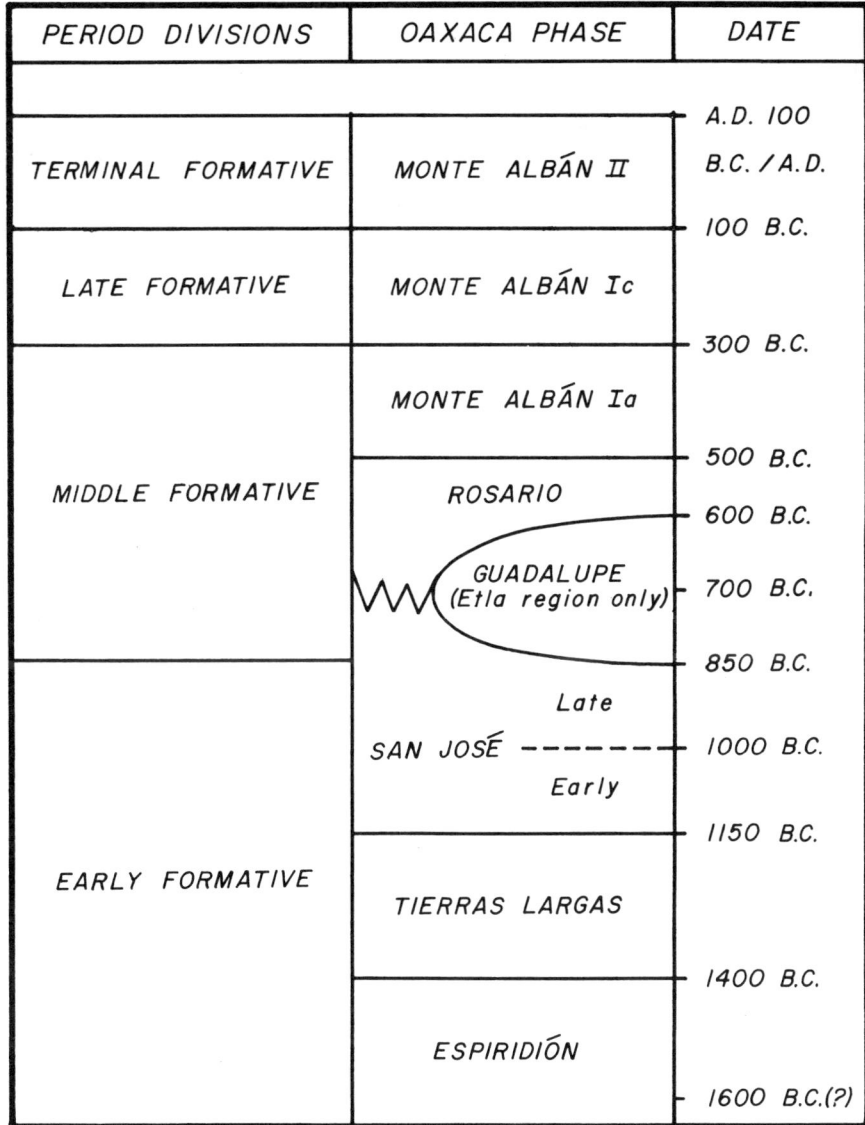

FIGURE 2. Chronology of the Formative period in Oaxaca.

differentiation, village composition and layout, and inter-and intra-regional interaction and development. It was with these sorts of questions in mind that the site of Santo Domingo Tomaltepec was selected for testing in 1969 and 1972 by Henry T. Wright and Susan H. Lees of the University of Michigan, and eventually chosen by the present writer for more intensive excavation in February, 1974. The site was a particularly appealing one for several reasons: 1) its location; 2) the environmental zone which it occupies; and 3) the history of previous work at the site. Each of these topics is briefly considered below, following a general description of the site itself.

THE SITE OF TOMALTEPEC

The site is small and fairly shallow, being some 2.0 ha in area and 0.5 to 2.0 m deep. There is only the slightest surface ceramic evidence of Early and Middle Formative occupation, although Late Formative sherds are relatively abundant and four Late Formative mounds are clearly visible. These are designated Mounds 1 through 4 in subsequent discussion. Mound 1, also referred to as the "Main Mound," is about 5 m high, Mound 2 is about 2 m high, Mound 3 about 1.5 m, and Mound 4 is less than one m. Locations of all mounds are given in Figure 3, and Plates 1 and 2 present views of several of the mounds.

The site is divided by a small dirt road which is thought to date from the Colonial period. The road cuts through the piedmont spur upon which the site is located, sinking to a maximum depth of about 1.5 m in the center of the site, and thereby providing two complete profiles of the artifact bearing strata. The profiles served as convenient starting points for all archaeological work at the site, as shown in Plate 3.

The site is located in the eastern (or Tlacolula) arm of the Valley of Oaxaca, at approximately 17°40′ N and 96°36′W, lying in the piedmont zone of the mountains surrounding that part of the valley. The shortest distance from San José Mogote to Tomaltepec is nearly 23 km (some 17 mi) along the valley. This point is significant because, prior to 1974, all Early and Middle Formative sites excavated on a moderate or large scale in the Valley of Oaxaca had been located in the northern or Etla arm, and all lay within 10–12 km of San José Mogote (see Fig. 1). It therefore was deemed important to broaden our understanding of the variety extant among Early and Middle Formative settlements in the valley by investigating communities that are not proximate to the major cere-

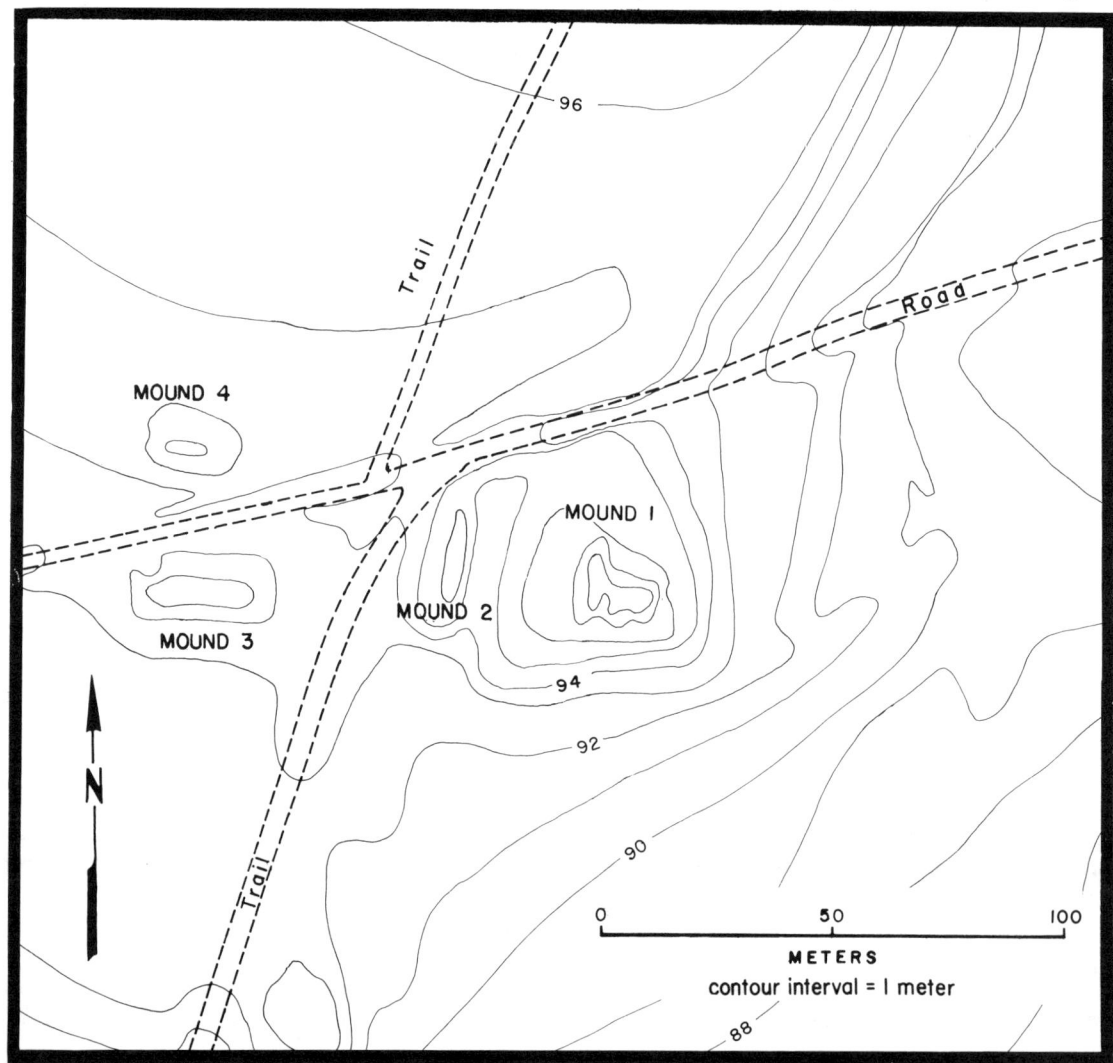

FIGURE 3. The Santo Domingo Tomaltepec site, showing Mounds 1–4. Contour interval is 1 m., starting from an arbitrary datum of 100 m.

PLATE 1. Two views of Mound 1, Tomaltepec. Top, view from the north. Bottom, view from the southwest.

PLATE 2. Views of Mounds 2 and 4. Top, Mound 2 as seen from Mound 1. An exploratory trench is visible on the left. Bottom, Mound 4.

monial-civic center, and in which organizational, formal, or functional variations may have existed. If such variation could be documented at sites more distant from San José Mogote, one could suggest that such villages were more autonomous in economic, ceremonial, and political affairs, than other small communities, nearer San José Mogote. The degree of autonomy of the outlying communities is clearly a significant factor in understanding processes of intra-valley integration during the Early and Middle Formative periods.

Environmental Situation

No less significant than the location of Tomaltepec is the environmental zone which it occupies. As previously mentioned, the site lies in the piedmont zone of the valley overlooking a high alluvial terrace at the mouth of a permanent tributary stream which descends from the mountains (Plate 4). The site is some 80 m above the floor of the main valley and its absolute elevation is about 1630 m above sea level. The site is well situated for farming on the alluvial terrace and piedmont slopes, as well as for collecting a wide variety of alluvial, piedmont, and mountain resources. There also exists the distinct possibility that water control techniques such as gravity-flow canal irrigation on the nearby slopes may have been practiced. There is, in fact, some tentative indication of irrigation systems at Tomaltepec in Late Formative times, and other Late Formative irrigation systems are known in the region: at Hierve el Agua, Oaxaca, for instance (Neely, 1967).

The piedmont location of the site was originally thought to be something of an anomaly, as the better known Early Formative settlement pattern in the Etla arm of the Valley of Oaxaca was one of concentration of sites in the low alluvium along the banks of the Atoyac River. However, a new survey by Kowalewski (1976) now suggests that there may have been a discernible tendency toward Early Formative occupation near piedmont tributary streams in the drier Tlacolula arm of the valley. The Tlacolula arm of the Valley of Oaxaca, wherein Tomaltepec is located, lacks a perennial, centrally-located river, in marked contrast to the Etla arm. In the Tlacolula valley, the low alluvium of the Río Salado is also poorly drained and slightly salty over much of its length. Finally, as noted by Kirkby (1973), the Tlacolula branch of the Valley of Oaxaca suffers from a rainshadow effect produced by topography and storm direction, as well as from highly variable rainfall (Kirkby, 1973:21).

These impediments to agriculture are, however, generally lessened in the Tlacolula piedmont. Here, streams descending from the mountains are perennial, non-saline, and slow-flowing (Kirkby, 1973: 24): well-suited, in other words, for small-scale irrigation.

Given these conditions, the piedmont location of the site is quite understandable, even though piedmont soils are somewhat thinner than their alluvial counterparts. As Kirkby observes (Ibid: p. 11), it is water rather than land resources which make the Valley of Oaxaca piedmont so valuable for agriculture.

Excavations at Tomaltepec

1969 and 1972 Excavations

The site of Tomaltepec was first recorded by Dr. Ignacio Bernal in the course of his survey of the Valley of Oaxaca. In 1969 the site was selected for mapping and brief test excavations because of its suitability for development of piedmont canal irrigation in the Monte Albán I period. Accordingly, the site was mapped and test excavations were begun by clearing one profile of the previously described road cut. Work was directed by Henry T. Wright and Susan H. Lees, both of the University of Michigan Oaxaca Project. Strata were identified and pottery and flotation samples were taken. The most interesting find, however, pertained not to the Monte Albán I period, but to the Tierras Largas phase. This was Feature 7, a large bell-shaped pit containing a considerable quantity of domestic refuse. As noted by Flannery et. al. (1970:80), this was the first Early Formative material recovered from the upper piedmont zone of the Valley of Oaxaca.

In 1972, the site was again tested by Henry T. Wright and a small group of assistants. Information in the following discussion was all taken from Wright's (n.d.) preliminary report. During his two week season, an intensive effort was made to locate enough Early Formative material to settle a basic

PLATE 3. Artifact-bearing strata exposed by the Colonial/modern road through the site. Top, looking east from the vicinity of Mound 2 toward the canyon of the Río Tomaltepec. Bottom, work beginning on the north road profile during Henry T. Wright's test excavations in 1972.

PLATE 4. View of the Tomaltepec site from the south side of the Río Tomaltepec canyon. Mound 1 is in the center of the photograph, and the undulating line of trees in the foreground delineates the river.

question raised by the 1969 find: whether any permanent Early Formative community existed at Tomaltepec, or whether the material represented no more than a seasonal campsite. At the other end of the Formative continuum, the 1972 investigations were concerned with recovery of Late and Terminal Formative features bearing on differentiation within the community.

Wright's work involved clearing both major profiles in the road area including that portion tested in 1969. He then excavated a short distance horizontally, following strata and investigating features. Feature 7—the Tierras Largas phase pit—was completely excavated, and a portion of the outside ground surface of House 4, discussed in Chapter IV, was recognized and cleared (Plate 5). Several other small Early Formative features of the San José phase were also investigated in the westernmost part of the road cut. These were tentatively assigned to a second San José phase household unit. Work on the south road cut exposed an extensive plastered surface dating to the Monte Albán Ic occupation of the site. Under this surface were the remains of a large Middle Formative structure, designated House 2. The house construction involved cutting a rectangular step into the sloping ground surface. A layer of adobe bricks then served to level the surface, and several packed earth floors were laid atop the adobes (Plate 6). The structure was very badly damaged both by the road cut and by Late Formative intrusions but enough remained to suggest a structure considerably more elaborate than the ordinary Middle Formative houses then known from several contemporary Oaxaca sites.

Wright's excavations also involved a deep shaft into Mound 1 (Plate 7). The shaft, in almost seven m, passed through a series of superimposed structures. From top to bottom, these were a Terminal Formative floor (Structure 14); a large Late Formative platform (Structure 13); a somewhat smaller Middle Formative platform (Structure 12); and, just above sterile soil, an Early Formative house floor (House 8) and several features (108, 109). All numbers were assigned by the present writer in 1974. Some Early Formative construction fill was encountered near the bottom of Wright's deep cut, and subsequent large-scale excavations in 1974 revealed this to be a corner of the San José phase house platform designated Structure 11 by the present writer (see Plate 7).

In sum, Wright's brief but extremely productive

PLATE 5. Early Formative features in the north road cut. Top, Feature 7 (partially damaged by the road cut) is marked by the meter stick. Bottom, a different view of the base of Feature 7.

PLATE 6. Adobe brick floor construction of Middle Formative House 2, as first discovered.

test excavations at Tomaltepec produced evidence of two definite and one possible San José phase household units. The work raised the possibility of the existence of some sort of San José platform beneath the main mound. Wright's excavations also tentatively established an occupational sequence for the community, pointing out the absence of Guadalupe phase remains, the existence of a Middle Formative and several Late Formative platforms, and other relatively elaborate architecture. Using data recovered in 1972, Jane Sallade, one of Wright's assistants, carried out a study of the uppermost occupation surface of Mount 1 (Plate 8), which dates to the Terminal Formative (Monte Albán II) period. Sallade's paper appears as Appendix XI of this study.

Wright's work and other surface surveys also demonstrated that no substantial Classic or Postclassic occupations existed at Tomaltepec. This point is extremely significant, as many shallow Oaxacan Formative sites were very badly disturbed by later occupations. Oaxaca Project archaeologists had come to regard horizontal excavation, or the clearing of large areas, as one alternative method of investigation of Formative communities, although the depth of Formative deposits at many sites greatly hampered this strategy. Accordingly, the lack of overburden at

PLATE 7. The 1972 shaft into Mound 1. The large rock rubble behind the workman if the fill of Middle Formative Structure 12. The small rock rubble in front of the workman is the fill of Early Formative Structure 11. The large bun-shaped adobe bricks beneath the workman's arm represent the footing of Structure 11. Upper layers of the shaft passed through Late Formative Structure 13.

Tomaltepec and the excellent preservation of Formative deposits documented in 1969 and 1972 made the community an ideal one for large-scale excavation.

The 1974 Excavations at Tomaltepec

As the preceding pages demonstrate, the 1974 excavations at Tomaltepec began with extremely valuable insights into the nature and location of many Formative deposits. Accordingly, the major strategy which was followed was to re-open the areas which produced Early Formative material in previous seasons and to expand these areas, more thoroughly investigating the cultural features which were observed in 1969 and 1972. Numerous other associated features were also discovered in the process.

Excavation was begun where Wright's work had ended two years previously: on the north road cut (hereafter referred to as Area B) and on the south road cut (Area D). Figure 4 shows all areas of excavation at Tomaltepec. The objective of the Area B excavations was clearing of House 4 and

PLATE 8. The Terminal Formative (Monte Albán II) stucco floor atop Mound 1. All fallen stones have been left in situ.

associated surfaces, while the Area D work aimed at clearing the Late and Middle Formative structures near Mound 1. Plate 7 shows these two areas under excavation. Another major objective was location of more San José phase features to document the transition from a residential area—House 4—to what was suspected to be a higher status area—the House 8/Structure 11 complex beneath Mound 1.

Excavation was horizontal in all cases, concentrating on the widest possible exposures in selected areas. Each of these was known to include several smaller provenience units such as house floors, burials, and pits. Within each of these macro-provenience units, excavation focused on definition of activity areas, clusters of artifacts, and debris from craft activities or food production, seeking to define both particular activities and utilization of space within the community. Plate 10 shows the extent to which Wright's excavations were extended. Plate 10 should be compared to Plate 5. Feature 7 appears in the foreground of each.

At the same time, a roughly systematic array of 25 m by 2m test pits was used to sample the remainder of the site. The pits were aimed at locating cultural features and at defining the size of the community for the various occupation periods. It is estimated that the Early Formative community covered a maximum area of 1.0 ha. The maximum Middle Formative area of occupation is

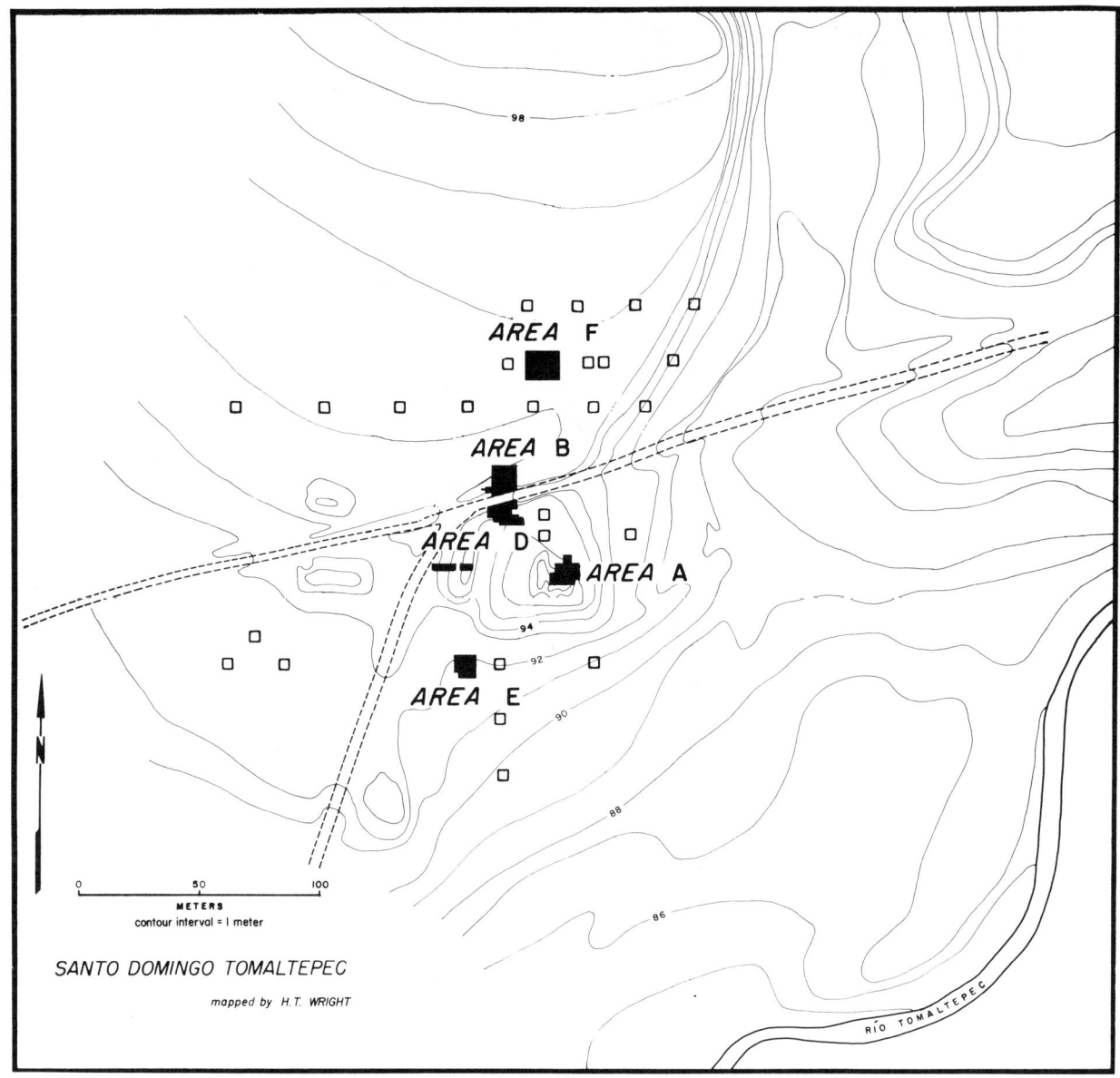

☐ Location of test pits (pit outlines not to scale).

■ Excavated area.

FIGURE 4. The Santo Domingo Tomaltepec site, showing test pits and major excavated areas.

roughly estimated at 2 to 3 hectares. The area of the Late Formative community is not well known, although surface debris and test excavation results suggest a size in the 3–4 ha range. Furthermore, it was by means of one of the test pits that the early San José phase cemetery discussed in Chapter III was discovered. As every expansion of the original test pit produced more burials, the area was designated Area F, and more extensive excavations were begun there to recover as many burials as possible.

With completion of work on Area D, large-scale excavations were begun on Mound 1 (Plate 11). The area of excavation included Wright's 1972 test

INTRODUCTION

PLATE 9. Excavation in progress on the north and south road cuts (Areas B and D). This photo shows something of the profusion of features and architectural traces encountered in little more than a meter of depth.

shaft, and was eventually expanded to 30 m² of the northeast quadrant of the mound (see Fig. 4). Excavations began, as had Wright's, in a large cavity left in the top of the northeast quadrant of the mound. Local men informed the writer that this cavity was made in 1937 to obtain construction stone for a dam built farther up the canyon by the federal government, allowing larger-scale irrigation in the area. The disturbance was fortunately confined to the upper levels of the mound construction, and it facilitated archaeological work in that it allowed larger exposure of the more enigmatic Middle and Early Formative constructions beneath.

The objective of work on Mound 1 was to clarify the sequence of construction suggested by Wright, with particular emphasis on the Early Formative house, features, and possible structures at the base of the deposits. Ultimately, some of the very badly disturbed Early Formative house floor and much of the overlying Early Formative platform were uncovered. A considerable amount of information on succeeding constructions was also gained. The Mound 1 construction sequence is schematically represented in Figure 5 (see also Plates 7 and 12).

From bottom to top, remains of Early Formative household clusters are covered by an early San José phase platform, designated Structure 11.

PLATE 10. The extent of excavations in Area B, 1974. The base of Feature 7 is visible in the foreground. The dashed line shows the northern limit of the 1972 excavations. (Compare Plates 5, Top, and 10.)

Structure 11 was succeeded by the much larger Middle Formative Structure 12, and the final major construction is the Late Formative Structure 13. Structure 14 is a Terminal Formative resurfacing which does not seem to have involved substantial additions to the Late Formative Structure 13. Each of the component structures will be more thoroughly described in terms of size, orientation, construction technique, and associated buildings in succeeding chapters of this study.

At the same time, excavations were carried out in Area E, a Late Formative activity area to the southeast of Mound 1, which is discussed in Chapter VI. Also present were several San José phase features, leading to designation of this area as the site of a probable Early Formative household unit. Brief excavations were also carried out on and around the other three mounds, all of which are Late Formative and are discussed in Chapter VI.

In this manner, some 400 m^2 in six areas in the central portion of the site were intensively excavated, while another 50 m^2 were covered by the test pits. It may be roughly estimated that sampled areas totaled about 4.0 percent of the total one ha area of the Early Formative occupation, about two percent of the three ha area of the Middle Formative occupation, and roughly one percent of the four ha Late Formative occupation. The sample was located largely in what was the most densely occupied portion of the community during every occupation.

This chapter has had as its objective consideration of the cultural and physical placement of the Tomaltepec site. Both the site itself and the specific methodology employed there have also been described. Succeeding chapters will concentrate on analysis and interpretation of the data recovered at Tomaltepec.

PLATE 11. Beginning work on the depression in the northeast corner of Mound 1.

PLATE 12. A portion of the Mound 1 construction sequence. The area of the 1972 test shaft (shown in Plate 7) is marked by the meter stick. Further excavation revealed the footing of a Middle Formative platform (Structure 12), which runs parallel to the meter stick and is indicated by the 30 cm rule and the white north arrow. The large stone wall and heavy adobe bricks on the left are parts of the Late Formative Structure 13.

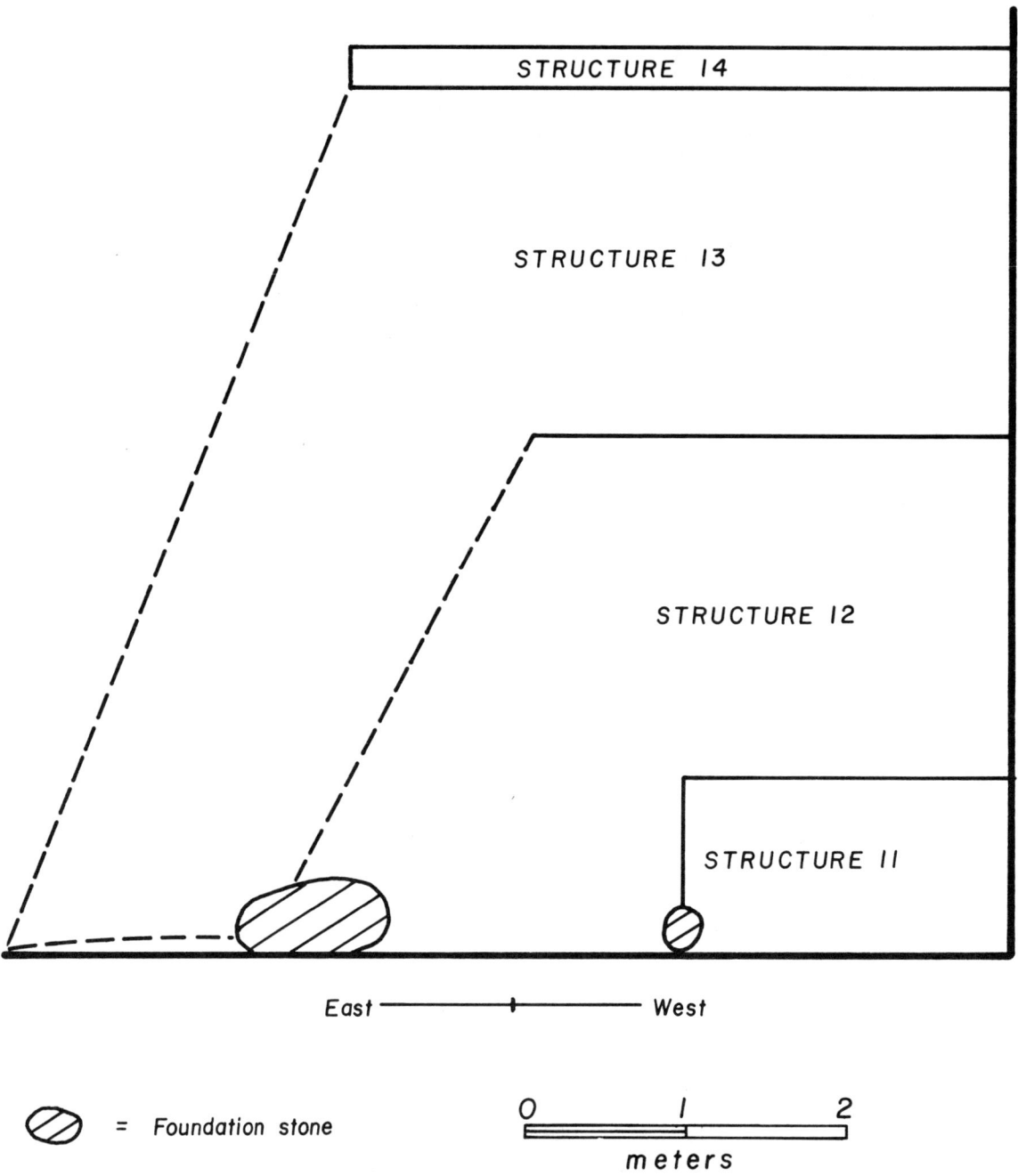

FIGURE 5. The Mound 1 construction sequence. This is a schematic representation of the south profile of the excavated area shown as Area A in Fig. 4. Structure 11 is Earl Formative, Structure 12 is Middle Formative, Structure 13 is Late Formative, and Structure 14 is a Terminal Formative floor atop Structure 13. The facing of Structure 12 was not preserved, and that of Structure 13 was not excavated. (See also Plates 7 and 12.)

Chapter II

Early Formative Occupation at Tomaltepec: The Tierras Largas Phase

**The Tierras Largas Phase
(ca. 1400–1150 B.C.)**

The initial Early Formative occupation at Tomaltepec was during the latter part of the Tierras Largas phase (perhaps 1300 or 1250 B.C. to around 1150 B.C.). The Tierras Largas phase is at present the earliest well-defined, sedentary occupation known in the Valley of Oaxaca, although recent excavations by Flannery and Marcus in press at San José Mogote have demonstrated that the area was occupied during an earlier phase by makers of simple, monochrome pottery of Purrón affiliations.

The Tierras Largas phase occupation at Tomaltepec is contemporary with the Barra and Ocós phases on the Chiapas coast (Green and Lowe, 1967; Ekholm, 1969); with the early Ajalpan phase in Tehuacán (MacNeish, et al., 1970); with the Ojochi and Bajío phases in Veracruz (Coe, 1970); and with the Nevada phase recently defined by Niederberger (1974) at Zohapilco (Tlapacoya) in the Valley of Mexico.

The late Tierras Largas phase occupation at Tomaltepec is unfortunately the only component of the site from which no in situ burials or house floors were recovered. The only evidences of Tierras Largas phase occupation were three pits (Features 7, 102, and 108) identified as belonging to that period by their ceramic contents. While this evidence is less than adequate to achieve the expressed goals of this study, some interpretations will be offered as a preface to the discussion of succeeding and better known periods.

The Tierras Largas phase is still not well known on a valley-wide basis at this writing. However, if so broad a generalization may be offered, an extremely important aspect of the Tierras Largas phase seems to have been the firm establishment of the sedentary agricultural village as the basic settlement type in the Valley of Oaxaca, thus paving the way for slightly later and more spectacular developments in social and political organization.

Composition of the Community

The late Tierras Largas phase occupation at Tomaltepec was most probably characterized by a small number of household units like those discovered by Winter (1976a:25) at the contemporary site of Tierras Largas. These usually consist of a single wattle-and-daub structure of some four by six meters, which seem to be nuclear family residences, several associated bell-shaped storage pits, human burials, trash middens, ovens, activity areas, and so forth. All of these features center around the house—the whole unit being the archaeological manifestation of an area in which the nuclear family performed many of its daily activities. At Tierras Largas, these units were found to be spaced some 30 to 40 m apart (Winter, 1976b:228).

Given the association of bell-shaped pits with such houses in Oaxaca, it seems reasonable to suggest the existence of household units in areas where well-defined late Tierras Largas phase pits were located, especially where masses of burned daub were recovered, as was the case in Feature 7. Proceeding by this logic, two possible late Tierras Largas phase household units can be located. These are designated Possible Household Units TL-1 and TL-2. Both are shown in Figure 6 and are discussed below.

TL-1

The existence of the household is suggested by two bell-shaped storage pits, Features 7 and 102 (see Fig. 7 and Plate 5). Feature 7 contained a considerable quantity of baked clay daub, the remnants of burning the walls of a wattle-and-

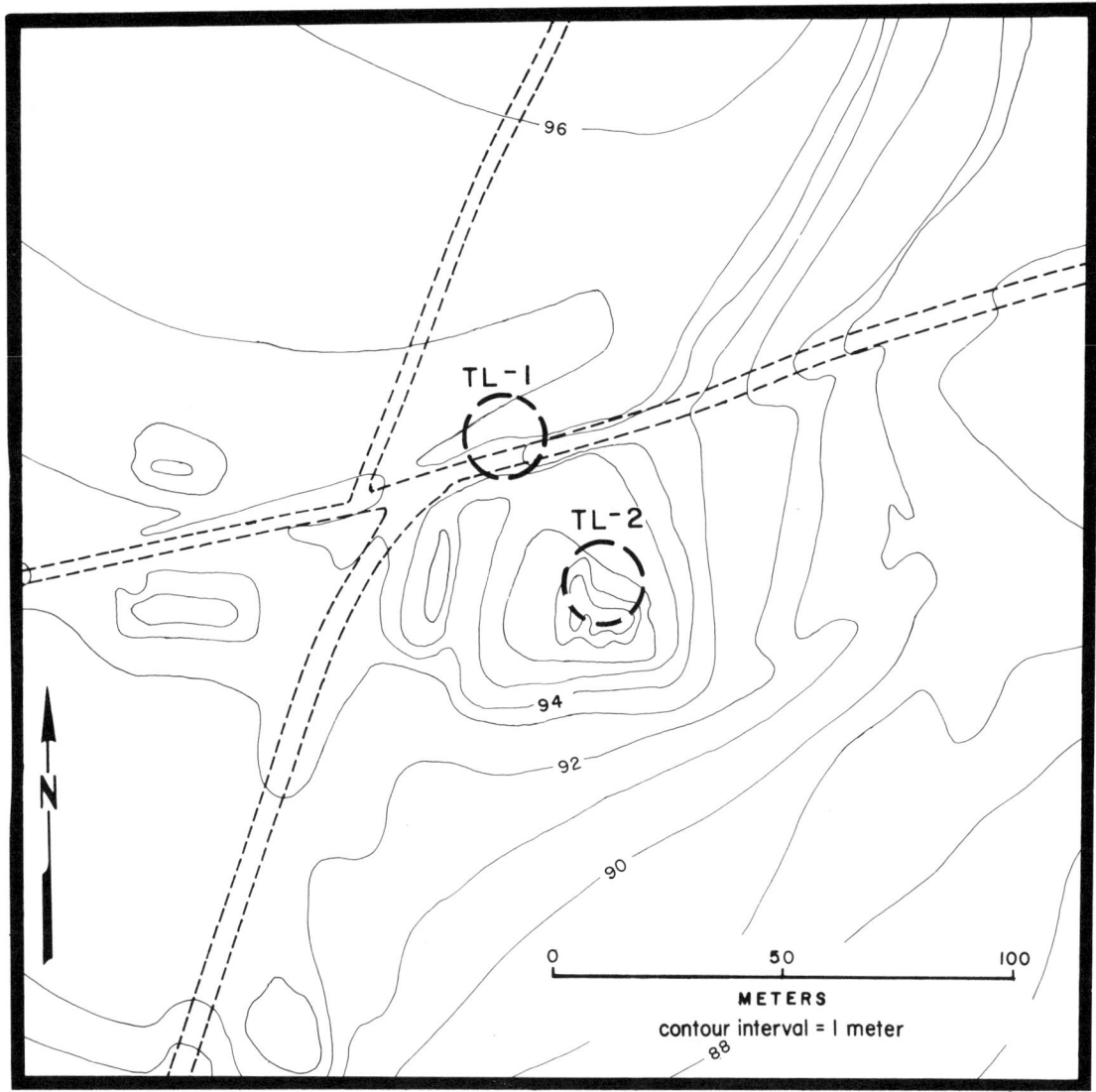

FIGURE 6. Late Tierras Largas phase occupation at Tomaltepec. Each possible household unit is represented by a dashed circle 20 m in diameter.

daub house. The implication is that such a house once stood nearby, and associated artifacts suggest that a wide variety of craft and food preparation activities took place in the vicinity.

The stone tool industry from Feature 7 is quite distinctive, containing a considerable quantity of angular debitage and cores, many of which were used for heavy chopping. Also present were exceptionally large quantities of retouch flakes removed from cores with prepared striking platforms, suggesting preparation of core tool edges. Most of these heavy duty tools were made from a locally available siltstone. Technique of manufacture was almost entirely hard-hammer percussion, largely lacking soft-hammer percussion, and virtually without pressure retouch. Little energy was expended in production of the tools, and locally available stone was used almost exclusively. Use of most tools seems to have been short-term.

Included in Feature 7 assemblage are a number of heavy, concave-edge scrapers and choppers appropriate for use on cylindrical surfaces. This, combined with wear indicative of woodworking, suggests that a major use to which the tools had

*a. Feature 7: Large, bell-shaped storage pit; E/W section.
Location: Possible Unit TL-1.*

*b. Feature 102: Small, bell-shaped storage pit; E/W section.
Location: Possible Unit TL-1.*

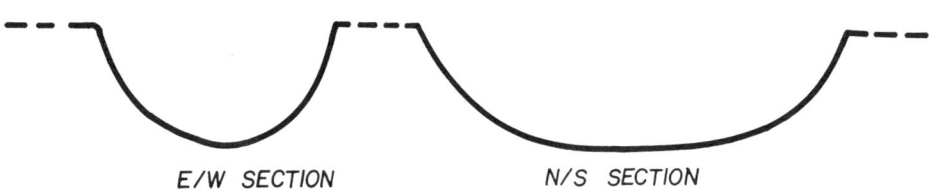

E/W SECTION   N/S SECTION

*c. Feature 108. Large, basin-shaped pit.
Location: Possible Unit TL-2.*

FIGURE 7. Late Tierras Largas phase features.

been put was cutting, chopping, and scraping of large branches or small tree trunks. Presence of large, angular debitage suggests also that the tools were made, used, and deposited over a relatively short period of time, such that tool kits and debitage were never spatially separated. The tool kit may very well have been used in construction of the wooden frame of a wattle-and-daub house, for which a number of posts would have been required.

TL-2

This household is represented by a large, oval, trash-filled pit of uncertain function (Feature 108), which is illustrated in Figure 7. Charcoal, animal bone, chipped stone, and other debris suggest the normal daily round of domestic activities. Artifacts associated with each household unit will be discussed presently.

As no in situ late Tierras Largas houses were recovered at Tomaltepec, very little can be said with confidence about house construction details and household orgaization. The cane-impressed daub fragments recovered from Feature 7 are entirely unremarkable, suggesting a wattle-and-daub house of the sort commonly found at Early Formative Oaxacan villages. As previously noted, the actual sizes of the late Tierras Largas phase houses at San José Mogote and Tierras Largas seem to have been some 6 m by 3m–4m, or 18 to 24 m^2 (Flannery, 1976:19; Winter, 1976a:25). Such houses may have accommodated a nuclear family. Whether this was the case in the late Tierras Largas phase community at Tomaltepec remains unclear. It may be supposed to have been, as houses of these dimensions do occur in the succeeding early San José phase community at Tomaltepec.

Based on his excavations at the type site of Tierras Largas, Winter (1976a:25) suggests that: 1) the household units were approximately evenly spaced; 2) in the Early Formative period, spacing between the margins of household units was some 20 m; and 3) distance between the centers of two adjacent units averaged 40 m. Reference to Figure 6 suggests that these spacing principles are also applicable to the late Tierras Largas phase settlement at Tomaltepec.

Feature 7, the defining feature of Possible Unit TL–1, lies some 40 m to 45 m from Feature 108, the defining feature of possible Unit TL–2. Furthermore, if circles of 20 m in diameter are drawn about the two features and are taken to approximate unit boundaries, some 20 m to 25 m remains between the two. Tests in this inter-unit area produced virtually no Early Formative debris, all of which accords well with Winter's spacing model.

As Tomaltepec was not sampled on any sort of probabilistic basis, no probability-based estimate for the total number of households can be reached. Some ten late Tierras Largas phase houses are estimated at the type site (Winter, 1972:91), and while there is space for an equal number of dwellings at Tomaltepec, the general paucity of late Tierras Largas cultural remains there suggests a smaller number of dwellings. A more likely, although largely subjective, estimate is on the order of two to five households. This is based on the spread of Early Formative materials over the site as revealed by the test pit program.

Artifacts associated with each of these possible household units are shown in Table 1. Pottery, chipped stone tools and debitage, animal bone, and carbonized plant remains were the most common items found in each unit, implying that the round of daily activities was much the same in both households. Chi-square tests were used to check randomness of distribution of major classes of artifacts between possible Units TL–1 and TL–2. One distribution of particular interest was that of finer quality chert tools, versus somewhat lower quality—but more readily available—local silicified siltstone tools. As Table 1 shows, the local siltstone tools are much more common in both units, the ratio of chert to local stone being 0.084 in TL–1 and 0.154 in TL–2. The distribution is not significantly nonrandom, however (Chi-square = 2.14 for 1 degree of freedom, associated probability less than 0.1).

Table 1: Artifacts Associated with Possible Units TL–1 and TL–2†

Artifacts	TL–1	TL–2
Total Sherds*	467	132
Bowls*	60	12
Jars*	407	120
Local Stone	450	52
Chert	38	8
Obsidian	3	4
Deer Bone	8	1
Rabbit Bone	13	2
Ground Stone	9	0
Bone Tools	1	0
Mica	1	0
Figurine Fragments	2	0
Shell	0	1

*Rim sherds only.

†More complete descriptions of all artifacts may be found in the appropriate appendix. All counts are numbers of pieces present in this and all succeeding tables.

Distribution of obsidian, on the other hand, was found to be distinctly nonrandom. The cell frequencies in the obsidian-versus-non-obsidian chipped stone conteingency table did not meet minimum criteria for the chi-square test as given in Siegel (1956:46–47), so that Fisher's Exact Probability was calculated instead (p = 0.0043), indicating significant departure from randomness of the obsidian distribution between the two household units). This test was also performed as described by Siegel (op cit.:97–98). The chi-square statistic, although not absolutely reliable in this case due to low cell frequencies, was calculated to be 14.46 for 1 degree of freedom, with an associated probability of less than 0.001—in agreement, in other words, with the Fisher solution.

The greatest density of obsidian at this time period occurs in Possible Unit TL-2, although it should be emphasized that the absolute quantity of obsidian at Tierras Largas phase Tomaltepec is very small. The concentration is a revealing one, however, in light of the subsequent history of the area where Possible Unit TL-2 is located. As we shall see, this area developed into a high status residence/public building area in slightly later times and maintained this position in spite of its non-central location, as long as the Tomaltepec site was occupied, or ca. 700-800 years. This topic will be elaborated upon in subsequent sections of this study.

Both units have maize among their carbonized plant remains, so that the lack of grinding stones in Possible Unit TL-2 should be taken as an example of sampling error, rather than as indicative of lack of maize consumption. Mica fragments, a small cut piece of shell (see Appendix VI for description of shell from Tomaltepec), figurine fragments, and bone tool fragments are too thinly scattered for meaningful interpretation. All evidence, however, suggests that much the same activities took place in both households.

Social Differentiation

The level of social differentiation within the Tierras Largas phase community at Tomaltepec is unfortunately ambiguous, as neither burials, nor much house construction evidence, nor large artifact samples were recovered. It has already been observed that Feature 108 of Possible Household Unit TL-2 contained more obsidian and a higher ratio of chert to local silicified siltstone than did Features 7 and 102, the defining elements of Possible Household Unit TL-1.

Ceramic assemblages are quite uniform between the two possible units, however. In each case, utilitarian jars and bowls are found in nearly equal proportions: 71 percent jars to 19 percent bowls in Unit TL-1, and 68 percent jars to 13 percent bowls in Unit TL-2. Also, as will be evident in the next section of this chapter, there seem to have been no substantial differences in food consumption between the two possible household units investigated. It should be noted that the sample of relevant evidence was quite small, however. In general, the small samples of Tierras Largas material recovered preclude meaningful estimates of differentiation beteween individuals and households during this early phase.

Subsistence Activities

Activities performed in possible Late Tierras Largas phase Household Unit TL-1 can be partially defined by artifacts recovered from the fill of Feature 7. Corn and other seed grinding and preparation is indicated by six grinding stone fragments (five manos and one metate), three of them showing fairly heavy wear. Also recovered were a number of carbonized maize kernels (*Zea mays*), as well as a number of small teosinte seeds (*Zea mexicana*), identified by Judith Smith of the University of Michigan (see Appendix IX) and C. E. Smith of the University of Alabama. C. E. Smith (nd.:2) suggests that the quantity of carbonized teosinte seed recovered at Tomaltepec implies that the plant was probably being interplanted, or at least tolerated in quantity in the maize field, harvested, and eaten along with the maize. As observed by Ford (in Drennan, 1975, Appendix VIII), maize and teosinte readily hybridize, such hybridization producing a tougher plant which is more resistant to drought, an especially important consideration in Oaxaca. However, Ford (op. cit.) notes that such hybridization would also effectively lower the productivity of more primitive varieties of corn. Balanced against this loss, however, is the addition of another edible grain (i.e., the teosinte) and an increase in drought resistance.

Other plant remains recovered from the late Tierras Largas phase deposits at Tomaltepec include the common bean, *Phaseolus vulgaris*, two fragments of which were identified by C. E. Smith (Ibid.:2). "Unfortunately," he writes, "the carbonized bean fragments have lost their seed coats . . . and the cotyledon fragments indicate only that the original beans were too large to have been gathered from wild *Phaseolus* plants in the area."

Consumption of avocados, *Persea americana*, at late Tierras Largas phase Tomaltepec is also in evidence. C. E. Smith (op. cit.) reports several carbonized fragments of avocado cotyledon which may have come from wild or cultivated trees.

Unfortunately, the fragments were not sufficiently large for the measurements necessary to resolve the wild or domestic question. However, Smith observes that "the presence of carbonized cotyledons ... does indicate that avocados were being consumed in sufficient quantities to have been preserved" (op. cit.).

In summary, it may be inferred that at late Tierras Largas phase Tomaltepec the principal crop, maize, was accompanied by teosinte, by some cultivation of beans, and by cultivation or collection of avocados. As Ford (Drennan, 1975, Appendix XIII) has suggested, the abundant evidence of avocados at several other Oaxacan Formative sites suggests that avocados and corn were an important combination at that time. That beans were so poorly represented in the Tomaltepec remains at least tentatively implies that they had not yet become as vital an element of the subsistence assemblage as they were in somewhat later times.

Animal bone from both Tierras Largas phase households units at Tomaltepec, identified by Kent V. Flannery of the University of Michigan, included some whitetail deer and collared peccary. Cottontail rabbit is also prominent, and Flannery (1966:803) observes that these animals are easily taken in traps. Bone frequencies are given in Appendix V.

The Tomaltepec data, then, suggests that maize cultivation, supplemented by other wild and cultivated plants, as well as hunting and trapping of large and small game, sustained the Tierras Largas phase households. Also, although the sample is quite small, and therefore can provide only a tentative indication, it can be suggested that there were no substantial differences in food consumption between the two household units investigated.

Craft and Exchange Activities

As far as can be determined from the scanty evidence, limited exchange of non-local items characterized the Tierras Largas phase community at Tomaltepec. Obsidian, apparently a basic household commodity, appears in both possible household units at Tomaltepec. A single cut piece of shell (identified by Dr. L. H. Feldman, University of Missouri, see Appendix VI) was found in Feature 7 (possible Household Unit TL-1). We remain ignorant of the mechanisms by which this material entered the community, but if we accept Flannery's (1972) assertion that particular levels of sociocultural complexity are characterized by particular kinds and levels of exchange, then we may suggest that Tierras Largas phase trade in non-local goods was rather simply organized.

Summary

As observed at the outset of this discussion, little detailed information about the late Tierras Largas phase community at Tomaltepec was recovered so the workings of the community as a whole, unfortunately, can only be discussed in the most tenuous terms. For some period of time, very roughly between 1300 and 1150 B.C., a hamlet of at least two and probably not more than five households, sheltering on the order of 10 to 20 persons, existed at Tomaltepec. It seems that this occupation can best be characterized as permanent rather than seasonal. The large and small storage pits, house remains, domestic refuse, and agricultural products recovered, all lend support to such an interpretation.

Tentative indications are that the hamlet was composed of the sort of nuclear family, wattle-and-daub houses previously known for the phase, and that the spacing principles governing the distribution of the components of the community were also quite comparable to contemporary sites in the region. Two household units were tentatively defined on the basis of several large, trash-filled pits. Unfortunately, no in situ houses or burials were discovered, although the burned and redeposited remains of a wattle-and-daub house were associated with possible Unit TL-1.

Chi-square tests, where admissible, showed that of the various classes of artifacts recovered, only obsidian showed a significantly non-random distribution. While this result is statistically significant, however, the fact that it was drawn from only three pits renders it questionable in practical terms. None of the variations between households in the distributions of the classes of artifacts recovered departed significantly from randomness. It seems, then, that activities carried out in both households were quite similar and that intra-community differentiation was most probably at a relatively low level.

The Tierras Largas phase inhabitants of Tomaltepec were farmers, cultivating maize (intermixed with teosinte), beans, and perhaps avocados. Farming was most probably done on the high alluvial terrace just below the site. Hunting and collection of mountain, piedmont, and a few riverine resources were also engaged in, and woodworking tool kits suggest adaptation to the probably then forested piedmont slopes. The prevalence of tools made from locally available siltstone over finer quality chert (sources of which are located 10–15 km from Tomaltepec [Whalen, n.d.]) implies some limits at least on this resource exploitation zone.

Finally, with reference to the criteria of complexity discussed in the preceding chapter, the community at Tomaltepec evidences relatively few parts, relatively little differentiation of these parts, and we may suspect that a low level of integration of the component individuals and households was also characteristic of the hamlet. It may also be tentatively suggested that relations between the essentially similar segments of the community were virtually self-regulating, or were mediated in some extremely generalized, and perhaps sporadic, fashion. With the data currently available, very little more can be said about the regulation of relations within the community, save to suggest that it probably did not rise far above the level of the component households. As this study follows the development of the community, however, we will see the control hierarchy gradually grow in "height" until it towers far above the level of the ordinary household.

Chapter III

Early Formative Occupation at Tomaltepec: The San José Phase

**The San José Phase
(Ca. 1150 B.C.–850 B.C.)**

Occupation at Tomaltepec continued without interruption into the early part of the San José phase. The early San José phase community, dating from around 1150 B.C. is better defined and less enigmatic than the Tierras Largas phase occupation. Contemporary phases in other parts of Mesoamerica include the latter part of the Ocós-Cuadros transition on the coasts of Chiapas and Guatemala (Coe and Flannery, 1967; Green and Lowe, 1967; and Ekholm, 1969), the earliest Cotorra phase in the Grijalva depression of Chiapas (Lowe, et al., 1960), the Middle Nexpa phase in Morelos (Grove, 1970), the early part of the Ajalpan phase in Tehuacán (MacNeish, et al., 1970), the early part of the Ixtapaluca phase in Central Mexico (Tolstoy and Paradis, 1970), and the Chicharras phase in Veracruz (Coe, 1970).

Most interestingly, no substantial remains were recovered at Tomaltepec from the latter part of the San José phase (probably 1000 B.C. to 850 B.C.) as defined in the Etla region (Flannery, et al., 1970). It is not clear whether this reflects a partial abandonment of Tomaltepec, or an absence of some of the late San José phase ceramic horizon markers which are so common near Etla. We are only beginning to appreciate the regional differences in ceramics among the various arms of the Valley of Oaxaca at this time period, and there is no room to discuss them here. Accordingly, the remainder of this chapter will be concerned with discussion and analysis of the early San José phase community at Tomaltepec. Starting from the Tierras Largas phase base, the object of the chapter will be to use the concepts set forth in Chapter I to consider evolutionary change within the community. These next few sections will suggest four points: 1) multiplication of different kinds of parts of the social body, 2) differentiation of these parts, 3) centralization of authority within the community, and 4) development of more complex linkages between these parts. All four of these represent essential concomitants of increasing social complexity.

Composition of the Early San José Phase Community

It is estimated that the early San José phase village at Tomaltepec consisted of five to eight household units, containing a total of 25 to 40 people. The three best defined household units at Tomaltepec are designated ESJ-1, ESJ-2, and Structure 11. Possible Household Units ESJ-3, 4, and 5 were also designated, although very little was recovered from these locations. Finally, a San José phase cemetery area entirely disassociated from any other contemporary cultural feature was discovered and will also be discussed as a component of the community. The "possible" household units of this phase should be regarded with caution, since any spatially separate early San José phase feature of the type known to be typical of household units was used to define a possible unit. In this manner, Possible Units ESJ-3, 4, and 5 were distinguished even though no actual house post molds were found. It is possible that these three proveniences do not represent household clusters at all, but are simply isolated caches, dumps, or activity areas. Figure 8 shows the location of each proposed unit and the cemetery. Table 2 summarizes artifacts recovered from each unit. Artifacts and proveniences are discussed in more detail in the appendices to this study. A discussion of each of the components of the community follows.

ESJ-1

There are actually two superimposed constructions here, although both belong to the early part

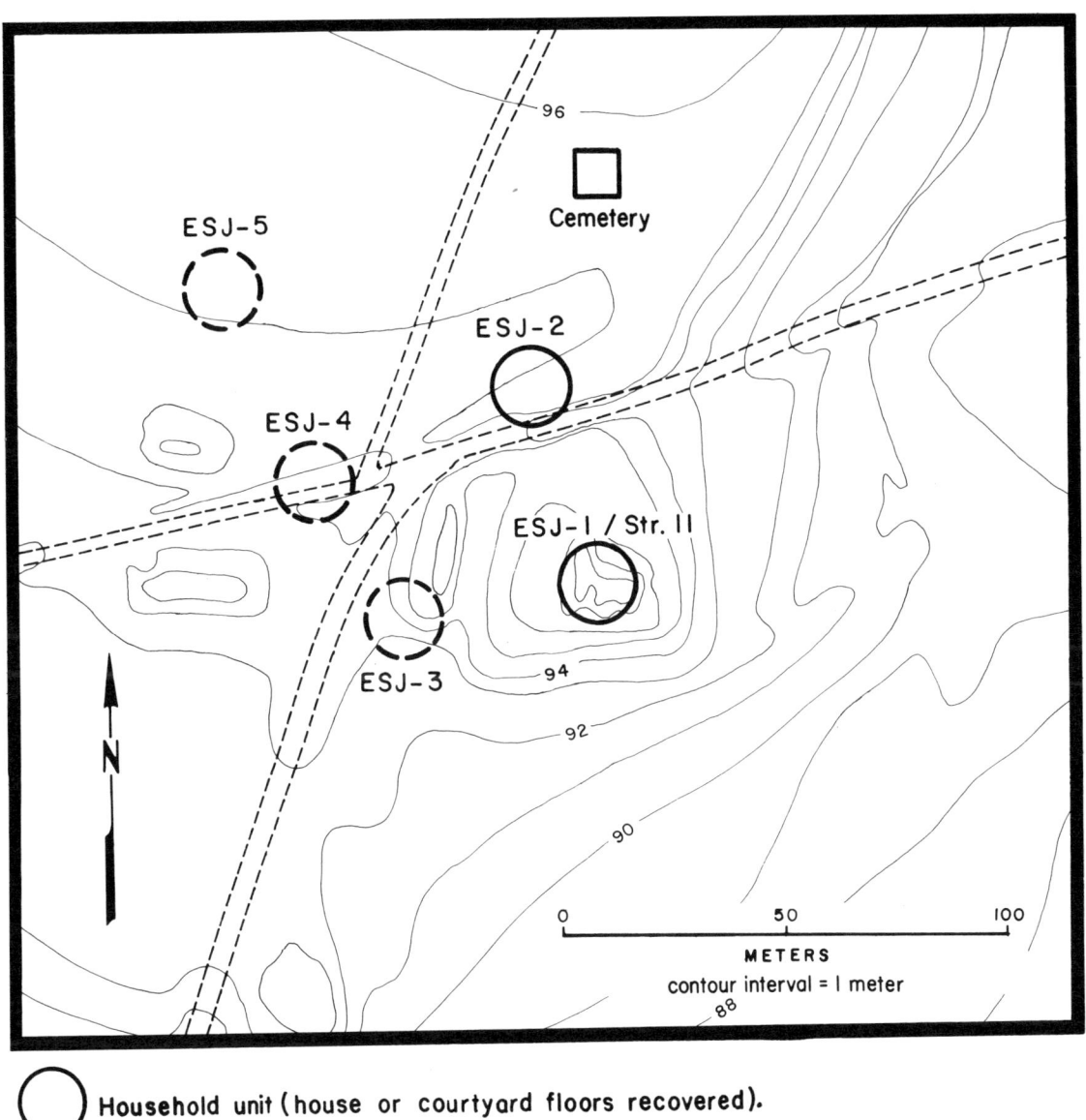

FIGURE 8. Early San José phase occupation at Tomaltepec.

of the San José phase, and are thus not far removed in time from each other. Household Unit ESJ–1 is represented by the large, bell-shaped storage pit (Feature 109), a midden area (Feature 117), and about 10 m² of hard-packed earth surface, designated House 8. Components of ESJ–1 are illustrated in Figure 9 and Plate 13. Insights into Early Formative house construction gained in excavation of Unit ESJ–2, to be discussed pres-

ently, suggest that the "House 8" surface associated with Feature 109 is not actually an interior house floor. No post holes were found, and the surface seems rather to be part of the hard-packed exterior ("courtyard") area which was found to surround the other Early Formative house at Tomaltepec. It thus seems very likely that an Early Formative house once stood in the immediate vicinity of Feature 109, but its remains were not uncovered.

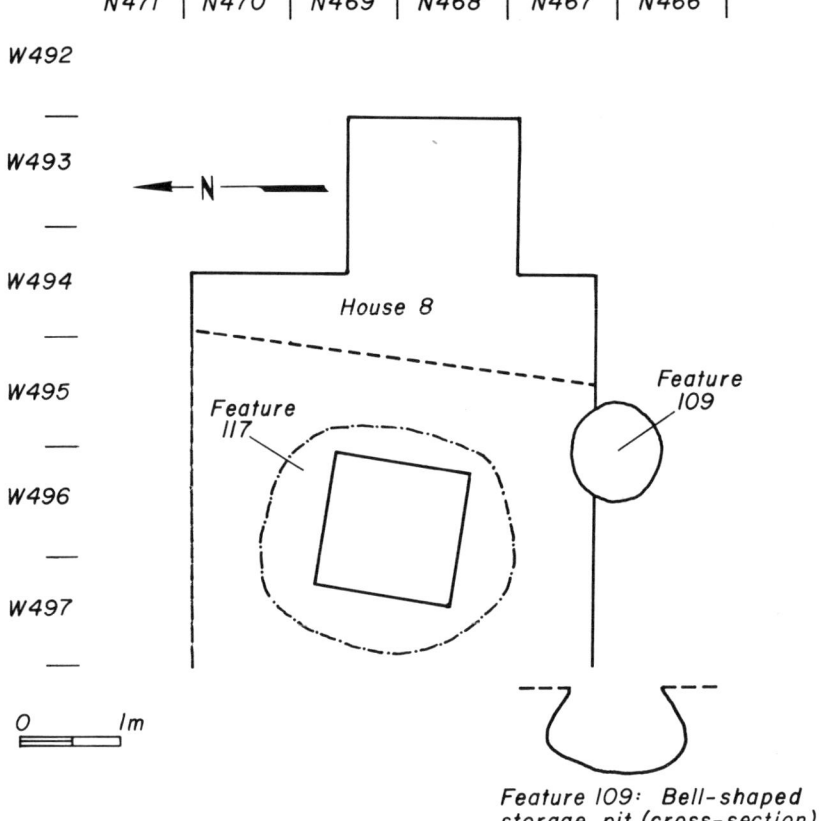

FIGURE 9. Components of Household Unit ESJ-1. Feature 117 lay beneath Structure 11. Limits of House 8 not defined.

Artifacts associated with Feature 109 include substantial quantities of splintered deer bone as well as the distal metapodial of a deer with the shaft of the bone neatly cut off, possibly for further use as a haft or as a source of bone splinters for awls or needles. Throughout the early San José phase, in fact, bone tool making and use were to characterize this area of the community, as we shall see in the course of this discussion. As is apparent from Table 2, fully 87.5 percent of the early San José phase bone tools recovered at Tomaltepec are from this area.

The stone tool assemblage from Feature 109 also suggests an emphasis on bone tool production, hide scraping, and other light bone or wood chopping and scraping activities, as discussed by

Table 2: Artifact Counts and Distributions Among Known and Possible Early San José Household Units

Artifacts	ESJ-1	STR.11	ESJ-2	ESJ-3	ESJ-4
Total Sherds*	169	345	87	147	19
Jars*	68	148	49	85	11
Bowls*	101	197	38	62	8
Jar/Bowl Ratio*	0.673	0.751	1.289	1.371	1.375
Deer Bone	148	150	13	66	18
Other Bone	51	18	2	3	1
Bone Tools	3	3	2	0	0
Chert/Local Stone Ratio†	0.377	0.575	0.095	Insuf. Data	0.200
Obsidian	22	38	8	0	0
Ground Stone	7	4	1	0	1
Mica	1	2	0	0	0
Figurines	1	0	0	4	1
Shell	3	1	0	0	0

*Only rim sherds counted. Ratio of jars to bowls is the number of jar rims/number of bowl rims.

†Chert/local stone ratio is the number of pieces of chert/the number of pieces of local silicified siltstone.

EARLY FORMATIVE: THE SAN JOSÉ PHASE

PLATE 13. Components of Household Unit ESJ-1. Top, Feature 109 and the House 8 surface, both overlain and disturbed by the later Structure 11. Feature 108, a Tierras Largas phase pit, is also indicated. The dashed line indicates the original limit of Structure 11. Bottom, excavation of the badly disturbed House 8 surface. The two large stones indicated by arrows are remaining foundation stones from the overlying Middle Formative Structure 12.

Rick in Appendix VIII. As was the case in the late Tierras Largas Feature 7 assemblage described in Chapter II, the Feature 109 assemblage includes everything from raw chunks of stone to retouch flakes, suggesting that the tools were made, used, and deposited in a restricted area and over a fairly short period of time. In addition, as in the preceding phase, the lower quality local silicified siltstone continues to vastly outweigh the finer quality cherts available 10-15 m from the community (Whalen, n.d.). A very small quantity of black and striated gray obsidian in the form of debitage and retouch flakes was also found.

The tools themselves include light duty, short-term use choppers; a notched tool suitable for shaping wooden shafts or bone needles, or for fiber scraping; a spokeshave-like, concave scraper with extensive wear; a thick, steep-edged scraper, suitable for light scraping of wood, bone, or hide; and several cores. More precise discussions of these tools appear in Appendix VIII.

Ground stone tools from Feature 109 included a fist-sized river cobble of dubious grinding and pounding function, a fragment of a mano, or grinding stone, and two small stone balls 1.6 cm and 2.2 cm in diameter respectively. Several of these reasonably carefully ground stone balls were found in Early Formative contexts (Plate 14), but their function remains unclear.

Floral remains consisted largely of carbonized maize cupules and kernels. Assorted small seeds were present, but maize seems to have been the major staple in Unit ESJ-1.

A figurine head, a small fragment of mica, and three fragments of cut and drilled marine shell, including a small bivalve shell drilled for hanging at the hinge, complete the Feature 109 assemblage. The ceramic contents of the feature are discussed in Appendix II.

The exterior "House 8" surface referred to earlier in association with Feature 109 was so badly disturbed by Middle Formative intrusions (refer to Pl. 13) that artifacts recovered from it will not be tabulated here. It seemed clear on stratigraphic grounds, however, that the surface antedated the intrusions and was once associated with Feature 109.

Structure 11

At a slightly later point in the early San José phase, the platform designated Structure 11 was constructed over the remains of Unit ESJ-1. This platform, the first of its kind to be discovered at one of the smaller Oaxacan Early Formative sites, measured very roughly 4 m by 6 m, and its approximately vertical sides were about 1 m high. The platform was oriented with its long axis about 8° east of magnetic north (16°-17° E. of true north). No evidence of a stairway of any sort was recovered, although the south, west, and north sides of the platform were only partially cleared due to the heavy overburden of more than 4 m of later mound construction and fill. It is possible, therefore, that some sort of stairway may still be hidden. The platform was built upon a layer of larger foundation stones, followed by alternating layers of adobe—sometimes puddled and sometimes in the form of "bun-shaped" adobe bricks—and fist-sized stones set in a puddled adobe matrix. The most interesting feature of Structure 11 is a large, adobe-plastered cell positioned so as to lie under the floor of any structure atop the platform. Figure 10 shows a plan and section of Structure 11, including the cell just described, as well as a view of the platform's construction technique (see also Plate 15). Table 2 lists associated artifacts. The cell itself measures some three by five meters and is about 0.6 m deep, with well-defined vertical walls coated with hard adobe plaster. The bottom of the

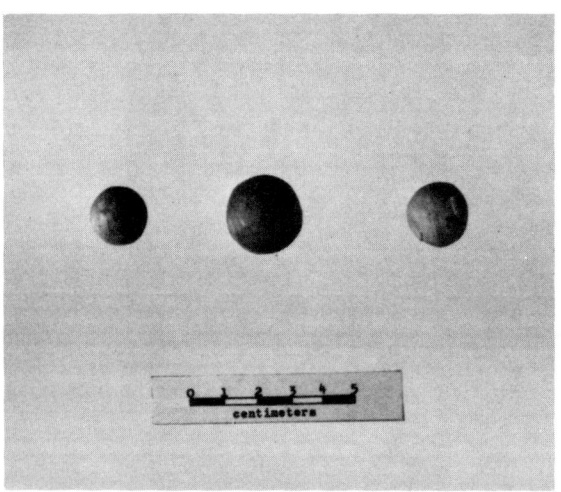

PLATE 14. Examples of the stone balls occasionally found in Early Formative contexts.

EARLY FORMATIVE: THE SAN JOSÉ PHASE

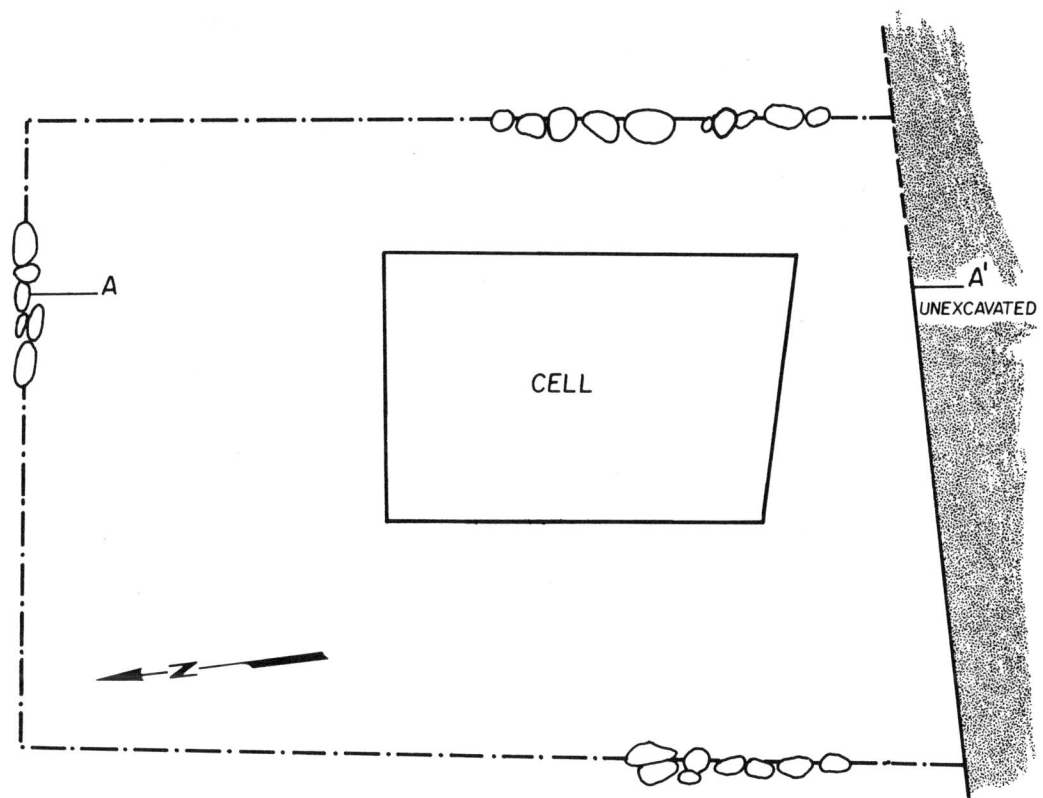

A. PLAN VIEW OF STRUCTURE 11 (RECONSTRUCTED).

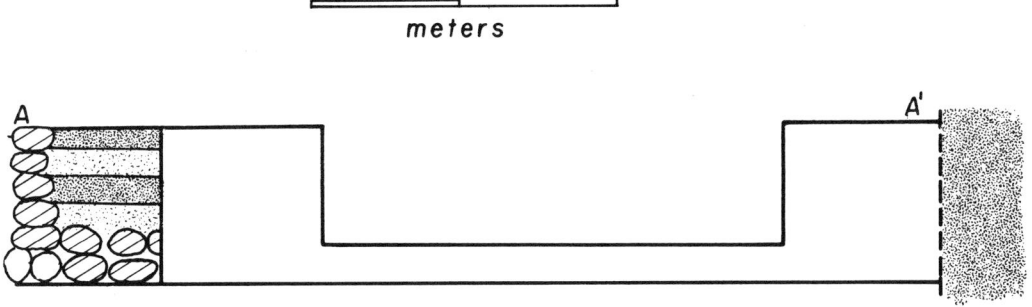

B. SECTION OF STRUCTURE 11, SHOWING CONSTRUCTION TECHNIQUE.

○ = FOUNDATION STONES.
⊘ = PLANO-CONVEX ADOBE BRICKS.
▨ = PUDDLED ADOBE.
▦ = EARTH AND SMALL-ROCK RUBBLE.

FIGURE 10. Structure 11 (southern limit of Structure poorly defined).

PLATE 15. Lateral view of Structure 11. The arrow indicates the bun-shaped adobes which formed the footing of the platform. A portion of the wall under and in front of the meter stick has been removed. Note the layers of sherds, stone rubble, and adobe bricks of which the walls are constructed. The interior cell lies directly behind the meter stick. The heavy stone wall crossing the platform (right side of the photo) is part of Late Formative Structure 13.

cell was also plastered with the same material, although it was in a rather deteriorated condition at excavation. The volume of the cell is about 9 m³, or approximately 6 times the capacity of the average bell-shaped food storage pit at Tomaltepec, San José Mogote, and Tierras Largas.

That Structure 11 was used as a house platform is suggested by the enormous quantities of associated domestic garbage, including utilitarian pottery, bone, charcoal, and carbonized plant remains. Unfortunately, however, no evidence of the house itself was preserved, as the top of the Early Formative platform appears to have been leveled when construction of a larger platform was begun upon reoccupation of the site in Middle Formative times. It is further suggested that Structure 11 served as a large-scale storage facility, although on what scale or for what ends goods or produce were stored remains unclear. This and related concepts will be considered in more depth when the early San José phase community is discussed as a whole in the final section of this chapter.

The artifact assemblage associated with Structure 11 is also somewhat distinctive. As with the underlying Feature 109 complex, unusually large numbers of deer and rabbit bones were present, as were several bone awl fragments (Plate 16). The associated stone tool industry also most strongly suggests specialization in light woodworking, especially shaft scraping, hide scraping, and butchering. Tools identified by Rick in Appendix VIII included 8 flake knives, 2 shallow edge-angle knife/scraper tools, 5 choppers (including light and heavy duty specimens), and 10 scrapers. Wear indicative of the suggested uses was noted by Rick in each case. One projectile fragment was positively identified, and two other possible fragments were noted. These, together with the notched scrapers and spokeshave-like tools referred to above, suggest that at least some of the deer were taken with hafted projectiles. Local silicified siltstone, finer quality chert, and obsidian were the materials utilized. It is interesting to note that the ratio of chert to local siltstone associated with Structure 11 is .570, a considerable increase over the earlier Unit ESJ-1 ratio of .337 and the Unit

EARLY FORMATIVE: THE SAN JOSÉ PHASE

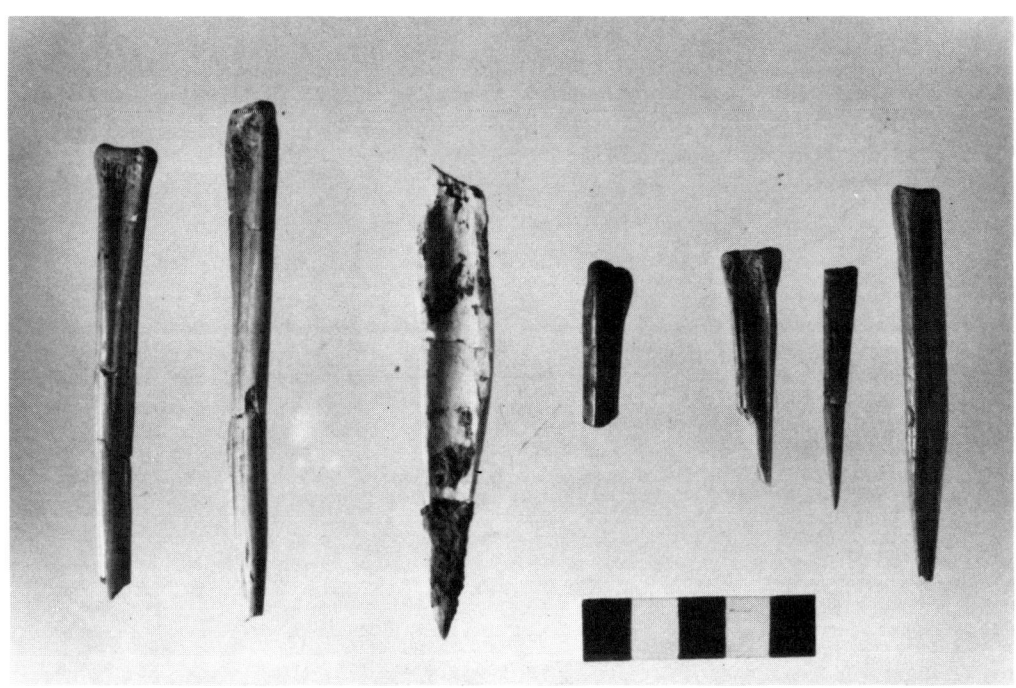

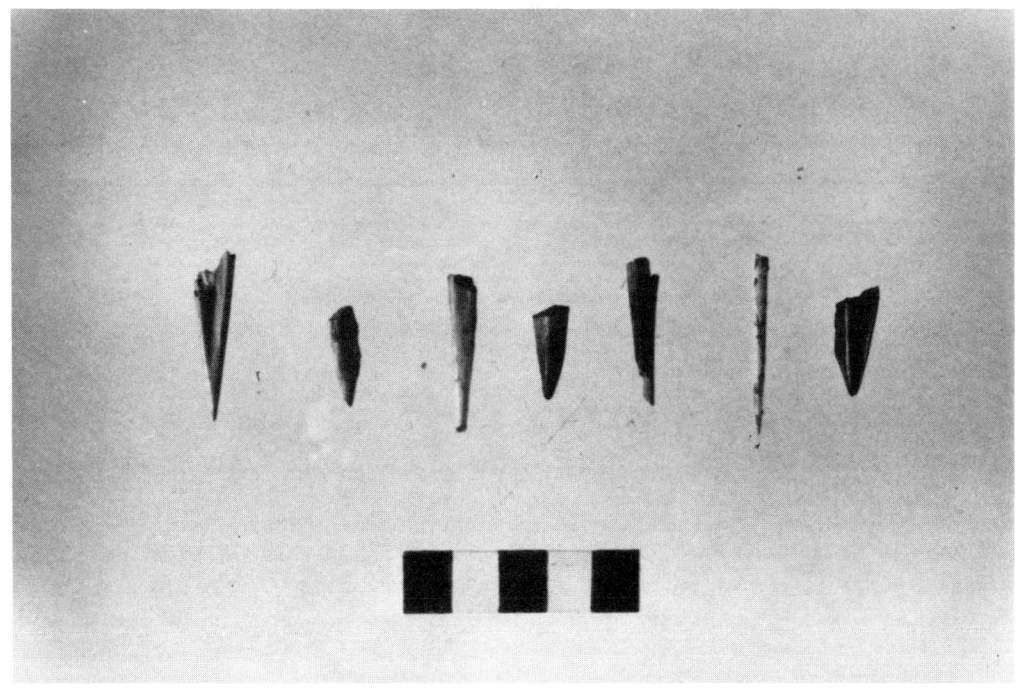

PLATE 16. Bone awls (Top) and awl tips (Bottom) from Early Formative proveniences. (Scale in cm.)

PLATE 17. Ground stone tools from Structure 11. Top row, side view of heavily worn pestles. Middle row, end view of same pestles. Bottom row, broken manos.

EARLY FORMATIVE: THE SAN JOSÉ PHASE

TL-2 ratio of .348. Units ESJ-1 and TL-2, it will be recalled, both underlie Structure 11. They seem fairly close together in time. The quantity of obsidian tools and—mostly—debitage associated with Structure 11 also reaches an all-time high for the Early Formative at Tomaltepec: over 50 percent of the Early Formative obsidian from the site comes from this one provenience (i.e., 38 of 59 pieces).

Floral remains associated with Structure 11 include large quantities of charcoal, almost all of which is pine from the nearby mountain zone (see Appendix IX). Also present were maize cupules, kernels, and cob fragments as well as teosinte seeds, and avocado pits. The floral complex, in other words, is nearly identical to that of the other late Tierras Largas and early San José households thus far described.

Numerous whole and fragmentary ground stone tools were also recovered from Structure 11. Smaller one-hand grinding stones, elliptical manos, and trunco-conical, pestle-like grinding stones were recovered, both of which seem to have been first pecked and then ground to shape. The pestles are doubtless for use with the stone grinding bowls or mortars which also characterize the Early Formative ground stone assemblage at Tomaltepec. All of these forms are described in Appendix VII.

A small, cut, sub-rectangular piece of marine shell with a partially drilled hole in the center attests to production, as well as simple consumption, of items of imported raw material in the Structure 11 area. Several small bits of mica were also found in this area although, interestingly enough, no figurine fragments were recovered. It should be noted, however, that there is a general paucity of figurines from Early Formative proveniences at Tomaltepec.

Before concluding this discussion, it should be emphasized that while all of the proveniences just described belong to the early part of the San José phase (ca. 1150–1100 B.C.), there are at least three phases of activity represented here. The first of these is the Feature 109-House 8-Feature 117 complex, designated Household Unit ESJ-1; the second is the platform designated Structure 11; and the third is the refuse with which the cell of Structure 11 was filled. It might be suggested that this fill was collected on a site-wide basis, but the artifact continuities (i.e., relatively large quantities of chert as opposed to local stone, and similarly large quantities of deer bone, obsidian, and shell) all suggest that the fill does, in fact, derive from the same area. It may, therefore, be reasonably suggested that the debris used to fill the then-defunct cell was more or less contemporary trash scraped up from the immediate area of the structure, and very possibly originally associated with Structure 11. It might be added that no evidence of early San José phase occupation apart from ESJ-1 and the succeeding Structure 11 were found in the immediate area.

ESJ-2

Early San José phase Household Unit 2 is an unusual and interesting find. It contained a virtually intact house floor, complete with posthole alignments forming four walls and internal and external features, and a large exterior courtyard-like area. The house is illustrated in Figure 11, and associated artifacts are listed in Table 2. The structure itself (House 4) measured 2.2 m by 4.9 m, with a floor area of 10.8 m^2. The house is thus quite comparable in size to houses excavated at other Early Formative sites in the area. Flannery (1976: 19) reports that most San José phase houses from the Valley of Oaxaca measure between 3 m by 5 m and 4 m by 6 m. The Tomaltepec house thus falls at the smaller end of this continuum.

House 4 was oriented with its long axis almost due east. A door, apparently protected by a wattle-and-daub wind screen, seems to have been located

PLATE 18. Partially-drilled shell ornament from Structure 11. (Diameter, 19.2 mm.)

44 EXCAVATIONS AT SANTO DOMINGO TOMALTEPEC

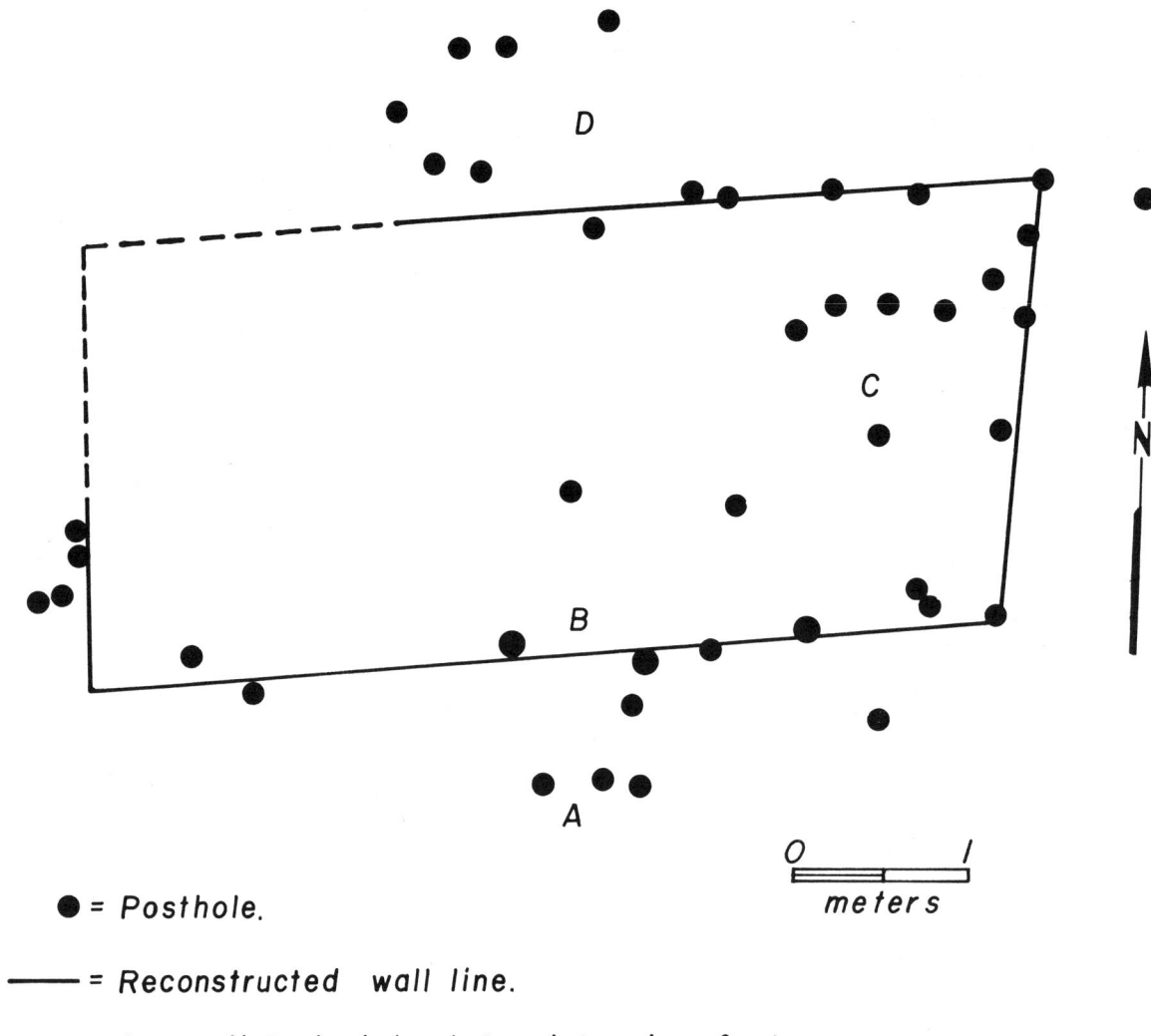

FIGURE 11. House 4, a part of Household Unit ESJ-2. It is suggested that A was a windscreen in front of the door, B; C was a firestand; and D was some type of auxiliary feature.

near the center of the southern side. The construction technique involved a slightly staggered, unevenly-spaced row of posts with diameters in the 8–13 cm range, along each of the four walls. These formed the framework of the house, over which vertical, finger-sized canes were tied and covered with a layer of mud plaster. There were several superimposed packed earth layers, representing resurfacings of the original floor. There were also apparently three auxiliary features attached to the house, including what seems to be a wind screen across the door—such as are still seen on contemporary wattle-and-daub structures in the Valley of Oaxaca—a fire stand inside the house, and a small lean-to or other construction of unknown function at the rear or north side of the house.

The house itself was surrounded by a wide area of packed earth, and this exterior surface was in all respects nearly indistinguishable from the actual interior floor surface of the house. Including the area of the house itself, the entire space covered by packed earth surfaces was at least 6.5 m by 7.0 m, or some 45.5 m² in extent. The actual area of the

EARLY FORMATIVE: THE SAN JOSÉ PHASE

PLATE 19. The House 4 surface, looking west. The door of the house is immediately to the south of the meter stick. (Compare with Figure 11.)

house itself was about 10.8 m², leaving a total *exterior* surfaced area of at least 37.7 m². The ratio between exterior packed earth surface and interior packed earth floor in this Early Formative house, then, is at least 3/1. For future reference, it may therefore be noted that: 1) not all postholes found in association with Early Formative houses are wall posts, and 2) not all packed earth surfaces are actual house floors.

The interior floor of House 4 was quite well preserved, with the exception of an intrusive feature which removed the northwest quadrant of the surface, or about 23 percent of the total. The house and surrounding exterior surfaces were excavated in 50 cm quadrants of the 1 m² grid which covered the site. Within each quadrant, all of each of the three successive surfaces was saved and floated in water. This allowed a very high recovery rate of seeds and tiny flecks of charcoal which had been trodden into the floor surface, and which would have been extremely difficult to recover by conventional screening techniques. Other major classes of data recovered from the floors of House 4 included ceramics, lithics, animal bone, and fragments of burned daub, i.e., the clay used on the walls of the house.

Artifacts from the last and best preserved floor were used in a nearest neighbor analysis of activity areas inside the structure. This analysis, carried out by Charles S. Spencer of the University of Michigan Museum of Anthropology, is described in detail in Appendix X. Artifacts used in the analysis included only those which were actually trodden into the floor or lying in direct contact with it. Some 2–4 cm separated each of the successive floors, and it was felt that to have included all material within this 2–4 cm layer as contemporary with the floor below it would be unjustified, as the layer itself was presumably laid down to serve as fill over the old floor and under the new.

Briefly, the analysis shows that cooking and some associated food preparation appears to have been confined to the eastern end of the house, especially around the semicircle of postholes which very possibly represent the supports of a fire stand of the sort most commonly found in wattle-and-daub houses in the area today. Several observations are all consistent with interpretation of this feature and area as the remains of a fire stand and food preparation area. These are: the absence of any hearth or similar feature on the floor of the house; the quantity of charcoal and other carbonized materials trodden into the floor in the immediate vicinity of the posthole configuration; and the number of jar as opposed to bowl sherds (the bowls apparently being very seldom used for cooking, as blackening is seldom found on them; jars, on the other hand, were often blackened).

It is unfortunately more difficult to identify any other activities which might have taken place inside the house, due both to the previously mentioned intrusion and to the fact that garbage was probably not allowed to accumulate on the floor of the house during the period of its use. The problem is considered in more detail in Appendix X.

No concentrations of materials were evident on the exterior ground surfaces of the house. Unfortunately, preservation here was much poorer due to later intrusive features. Also, the sunken road which cuts through the center of the site removed a large portion of this surface. The use of exterior space, then, must remain unclear, although a number of activities were most probably performed there. It is also most unfortunate that no bell-shaped pits were recovered in association with the house. Several such pits were commonly associated with Early Formative houses at other Oaxaca sites, and Feature 109/House 8 association suggests that early San José phase houses at Tomaltapec were not without storage facilities.

ESJ-3

Although the area thus designated probably represents the latest San José phase occupation at Tomaltepec, it still may fall within the first half of the phase. Its relatively late date is shown by the form, surface finish, and decoration of the jars, the decline in frequency of Leandro Gray ware, and the dramatic increase of Atoyac Yellow-white outleaned-wall bowls. These bowls still almost entirely lack the incised decoration which is so common in the late San José phase in the Etla region, but this could turn out to be a regional difference (see Plog, 1976).

At this writing, it remains unclear exactly what Possible Household Unit ESJ-3 represents. No house remains of any sort were found, the unit being defined by two small features (Feature 62 and 72) and a midden heap most probably associated with them on ceramic grounds. Feature 72, illustrated in Figure 12, is a shallow, trash-filled pit containing ceramics, a moderately large quantity of smashed deer bone, and one cut deer metatarsal. Very little charcoal and virtually no other carbonized plant remains were recovered. Four figurine fragments were present, including limb and body fragments from small, solid, apparently human figurines. It has also been noted that figurines are less than abundant in the Early Formative proveniences at Tomaltepec. Feature 72 thus very tentatively suggests that figurines began to be more common toward the end of the early part of the San José phase at Tomaltepec.

Other deposits associated with Possible Unit ESJ-3 are from the lower levels of Test Pit number 2. The location of Test Pit 2 relative to Features 72, 65, and 62 is shown in Figure 12. Test Pit 2 seems to have cut through a thick, amorphous layer of refuse which was probably dumped downslope from the Feature 72 area.

In conclusion, no definitive statement can be made as to exactly what is represented by the remains designated Household Unit ESJ-3. As the three recorded proveniences seem to be domestic garbage heaps, the existence of an undiscovered or entirely obliterated house in the vicinity is implied.

ESJ-4

The existence of this "possible" unit is extremely unclear. Its identification is based on Feature 112,

EARLY FORMATIVE: THE SAN JOSÉ PHASE

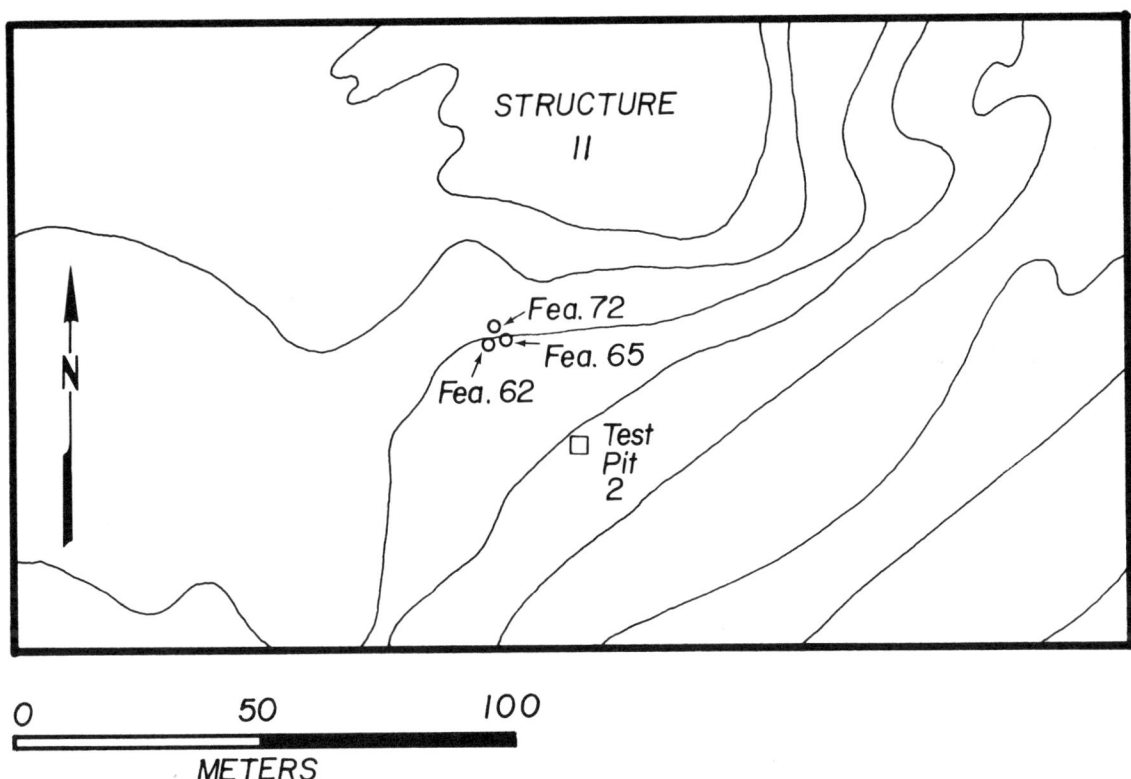

a. Location of the components of Possible Household Unit ESJ-3 with respect to Test Pit 2.

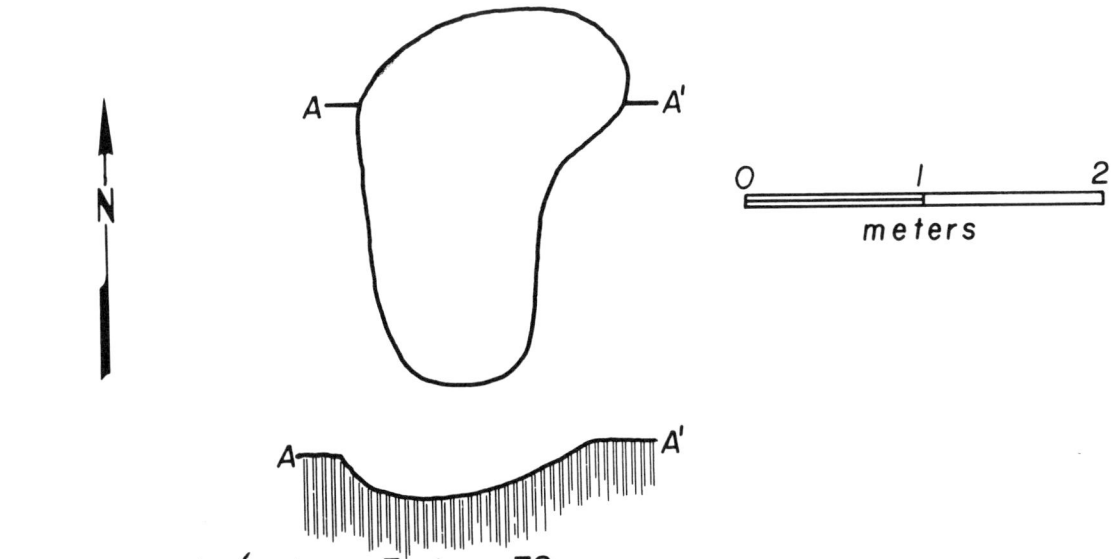

b. Early San José phase Feature 72.

FIGURE 12. Components of Possible Household Unit ESJ-3.

which appears to once have been a large, straight-sided pit. The feature had been extensively disturbed both by leveling and filling for an immediately-overlying Late Formative plastered courtyard, and by the sunken road that also passed through this part of the site.

A few other San José phase sherds were discovered at the base of Mound 3, revealed by the road cut through the area (refer to Fig. 3). The mound itself was not investigated in this field season. The bulk of the construction, however, seems to be Late Formative. Sherds found in association with mound fill must always be interpreted with caution. Nevertheless, the fact that the Mound 3 sherds came from the bottom of the mound and were not mixed throughout the fill at least raises the possibility of early San José phase occupation in this area. The existence of nearby Feature 112 also points in this direction.

ESJ-5

A single rather dubious provenience located on what seems to have been the outskirts of the community comprises "possible" Unit ESJ-5. Feature 70 consists of three whole vessels sitting upright in a pit. Stylistically, the vessels date to the Tierras Largas/San José transition period, or the initial part of the San José phase. The pit contained none of the domestic garbage characteristically associated with other contemporary features; however, several bell-shaped pits associated with household units at Tierras Largas contained stored whole vessels. Nevertheless, the distance from Feature 70 to the apparently more heavily occupied section of the community is such that we cannot rule out the hypothesis of an isolated cache on the periphery of the village. This area of the site could not be extensively investigated due to budget limitations, and the question cannot be resolved with the data currently in hand.

The Cemetery

In describing the structure of the early San José phase community at Tomaltepec, the final area requiring consideration is the village burial area, illustrated in Figure 13. To date, this is the largest such Early Formative cemetery known in the region. This is not to suggest that comparable burial areas did not exist at other contemporary Oaxacan sites; on the contrary, there is no indication that the Tomaltepec community was in any sense extraordinary. However, at this writing the only burial areas known are small "neighborhood" cemeteries of 8-15 individuals such as those in Area C at San José Mogote (Flannery and Marcus, unpublished). The much larger area used for burial at Tomaltepec was evidently devoted entirely to this function, as no contemporary cultural features of any sort whatsoever have ever been found in its vicinity. The cemetery evidently contained a substantial portion of the adult population of the village during the period of its use. As suggested by ceramic evidence presented in Appendix II, this period seems to fall entirely within the early San José phase.

Nearly 70 burials, containing the remains of some 80 individuals, were recovered in the cemetery excavation. A number of these burials and all burial offerings are illustrated in Appendix III. The underlying assumption about mortuary practices from which this section of this study will proceed is best expressed by Binford, who asserts that:

> . . . the form and structure which characterize mortuary practices of any society are conditioned by the form and complexity of the organizational characteristics of the society itself. Change or variability in either form or structure must take into account the limiting or determining effects exerted on these practices by the nature of the organizational properties of the society (Binford,1971:23).

In the same paper, Binford also asserts that there are at least two necessary evaluations when attempting to extract the social phenomena symbolized in mortuary ritual. These are 1) the social position of the deceased, and 2) the composition and size of the social aggregate recognizing status responsibilities to the deceased (Ibid.:21). Both of these are frequently rather enigmatic, although some tentative conclusions will be reached in the course of this discussion

It was previously observed that some 70 burials representing nearly 80 individuals were recovered from the cemetery. Of these, 60 burials, representing 75 primary and secondary individuals, were complete and preserved well enough for further analysis. Age and sex of the 60 primary burials are shown in Table 3.

As is apparent from the table, the sex distribution is very close to equal in the cemetery (this

EARLY FORMATIVE: THE SAN JOSÉ PHASE

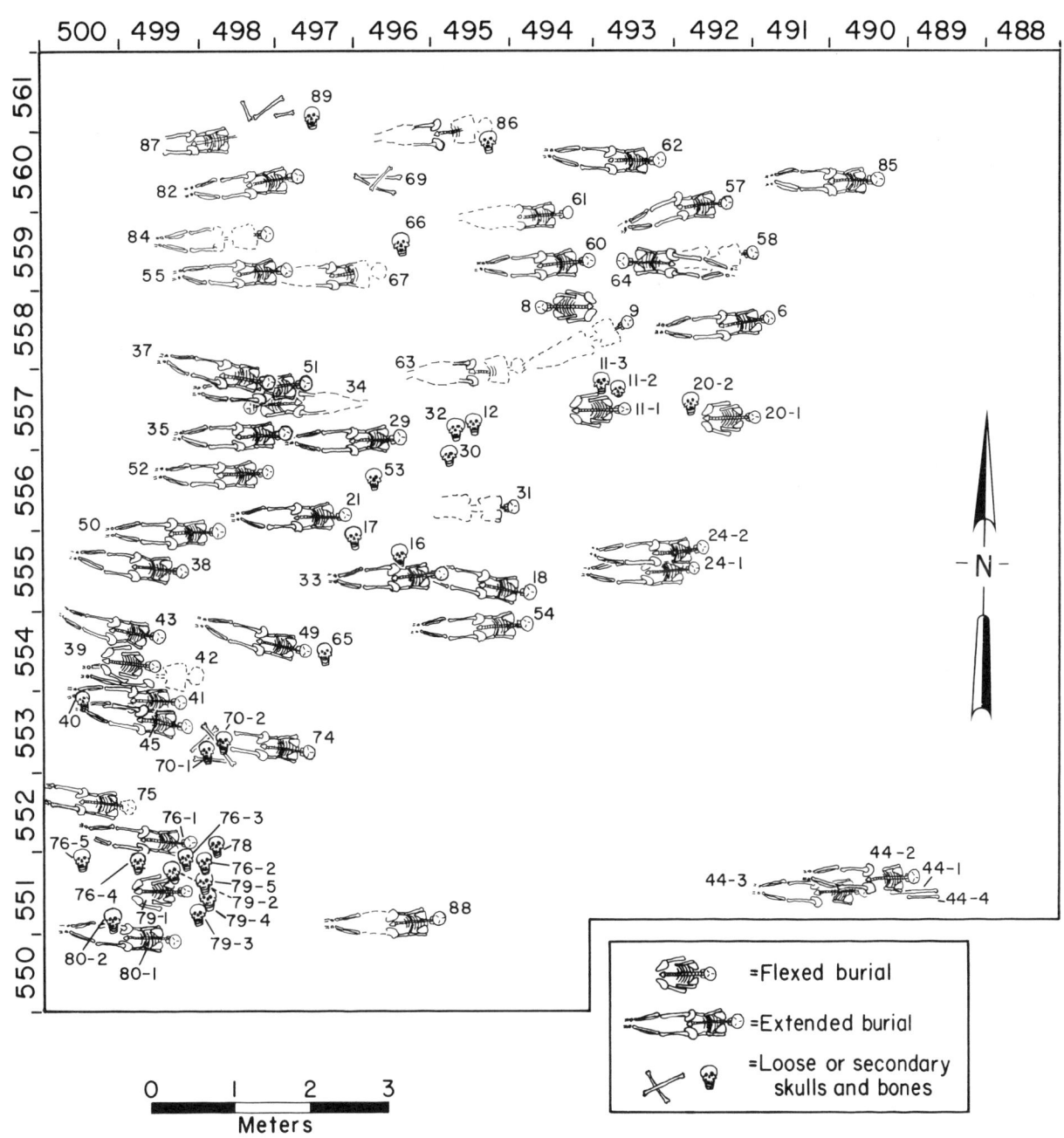

FIGURE 13. The San José phase cemetery at Tomaltepec.

statement is, of course, based on the assumption that the burials unidentifiable as to sex include about equal numbers of males and females). Time and resources did not allow complete excavation of the cemetery, but testing in the cemetery vicinity suggests that the majority of the burial population was recovered. It may therefore be suggested that males and females were buried in the cemetery in nearly equal proportions. There is, in other words, no apparent differential selection by sex for interment in the cemetery.

Selection for age in the cemetery is quite evident from Table 3. It can be observed that there is only one child burial, and no infant burials at all. There are several adolescents, but these may well have been considered functional adults.

Table 3: Ages and Sexes of Primary Tomaltepec Cemetery Burials

Sex	Adolescent 13–19 yrs.	Adult I 20–29 yrs.	Adult II 30–39 yrs.	Adult III 40–49 yrs.	Adult IV 50 + yrs.	Adult (?) Age (?)	Total
Male	0	4	7	3	0	7	21 (38%)
Female	0	11	2	2	1	4	20 (36%)
Sex Unknown	3	3	2	0	1	5	14 (26%)
TOTAL	3 (5.5%)	18 (32.7%)	11 (20.0%)	5 (9.1%)	2 (3.6%)	16 (29.1%)	55 (100%)

Beyond the simple requirement of adult status for interment in the cemetery, one must ask if there is selectivity for any particular age/sex combinations. Consultation of Table 3 shows that the sexes are differentially represented within the age categories, but it is suggested that this can be explained in terms of the dynamics of the population. The imbalance, in other words, may be taken as a reflection of different high-risk periods for males and females. Table 3 represents the cumulative totals of males and females in the cemetery for each age group. From this table and from Figure 14, it is evident that the death rates for males and females increase markedly, although unequally, between adolescence/young childhood (13–19 years) and the Adult II stage (20–29 years). It is also clear, however, that this period is the highest risk period for females, 67 percent dying then. Moreover, after age 29, female mortality dropped sharply showing a fairly steady decline to old age. The male situation, on the other hand, is markedly different, their highest risk period extending into the 30–39 year age bracket, at the end of which time 83 percent were dead. As with the females, the male death rate then declines steadily to old age.

This situation is quite similar to that hypothesized by Saxe for the Mesolithic Nubian population which he studied. He observes that:

> Females would begin bearing children sometime during the subadolescent period. During the first few pregnancies, those women with obstetric and gynecological problems would be selected out of the population. Unlike men, the women's risky activity peak would last only into young adulthood (20–25 years), the women's mortality rate thereafter declining until old age set in (Saxe 1971:44–45).

Males, on the other hand, seem to have suffered a lower intensity but longer lasting attrition rate, probably perishing in the course of hunting, raiding, and other activities, in addition to the disease and accidents which can be expected to strike both males and females. The observed distribution, in the Tomaltepec cemetery, then, could be attributed to the dynamics of the population.

Positioning of corpses in the cemetery is quite uniform, all being prone, with the heads in the normal face-forward position (see Plate 20). Moreover nearly every corpse was oriented with the head to the east. Burial orientation was possibly accomplished with reference to some natural phenomenon, such as the rising sun. The slight variation which exists in precise direction of orientation may be attributable either to random error or to seasonal variations in the positioning phenomenon. The latter explanation would seem to be more likely, since, in the event of simple random error, one would expect deviations from east to be roughly equal in either direction. This is, however, not the case, the great majority of burials (95 percent) being oriented either directly east or slightly south of east. The four non-eastern oriented burials occur in reverse position from the rest of the cemetery burials, i.e., heads to the west, though still face down. These represent both male and female as well as old and young adults, and it is not felt that any special significance can be assigned to this group.

Beyond the near-universals just described, there is significant variability in body position, associated burials, and presence of offerings of both utilitarian and exotic sorts. Burial attributes are displayed in Figure 15 in the form of a "key diagram." Very briefly, a key diagram, following Saxe (1970:40), may be described as a branching structure in which the first branching node represents a division on the basis of the state of a particular variable or attribute. Succeeding

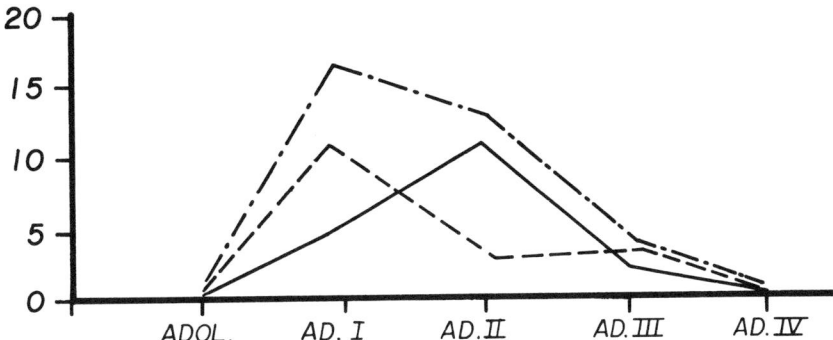

a. Total number by age group in cemetery.

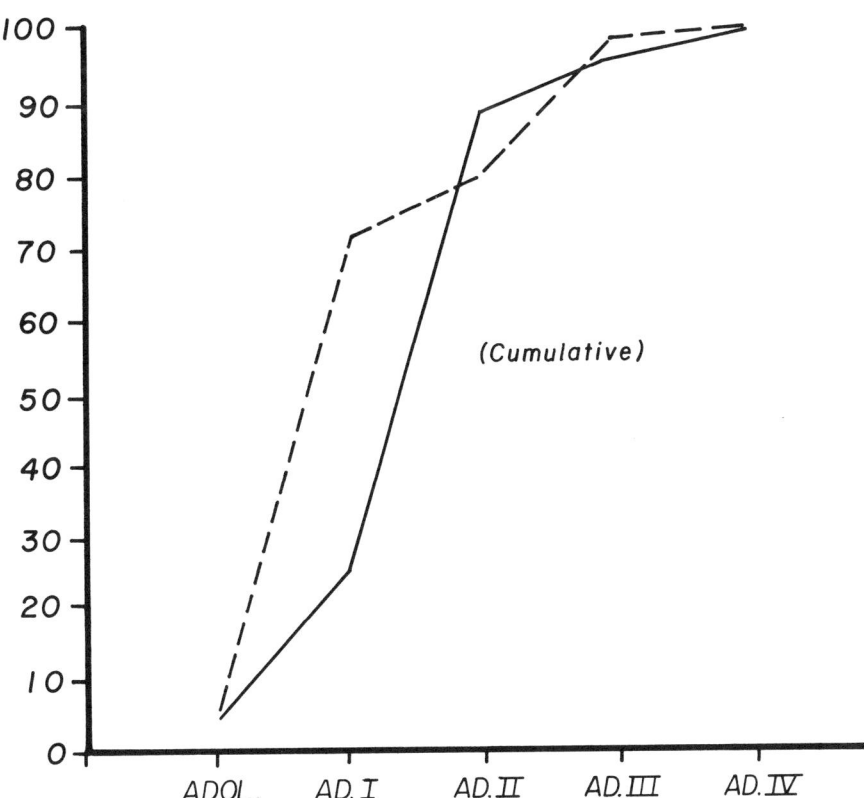

b. Percentage of population deceased, by age group, based on cemetery data.

 = females
———— = males
—·—·— = whole population

FIGURE 14. Numbers and percentages of dead by age group within the Tomaltepec cemetery.

PLATE 20. A typical extended, face-down burial from the San José phase cemetery.

branching nodes represent divisions on the basis of states of other attributes, taken sequentially.

Examination of the key diagram emphasizes several interesting phenomena:

1) There exists a distinct sub-group of tightly flexed burials, of which five are males and five are of indeterminate sex (Plate 21). No flexed burial was identified as female.

2) Both senior and junior males belong to the flexed group.

3) Secondary burials occur both with flexed and extended burials, but are most commonly associated with the flexed burials: 40 percent of all flexed interments have associated secondary burials, whereas only 9.1 percent of all extended burials are so accompanied.

4) Although this flexed category of male burials makes up only 16.6 percent of all cemetery burials, they possess 50 percent of the occurrences of excised "fire-serpent" motifs (Pyne 1976) on ceramic vessels (see Plate 22). Such motifs are here termed "supra-local symbols," following Peebles' (1971) usage, and their significance is considered in more detail presently. Also, 66 percent of the occurrences of stone covers were with flexed burials. These covers consist of small stones (ca. 10 x 20 x 5 cm) which were occasionally laid down over the backs of the burials (Plate 23). Finally, 88 percent of the occurrences of jade or "greenstone" beads in the cemetery were with flexed burials. Plate 24 shows a necklace of small, flat beads found around the neck of a senior flexed male.

EARLY FORMATIVE: THE SAN JOSÉ PHASE

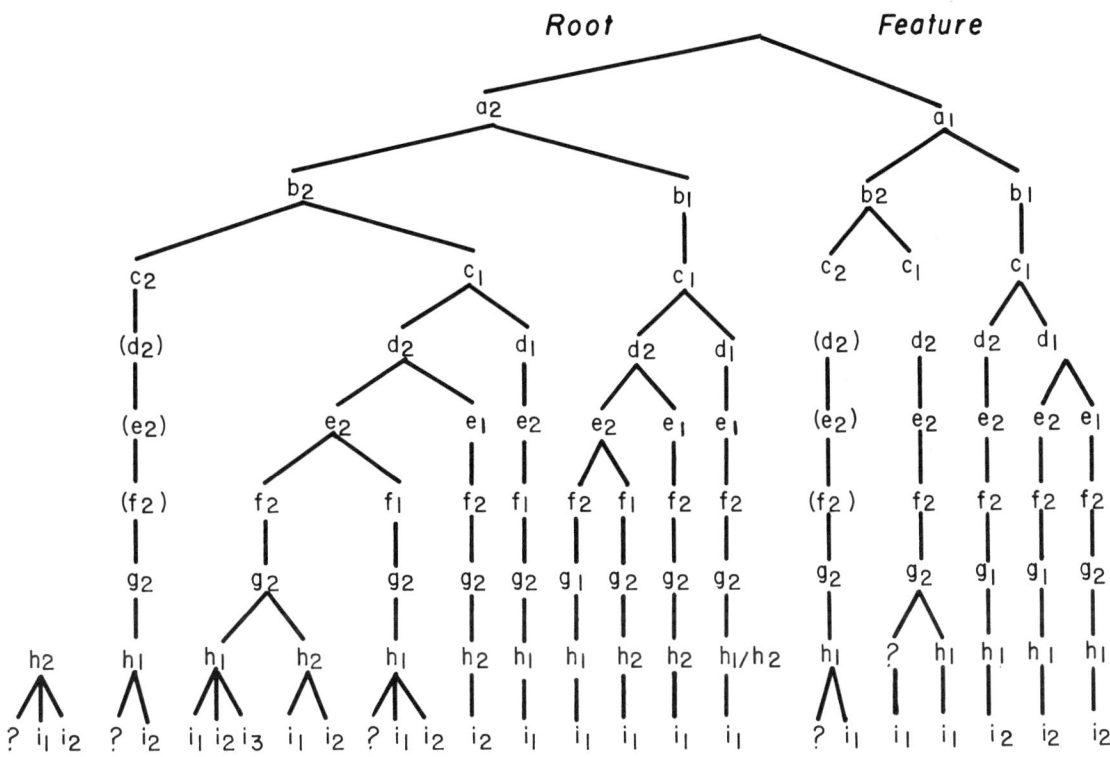

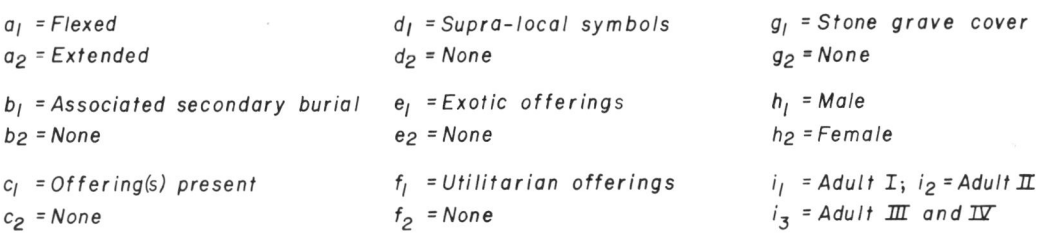

FIGURE 15. Key diagram of attributes of burials, Tomaltepec cemetery. The root feature common to all burials is the prone position with head to the east.

Flexed burials never had utilitarian objects, such as awls or grinding stones, among their offerings, although these do occur at times in the unflexed category (see Plate 24).

5) Within this flexed category, secondary burials, ceramic offerings, and supra-local symbols on pottery occur only with senior males, and never with their juniors.

These flexed burials seem to form a distinct, internally graded sub-group, at least the senior members of which may be seen to have received more elaborate treatment than 1) their juniors within the flexed category; 2) all other males, including some who were older still in the population at large; and 3) all females, regardless of age. It may be further suggested that the sub-group represented by the flexed burials was something entered into by some, but not all younger men, some of whom later rose to prominence within its ranks. It may also be suggested that its members were not elevated far above the rest of society, as the quantitative and qualitative differences between offerings with flexed and those with unflexed burials is not extreme.

The ceramic offerings recovered with both groups are also consistent with this conclusion.

PLATE 21. A flexed burial from the San José phase cemetery. Black arrows indicate the bones of a secondary burial accompanying the primary burial.

Without exception, they are ordinary household vessels which (as the heavy basal wear shows) have been well used before interment. Fisher's Exact Probability scores were calculated between all vessel types occurring in the cemetery and the attributes of age, sex, flexure, etc. shown in the key diagram in Figure 15, and the very few significant associations arrived at (even at the 0.1 level) attest to a marked lack of formality in the association of particular vessels with particular types of burials. If we assume that every person went to the grave accompanied by vessels used in his household during his life, then we may conclude that much the same sorts of vessels were in use in every household. Evidence from household proveniences also suggests such an interpretation.

The society appears to have been crosscut by a second group as well, composed entirely of males and displaying the "fire-serpent" motif on associated pottery. The group includes both the flexed and extended corpses of older and younger males, many of whom were also relatively well-provided with other offerings. The "fire-serpent" and "were-jaguar", both motifs in the Early Formative Olmec style, are thought by some to represent mythological beings of supernatural significance. A recent

EARLY FORMATIVE: THE SAN JOSÉ PHASE

PLATE 22. Bowl with excised decoration which accompanied the burial shown in Plate 21.

study by Pyne (1976) suggests that the two motifs tend to be "antagonistic" or mutually exclusive within particular residential units at San José Mogote, Tierras Largas, and Huitzo. Furthermore, burials so far recovered from the Valley of Oaxaca suggest that fire-serpent and were-jaguar symbols on ceramics occur almost exclusively with male burials (*Ibid.*). There are also examples of occurrences of fire-serpent motifs with infant burials (e.g. Flannery, et al., 1970). From this, Pyne (*Ibid.*) suggests that association with the symbols may have been hereditary and passed largely through the male line, representing descent from a mythological apical ancestor of some type.

PLATE 23. A flexed burial from the San José phase cemetery, covered with irregular stones.

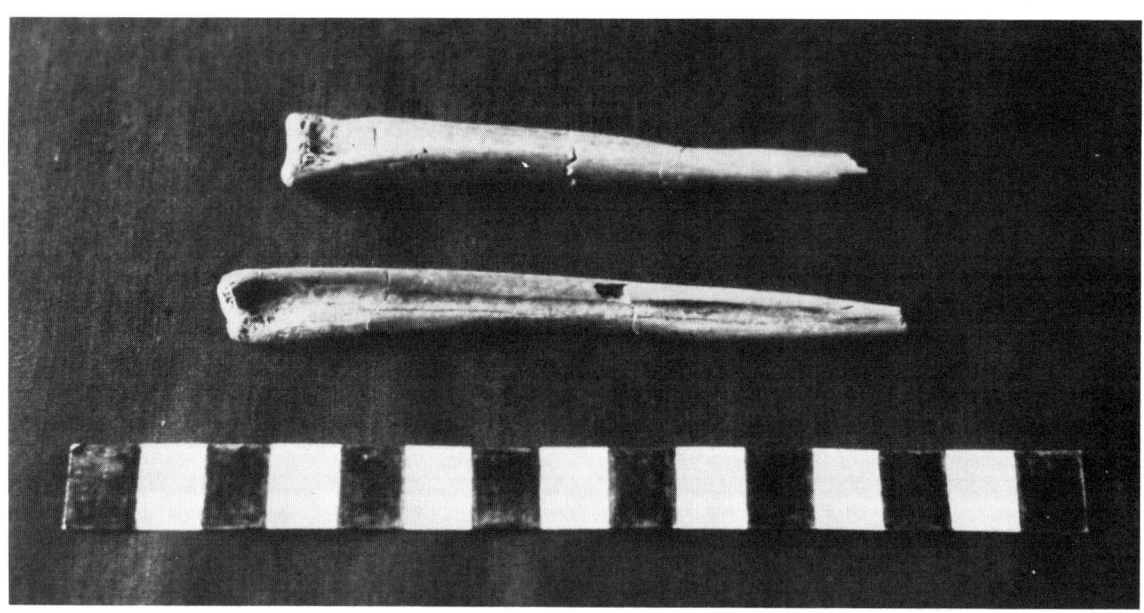

PLATE 24. Grave goods from the San José phase cemetery. Top, greenstone beads (Burial 11-1). Bottom, deer bone awls (Burial 80). Scale in cm.

At Tomaltepec, only fire-serpent symbols are found excised on ceramic vessels. Furthermore, only male burials have serpents on ceramic offerings. It should be noted, however, that a small magnetite mirror in the form of a "U" motif was found under the chest of one of the cemetery burials: a female of 20–29 years. The mirror was about 5 cm long, 1 cm wide, and 0.2 cm thick, and was finely ground from three small, separate pieces of magnetite (see Plate 25). Very probably the mirror was an inlay, as no hanging or joining holes were present on any of the three component pieces, and once decorated a pendant or pectoral of some perishable material.

The elongated "U" motif of the mirror is one component of the fire-serpent design (see Pyne, 1976:273, Figs. 9–7a,b), and is thus consistent with the predominance of the fire-serpent motif at Tomaltepec. In fact, the female with whom the mirror was associated was part of a double

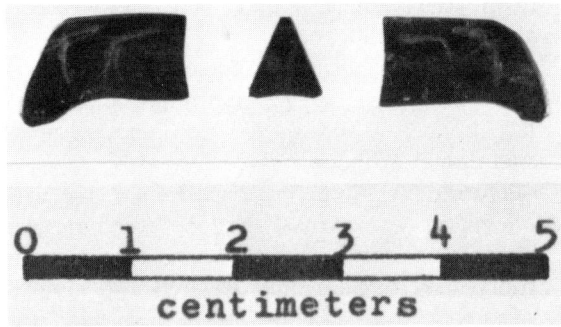

PLATE 25. Magnetite "U-motif" which accompanied Burial 24, Individual 1.

Table 4: Age, Sex, and Association of Secondary Burials from the Tomaltepec Cemetery

Secondary Number	Age	Sex	Association w/Primary Number	Age	Sex
11–2	Adult	?	11–1	Adult II	M
11–3	Adult III	F(?)	11–1	Adult II	M
20–2	Adult I	F	20–1	Adult II	M
40–1	Adult	M	41	Adult I	F
40–2	Child	?	41	Adult I	F
69	Adult	?	None	—	—
70–1	Adult II	F	None	—	—
70–2	Child	?	None	—	—
76–2	Adult III	?	76–1	Adult I	M
76–3	Adult II	M	76–1	Adult I	M
76–4	Adult	?	76–1	Adult I	M
76–5	Adult	?	76–1	Adult I	M
79–2	Adult	?	79–1	Adult III	M
79–3	Adolescent	?	79–5	Adult IV	?
79–4	Adult	M	79–5	Adult IV	?
80–2	Adult II	?	80–1	Adult	F

primary burial, the other member of which was a 20–29 year old male accompanied by a large cylinder bearing the fire-serpent motif.

It may be tentatively suggested, then, that such symbols served to link their bearers at Tomaltepec and other contemporary communities on an inter- and intra-community basis, although the intensity and significance of these linkages are still not well understood.

Another interesting phenomenon in the Tomaltepec cemetery is the presence of secondary burials. These frequently occur accompanying primary interments in the flexed category, where, 42.8 percent of all primary burials have secondary accompaniments. Secondary burials are less frequently found accompanying primary burials in the extended category, where only 9.1 percent have secondary interments. Detached skulls were frequently found arranged around the head and upper body of the primary interment, which was also occasionally covered with a layer of loose long bones and skull fragments. Particulars of age and sex of secondary burials and of the primary burials which they accompany are shown in Table 4.

In general, the secondary interments were poorly preserved, and therefore quite difficult to assign age and sex. Accordingly, the results are not complete enough to be reliably subjected to any tests of association of age and sex among the primary and secondary burials. Nevertheless, one association that is apparent is the prevalence of secondary burials with senior male interments. Table 4 shows that in four of the six cases identifiable to age and sex, the primary burial was male. Moreover, in three of these four cases, the male was an older one (i.e., Adult II or III, or 30–49 years).

The picture seems to be further complicated by the presence of both sexes and all ages among the secondary burials. It will be noted from Table 4, however, that male primary burials are accompanied only by adult secondary burials, although these may be either male or female, and they may be senior or junior in age to the primary interment. It is suggested that Secondary Burials 69 and 70 may be disregarded for the moment, as they do not accompany primary burials, and so would seem to have been buried under somewhat different circumstances. This leaves but a single non-adult secondary burial (Burial 40-2, a child of 5-6 years), which, together with a male of unknown age, accompanies a ca. 20-29 year old female primary burial.

Considering the general case, we may conclude that the secondary burials which accompany primary interments in the Tomaltepec cemetery are predominantly adults (13 of 14 cases), that most are adults, ranging in age from young to old, that they may be male or female, and that male primary burials have accompanying secondary burials twice as often as do their female counterparts. Furthermore, the average number of secondary burials per primary male burial is 2.5, whereas the figure per primary female burial is 1.5. Males, then, not only have associated secondary burials much more frequently than females, but have markedly more secondary individuals per interment. It is suggested here that these secondary burials reflect multigenerational descent lines, and that the saving and reburying of the remains of ancestors, as well as the very existence of the cemetery itself, are artifacts of the territorial organization of the society.[1]

Flannery has argued that

> ... the origins of sedentary life had more to do with the installation and maintenance of permanent facilities, and the establishment and maintenance of hereditary ownership of limited areas of high resource potential than it did with agriculture per se ... The placing of permanent, nucleated communities on or near localized areas of strategic resources probably changes group ideology from one of weak territoriality to a pattern of a small, defended core area versus a large, undefended periphery, further emphasized in concepts of descent (Flannery 1972:28–29).

Flannery goes on to argue that repositories for multiple secondary burials or saving of ancestor skulls are one possible result of this emphasis on descent, and he notes that "without written deeds, the presence of the ancestors frequently serves as the group's best evidence that the land was theirs 'since time began'" (*Ibid.*:29).

Furthermore, using ethnographic data to consider the significance of cemeteries in tribal level societies, Saxe (1971) cites a study by Meggitt (1965) to suggest that, generally speaking, the importance of ancestors as measured by the degree of permanence of burials and by degree of increasing specialization of burial areas does co-vary with degree of agnation. It is not clear, however, how relevant this point would be in Oaxaca, where all known Indian groups were cognatic at the time of the Spanish Conquest. As Saxe notes, further research on the ethnographically recorded conditions under which cemeteries appear is certainly in order, although it cannot be undertaken here.

In conclusion, then, the following observations may be made based on the Tomaltepec cemetery:

1) The burial population is not highly differentiated, the main determinants of status in the cemetery population being age and sex.

2) There existed a distinct, internally graded subgroup of males (distinguished by flexing), the senior members of which were buried slightly more elaborately than the rest of the population.

3) There exists a group of males, the members of which display the fire-serpent motif on the associated ceramic offerings. Both flexed and extended males are represented in this category. Pyne's (1976) study suggests that these motifs are of valley-wide significance.

4) Secondary burials associated predominantly with male burials suggest the importance of the male household head, and perhaps his multi-generational affiliation as well.

Before concluding this discussion of the components of the early San José community at Tomaltepec, it is necessary to consider the spatial arrangement of the whole. Reference to Figure 8 shows that houses themselves seem to have been about 40 meters apart, while boundaries of household units seem to have been separated by 20m–30m. Testing in the area between units ESJ–1/Structure 11 and ESJ–2 produced little or no Early Formative debris. Likewise, the features defining possible unit ESJ–3 lie 40–50 meters from both ESJ–1/Structure 11 and ESJ–2, and the edge of a circle of 20m in diameter drawn around these features is separated by 20m–25m from the ESJ–1/Structure 11 boundary and by 35m from the ESJ–2 boundary. Finally, the cemetery is located some 30 m northeast of the ESJ–2 boundary, with no intervening evidence of household units. Apparently, therefore, roughly the same distance was considered adequate for separating households and for segregating the cemetery area from the nearest household.

Social Differentiation

In order to deal adequately with this topic, it is clearly necessary to go beyond mortuary data, which can be somewhat misleading, as Ucko (1969) suggests. Also to be considered are several additional classes of archaeological evidence, including artifact distributions and associations, and attributes and distribution of structures. These two classes of data have already been introduced in other contexts, but require further consideration here in light of this particular questions.

Based on the artifact distributions discussed in Section 1 of this chapter, it is possible to divide the early San José phase community at Tomaltepec into two distinct residential zones: one of relatively higher status, and the other of relatively lower status. The relatively higher status residential zone corresponds to the area wherein are located Unit ESJ–1 and Structure 11. It is further suggested that Units ESJ–2,3, and 4 represent relatively lower

---

[1] An alternative interpretation would be that less-important family members were added to the burial of the adult male household head when he died (Ed.note).

status residences ringed around the higher status zone. Unit ESJ-5 is so poorly defined that it is not considered here. Variance in the within-unit ratio of finer quality chert to siltstone seems to be significant to this status distinction. The nearest known chert sources are 10–15 km from Tomaltepec, while siltstone is locally available. A Chi-square shows that chert is not randomly distributed among the four early San José phase household units. Low frequencies of the contingency table necessitated the regrouping of ESJ-2,3, and 4 into one column. ESJ-1 and Structure 11 were than grouped into another, giving a two-by-two table of chert versus local stone in the proposed higher status area, as opposed to all of the proposed lower status areas. Chi-square = 65.43 for one degree of freedom, with an associated probability of less than .001, indicating that chert is not randomly distributed between the higher and lower status zones. The three late Tierras Largas Features, 7, 102, and 108, reflect a similar distribution of stone. Thus it may also be noted that the use of higher quality chert was already more prevalent in this area in the late Tierras Largas phase.

As pointed out earlier in this chapter, the cost of a commodity in primitive economics is best measured in terms of the relative difficulty of obtaining it. By this logic, the Structure 11 tool kit, in which 73 percent of the identified tools were of chert and 27 percent of local silicified siltstone, is clearly a more "expensive" one than that of any other contemporary household unit. There is also a functional consideration, in that the chert is somewhat harder than the siltstone; has a finer and more predictable fracture; and would thus produce higher quality, more durable tools. Obsidian is another high-quality, non-local tool-making material which shows a similarly uneven distribution within the community. The proposed higher status area has 88.2 percent (by count) of all early San José phase obsidian recovered at Tomaltepec. The actual counts per unit are listed in Table 2.

Shell at Tomaltepec is found only within the proposed higher status area. Also, as previously observed, unfinished pieces attest to production as well as simple consumption of shell ornaments. In addition, mica, which was presumably also used in ornament manufacture, is present only in the proposed higher status zone.

To summarize, the ESJ-1/Structure 11 area is designated a relatively high status residence area on the basis of concentration there of a number of items which are "expensive" in terms of effort expended in procurement. These items are also less plentiful or even absent in other parts of the village. These include obsidian, shell, and non-local chert. The source of the mica that is concentrated in this area is not positively known, although mica is today commercially mined near the town of Zimatlán in the Zaachila branch of the Valley of Oaxaca (K.V. Flannery: personal communication).

Moreover, a Chi-square test indicates that bowls and jars are not randomly distributed among the four early San José phase households considered (Chi-square = 74.54 for 3 degrees of freedom, associated probability less than 0.001). Drennan (1975:137) also notes this imbalance between Middle Formative households at Fábrica San José, arguing that higher status houses possessed more of the finer serving vessels. The basic assumption was that "the balance of functions performed in houses of varying statuses differed" (op.cit.). Simple nonrandomness of distribution of jars and bowls is of course insufficient to lead one to conclude that the difference was a status-based one at Tomaltepec, but it can at least be suggested, based upon this research and upon Drennan's previously cited study, that a higher bowl/jar ratio is one characteristic of Early and Middle Formative Oaxacan higher status residences.

Finally, it has been noted that Structure 11 had facilities for large-scale storage. Whether the stored material was consumed by this household alone or redistributed in some manner, such a situation is certainly consistent with designation of the Structure 11 area as one of relatively higher status in the community.

Consideration of mortuary, architectural, and artifactual evidence from Tomaltepec in early San José times, then, certainly leads to the conclusion that some status differentiation existed within the community. Nevertheless, it should be emphasized that the absolute level of social differentiation within the community still seems to have been fairly low relative to succeeding periods.

Subsistence Activities

As during the preceding Tierras Largas phase, the dominant subsistence activity during the early San José phase at Tomaltepec appears to have been maize farming. Maize kernels and cupules are included in every contemporary feature containing appreciable quantities of carbonized plant remains (see Appendix IX for a continuation of this discussion).

Large quantities of animal bone recovered from early San José phase deposits at Tomaltepec show that hunting, especially of deer, continued to be an important element of the subsistence pattern. From the associated bones, it appears that deer were butchered in every household: skull, vertebra, pelvis, tooth, and jaw fragments everywhere appear along with larger quantities of thoroughly splintered long bones, from which the marrow appears to have been systematically extracted. Table 2 also suggests that deer were not consumed in equal amounts in each of the five household units defined. The area of household ESJ-1 and Structure 11, the apparent higher status area, seems to reflect higher-level consumption of deer, although it should be kept in mind that the volume of midden debris excavated in conjunction with each household unit is not identical. Some additional support for this suggestion can be drawn from the specialized butchering/hide scraping tool kit associated with Structure 11 (see Appendix VIII).

Beyond this observation, we are venturing onto very shaky ground in attempting to specify proportions of different animals consumed in different households. It is evident, nevertheless, that a wide variety of animals were taken in addition to deer, including rabbit, peccary, gopher, and opossum. Dog appears for the first time at Tomaltepec in minute quantity in the Structure 11 cell fill, in Feature 65, and in Feature 112. There is, however, no indication of large-scale use of dogs as a meat source. We know from evidence from other Oaxacan sites that consumption of dog was widespread in the latter part of the San José phase, and dog remains were plentiful in Middle Formative period deposits at Tomaltepec.

In summary, the Early Formative inhabitants of Tomaltepec were maize farmers and hunters, most probably farming the alluvial terrace immediately below the site and hunting and trapping deer and other animals on the overgrown piedmont and lower mountain slopes. There seems to have been little or no use of riverine resources, as only one mud turtle plastron fragment was recovered from Early Formative deposits at Tomaltepec.

Craft and Exchange Activities

As noted in Chapter I, the Early Formative period was one of considerable contact and exchange among the several distinct regions of Mesoamerica. That the San José phase community at Tomaltepec participated to some degree both in the exchange and in the display of supra-local symbols which represented this exchange is clear. It is also clear, however, that consumption of exotic goods and display of esoteric or mythological symbols at Tomaltepec was at best a small-scale affair.

The quantity of shell present at Tomaltepec increases over Tierras Largas phase totals in the early San José phase, paralleling a similar increase at Tierras Largas (Winter, 1972:179). At no time, however, is there any impressive quantity of shell at Tomaltepec, the increase being from one to four pieces. All of the pieces of shell at Early Formative Tomaltepec were cut or drilled in some fashion (see Appendix VI). There also exists a single sub-rectangular piece with a partially drilled hole, which perhaps implies production as well as consumption of shell ornaments. It must be conceded, however, that if shell ornaments were being made at Tomaltepec, it was on a very small scale. No other marine products of any sort were recovered.

As mentioned earlier in this chapter, obsidian, another imported commodity, appears more frequently in the early San José phase community than in the preceding Tierras Largas phase village. Also like shell, however, the absolute quantity of obsidian recovered at Tomaltepec is small. In all probability, the obsidian was brought to the community in lumps and broken on the spot into more usable pieces. Angular fragments and retouch flakes make up most of the obsidian debitage recovered, and most pieces occupy considerably less than 0.5 cm^3. Prismatic blades at Tomaltepec and at other contemporary Oaxacan sites are extremely rare. Also entirely absent is the distinctive translucent green obsidian that becomes so common in Late Formative times. Early Formative obsidian at Tomaltepec is uniformly either pure black or translucent, striated gray. Winter and Pires-Ferreira (1976:308) report that the obsidian recovered in Tierras Largas/San José deposits at Tierras Largas seems to be largely from the Guadalupe Victoria and Barranca de los

Estetes sources, both lying to the north or northeast of the Valley of Oaxaca.

Magnetite, a local but evidently restricted resource, appears at Tomaltepec only once in worked form: a small, three-piece mirror in the form of a "U" motif, which was found under the chest of one of the prone cemetery burials and which has already been described in this chapter. A small holder carved from a thick section of conch shell, and seemingly designed for a round magnetite mirror, was also recovered from the cemetery, although its association is unclear (see Appendix VI).

No evidence of any sort suggesting magnetite mirror production was found at Tomaltepec, and a similar situation also exists at Tierras Largas. Magnetite ornaments were quite scarce in both communities. In contrast, Flannery's (1968a:89) work at San José Mogote shows that mirrors were produced in quantity in one localized area of that site, where hundreds of magnetite fragments were found scattered over the ground surface. No comparable evidence has been found at any other contemporary site anywhere in the Valley of Oaxaca. This being the case, it may well be that San José Mogote monopolized production of this particular exotic item. Whether the mirror from Tomaltepec arrived there through direct contact with San José Mogote or whether by passage from village to village is of course unknown. The implications for elite exchange within the Valley of Oaxaca exist, however, in either case.

Fine greenstone of unknown origin appears in the form of beads and small celts in the early San José phase cemetery. A senior male of the flexed subgroup discussed earlier wore a necklace of some 14 small, flat, greenstone beads and had an additional three in his mouth. Several more beads and several small celts were also recovered from various of the flexed and extended burials, although nowhere on a large scale. These beads represent very early occurrences of greenstone ornaments, which become much more common in the succeeding Middle Formative Period. They could have been manufactured at Tomaltepec, but whether they were has not been established.

Finally, attention should be called to the occurrence of what may be termed "Olmec"-style objects at Tomaltepec. These include the fire-serpent motifs as well as figurines recovered from cemetery burial offerings. It should be emphasized that Olmec-style objects do not demonstrate direct participation by the Tomaltepec community in extra-regional exchange networks. Nevertheless, their presence does suggest some degree of participation in the display of supra-local symbols which characterized much of Early Formative Mesoamerica.

In summary, a number of things seem to have been acquired by the Tomaltepec community from the outside in Early Formative times. Obisdian, shell, mica, greenstone, and magnetite materials or finished tools and ornaments were brought into the community, and pan-regional symbols were employed. Unfortunately, we understand very little as yet about the precise mechanisms by which these commodities and concepts moved. This is especially true at smaller Valley of Oaxaca communities such as Tomaltepec. It does seem clear that all of these classes of items were either absent or less well represented in the preceding late Tierras Largas phase. We may thus conclude that the community at Tomaltepec had begun to interact on a somewhat greater scale with the wider world, probably both regional and extra-regional.

Summary and Discussion of the Early Formative Evidence

A general picture of the early San José phase community at Tomaltepec emerges from the preceding discussion. Between about 1150 B.C. and perhaps 1000 B.C., a community of five to ten households totaling 25 to 30 people was located at Tomaltepec. Based on architecture and artifact associations, the community can be divided into three distinct zones: an area of relatively higher status residences, several areas of relatively lower status residences, and a cemetery area.

Houses seem to have been small wattle-and-daub structures, measuring some 2m–4m by 5m–6m and accommodating nuclear families. Such houses were usually accompanied by storage and cooking facilities as well as by areas for performance of the activities of daily life. Evidence indicated that this house type persisted even in the higher status residence area. Prior to the building of the Structure 11 platform, then, it appears that the community was composed of a number of basically similar parts. With the construction of Structure 11, however, a difference of kind between households was introduced for the first time at Tomaltepec.

The community subsisted by a combination of farming and hunting. The alluvial terraces below the site probably served as farmland, while deer, peccary, rabbits, and other small animals were taken from the piedmont slopes around and above the village. The extent of interaction between the Tomaltepec village and other contemporary communities is difficult to assess, although the small number of non-local items found in the community indicate only limited participation in inter- or intra-valley exchange networks.

Cemetery data suggest that the Tomaltepec community was cross-cut by several groups, membership in which was restricted to males. The first of these, the group with "fire-serpent" vessels, must somehow be related to males buried with similar vessels at San José Mogote and Tierras Largas, though the exact relationship cannot be specified. The second male group at Tomaltepec was distinguished by flexure of the corpse at burial. Some, but not all, senior and junior men were so treated. This group also includes some, but not all, men with fire-serpent vessels. It is tentatively suggested that this flexed group may have some significance at the local (Tomaltepec) level, as this burial pattern is not yet known from other Oaxacan sites.

Further clues to the nature of the social order at Tomaltepec during early San José times are provided by the Structure 11 platform and its postulated storage facility. It will be recalled that the postulated storage cell is some six times larger than the ordinary single-household, bell-shaped storage pits at Tomaltepec and other contemporary communities. The existence of this facility suggests that the economic structure of the village may have involved some form of redistribution, or the pooling and distribution of goods by a central family. Ethnographically, redistribution is recognized as one method by which ambitious individuals are able to attract followings and form factions, and various anthropologists have argued for the evolutionary potential of redistributive institutions. For example, Sahlins (1961:208) terms them potential "starting mechanisms of rank and leadership."

As Winter and Pires-Ferreira (1976) have pointed out, however, one cannot simply infer pooling and redistribution from storage facilities; it must be demonstrated by independent means, such as their statistical analyses of obsidian sources represented house by house at San José Mogote and Tierras Largas. The available data does not permit such a statistical analysis at early San José phase Tomaltepec. Unfortunately, occupation at Tomaltepec either ceases or is greatly diminished before late San José times, and the writer is thus unable to trace further developments centered on the Structure 11 platform.

Processes of Change

The initial Tierras Largas phase occupation at Tomaltepec is so poorly defined that little detailed analysis of the late Tierras Largas-to-early San José phase transition can be attempted. Nevertheless, directions of change can be indicated by pointing out features of the early San José phase occupation which apparently did not exist in Tierras Largas times. First, it has been suggested that the absolute level of differentiation among community components was increasing in the early San José phase, although this differentiation was still at a low level relative to succeeding periods. The level of specialization of community components also appears to have been on the rise in the early San José village. It has been suggested that a relatively high status family occupied a house on a raised platform equipped with unusual storage capacity, perhaps implying creation of a new and distinctive role within the community. It has also been argued on the basis of cemetery data that several different groups existed among the male members of the village, providing some degree of intra- and inter-community integration. In a word, multiplication of parts, increasing specialization of function of parts, and formalization of definition of different sorts of parts characterized the early San José village at Tomaltepec. In Flannery's (1972c) terminology, the San José phase community can be characterized by a low, but increasing, level of "segregation" when compared with late Tierras Largas phase times.

Formation of more complex linkages between components, and between components and their surroundings, is also apparent in the early San José phase. Increasingly elaborate modes of community organization and integration are suggested by the postulated men's groups and by the Structure 11 platform and storage facility. The widespread distribution of burial vessels with were-jaguar and fire-serpent symbols in Early Formative

Oaxaca also implies an increasingly valley-wide significance for some of the men's groups, although it should be emphasized that appreciable levels of valley-wide socio-political organization were not to exist in Oaxaca for many centuries.

In summary, this section has been concerned with 1) multiplication and differentiation of the parts of the Tomaltepec community, and 2) an increase in complexity of the linkages existing between these parts. As succeeding chapters will make clear, these trends continued and intensified during the Middle Formative at Tomaltepec.

Chapter IV

Middle Formative Occupation at Tomaltepec: The Rosario Phase

**The Rosario Phase
(Ca. 700?-500 B.C.)**

In the Etla arm of the Valley of Oaxaca, the Middle Formative period begins with a complex of pottery diagnostic of the Guadalupe phase. This phase was originally defined at Huitzo and San José Mogote (Flannery et al. 1970). Since 1970, surveys and excavations suggest that the ceramic and figurine types used to define the Guadalupe phase are rare to absent outside the Etla region. For example, it cannot at present be shown that either the Tlacolula arm of the valley, or the Zaachila-Zimatlán-Ocotlán arm, went through a Guadalupe phase comparable to that in Etla. Flannery (personal communication) suspects that most of the diagnostic types involved originated at Huitzo, and become rarer and rarer as one moves east and south out of the Etla region. It is no surprise, therefore, that very little evidence of Guadalupe phase material appeared at Tomaltepec.

However, Tomaltepec was definitely occupied during the Rosario phase, a much more widespread Middle Formative horizon which seems to occur throughout the Valley of Oaxaca. The Rosario phase may have begun as early as 650 or 700 B.C. and lasted until at least 500 B.C. In terms of its interregional style characteristics, it appears to be broadly contemporary with the Escalera phase in the Central Depression of Chiapas (Lowe, et al. 1960); the Conchas II phase on the Chiapas Coast (Ekholm, 1969), the initial part of the Late Santa María phase in Tehuacán (MacNeish, et al. 1970), the final part of the Zacatenco phase in the Valley of Mexico (Tolstoy and Paradis, 1970), and the latter part of the Palangana phase in Veracruz (Coe, 1970).

It seems likely that the Tomaltepec site was occupied for the entire Rosario phase, as will become apparent in the course of this discussion. There are also three proveniences at the site which contain some Guadalupe-like elements. One of these is Burial 68, which is accompanied by a single large, undecorated Atoyac Yellow-white cylinder. The burial is just below the floor atop the Structure 12 platform, which was erected over the ruins of Structure 11. Burial 47, located under the same floor, was accompanied by an eccentric-rim bowl of the type pictured by Drennan (1975:41, Fig. 11; refer to Appendix III, Figure 43 for vessel drawings). Finally, a figurine recovered from layer H of Area B is in Guadalupe phase style. Such scattered finds suggest that Tomaltepec was well outside Huitzo's main sphere of influence (cf. Plog, 1976).

Composition of the Community

One definite and one probable Rosario phase household unit (R-1 and R-2) and a larger Rosario phase public building (Structure 12) were located at Tomaltepec. It is very likely that this represents a fairly small sample of the original community. Drennan's (1976) excavations at Fábrica San José in the Etla sub-valley produced eight, or possibly nine, Rosario phase household units on a site of about the same size as Tomaltepec. Unfortunately, time and resources were not sufficient for investigation of the north and northwestern areas of the Tomaltepec site, where surface collections and test pits suggest that other Middle Formative houses are likely to have been located. Figure 16 shows the location of known and possible Rosario household units, and Table 5 lists the few associated artifacts. A discussion of each household unit follows.

STRUCTURE 12

This is the second construction found inside Mound 1, directly overlying the remains of Struc-

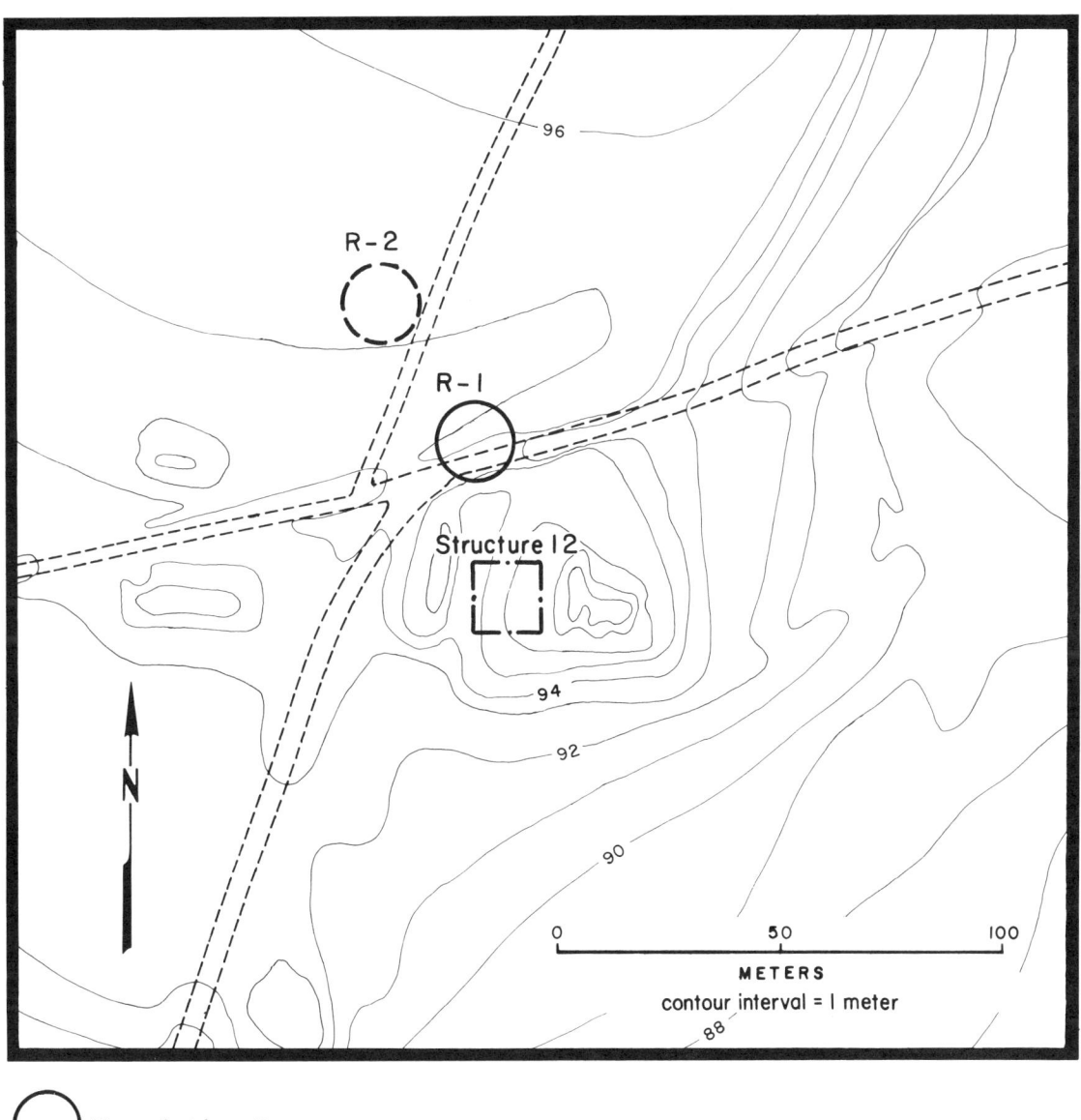

FIGURE 16. Rosario phase occupation at Tomaltepec.

ture 11 (refer to Fig. 5 and Plate 7). Due to heavy overburden of later mound fill, only some 20 percent of the top and side of the structure was uncovered. Thus the precise dimensions and nature of the structure remain unclear, although it is certainly many times larger than the early platform beneath it. As far as can be determined, Structure 12 was greater than three m high and was oriented with one axis north/south. However, it is not known whether this is a long or a short side, or indeed whether the platform was square or rectangular.

Table 5: Artifact Counts and Distributions Among Known and Possible Rosario Household Units

Artifacts	R-1	R-2
Total Sherds*	131	—
Jars*	71	—
Bowls*	60	—
Jar/Bowl Ratio*	1.18	—
Deer Bone	1	13
Other Bone	2	4
Chert/Local Stone Ratio**	0.41	0
Obsidian	7	2
Ground Stone	6	0
Mica	1	0
Figurines	1	3
Shell	***	0

*Only rim sherds counted. Ratio of jars to bowls is number of jar rims/number of bowl rims.

**Number pieces chert/number pieces local stone.

***Some of the pieces of shell tabulated with Ia-1 (Table 6) may have been associated originally with R-1.

The platform was founded upon a row of large stone slabs, each *ca.* 1.0 x 0.5 x 0.3 m and weighing more than 50 kg (Plate 26). The outer facing of the platform was not preserved in the small area excavated, although it may have been largely adobe brick or thick adobe plaster rather than masonry. The former could decompose rapidly, leaving few traces. The question must be left unresolved at this writing, as so small a section of the entire platform was exposed.

The fill of the platform seems to be largely earth and rock rubble, including numerous Early Formative sherds. A small quantity of plain gray Middle Formative pottery was mixed throughout the fill. There were present neither diagnostic Guadalupe phase sherds nor any substantial quantity of the characteristic fine-line incised gray Rosario ceramic types described in Drennan (1976). These

PLATE 26. Structures 12 and 13 (superimposed). The foundation stones of Structure 12 run beside the meter stick. The stone and adobe contruction in the foreground is the overlying Structure 13. (Compare Plate 12.)

proportions would be expected, assuming that during the early Rosario phase, the inhabitants collected all available fill and began construction of a new platform over the ruins of Structure 11.

It seems clear that refuse from the original occupation of Structure 11, which would have been immediately underfoot, was among the first fill collected for the construction of Structure 12. Structure 11 is covered first by a layer of Early Formative sherds in which occur a few Middle Formative sherds and then by layer upon layer of earth with decreasing proportions of Early Formative pottery. The fill at this point contained very little pottery at all, in fact.

Since time and funds did not suffice to clear off more than a small part of the upper portion of Structure 12, very little can be said about the sort of building which once stood atop it. It seems that much of the top part of the platform was destroyed after the Rosario phase. The size of the platform was doubled in Late Formative times, and this construction seems to have caused some damage to the older structure. There is also the problem of construction during the Monte Albán Ia Phase, to be dealt with in the next chapter. Altogether, the Middle Formative construction in this area is the most enigmatic of any of the occupation phases, as this and the succeeding chapter will make clear.

Preserved features of the upper portion of Structure 12 included a small charcoal-filled hearth, apparently on the floor, and four separate but closely spaced primary burials directly beneath the floor surface. These were identified as a male of some 40 years, and three females, aged ca. 14, 30, and 40. Briefly, the four burials were all face down, with heads to the east, and none was without offerings. Two of the females had greenstone beads in the face/neck area, and the single male burial had two marine shell discs under the chest. The remaining female was buried beneath four flat stone slabs. None of the burials lay more than 0.50 m below the upper surface of Structure 12. Plate 27 shows Burials 56 and 59. One of the female burials had a chert projectile point ca. 4 cm long under (and possibly originally in) her chest. The burials themselves, in spite of the presence of a few exotic items in three of four cases, are no more elaborate than many recovered from ordinary household units at Fábrica San José (see Drennan, 1976). The evidence, in sum, is too scanty to accurately define either the nature of Structure 12 or the circumstances of human burials within it.

R-1

This is the most complete Rosario phase household unit recovered at Tomaltepec, consisting of two presumably contemporary houses, numbered 5 and 7. The houses intersect each other at the corners so as to form a right angle which encloses a patio or open work area. Several features, including a large oven or roasting pit (Feature 44a), a small hearth (Feature 35), and the burials of two infants (Burials 10 and 36) were found in or under the patio surface.

The two houses, illustrated in Plate 28, seem to have had roughly the same dimensions, although the ends farthest from their juncture were either disturbed or left unexcavated. The houses were long and narrow: minimally 7 m long by about 1.5 m wide, with an approximate floor area of 10.5 m². This is approximately equal to the floor area of the Early Formative House 4, which lay directly beneath the courtyard of R-1. Very possibly, then, each of these houses was also the residence of a nuclear family-sized group. What the exact nature of the residential group may have been, however, is not clear. Commonality of domestic activity can be suggested from the positions of the two houses, the courtyard, and the associated features.

Each house had a well-laid stone and adobe mortar foundation about 0.6 m in width. The size of these foundations suggests that they supported substantial adobe walls rather than light wattle-and-daub partitions. Doors were very possibly located near the far ends of each structure, opening out onto the common courtyard. The houses are not precisely aligned with the cardinal points of the compass, the long axis of House 7 being oriented about 105° and the long axis of House 5 about 15°.

The floor of House 5 had been extensively disturbed during the succeeding Monte Albán Ia phase, when another large structure (House 2) was built nearby. The then-abandoned House 5 apparently served as a trash dump for Monte Albán Ia House 2. House 7 was better preserved, but the floor could not be excavated due to insufficient time. Virtually nothing was recovered from the surface of the patio. Here, mixing with overlying Late Formative material was a serious problem, so that Features 44a and 35 provide the only dependable clues to activities performed in Unit R-1.

Feature 44a (Plate 29), a large oven or roasting pit located near the intersection of Houses 5 and 7, contained fire-cracked rock, pottery, chipped and

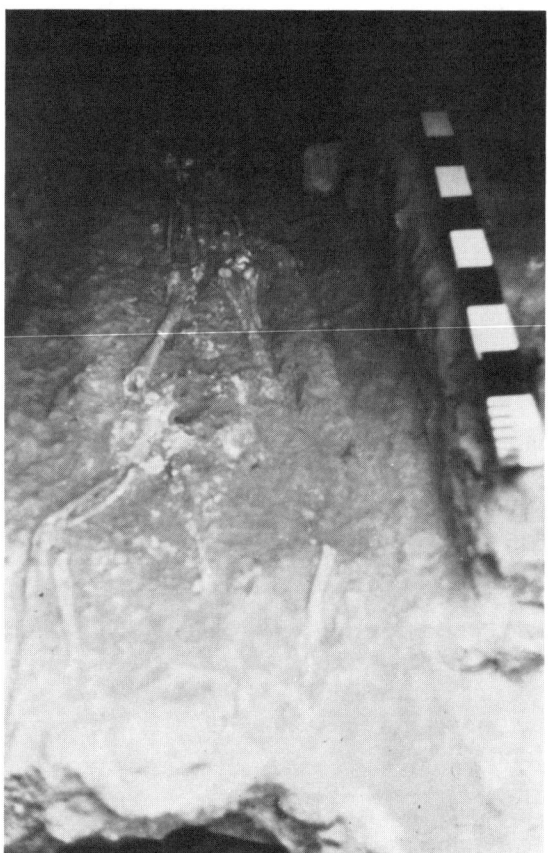

PLATE 27. Burials discovered beneath the upper surface of Structure 12. Top left, the stone slabs covering Burial 59 before excavation. Top right, Burial 59 with stone slabs removed. Bottom, Burial 56.

PLATE 28. Views of Household Unit R–1. Top: all that remained of House 5 appears on the left of the photo. Bottom: remains of the better-preserved House 7. The dashed line in the background indicates the location of House 5 relative to House 7.

PLATE 29. Feature 44a, a large roasting pit associated with Houses 5 and 7 of Unit R-1. The north arrow and scale are in Feature 44a; the pit in the foreground is an intrusive Late Formative feature.

ground stone, and carbonized corn and other small seeds. A single figurine fragment and a single piece of mica complete the inventory; no shell was found.

Most interestingly, jar and bowl fragments were present in nearly equal proportions: 60 bowl to 71 jar sherds. In Drennan's (1976) Rosario deposits from Fábrica San José, on the other hand, jar sherds always outnumber bowl sherds—even in small lots—by at least 2:1. The Feature 44a assemblage, then, would not seem to be the result of "typical" cooking/serving activities. It may be that an additional food preparation area remained undiscovered within the Unit R-1 boundary, but the evidence is too unreliable to do more than raise the possibility.

Obsidian was present, although very rare, and the ratio of chert to local silicified siltstone was low (0.41). A number of large and small grinding stones, as well as carbonized corn kernels, other small seeds, and a single splinter of deer bone attest to some food preparation activities within the household unit.

Burials associated with Unit R-1 include one child of about 2 years, and another evidently newborn or stillborn (Plate 30). No adult burials were discovered. Drennan (1976) observes that two areas of his Rosario phase community seem to have been used as burial grounds for male and female adults and children, although infants were generally not included. These areas are quite different from the Tomaltepec cemetery, however,

PLATE 30. Infant burial associated with Household Unit R-1.

and probably represent burial areas for units smaller than the whole village. Small cemeteries were common features of Rosario phase communities, the lack of adult burials at Tomaltepec might simply reflect the fact that the excavation of R-1 did not include the burial area used by that household unit.

R-2

Probable Household Unit R-2 is defined by a single large, bell-shaped storage pit (Feature 50) located to the northwest of Unit R-1. Previous experience with Early and Middle Formative Oaxacan villages suggests that such storage facilities are usually found near houses. Accordingly, R-2 is designated a "possible" household unit. Feature 50, illustrated in Figure 17, is a typical Middle Formative storage pit, these being about 90% larger than their Early Formative predecessors. As about one-half of the Rosario pit had been destroyed by a Postclassic intrusion, no bowl/jar ratio was computed. In general, in fact, the artifact assemblage from Feature 50 is not a rich one, providing minimal information about activities carried out there.

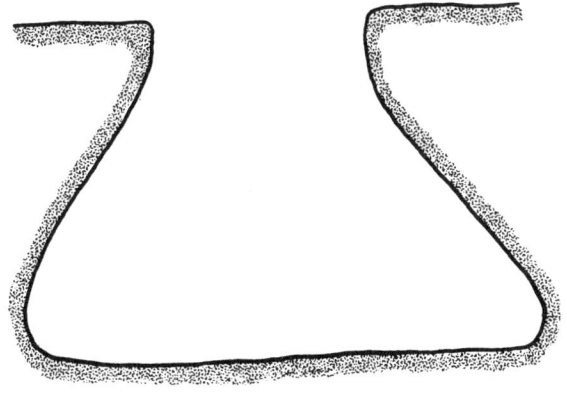

FIGURE 17. Feature 50, Possible Household Unit R-2.

Three figurine fragments were recovered from the pit, as compared to a single one from the entire Unit R-1 complex. Drennan (1976) notes that distribution of figurines during the late Guadalupe and Rosario phases at Fábrica San José was nonrandom among the household units sampled. The same situation seems to exist at Tomaltepec, but exactly what this distribution implies is still unclear. Drennan tentatively suggests that houses of ritual practitioners might contain more figurines than the average. It is also observed that this difference does not appear to be a rank-related one (op. cit.).

Feature 50 at Tomaltepec also contained two chips of obsidian, as opposed to seven pieces from Unit R-1, but the totals involved are so small as to preclude meaningful interpretation. No ground or chipped stone was recovered. Subsistence activity remains included carbonized corn kernels, a carbonized avocado pit, and other small seeds. Deer and dog seem to have provided meat for the household.

From the tabulation of Rosario phase artifacts in Table 5, it will be apparent that several very common categories of artifacts are absent from each column. The Unit R-1 artifacts are largely from Feature 44a, while the R-2 totals are entirely from Feature 50. We thus have two distinct but contemporary features which have rather different assemblages: 44a has no bone and 50 has no chipped or ground stone. Chipped stone and bone were also nonrandomly distributed at Fábrica San José, it should be noted (Drennan, 1976). This is in marked contrast to the Early Formative situation at Tomaltepec in which nearly all features contained the same kinds of artifacts, i.e., refuse from many of the activities of daily life.

It is suggested that this situation reflects increasing formalization of the use of space within the Middle Formative community. During the early San José phase, activities and use of space seem to have been on a somewhat more uniform basis, thus producing the more or less homogeneous spread of domestic garbage which is reflected in Table 2. The Middle Formative situation, on the other hand, might have been produced by a more formalized definition and use of cooking, eating, working, and living areas. It was implied in Chapter 3 that increased formalization of many aspects of social life, from leadership and status differentiation to utilization of space within the community, was a concomitant of increasing social complexity. Rosario phase artifact distributions at Tomaltepec, while scanty, are consistent with this hypothesis.

Before concluding this discussion of the components of the Rosario phase community at Tomaltepec, it should be added that no cemetery of the sort found with the Early Formative village was recovered. It is suggested that the social circumstances which supported the village cemetery of early San José times had changed. This topic will be pursued in more detail in the concluding section of the next chapter. At present, suffice it to say that evidence from Fábrica San José (Drennan, 1975), Tierras Largas (Winter, 1972), and San José Mogote (Flannery and Marcus, personal communication) suggests that smaller burial grounds existed in several locations around those communities during the Formative. The absence of adult or adolescent burials in the Rosario household units located at Tomaltepec may mean that such small cemeteries remain to be discovered there.

Examination of Figure 16 shows that the Rosario phase household units at Tomaltepec may have been spaced much like their Early Formative predecessors, with about 30 m between central features. Drennan's map of Fábrica San José in the Rosario phase also shows roughly 25 m–35 m between features defining units and their nearest known neighbors, although he observes that it is most probable that not all units were occupied simultaneously (Drennan 1976: Fig. 63). A rough distance of 30 m would seem to be a minimal spacing unit between household unit centers, however.

With specific reference to the Tomaltepec community, Structure 12 is about 30 m from Houses 5 and 7 in Unit R-1, while Feature 50, the defining feature of Unit R-2, is also about 30 m from the two houses. As in the early San José phase community, it would seem that Structure 12, the presumed focal point of the community, was separated from residential areas by roughly the same distance used to separate ordinary households from each other.

The sorts of Chi Square tests carried out in preceding chapters are not appropriate here, as there are so few good Rosario phase deposits with which to work. Some comments have already been made in this chapter about functional differentiation of activities and areas, and the following section will consider artifactual and other evidence that may be related to status differences within the community.

Social Differentiation

This aspect of the Rosario phase community at Tomaltepec is also less than clear cut. As previously mentioned, so few artifacts were recovered from good proveniences that study of their distribution over the site is of somewhat limited utility. Furthermore, as no primary midden deposits were recovered from the Structure 12 (Mound 1) vicinity, it is somewhat difficult to compare this area with the other two. Nevertheless, it seems that some tentative conclusions can be reached.

The construction technique of Houses 5 and 7, as described earlier in this chapter, seems to be much more substantial than the small, foundationless, wattle-and-daub houses known from several Oaxacan Middle Formative sites. Drennan (1976) recovered a structure similar to Houses 5 and 7 at Fábrica San José (his House 9) although it is not clear whether there was a single building or a pair comparable to that at Tomaltepec. House 9 at Fábrica San José is more than 11 m long by 2.5 meters wide, while House 5 at Tomaltepec was more than 8 m long and of undetermined width. Tomaltepec House 7 is 1.5 m wide, suggesting the possibility of somewhat smaller buildings at that site. However, the general order of magnitude seems to be quite similar in both communities. Orientation is also similar, Tomaltepec House 5 being oriented some 25° east of north. Its free end lay to the south, where a door seems to have been located; its end joined with House 7 was to the north. Fábrica San José House 9 is oriented about 15° east of north, with one free end to the south, where Drennan suspects a door to have been located. Its northern end was not uncovered, but if it was like the Tomaltepec complex, there may in fact, be another similar structure joined to it at the buried northern corner and extending away to the east. This assumes that Drennan's suggestion as to the location of the door is correct, and that the door opened onto the courtyard between the buildings, as in the Tomaltepec examples.

Drennan observes that House 9 at Fábrica San José does not seem to be that of a particularly high status family, based on artifact and design motif associations. Indeed, compared with some Rosario phase houses recently found at San José Mogote, no house at Tomaltepec or Fábrica San José appears to belong to anyone of extremely high status (Flannery and Marcus, personal communication). Our total sample of Rosario phase houses is still quite small, and variation among them is not well understood. Associated with House 5 of Unit R-1 was found a thick, polished fragment of lowland turtle shell (*Dermatemys mawii*), which very probably once formed part of a turtle shell drum. As already indicated, more obsidian and a little mica also came from this unit, which seems to be the nearest household unit to Structure 12, the public building.

So little is known of Household Unit R-2 that it is difficult to compare it to the other units, although one is left with the impression that it may have belonged to a relatively lower status family. First, no exotic items, such as marine shell, greenstone, or mica, were present. Obsidian, while present, occurred in relatively lower amounts. Second, the household would have been about 60 m from the public building area, placing it well out into the area where the rest of the community is presumed to have been. These indications, while admittedly rather tenuous, suggest the possibility that Unit R-2 may have been of lower status than Unit R-1.

There are therefore no data from Tomaltepec for anything beyond a continuum of status differentiation. This distinction, as it is based entirely on associations of not overly abundant artifacts, is of the most tentative sort, although it is consistent with the idea of ranking (i.e., a gradation of status as argued by Service [1962, 1971]) by which we usually characterize Middle Formative society (see Flannery, 1968a, and Drennan, 1976, for instance).

Subsistence Activities

Subsistence activities at Rosario phase Tomaltepec cannot be adequately characterized with the small artifact samples currently available. Carbonized plant remains suggest that maize farming continued to be an important subsistence activity. The bell-shaped pit (Feature 50), which is the defining feature of Possible Unit R-2, suggests that food was still stored on a residential unit basis. Hunting of deer and other wild animals continued, and domestic dog was apparently eaten in some households. The question of the kinds and proportions of animals which were eaten by particular households is still unanswered due to sample size.

Craft and Exchange Activities

The relatively small quantity of Rosario phase artifacts recovered at Tomaltepec precludes extensive development of this topic as well. Some obsidian was present, although it composed only .05 percent of all chipped stone. No marine shell was found. Non-local chert, as opposed to local silicified siltstone, was present in very small quantity, the ratio of chert to local stone in Unit R-1 being 0.41. If these bits of information may be taken as representative of the general situation, then it may be suggested that extra-community trade relations were maintained, but on a lower level relative to the Early Formative.

Summary of the Evidence

As should be clear from the preceding sections, the Rosario phase occupation at Tomaltepec is not well defined as regards either extent or character. Occupation seems to have been continuous throughout the Rosario phase and into the Monte Albán Ia phase of the Middle Formative period. The size of the community was most probably below 2 ha, although this cannot be precisely determined with the data currently in hand. Likewise, the number of households composing the village cannot be rigorously determined, although it may be estimated at 10 or 15. A population of 50 to 100 persons is thus implied. These estimates are, of course, of the most tenuous sort, and they are offered simply to provide some concept of the order of magnitude of the Tomaltepec Rosario occupation.

Two Rosario phase household units were discovered. One of these is well defined and was suggested to have been of relatively higher status in the community. The second (possible) unit was poorly defined, but its location and artifact assemblage suggest that it may have held a position of relatively lower status. Other Rosario residences are very poorly known, as they appear to lie outside the limits of extensive excavation.

An apparent public building is located on the edge of the piedmont spur, covering the ruins on the early San José phase higher status area. Structure 12 is a solid earth, stone, and adobe construction at least 3 m high and of unknown dimensions. It represents an entirely different order of magnitude of construction from the Early Formative house platform (Structure 11) beneath it. It seems likely that Structure 12 was the result of large-scale community effort, whereas Structure 11 need not have been. The only other Rosario phase public buildings excavated at present in the Valley of Oaxaca are at San José Mogote and Huitzo. This situation will be discussed in more detail in Chapter 8 of this study.

Subsistence appears to have been based on maize farming and hunting of deer and other wild animals. Consumption of domestic dog may also have been significant. Data from the succeeding Monte Albán Ia phase of the Middle Formative strongly suggest that the distribution of deer and dog bone followed status lines: i.e., higher status houses consumed larger quantities of deer. It is not clear whether this situation existed in Rosario phase Tomaltepec, as absolute quantities of animal bone recovered are too small to apply to such considerations.

That some exchange in non-local exotic goods existed is attested to by the presence of obsidian in the community. The extent of this exchange is unknown, although tentative indications are that it was not great.

Chapter V

Middle Formative Occupation at Tomaltepec: The Monte Albán Ia Phase

The Monte Albán Ia Phase (ca. 500-300 B.C.)

The Monte Albán Ia phase represents the final phase of the Middle Formative period in the Valley of Oaxaca. It also marks the initial occupation of the mountain-top ceremonial center of Monte Albán, which eventually came to dominate much of the Southern Highlands of Mexico. Surveys in the central part of the Valley of Oaxaca (especially by Kowalewski, 1976:2) suggest that considerable increases in numbers and size of communities took place in the Monte Albán Ia phase. At least two canal irrigation systems were also begun in the area at this time: one at the base of Monte Albán itself and one in the western Tlacolula Valley (Kowalewski, op. cit.).

The Monte Albán Ia phase also marks the beginning of a shift in power centers in the Valley of Oaxaca and the beginning of a developmental process which by the Late Formative/Early Classic (i.e., about 300 B.C.-A.D. 500) culminated in centralized political domination of much of the region. This period also seems to mark the beginning of the process whereby the Etla sub-valley, where San José Mogote lies, became subordinate to Monte Albán. This is not to suggest that the Etla sub-valley, with its high population and productive farm lands, became insignificant, for substantial communities continued to be located there. It does seem, however, that the long pre-eminence of the Etla sub-valley began to come to an end in the Monte Albán Ia phase. As will be seen in subsequent chapters, this process accelerated throughout the Monte Albán I phase.

The Monte Albán Ia phase (ca. 500-300 B.C.) in the Valley of Oaxaca is contemporary with the Francesa phase in the Chiapas Highlands (Lowe, et al., 1960), with the latter part of the Late Santa María phase in Tehuacán (MacNeish, et al., 1970), with the Atoto-Cuautepec sub-phase in the Valley of Mexico (Tolstoy and Paradis, 1970), with the end of the Palangana phase in Veracruz (Coe, 1970), and with the end of the Cerro Chacaltepec I phase in Morelos (Grove, 1970).

Composition of the Community

Three Monte Albán Ia household units were designated (Ia-1, Ia-2, and Ia-3), and a fourth "possible" unit (Ia-4) was defined by midden debris. It seems likely that Structure 12, the Rosario phase public building, continued in use without substantial modification. These units are located on the site map in Figure 18, and associated artifacts are listed in Table 6. A discussion of each follows:

STRUCTURE 12

This public building is still designated by the number used in the Rosario phase discussion, as it is not clear that any really substantial additions

Table 6: Artifact Counts and Distributions Among Known and Possible Monte Albán Ia Household Units

Artifacts	Ia-1	Ia-2	Ia-3	Ia-4
Total Sherds*	238	467	—	UNRELIABLE DATA—MIXED
Jars*	52	234	—	
Bowls*	186	233	—	
Jar/Bowl Ratio*	0.28	1.00	—	
Deer Bone	18	6	6	
Rabbit Bone	4	0	0	
Dog Bone	1	10	ca. 100	
Chert/Local Stone Ratio**	0.19	0.08	0	
Obsidian	31	0	2	
Ground Stone	2	10	0	
Mica	5	0	0	
Figurines	2	5	0	
Shell	6†	0	0	

*Only rim sherds counted. Ratio of jars to bowls is the number of jar rims/the number of bowl rims.
**Number pieces chert/number pieces local stone.
†Most of this shell appears to have been associated with Ia-1. A small quantity may have been associated originally with R-1.

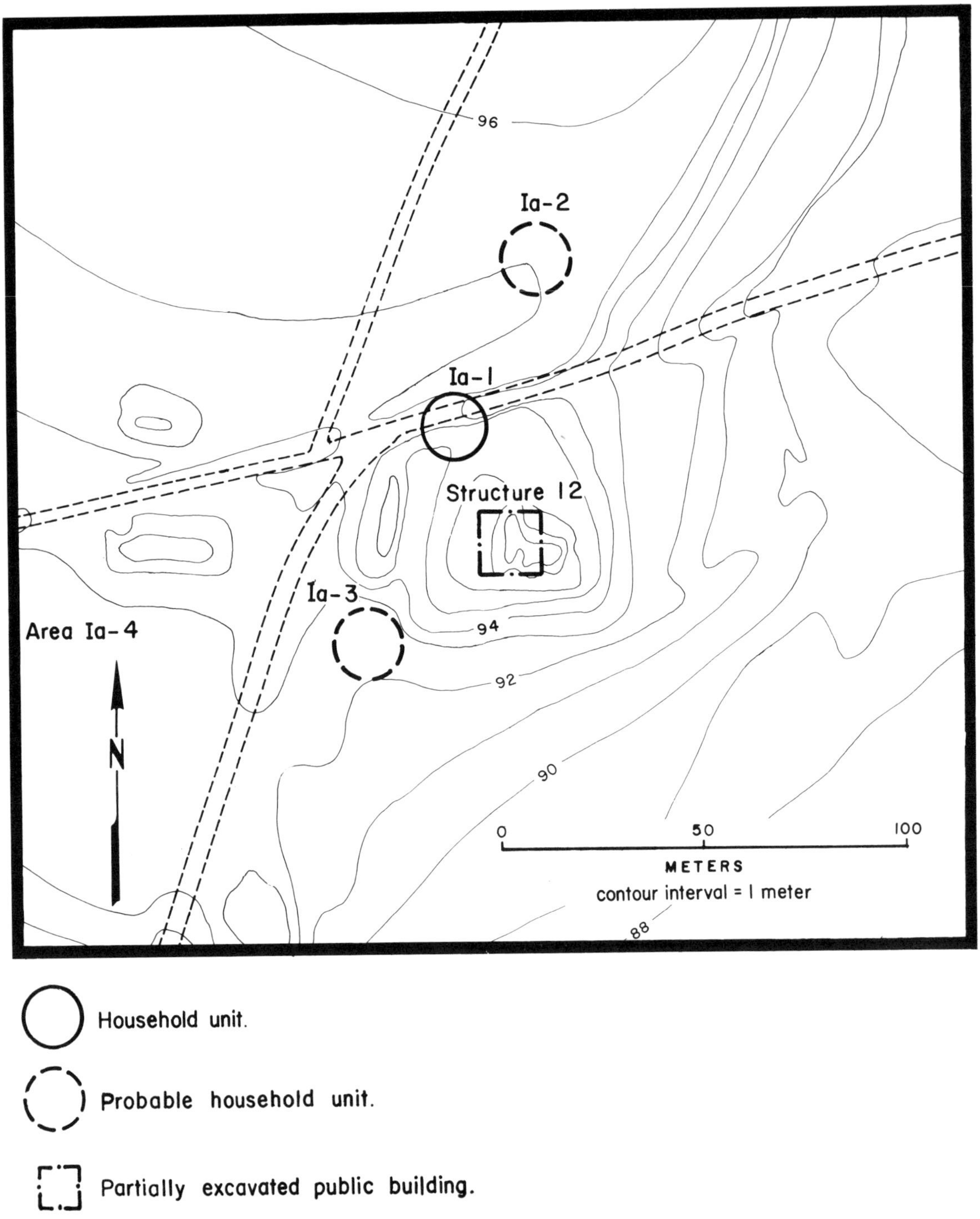

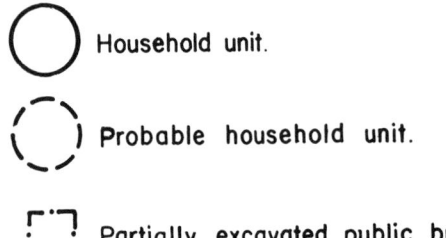

96
Ia-2
Ia-1
Structure 12
Ia-3
Area Ia-4
N
94
92
90
88
0
50
100
METERS
contour interval = 1 meter
Household unit.
Probable household unit.
Partially excavated public building.

FIGURE 18. Monte Albán Ia occupation at Tomaltepec.

were made to the structure in Monte Albán Ia times. It seems likely that such Ia additions as were made involved leveling and small-scale filling for new floors atop the old platform. It is suggested, in other words, that the Structure 12 platform was built early in the Rosario phase, and that it was maintained throughout the Rosario and Monte Albán Ia phases. The next substantial enlargements of the structure are made at the apogee of the site's developmental history in the succeeding Monte Albán Ic phase. No Ia burials were recovered in association with the platform, and it is

MIDDLE FORMATIVE: THE MONTE ALBÁN IA PHASE

unclear what ceremonial and/or civic functions it may have discharged in the community. Before any such conclusions can be substantiated, more work on this structure is certainly in order.

Ia-1

This unit consists of two superimposed structures—three human burials, and four features, ranging from bell-shaped storage pits to hearths. The uppermost of the two structures in this unit, designated House 2, had a sequence of four hard-packed sand floors (Plate 31). The upper floor surface was very poorly preserved, however, due to heavy occupation directly above it during the succeeding Monte Albán Ic phase. The surface is fairly large, possibly originally including as much as 70 m². However, it should be noted that this may include two nearly contemporary and slightly overlapping surfaces. Disturbance was so extensive that the entire picture is rather unclear. Whether surface is a courtyard or an interior is unknown. The orientation of the surface is also poorly known, although its long axis may have been oriented roughly east/west. All that does seem clear is that a Monte Albán Ia phase structure once stood here or in the immediate vicinity.

The second (underlying) structure of Ia-1, designated House 3, is of a somewhat different sort. Unfortunately it could not be investigated during the 1974 field season. Wright's field notes from his brief 1972 sampling at Tomaltepec (Wright, n.d.) describe the structure as follows:

> This house was built by cutting a rectangular step into the sloping surface of Layer I, which dips to the west. This step was 6.0 by 4.1 meters in size. Most of it was filled with a layer of adobes of various colors, made from Early Formative refuse, and laid in a similarly composed mortar.

The bricks were quite clearly visible when scraped, and several modal sizes seem to be present: one

PLATE 31. Upper surface of floor, House 2, Household Unit Ia-1. The only well-defined posthole associated with this house appears to the left of center.

30.5 by 20 cm and one 33.5 by 23.5 cm (Ibid.). (Refer to Pl. 6). A single sand floor was laid over the adobe layer, suggesting that the structure was not long or heavily used. At some point in the Monte Albán Ia phase, House 3 was covered over with 10-15 cm of fill to serve as a base for the previously described House 2. This surface is illustrated in Figure 19.

Features associated with the House 2/3 complex included a number of small and large amorphous, trash-filled pits, and two small, bell-shaped storage pits (See Fig. 20 and Plate 32). Bone, ground stone, a few figurine parts, and a number of pieces of burned daub were recovered. Chipped stone tools and debitage as well as ground stone and carbonized remains of maize and other small seeds attest to the usual domestic activities.

Human burials associated with Unit Ia-1 numbered two, including a male of 30-40 years, and a female of some 20 years. These are Burials 1 and 8a (Plate 33). Presumably, this pattern represents burial of residents of the household unit within its boundaries. No infants or children were recovered in association with this or any other Monte Albán Ia household cluster.

Ia-2

This household unit overlay and partially disturbed the early San José phase cemetery. While no actual house floor was recovered here, substantial quantities of burned, cane-impressed daub mixed with Monte Albán Ia refuse attest to the presence of a structure in the immediate vicinity. The household unit was defined by: a) the aforementioned daub remains; b) at least three adult burials: numbers 26, 42, and 72 (see Appendix III); and c) seven features: numbers 40, 69, 77, 82, 88, 104, and 107, including middens, hearths, and small pits. All of these features and burials were found within an area of some 80 m². The entire complex is illustrated in Figure 21.

The burials associated with Ia-2, like those

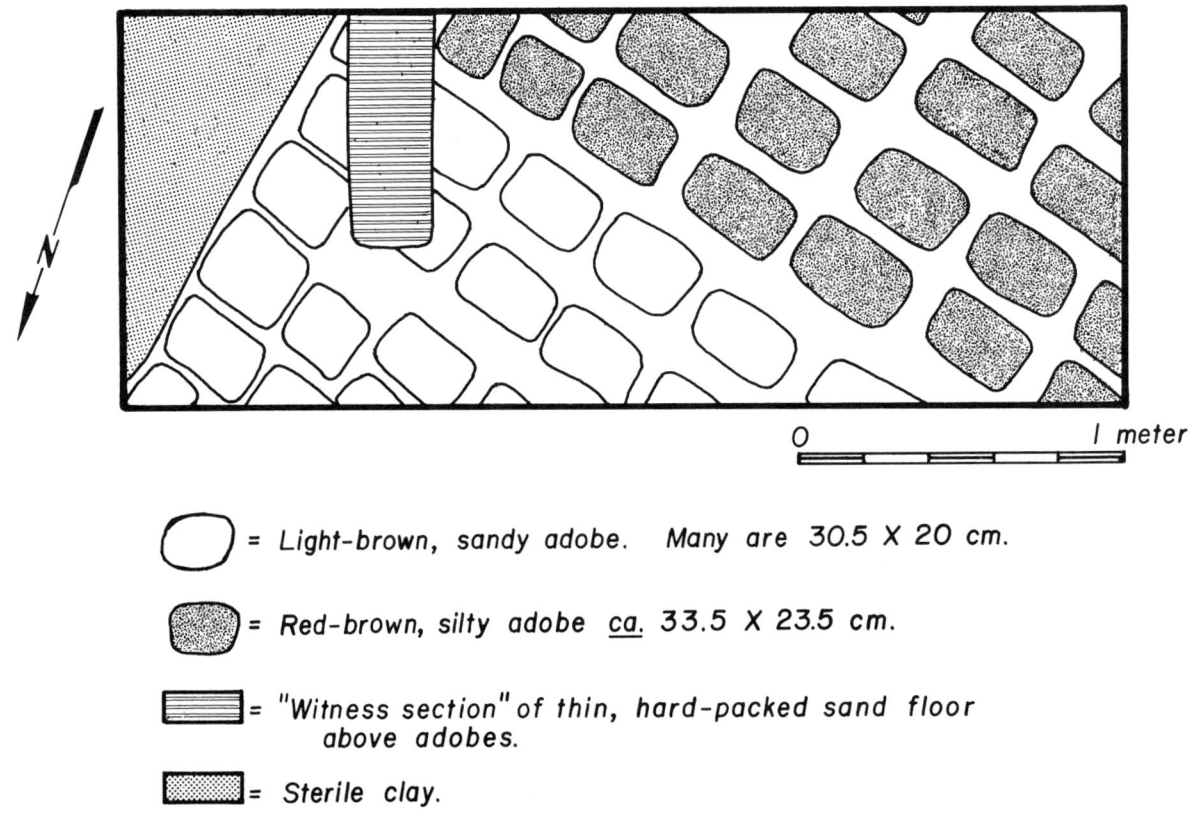

FIGURE 19. Construction of House 3 floor. (Diagram adopted from Wright, n.d.)

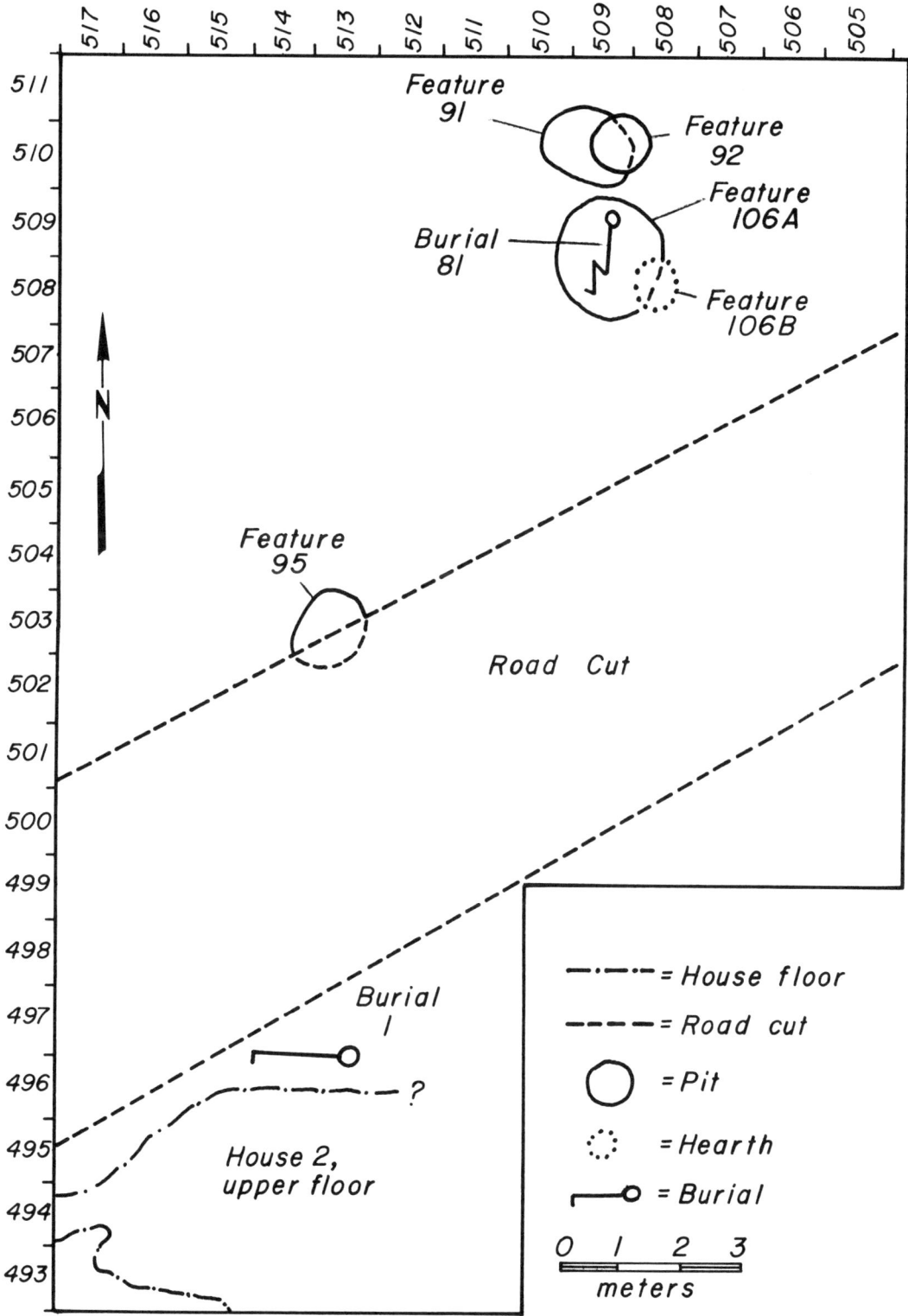

FIGURE 20. Components of Household Unit Ia-1. In addition to the features and burials shown, Monte Albán Ia pottery refuse was spread throughout the area.

PLATE 32. Features from Household Unit Ia-1. Top, Features 91 and 106. Bottom, Feature 95.

MIDDLE FORMATIVE: THE MONTE ALBÁN IA PHASE

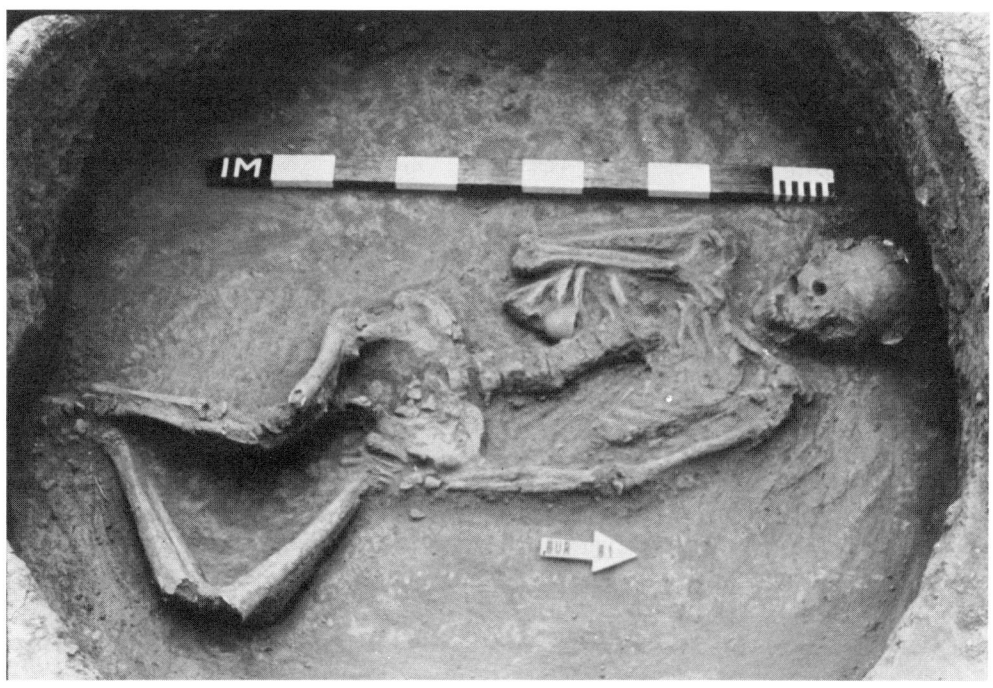

PLATE 33. Burial from Household Unit Ia-1. Top, Burial 1, Bottom, Burial 81.

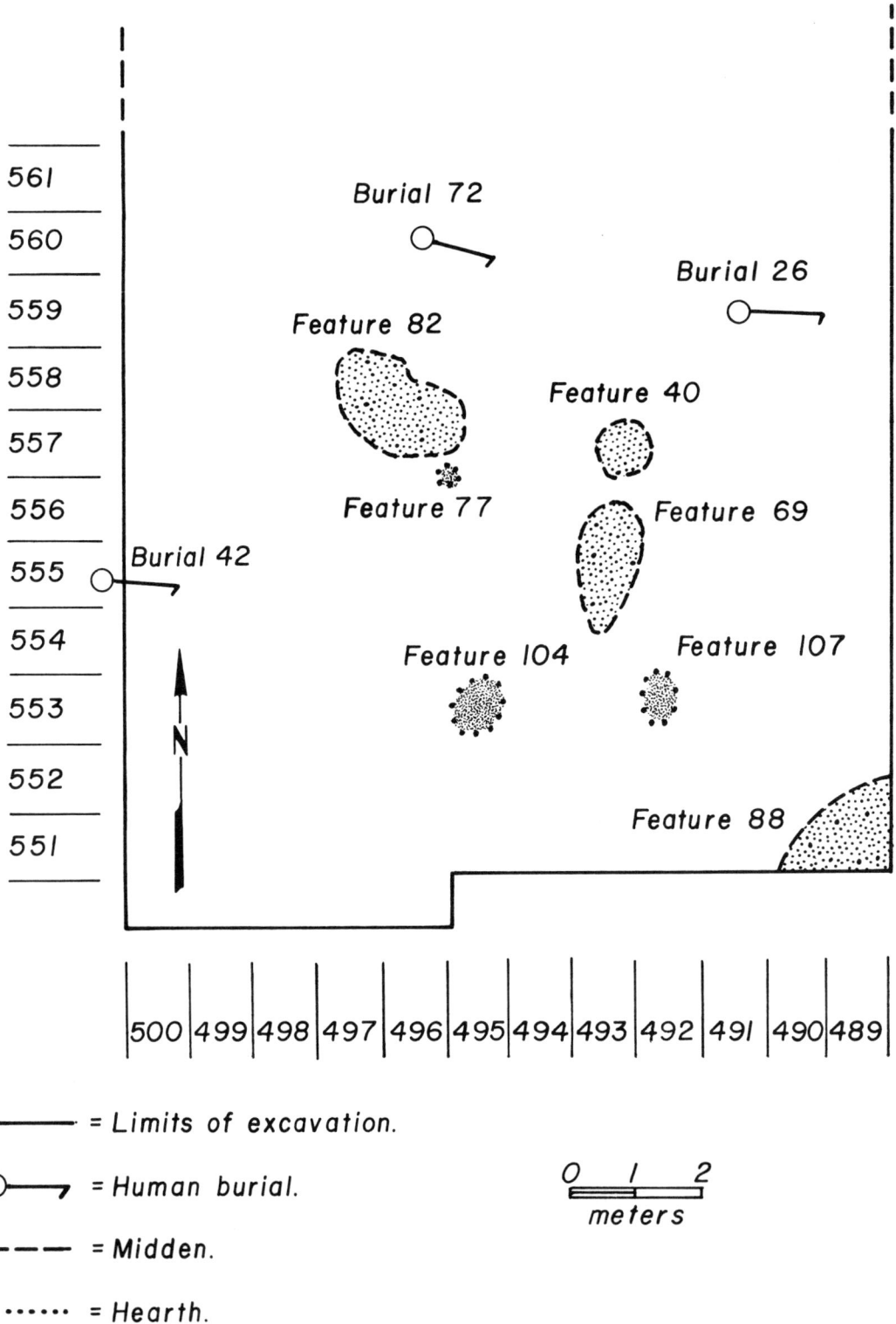

FIGURE 21. Components of Possible Household Unit Ia-2. In addition to the features and burials shown, Monte Albán Ia pottery refuse was scattered throughout the area. Burned daub was recovered from Feature 40 and (in even greater quantity) from Feature 82.

PLATE 34. Burial from Household Unit Ia-2.

found with Ia-1, were all adults. Also, like the Ia-1 burials, both males and females were present. All burials in Ia-2 were oriented with heads to the west, and might be placed either on the back or face down, with the supine position predominating. The Ia-2 burials invariably had their offerings placed over, around, and beneath their knees. The only Ia-1 burials with offerings, in contrast, had these placed over and around the head and face. Features 77, 104, and 107 appear to be small, shallow hearths, usually consisting of burned earth, charcoal, and a few stones. The size ranges from 30 to 60 cm in length and 5 to 20 cm in depth, so that we are clearly dealing with rather small scale facilities. Feature 40 represents a small (ca. 50 cm in diameter), shallow pit of uncertain function, while Features 69, 82, and 83 are midden heaps.

Maize and other carbonized plant remains, animal bone, chipped stone, and ground stone suggest that the usual kinds of household activities were carried out in unit Ia-2.

PLATE 35. Feature 107 from Household Unit Ia-2.

Ia-3

This unit is less extensively defined than the preceding two, but it does seem very likely that a Monte Albán Ia house once stood in the vicinity of the two features recovered. One of these (Feature 79) was a small bell-shaped pit (about 0.6 cubic meters in capacity) which yielded carbonized remains of maize and other small seeds, animal bone, chipped stone, and pottery. Feature 30 lay slightly downslope from Feature 79, and was evidently a midden heap. Features 79 and 30 overlay early San José phase Feature 72 and the associated Test Pit #2 midden. Features 79 and 30 were also in exactly the same relation to each other as Feature 72 and the Test Pit #2 midden. Both Early and Middle Formative houses, in other words, stood in about the same places, and the residents threw their garbage in about the same spot. Feature 79 of Unit Ia-3 is illustrated in Figure 22. Artifacts associated with Unit Ia-3 allow the assumption that domestic functions were

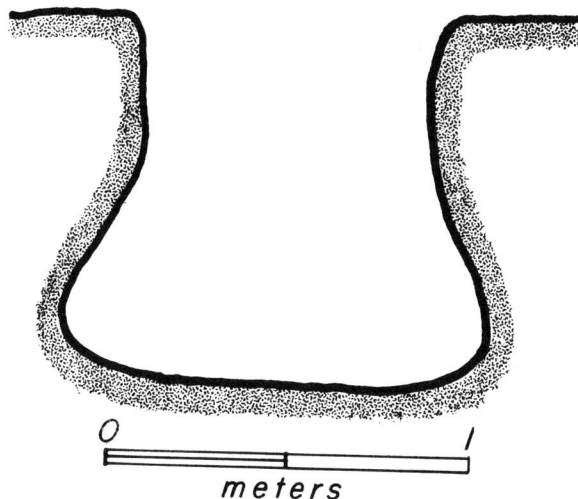

FIGURE 22. Feature 79, Possible Household Unit Ia-3.

performed there. In general, however, the entire area was very badly disturbed by a subsequent Late Formative activity area, to be discussed presently. No human burials were recovered from Ia-3.

IA-4

This is one of the least clear-cut Monte Albán Ia occupation areas recovered at Tomaltepec. Feature 74 of Unit Ia-4 was a large and irregularly-shaped pit with an 80 cm deep shaft in one end. The feature was not completely excavated, so its exact shape and size are unknown (Fig. 23). Fill consisted of fist-sized rock and domestic refuse. The abundant pottery was mostly of the Monte Albán Ia phase, with a little redeposited Rosario phase pottery and some intrusive pottery from a Monte Albán Ic disturbance. There was also a considerable quantity of cane-impressed daub in large chunks. It may be that in this area the remnants of a Period Ia house were later used as fill in Feature 74. It is further suggested that the Ia refuse came from the immediate area of Feature 74, as surface collections made there produced a relatively large quantity of Ia pottery.

What Feature 74 originally represented is unknown. The fist-sized fire-cracked rocks suggest roasting of some sort, although almost no charcoal came from the fill (it should be noted that charcoal is preserved in abundance over the rest of the site).

Spacing of the components of the Ia community corresponds quite well to that of previous occupations. The public building (presumably the focal point of the community) continued to be Structure 12. Household Unit Ia-1 was located about 30 m to the north, overlapping the areas covered by previous households TL-2, ESJ-1, and R-1. Unit Ia-2 lay about 50 m to the northeast of Ia-1, overlying the early San José phase cemetery. Unit Ia-3 lay about 50 m to the southwest, while "possible" Unit Ia-4 lay roughly 50-70 m from Ia-3, its nearest known neighbor.

Social Differentiation

One of the most striking differences among households can be found in the distribution of dog and deer bone over the site. It appears that inhabitants of Unit Ia-1 may have consumed more deer and less dog than Units Ia-2 or Ia-3, both of which show more dog than deer. Unit Ia-1 also contains rabbit bones, which are absent in Units Ia-2 and Ia-3.

Obsidian occurs in relative abundance in Unit Ia-1–38 pieces, compared to none in Ia-2, and 2 pieces in Ia-3. Local silicified siltstone and chert were also recovered from Ia-1 and Ia-2, although in different ratios: about 0.19 (chert:siltstone) in Ia-1 as compared with 0.08 (chert:siltstone) in Ia-2. More figurines were present in Ia-2 than in any other unit, but as was mentioned earlier, we do not know how these objects relate to status. Shell (in the form of an ornament interred with Burial 1) and a few bits of mica (scattered over the floor of House 2) were both present in unit Ia-1 and in no other Period Ia proveniences excavated. Several stone beads (possibly of quartzite) were found with Burial 42, Unit Ia-2. Also to be considered is the architecture of House 3, the lowermost structure in Unit Ia-1. The large step cut into the ground, as well as the pavement of adobe bricks, reflects a labor investment of unusual proportions.

The evidence, then, seems to lead to designation of Unit Ia-1 as a household of relatively higher status. To the evidence from artifact distributions and construction technique, we may add the proximity of Unit Ia-1 to Structure 12, the public building. It may also be suggested that as one proceeds outward from the public building, simpler wattle-and-daub residences of relatively lower status are encountered. Here, deer may have been replaced by dog as the primary meat source. Here

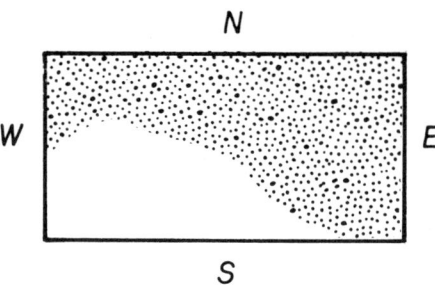

a. Test pit plan at 1 meter below surface.

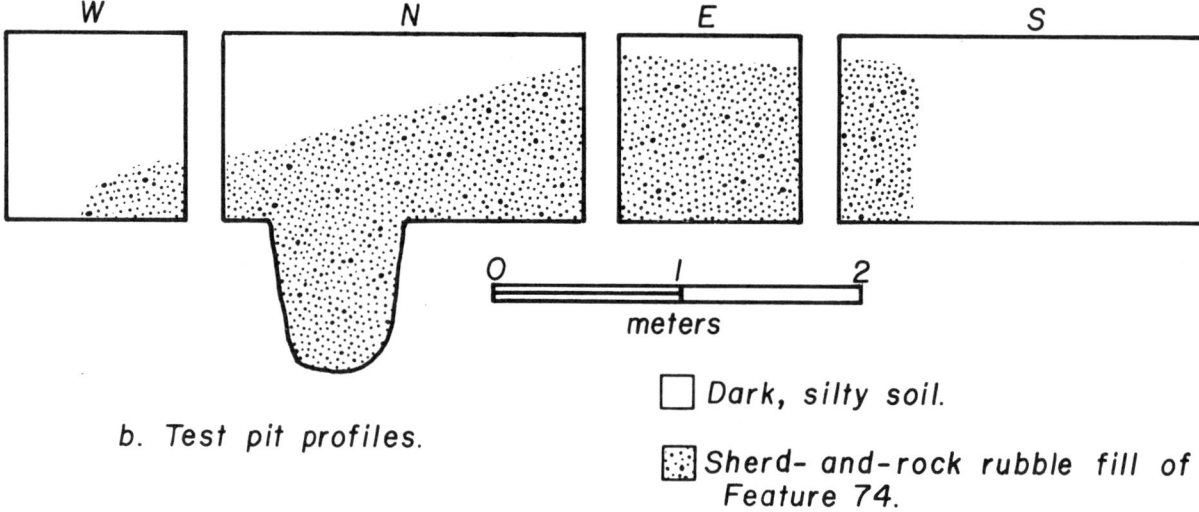

b. Test pit profiles.

Dark, silty soil.

Sherd- and-rock rubble fill of Feature 74.

FIGURE 23. Feature 74 of Household Unit Ia-4, as revealed in a test pit.

also, considerably less obsidian was used (relative to Unit Ia-1), and the ratio of finer chert to lower quality local silicified siltstone was appreciably lower. Shell and mica also seem to have been absent. Beyond these differences, however, the range of subsistence activities performed in each household seem to have been much the same.

Human burials associated with the household units provided little indication of relative social differentiation between households. However (although the sample is small), there seems to be some differential treatment of burials *within* a household unit. In both Units Ia-1 and Ia-2, there was one burial with relatively more elaborate ceramic offerings and with exotic or imported ornaments, albeit in miniscule quantities. These included several quartzite beads in Unit Ia-2, and a small shell ornament in Ia-1. Nevertheless, none of these burials display much social differentiation.

To this point, Structure 12 has not been considered, as neither reliable midden deposits, nor sizable floor areas, nor burials were recovered from it. It has been maintained, however, that the public building which stood atop it was modified and used throughout the Ia phase. As much of this structure seems to have been destroyed by subsequent construction and modern looting, very little of the Ia resurfacing was exposed. Thus, whether there are more elaborate Ia burials beneath the floor in the unexcavated 80 percent of the structure is unknown. Such was the case, it will be recalled, with the antecedent Rosario phase building.

At any rate, it may again be suggested that there existed within the community a public building, a relatively higher status residence near the foot of the public building, and a number of relatively lower status households farther removed from the center of the community.

Subsistence Activities

As observed in the introduction to this chapter, small irrigation systems began to make their appearance in the Valley of Oaxaca at this time. No canals definitely identifiable as Middle Formative were discovered at Tomaltepec, although the remains of two apparently Postclassic canals were found. It was the irrigation potential of the site's location which first attracted the notice of the Oaxaca Project (Wright and Lees, 1970:79).

Carbonized plant remains indicate that maize continued to be the major staple crop of the community. Hunting at Tomaltepec during the Monte Albán Ia phase seems to have remained at the generally lower level which characterized the Rosario phase community. Deer, rabbit, and peccary bones are present, but relatively few in number. The distribution of these bones, as already noted, might be construed as following status lines, with very nearly all identifiable deer, rabbit, and peccary bone coming from the higher status Household Unit Ia-1. Most dog bone, on the other hand, was associated with other, more distant households, both of which seem to be of lower status.

Craft and Exchange Activities

As in the preceding Rosario phase, there appears to have been a small amount of exchange in non-local items during the Monte Albán Ia phase at Tomaltepec. Obsidian composed about 10.4 perent of all chipped stone, and marine shell was present in small quantity. Neither, however, seems to have been distributed throughout the community. Rather, obtaining and using nonlocal goods would seem to have become increasingly a prerogative of higher status people, suggesting that exchange both within and without the Valley of Oaxaca had become a somewhat less egalitarian affair relative to the Early Formative Period.

Pires-Ferreira (1975:90) argues that pooling and distribution of imported obsidian blades by resident elites became more common even at smaller communities (such as Tierras Largas) by the Middle Formative Period, and we may suppose that certain categories of non-local items exchanged in the Valley of Oaxaca at smaller communities were increasingly controlled by the elite segment of society. It should be added that the trade in obsidian blades, in which this change is particularly clear, composed a substantial proportion of the non-local exchange in Middle Formative Mesoamerica.

Summary of the Evidence

Occupation at Tomaltepec seems to have been continuous throughout the Monte Albán Ia phase (ca. 500–300 B.C.). As with the preceding Rosario phase village, the exact size of the Ia community cannot be reliably determined. It does appear that the community increased in size from Rosario to Ia times, although in all probability this increase was not great.

Also like the Rosario community, the Ia village at Tomaltepec seems to have been composed of at least three different zones: (1) a ceremonial-civic zone; (2) a nearby zone of higher status residences; and (3) a zone of lower status houses scattered in a wide arc around the higher status zone. Differences in house construction technique between the higher and lower status zones were substantial, ranging from relatively elaborate structures with adobe brick floors, to small wattle-and-daub houses of the familiar Oaxacan Formative sort.

Subsistence in the Ia community continued to be based on maize agriculture, although hunting appears to have declined from its Early Formative levels. The meat of the domestic dog was more heavily used in Ia times at Tomaltepec than previously. Most dog bone was associated with what appear to be lower status units, while deer bone showed a much greater tendency to occur in their higher status counterparts. Marine shell and obsidian occur in small quantity in Unit Ia-1, and it has been argued that obtaining and perhaps distributing non-local goods such as obsidian became increasingly a prerogative of higher status community members in Middle Formative times.

It is impossible to attempt any detailed reconstruction of community organization and integration during the Middle Formative, as Middle Formative data from Tomaltepec are the least complete of that of any of the three Formative periods.

Chapter VI

Late Formative Occupation at Tomaltepec: The Monte Alban Ic Phase

**The Monte Albán Ic Phase
(ca. 300–100 B.C.)**

The Monte Albán Ic phase marks the apogee of Formative development in the Tomaltepec community. At this time, a minor ceremonial center consisting of four platforms, wide expanses of plastered courtyard, and high status house platforms of cut stone existed there. The Monte Albán Ic phase in Oaxaca is contemporary with the Tezoyuca and Patlachique phases in Central Mexico (Millon, 1967); with the Late Santa María phase in Tehuacán (MacNeish, 1964); with the Chiapa V and VI levels in the Chiapas highlands (Lowe, et al. 1960); and with the Cerro de las Mesas I — Tres Zapotes I phases in Veracruz (Drucker 1943).

In Chapter 1 of this study, it was suggested that the Monte Albán Ic phase was one of considerable political growth for the Valley of Oaxaca, during which time its influence began to be felt in other areas of Mesoamerica (see, for instance, MacNeish, 1964, and Flannery, et al., 1967). The Monte Albán Ic phase also appears to have witnessed major growth in the region, especially in the vicinity of Monte Albán. There, Kowalewski's 1974 survey recorded 194 Monte Albán Ic sites, which represents a vast increase in population over preceding periods (Kowalewski and Varner, 1975). In addition, the mountain-top center of Monte Albán, first occupied in the preceding Monte Albán Ia phase, had grown enormously in size (see Blanton, 1978) by the Ic phase.

As observed in Chapter II, the Late Formative Period all over Mesoamerica seems to have seen the dichotomy between center and subordinate area widespread and intensified as never before (Sanders and Price, 1968). It is also apparent that social differentiation between individuals widened in the Late Formative Period. In Oaxaca, Late Formative burials recovered from a number of Oaxacan sites range from simple pit graves with no offerings to elaborately constructed and furnished tombs. There also seems to have been a similarly wide difference in house construction technique, to be discussed presently.

Finally, it was suggested in Chapter II that by Late Formative times in Oaxaca (i.e., Monte Albán Ic) social integration was achieved by the exercise of genuine political authority in highly differentiated society. The following sections of this chapter will consider Late Formative developments in the Tomaltepec community, which by that time appears to have been a minor ceremonial-civic center.

Composition of the Community

The overall structure of the Late Formative community is somewhat obscure, due largely to the explosive Late Formative expansion of the central portion of the site (i.e., the vicinity of Mound 1). This same area was also the focal point of the Early and Middle Formative villages although it was considerably smaller in those periods. The excavated area, in other words, covered a larger and more diverse proportion of the smaller Early and Middle Formative occupations whereas only the central portion of the Late Formative community was within the area of investigation. Unfortunately, to extend the area of excavations in search of the presumed outlying lower status residence areas was beyond the capacity of the project. Nevertheless, several distinct components of the Late Formative community were isolated in the vicinity of the mound and plaza area, each of which is located in Figure 24. Artifacts associated with each area are listed in Table 7. Each excavated component is described below.

STRUCTURE 13 AND THE PLAZA AREA

Structure 12, the Middle Formative public building, was partially leveled and covered by Structure 13 in Late Formative times. Structure 13 was an extremely substantial platform, at least

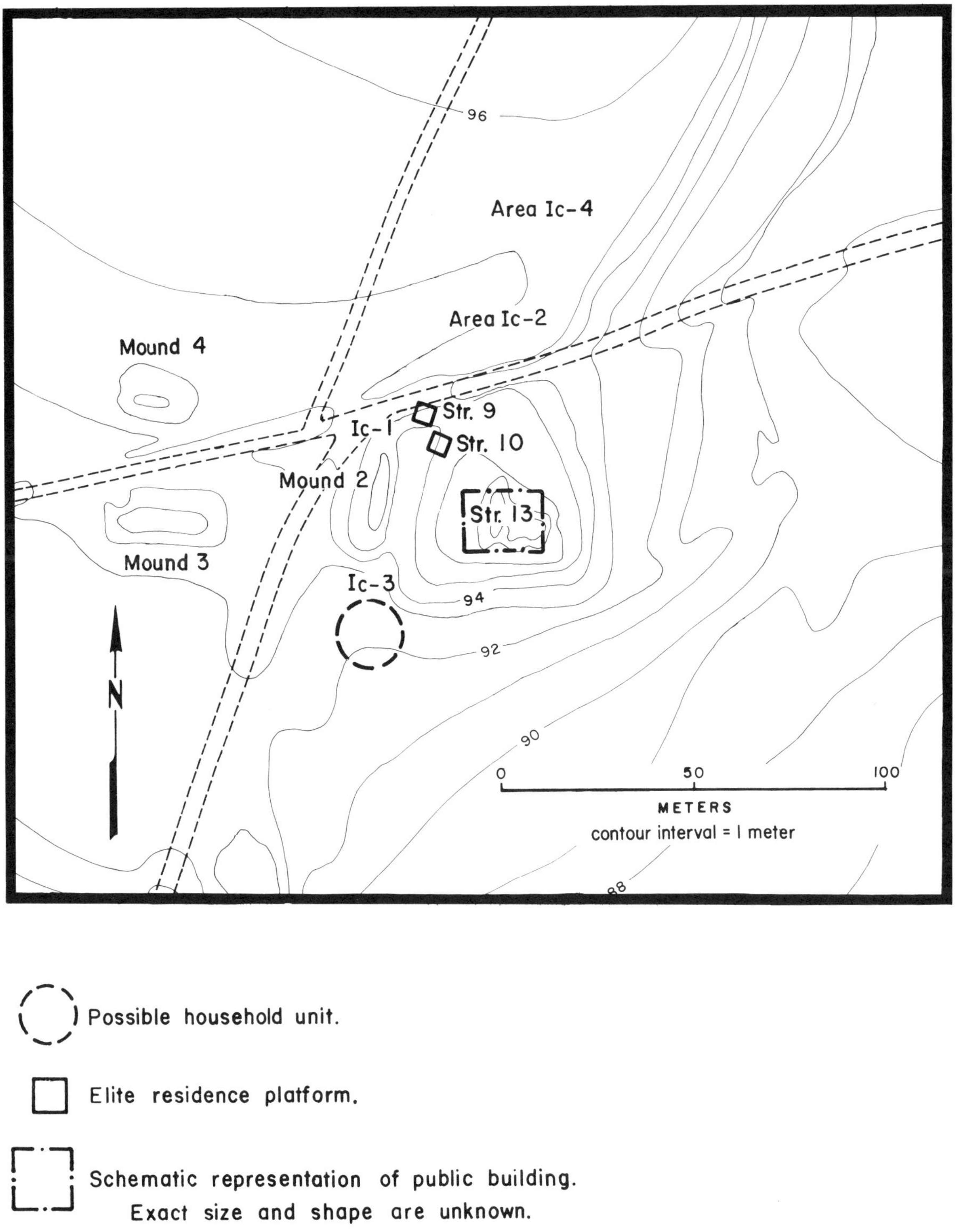

MIDDLE FORMATIVE: THE MONTE ALBÁN IC PHASE

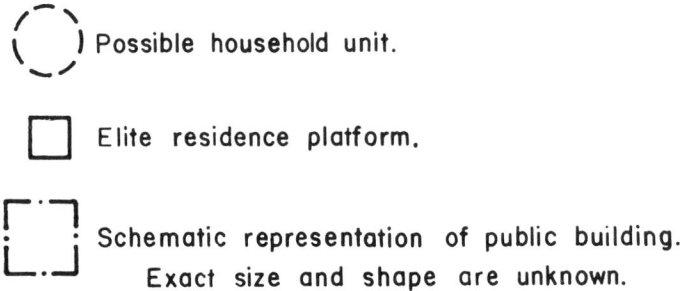

FIGURE 24. Monte Albán Ic occupation at Tomaltepec. The area between Mound 2 and Structure 13 seems to have been plastered, and additional plaster floors extend toward Mounds 3 and 4.

Table 7: Artifact Counts and Distributions Among Known and Possible Monte Albán Ic Household Units

Artifacts	Ic-1	Ic-2	Ic-3	Ic-4
Total Sherds*	527	700	524	
Jars*	127	200	127	
Bowls*	400	500	397	
Jar/Bowl Ratio*	0.32	0.40	0.32	UNRELIABLE DATA
Deer Bone	1	29	9	
Other Bone	6	22	7	
Chert	1	3	4	
Local Stone	1	47	0	
Obsidian	0	1	5	
Ground Stone	5	6	7	
Mica	0	1	0	
Figurines and Figurine Fragments	31	38	15	
Shell	4	3	5	

*Rim sherds only counted. Ratio of jars to bowls is the number of jar rims/the number of bowl rims.

partially faced with cut stone and strengthened with fill of large adobe blocks laid in adobe mortar (Plate 36). A small part of the structure which stood atop this platform was excavated in the course of Wright's 1972 preliminary testing at Tomaltepec (Wright, n.d.). The surface is described in Wright's report as:

> .....a mud floor into which ash, sherds, and other debris had been trodden. This floor covered the remains of a burial not yet excavated, oriented east/west, with head to the west. Immediately above this was a rectangular hearth edged with adobes and filled with ash. Just south of this was a tiny patch of white plaster, indicating that the floor may have initially been plastered. (op.cit)

The floor just described stood some 4 m above the top of early San José phase Structure 11, and about 2 m above the later Middle Formative Structure 12. The area of Structure 13 seems to have been nearly twice that of the Middle Formative platform as well, so that a construction of an entirely different order of magnitude is at issue here (refer to Fig. 5, Chapter I).

Three other platforms were also constructed during this period. None of these was as large as Structure 13, and none was either so well preserved or investigated in any detail. Mound 2 was tested and found to be entirely of Late Formative origin, while a convenient pit made by local farmers to remove stone from Mounds 3 and 4 (which may actually be two parts of the same large structure) allowed a similar conclusion.

Wide plastered floor areas, apparently amounting to hundreds of square meters, seem to have connected these structures. No further discussion of these structures is planned here, save to note that Structure 13 is the only one of the four with any evidence of residential debris on top. The Mound 2 platform is of unsuitable shape for a residence, and the Mound 4 platform is too small. The Mound 3 platform is considerably lower than the main structure and not so well preserved, so that its role is questionable. Although the evidence is inconclusive, probably all of the platforms discharged ceremonial and/or civic functions in the community, and one of them (Structure 13) may have had a resident staff. At the time of the Spanish Conquest, Zapotec "priests" or *bigaña* are known to have lived in the back rooms of temples (Marcus, 1978). Unfortunately, no primary middens, burials, or floors were excavated in association with any of these platforms, so that they enter the analysis only in architectural terms.

Ic-1

This area is evidently one of the elite residences clustered at the foot of and on the north side of Structure 13, the main platform. Here, two small but elaborately constructed platforms were excavated. Burials, hearths, fire pits, and middens associated with these structures suggest they are house platforms, and every indication is that they are unique at Tomaltepec. The platforms, called Structures 9 and 10, are illustrated in Figure 25 and Plate 37. They clearly form a small domestic group. It is inferred that each platform measured approximately 4 m north/south by 5-6 m east/west, was about 0.6 meters high, had walls and steps built of cut stones, and was surmounted by a white plastered floor. Also associated with the platforms were an oven, several hearths (Features 46, 47, and 48), and a large fire pit (Feature 51) of uncertain—although probably specialized—function. The pit was constructed in a rather peculiar fashion, with an adobe brick wall dividing it into rough halves. These interesting features also occur elsewhere on the site and will be considered in more detail presently.

Built into the center of the northern-most of the two platforms (Structure 9) was a slab-covered, adobe-walled tomb designated Burial 5 (Plate 38). The tomb contained the remains of an adult female of less than 40 years, an adult of undetermined sex of 40 ± 10 years, and a child, possibly male, of

PLATE 36. Construction details of Structure 13. Left, adobe brick terracing, stone wall, and rock and earth fill. Right, rectagular adobe bricks laid over a foundation of rock rubble.

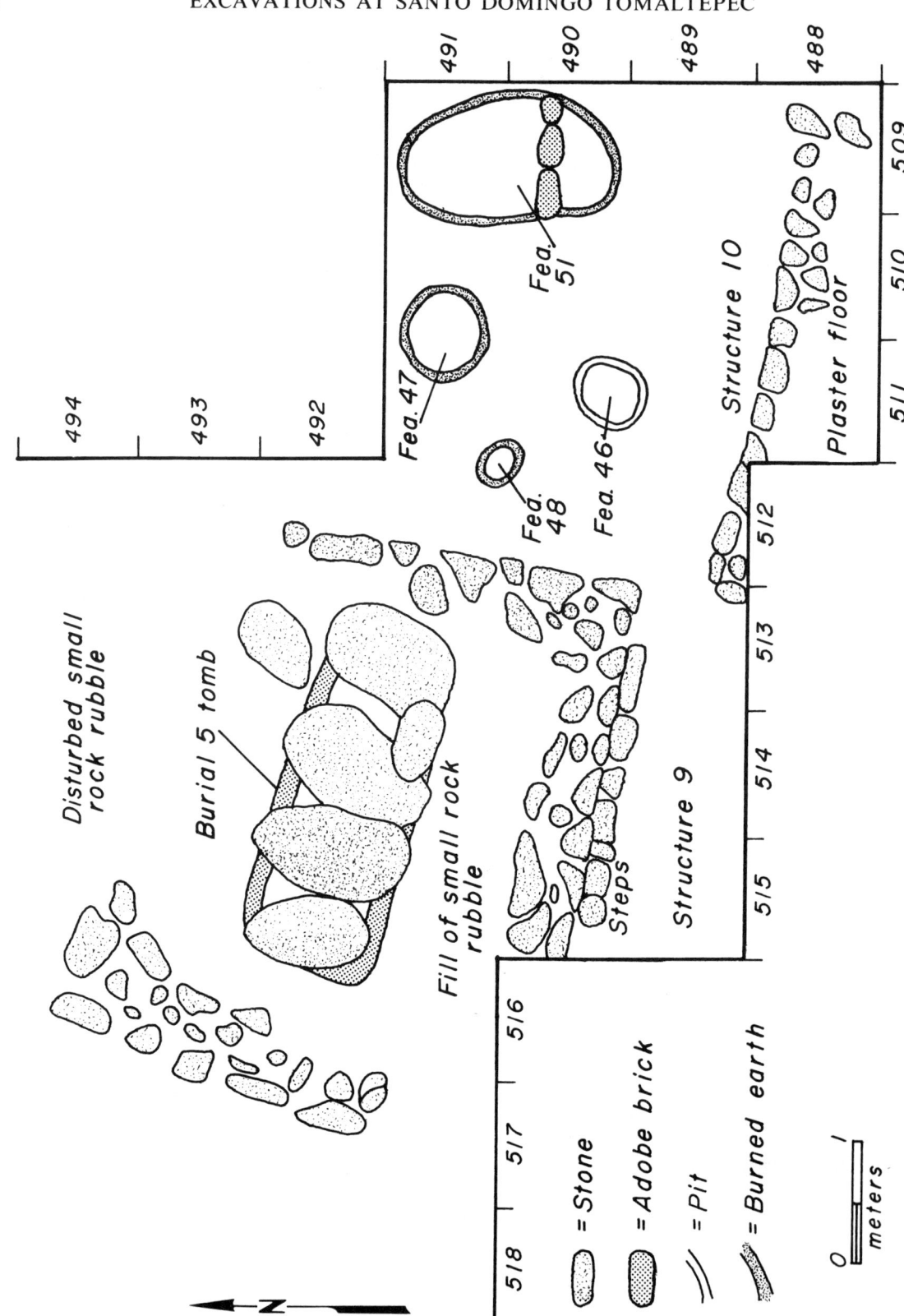

FIGURE 25. Components of Household Unit 1c-1.

MIDDLE FORMATIVE: THE MONTE ALBÁN IC PHASE

PLATE 37. Structures 9 and 10. Top, stone foundation of structure 9. Bottom, partially excavated Structure 10.

PLATE 38. The Burial 5 tomb before opening. The covering slabs have fallen in, and most ceramic offerings have been removed from atop the slabs. (See Plate 39, Top.)

ca. 12 years. An offering of 37 vessels accompanied the burials (see Plate 39, and Figs. 49–51 of Appendix III). There had also been an undetermined quantity of jade in the tomb, and several jade beads were still to be found in such inconspicuous places as inside vessels. The tomb appeared to have been opened, most of the valuables removed, and the ceramic offerings and covering slabs fairly carefully replaced. It seems likely that this reopening took place in Prehispanic times, most probably within the occupation span of Tomaltepec, while the tomb's location was still known.

The tomb measured 2.0 by 0.8 m, being about 0.4 m high. The four walls were constructed of adobe bricks, while the roof was formed of flat slabs of stone. This is a well-known type of tomb, with examples at Yagul and Monte Albán (Chadwick, 1966:246; Marquina, 1951:337; Covarrubias 1957:154). Refer to Fig. 48, Appendix III for drawings.

Artifacts associated with Unit Ic–1 are tabulated in Table 7, where it will be observed that, as in other excavated Ic households, Ic–1 contains a low jar-to-bowl ratio, little chipped stone, little animal bone, a number of mano and metate fragments, and a substantial number of figurine fragments. Carbonized remains of maize and other plants also occurred here (see Appendix IX). The general picture is one of an area in which domestic tasks were carried out, but on a relatively small scale.

PLATE 39. Ceramic offerings found with the Burial 5 tomb. These vessels were most probably once inside the tomb. They appear to have been dumped back on top of the replaced covering slabs after the tomb was opened and partially looted. Top, a portion of the offering at the west end of the tomb. Bottom, one of the more elaborate effigy vessels from the offering.

Ic-2

While no actual house remains were recovered from this area (located to the northeast of Ic-1), two Late Formative middens and a large Late Formative oven suggest that a residence may have been nearby. As Ic-2 lies only about 15 m from Ic-1, it is unclear whether one or two distinct household units were located here. In other words, the Ic-2 features could have been associated with Ic-1 structures. Unfortunately, a Colonial/modern road passes through the site at this point, removing the northern edge of Ic-1 and the southern portion of Ic-2, thus obscuring evidence of any connection or separation of the two areas.

As is evident from Table 7, artifacts recovered from Ic-1 and Ic-2 are not definitive on the question of the possible association of the two areas. Table 7 only suggests that Ic-1 and Ic-2 are no more similar to each other than either is to Ic-3, which is clearly a separate area. At present, then, it seems impossible to resolve the associational status of Ic-2, and it seems more satisfactory to divide it from Ic-1 for analytical purposes.

As mentioned earlier, Ic-2 was defined by two large middens, Features 32 and 34, and a small slightly bell-shaped pit designated Feature 44b (Plate 40). Pottery, chipped stone, ground stone, maize and other carbonized plant remains, a small quantity of animal bone, and a relatively large number of small, solid figurines complete the assemblage of artifacts recovered. No burials were recovered from this area.

Ic-3

This area overlies possible Household Units ESJ-3 and Ia-3. The area is classified as a possible Late Formative household unit, and is defined by adult and infant burials (Burials 13, 19, and 25, Plate 41), 167 chunks of burned daub, domestic refuse, and a remarkable concentration of ovens

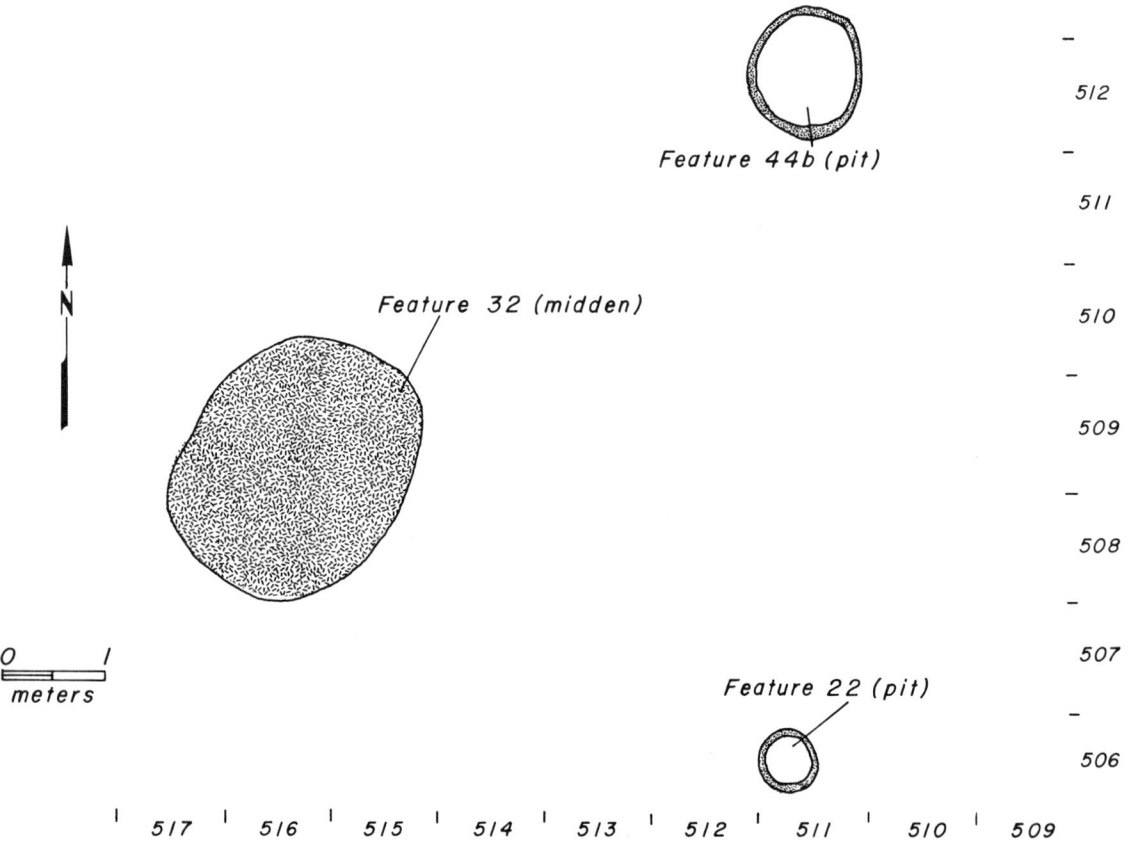

FIGURE 26. Components of Area Ic-2. These features lie directly across the Colonial/modern road from Unit Ic-1.

PLATE 40. Feature 44b of Unit Ic-2. The large pit in the background is Rosario phase Feature 44a (see Plate 29).

and fire pits (Features 53, 54, 61, 64, 65, 73, 75, 76 and 78, Plate 42). The entire complex is illustrated in Figure 27. Three of the pits (Features 53, 61, and 65) are of the peculiar type mentioned earlier in the discussion of Ic-1. These are medium-sized, basin-shaped pits measuring about 1.0 by 2.0 m. Each has a wall of substantial adobe bricks (ca. 10 cm across) built across the short axis of the pit. The walls of the pit, as well as both surfaces of the adobe wall, were heavily fire-reddened. The small areas where the adobe cross-wall intersected the sides of the pit, however, was never burned, indicating that the pit was dug, the wall constructed, and fires made in both halves. Specimens of this sort of pit are illustrated in Figure 28 and Plate 42.

Flannery (personal communication) believes that Features 51, 53, 61 are two-chambered pottery kilns, possibly for the reduced-firing of Monte Albán I gray ware. If so, this is the largest sample of Formative kilns so far found in the Valley of Oaxaca. Unfortunately, this interpretation cannot be confirmed by the fill of the features, as they all ended up being used for the disposal of ordinary domestic garbage. It should also be noted however, that the adobe-wall pits appear to have been cleaned out from time to time, as thick deposits of ash and charcoal were not found in them as they were in many other associated features. This, together with the adobe wall construction itself, suggests that the pits served some long-term purpose—an attribute consistent with the pottery kiln interpretation.

Four other features in the Ic-3 area (Features 54, 68, 73, and 78) are ordinary medium-to-large ovens or roasting pits, filled with charcoal and fire-cracked rock, and with heavily burned edges. They differ from the type just discussed, however, in that they are of irregular circular or rectangular shape and have no traces of the adobe walls found in Features 51, 53, and 61.

The features excavated in Ic-3 are generally 60–80 cm in diameter, and all have heavily burned edges. Ceramics show that all of the features are roughly contemporary, and their concentration in one small area suggests that we are dealing with a specialized activity area. The pits were possibly originally in association with a household unit, as

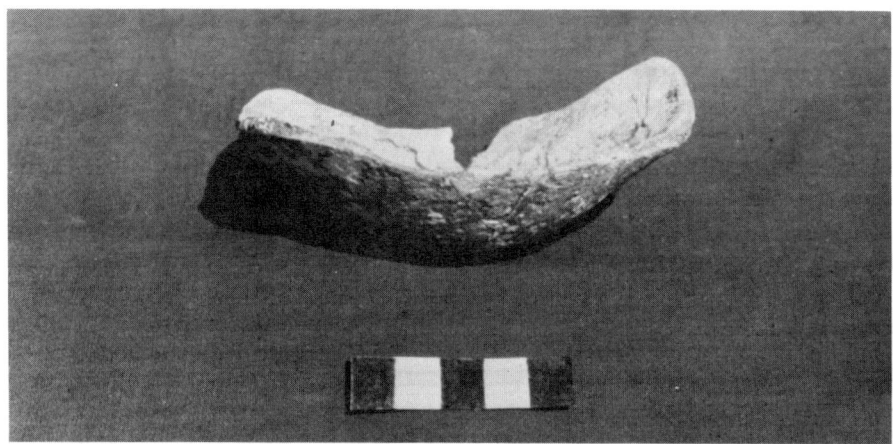

PLATE 41. Burials found in Household Unit Ic-3. Top left, Burial 19. Top right, Burial 25, which was partly disturbed by the large pit to the south. Note the secondary skull on the chest of the primary interment. Secondary long bones were also piled across the lower legs of the primary interment. Bottom, a cup made from human skull, found on the chest of Burial 25.

MIDDLE FORMATIVE: THE MONTE ALBÁN IC PHASE

PLATE 42. Features of Household Unit Ic-3. Top, Features 68, 75, and 76. Feature 75 was originally one of the adobe-walled pits discussed in this chapter; the black line shows its original extent before disturbance by another feature. Bottom, Feature 61, another adobe-walled two-chambered pit. The black line shows its original extent before it was removed in the course of further excavation.

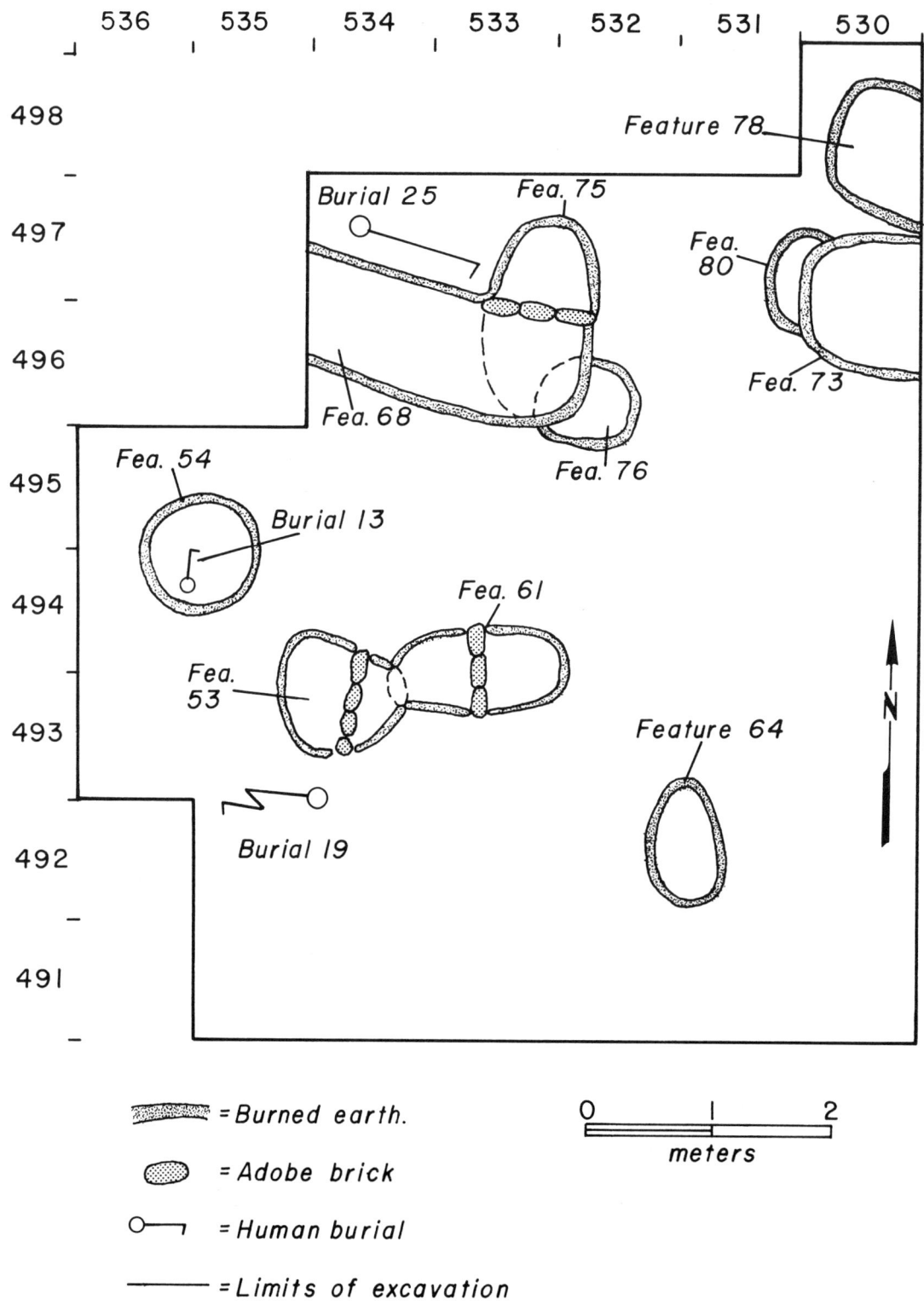

FIGURE 27. Components of Possible Household Unit Ic–3.

MIDDLE FORMATIVE: THE MONTE ALBÁN IC PHASE

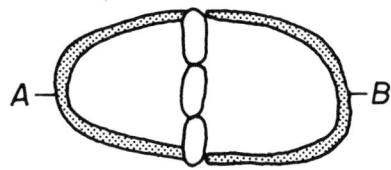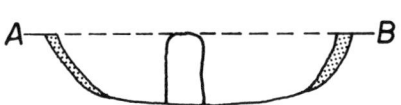

a. Feature 61 of Household Unit Ic-3.

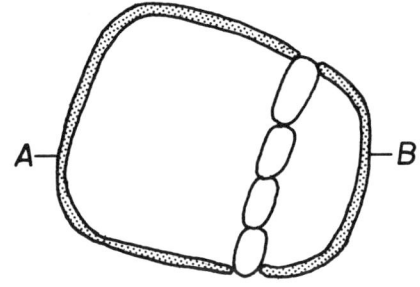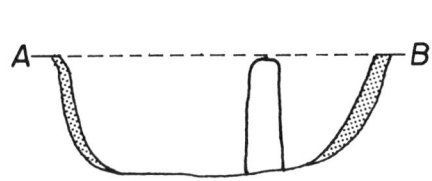

b. Feature 53 of Household Unit Ic-3.

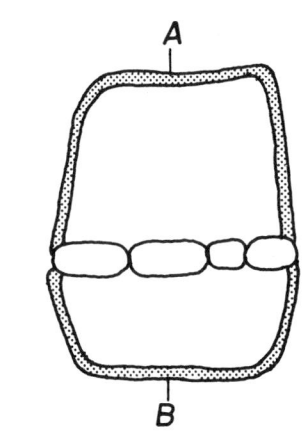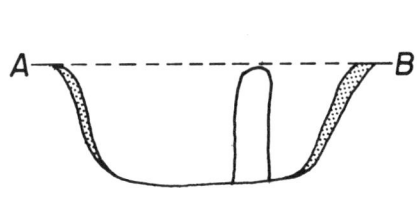

c. Feature 51 of Household Unit Ic-1.

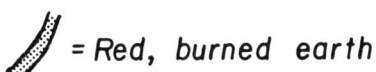 = Red, burned earth.

○ = Adobe bricks.

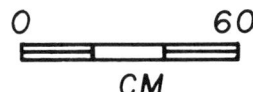

FIGURE 28. Adobe-walled pits from Monte Albán Ic areas.

associated adult and infant burials, as well as a large quantity of burned daub suggest.

It will be recalled that one of the adobe-wall pits which Flannery believes to be reduced-firing pottery kilns was also discovered adjacent to the high status house platform excavated in Ic-1, so that, whatever the special function of these facilities may have been, it evidently cross-cut status lines within the community. This point will be pursued further in the ensuing discussion of status differentiation at Late Formative Tomaltepec.

Ic-4

This Late Formative activity locus at least partially overlay and intruded into the early San José phase cemetery, as well as into Middle Formative Household Unit Ia-2. No features or house remains clearly assignable to the Monte Albán Ic phase were recovered here, although a great many large period Ic pottery sherds were found immediately overlying the thin strata containing the Early and Middle Formative remains. There exists the distinct possibility, therefore, that Ic-4 was an isolated trash dumping or activity area which was not associated with any house.

In addition, several burials intrusive into the early San José phase cemetery very possibly date to the Monte Albán Ic occupation. These burials—interred in simple pit graves—unfortunately lacked ceramic offerings, but were positioned quite differently from the early San José phase interments, being face up, head to the west. (The possibility also exists, it should be noted, that some of these burials without grave goods date to the Monte Albán Ia phase; it will be recalled that a number of features and several burials in this area were clearly Ia). The question cannot be resolved with the data in hand, however, and the nature of the entire Ic-4 area remains unclear.

In conclusion, the spatial organization of the components of the Late Formative community at Tomaltepec—like earlier occupations—was influenced by the local topography. The ceremonial/civic area of the community continued to be located at the end of the piedmont spur, but expanded westward, covering a much larger area than ever before (ca. 125 m east/west by 40 m north/south, or ca. 5000 m^2). Some elite residences were present in this zone (Household Unit Ic-1), but ordinary households would seem to have moved farther out to the north, northwest, southwest and west. As noted earlier, very few remains of ordinary residences lay inside the area of excavations, so that little is known of their spacing or composition. Also, it is most probable that, during Late Formative times, no simple distinction between "high" and "low" status individuals can be drawn, but that a more complex system of status differentiation existed. This was most probably reflected in an increasing number of different types of residential areas. The Tomaltepec data, unfortunately, are simply too limited to deal with these, or even to form any estimate of how many different types existed within the community.

It is clear, however, that the Late Formative community at Tomaltepec entailed an entirely different order of magnitude of construction and of architectural differentiation of components than any of the previous occupations, most of which seem to have involved a few houses grouped around a single larger structure. The extant data give no firm basis for an estimate of the population of the Late Formative community, but it was probably larger than ever before. The community itself may have covered 5-8 ha, although its density is unclear outside the central area.

Social Differentiation

Every indication is that social differentiation all over Mesoamerica reached unprecedented heights during the Late Formative period. In the Valley of Oaxaca, such differentiation is visible on both the individual and community levels.

Burials at Tomaltepec ranged from simple interments with few offerings to an elaborately accompanied tomb burial. The Tomaltepec tomb (Burial 5) has already been briefly described. The tomb contained, it will be recalled, an adult female of 30 to 40 years, another adult of undetermined sex and of 40 ± 10 years, and a child of about 12 years. The accompanying ceramic offering consisted of 37 vessels, several of them with elaborate appliqué faces, including tattooed or painted women, a monkey, a jaguar, and a masked human figure (refer to Figs. 49-51, Appendix III). This offering is equalled or surpassed by very few of the tombs from Monte Albán itself (see Caso, Bernal, and Acosta [1967] for descriptions of offerings). The tomb's implication is that even at smaller communities like Tomaltepec, individuals of considerable status were to be found. Architectural evidence also supports this conclusion, as previously discussed.

Unfortunately few of the Tomaltepec data concern the lower-ranking members of Late Formative society. Also, as pointed out earlier, it is clear that no simple distinction between "higher" and "lower" status individuals can be drawn, but that there were probably more specialized types of people, structures, and activities than ever before, as the data from Tomaltepec indicate.

Subsistence Activites

Relatively small numbers of animal bones were recovered from Late Formative deposits at Tomaltepec. These include deer, dog, rabbit, and peccary, in order of frequency of occurrence. The presence of carbonized corn in nearly every excavated feature demonstrates continued emphasis on cultivation of this staple.

As has been mentioned several times in the course of this study, canal irrigation systems were well developed in Oaxaca by Late Formative times, and the Tomaltepec site is well located for gravity flow canal irrigation. However, we located no clear traces of Late Formative canals. Two small canals, evidently used during the Postclassic period, were found (see Appendix XII), and it is at least possible that canal irrigated crops were also cultivated at Late Formative Tomaltepec. The quantity of social energy expended in construction of the central part of the community suggests that construction and maintenance of canal systems would have been a comparatively simple task. The point remains unproven, however.

An interesting characteristic of the Late Formative period at Tomaltepec is the apparent absence of the bell-shaped storage pits which had been so common during the preceding Early and Middle Formative Periods. While such pits are found with lower-status Monte Albán I houses elsewhere they seemingly did not occur (or occurred infrequently) at residences within the relatively higer-status zone of Tomaltepec. In adobe residences, storage rooms may have replaced storage pits.

The part played in the Tomaltepec subsistence system by vegetable foods, such as maguey, which require long roasting in large, stone-filled pits, is not entirely clear. However, the occurrence of large stone and charcoal-filled pits all over the site suggests that such foods may have been processed on a fairly large scale. Considerable numbers of maguey are grown in the piedmont of the Valley of Oaxaca today, and such could certainly have been the case in Late Formative times as well.

Craft and Exchange Activities

At least two different households in the central area of Tomaltepec engaged in activities which required a number of adobe-wall pits. If Flannery's interpretation of these as pottery kilns proves correct, we can say that households of at least two different status categories were engaged in this craft activity at Tomaltepec. The underground nature of these features suggests that, if they are kilns, they were for reduced firing of gray ware. Many very well-made gray ware pieces were found at Tomaltepec, as in the tomb already mentioned.

That there was some traffic in non-local goods is shown by the presence of obsidian and Pacific coast marine shell in the community. Thirteen pieces of shell were recovered in the higher status zones of the community (see Appendix VI). Obsidian was found in small quantity as compared to the Middle Formative, when some 50 pieces of obsidian were found; only 20 pieces of this material were recovered from Late Formative proveniences. Many of these were sections of prismatic blades made from translucent green obsidian, and substantially less obsidian debitage was recovered from Late (as opposed to Early) Formative levels. Whether the obsidian was distributed by some centralized mechanism or whether it was obtained by some less formal means is unclear. The Tomaltepec data suggest only that it did not reach that community in large quantities. We have already seen that non-local resources appear to have been channeled through resident elite during the preceding Middle Formative, and it such may also have been the case in the Late Formative. Clearly, more lower status households at Tomaltepec need to be excavated to obtain comparative data bearing on this question.

Finally, it has been suggested here that smaller civic-ceremonial centers such as Tomaltepec may have performed a range of specialized tasks. The discovery that pottery-making may have been one such task is consistent with Blanton's (1978) evidence that Monte Albán did not monopolize craft production for the Valley of Oaxaca the way Teotihuacán did for the Valley of Mexico. More "possible" kilns have been found at Tomaltepec than in any Period Ic area of Monte Albán itself.

Summary and Discussion of the Late Formative Evidence

By Late Formative times (ca. 300–100 B.C.), the Tomaltepec community had grown into a minor ceremonial center. Unfortunately, the extent and nature of Late Formative occupation outside of the central zone are poorly known. This is due largely to the dramatic increase in size of the central area and the concomitant wider dispersion of ordinary households. The community is estimated to have covered some 5–8 ha, although the occupational density is unknown. By all indications, the increase in size of the community was an explosive one. We know that the central zone consisted of public buildings and extensive plastered surfaces connecting all of these high status residence platforms. Within one of the high status residence platforms was discovered a tomb equalled, or surpassed, in quantity of ceramic offerings by only a few contemporary tombs from Monte Albán itself. Social differentiation had evidently been carried to unprecedented heights even at smaller communities such as Tomaltepec.

Subsistence in the Tomaltepec community may have been based on irrigated maize farming. Carbonized maize remains were found in nearly every excavated Late Formative feature, and the Tomaltepec community is quite well situated for small-scale water control. No definite evidence for canal irrigation is available at the site, although contemporary canals are known to exist at other sites in and around the Valley of Oaxaca. Canals were used at Tomaltepec in Postclassic and historic times, and they continue to be used to this day.

Whether hunting declined substantially from Middle Formative levels is unclear, although deer, rabbit, and peccary continued to be eaten. Dog was also eaten, possibly in smaller proportion in higher status households than in their lower status counterparts. Sizable and numerous roasting pits on the site may indicate large-scale roasting of vegetable foods such as maguey, and it was noted that considerable quantities of maguey are grown in the valley piedmont today. Another series of pits, divided into two chambers by adobe walls, may indicate that the manufacture of reduced-firing pottery was a craft specialization at Tomaltepec.

The Late Formative represents the culmination of sociopolitical development at Tomaltepec itself. The site reached its maximum size in Period Ic. The mortuary, architectural and artifactual data all show that Late Formative society was more highly differentiated than ever before. Likewise, specialization of Late Formative society's components was also increasing. Increasing ceremonial-administrative specialization in the upper ranks of society is suggested by the very structure of the Tomaltepec community. Throughout the occupational sequence at Tomaltepec, the tendency had been for the Mound 1 area to become increasingly distinct from the rest of the community. This trend included larger, more elaborate, and frequently unique structures, and sometimes more elaborate burials. The Late Formative period seems to have seen the culmination of this trend at Tomaltepec, when the central area contained platforms, elite residences, and a considerable amount of elaborate construction. It was also noted that much or all of this construction was apparently joined by plastered surfaces, further emphasizing both its internal unity and its separateness from the rest of the community, where no plastered surfaces of any sort were found. In early Formative times, every indication is that the area was a general purpose one, while by the Late Formative, it seems just as clearly to have evolved into a discrete, perhaps closed, special purpose area.

Only indirect evidence bears on the question of increasingly centralized social control within the community at Tomaltepec. The elaborate central zone and elite residences, which seem to have generated less of the refuse of ordinary domestic activities, may well be indicative of centralization of the affairs of society in the hands of ceremonial-administrative specialists. It seems most likely that impulses for change within the Tomaltepec community came mostly from the larger sociopolitical entity of which it formed a part, i.e., the entire Tlacolula region and perhaps the whole Valley of Oaxaca. This being the case, work at any one small site is likely to give an extremely narrow perspective on the conditions which resulted in the evolutionary processes described above. We can try to understand the structure of the smaller component, how it functioned, and how it changed; nevertheless, as at Monte Albán, the immediate relations between a community and its physical social environment are likely to take second place to wider systemic concerns as sources of change.

This chapter has concerned itself with the culmination of Formative developmental processes at Tomaltepec. The succeeding chapter will be concerned with the demise and final abandonment of the community at Tomaltepec.

Chapter VII

Terminal Formative Abandonment of Tomaltepec: The Monte Albán II Phase

The Monte Albán II Phase (ca. 100 B.C.–A.D. 100)

The Monte Albán II phase may be described as "Terminal Formative" or "Protoclassic" depending on one's point of view. By about A.D. 100, survey and excavation data agree, the Zapotec state was highly developed. The city of Monte Albán sat at the top of a four-tiered hierarchy which included secondary centers such as Dainzú and San José Mogote, tertiary centers such as Tomaltepec and Fábrica San José, and smaller villages which made up the fourth level of the hierarchy. In two key areas of Mesoamerica where some attention has been given to the problem (by Blanton, Kowalewski, Flannery and associates in the Valley of Oaxaca and by Sanders, Parsons, and Blanton in Central Mexico), there appears to have been considerable reorganization of demographic patterns by the end of the Terminal Formative.

This demographic reorganization in the Valley of Oaxaca included the final abandonment of the Tomaltepec community, which was never significantly reoccupied after the Monte Albán II phase. At the same time, a large early Classic Period site at Tlalixtac de Cabrera, some two km from Tomaltepec and in a similar piedmont location, seems to have been established.

It is suggested that this abandonment was not a result of pressures generated within the Tomaltepec settlement, but rather that the site was abandoned in the course of demographic changes in the whole Tlacolula arm of the Valley of Oaxaca. These changes are still poorly documented because the Tlacolula region has only recently been intensively surveyed.

The Monte Albán II phase at Tomaltepec appears to have been a period of decline from the heights reached there during the Late Formative. In spite of this, Tomaltepec remained at least a tertiary-level center in the valley-wide hierarchy, with a Monte Albán II temple. The Monte Albán II period in Oaxaca is contemporary with the Tzacualli and Miccaotli phases at Teotihuacán (Millon, 1967), with the end of the Late Santa María and the Early Palo Blanco phases in Tehuacán (MacNeish, 1964), with the Chiapa VII levels in the Central Depression of Chiapas (Lowe et al, 1960), and with the Cerro de las Mesas II–Tres Zapotes II phases in Veracruz (Drucker, 1943).

Composition of the Community

Only two components of Monte Albán II occupation were defined: a typical two-room temple (Structure 14) atop Mound 1 (see Sallade, Appendix XI), and a well-defined household unit partially overlying preceding households Ia-1, R-1, ESJ-2, and TL-1. Each component is shown in Fig. 29 and is considered below.

STRUCTURE 14

Apparently very little additional fill was added to Mound 1 during the Monte Albán II phase; virtually all substantial enlargements of the mound seem to belong to the antecedent Monte Albán Ic phase. However, at some point during Monte Albán II, the final Period Ic structure was leveled and a new plaster-floored structure erected over its ruins. Because of erosion, the precise dimensions of this structure could not be obtained, but it was at least 7 m north-south by 8 m east-west. These represent absolutely minimum dimensions, with the intact structure doubtless being somewhat larger. The floor of Structure 14 was cleared during Wright's (n.d.) test excavation in 1972 (see Plate 8, Chapter I). Distributions of artifacts on the floor were analyzed in detail by Jane Sallade (Appendix XI), whose work indicates that the building can be divided into two areas: 1) an eastern room, where considerable burning of the

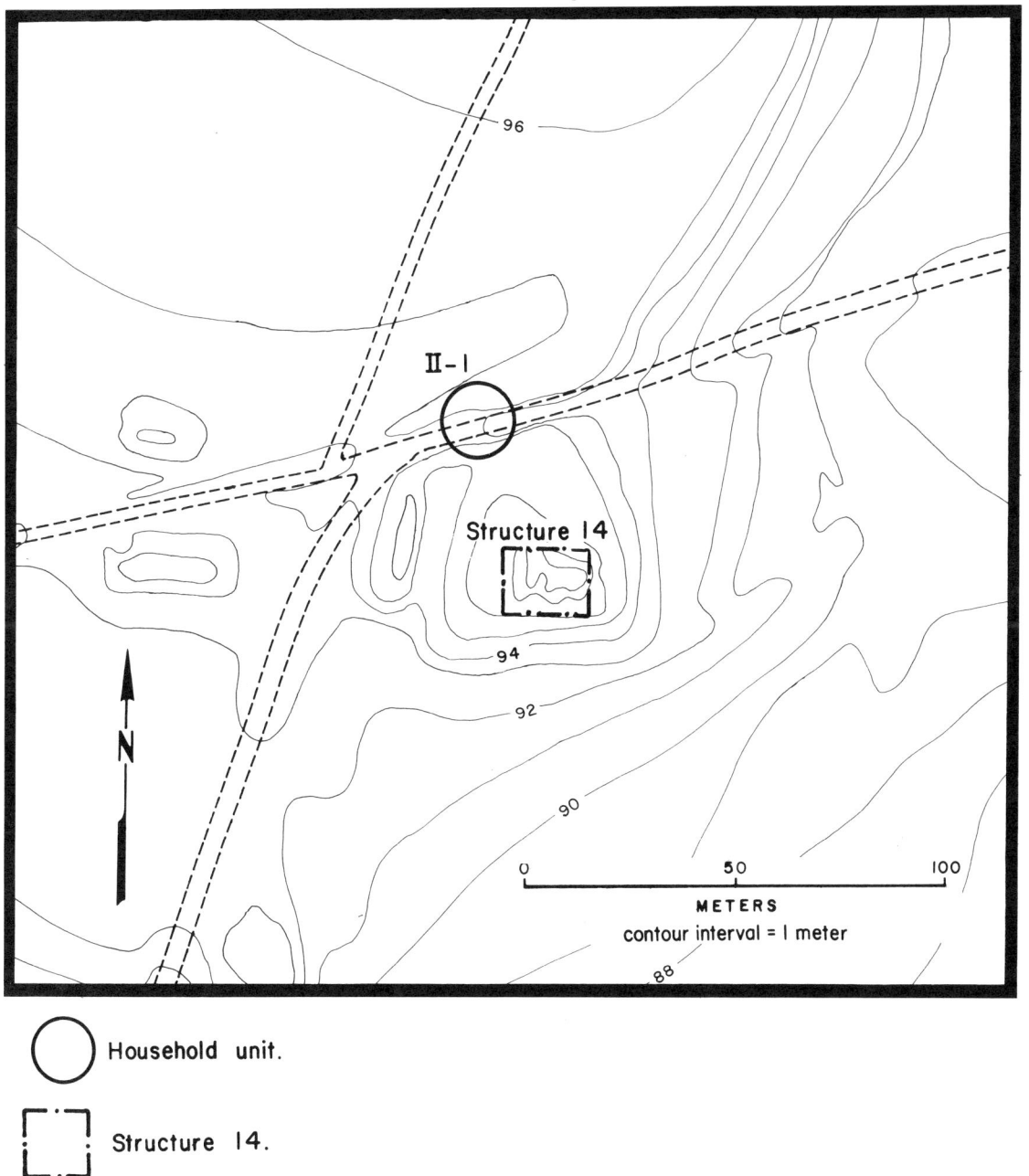

FIGURE 29. Monte Albán II occupation at Tomaltepec.

floor and some tasks involving utilitarian pottery were carried out; and 2) a western room where no burning occurred, and pottery debris was dumped after the building was abandoned. Most of the artifacts recovered here were pottery, chipped stone, small quantities of obsidian, and dog bone, with plaster and adobe fragments and fire-cracked rock also included. An adobe wall with a stone foundation separated the two rooms. According to Kent Flannery and Joyce Marcus (personal communication), most details of Structure 14 recall the remains of two-room Monte Albán II temples found on Mound 1 at San José Mogote (Flannery and Marcus 1976a, 1976b). It will be noted that the Zapotec *bigaña* or minor priests lived in the back room of the temple and burned incense in large braziers set on the floor (Marcus 1978). This would account for the utilitarian refuse and burned areas on the floor of the eastern room. These attributes also characterized Structures 13 and 21 at San José Mogote. The presence of such a temple suggests that Tomaltepec was still a fairly important place in Period II.

II-1

A well-defined household unit existed here, consisting of a structure (House 6) with a sand floor and stone foundations. Ovens (Features 20 and 26), middens (Features 34 and 56), pits (Features 18 and 19), and possibly associated infant burials (Burials 14a and 14b) were scattered to the north, east, and south of the structure. The area to the west was not excavated (Fig. 30 represents this domestic group). Little remained of the structure itself, all but a corner being destroyed by the Colonial/modern road which passed through the site. The dimensions of the house are unknown, although it is evident that the building was oriented roughly to the cardinal points. The house was probably wattle-and-daub, as burned daub fragments were present. There was a packed earth floor without traces of plaster, and a small stone foundation.

Unfortunately, this is all that is known of the plan and composition of the Monte Albán II community at Tomaltepec. It seems likely that more houses were scattered to the west and north of the main mound.

Unit II-1 lies about 40 m from Mound 1, and testing in the intervening area indicates that no other contemporary structures were located there. It may be suggested, then, that the Period II community more closely resembled Middle Formative Tomaltepec (a single major structure with residences scattered around it) than the Late Formative version of the community.

It cannot be asserted with any great degree of certainty that the community actually declined in absolute size during the Monte Albán II phase, although the writer believes this to be the case, based on relative numbers of Monte Albán Ic and Monte Albán II features and burials recovered from all excavated areas. It can, however, be suggested that the level of complexity of community organization did decline substantially in Monte Albán II times. This point will be discussed at greater length in the concluding section of this chapter.

Social Differentiation

The data suggest that status differentiation may also have undergone some simplification at Tomaltepec during the Terminal Formative period. It should be emphasized that this is by no means the case in the Valley of Oaxaca taken as a whole, where status differentiation continued to escalate. The Tomaltepec situation, by contrast, seems to be a result of the decline in importance of the community. The public architecture is the strongest line of evidence at Tomaltepec, reflecting a decline from the elaborate ceremonial/civic complex discussed in the preceding chapter to a single temple, the other mounds apparently remaining unused and without maintenance. Also suggested is the decline of the administrative specialist group postulated for Late Formative Tomaltepec. The Late Formative elite residence platforms at the foot of the main platform were evidently abandoned during Period II.

By the Terminal Formative period, in short, there was no longer a well-planned and integrated central zone with both public buildings and elite residences at Tomaltepec, which gives some indication of a descent from the apogee of administrative specialization postulated during the Late Formative. What is at issue is a simplification of the social control apparatus, which, it is maintained, also had implications for the level of complexity of social differentiation within the community. It may be suggested that the Tomaltepec community was simply no longer of sufficient importance to have an integrated complex like the one of Period Ic.

As no definite Monte Albán II adult burials were recovered at Tomaltepec, it is unclear whether the highest and lowest elements of society showed a smaller range of status differentiation than during the Late Formative, although such may well have been the case in this one community.

Subsistence Activities

Unfortunately, few data of relevance to this topic were recovered from Monte Albán II deposits at Tomaltepec. The only substantial midden

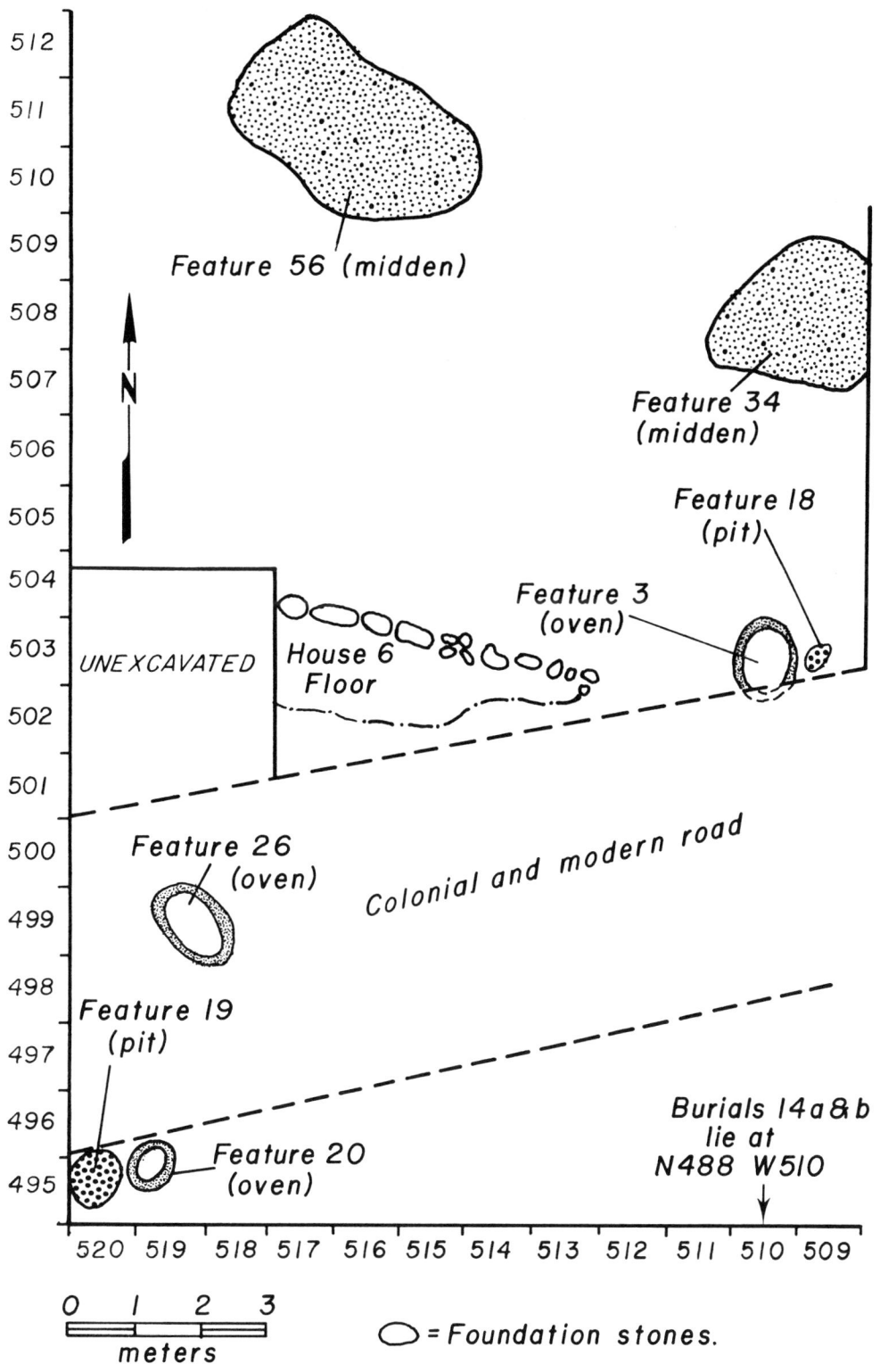

FIGURE 30. Components of Household Unit II-1.

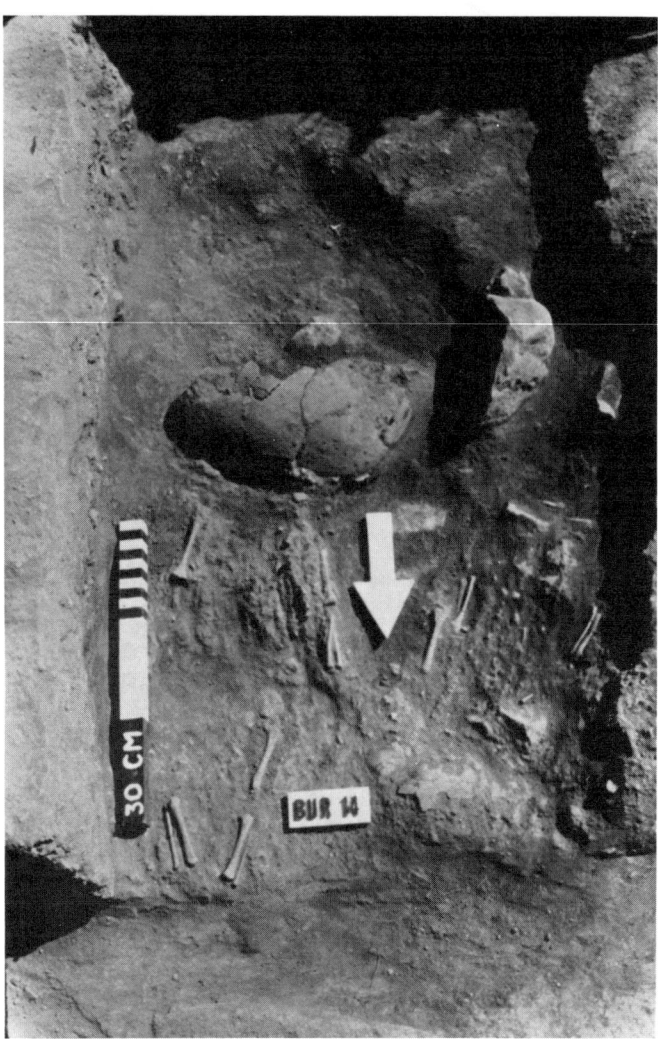

PLATE 43. Infant burials probably associated with Household Unit II-1.

excavated there (Feature 56) yielded maize as well as deer and pocket gopher bones, while other contemporary deposits from the community contained dog and deer bone in nearly equal proportions. Refuse associated with the House 6 area (Unit II-1) contained fragments of skull, vertebrae, pelvis, and foot of deer, as well as limb bone splinters, suggesting that in some cases whole animals were brought back to the village and consumed within the household unit. There is also evidence of use of domestic dog as a meat source.

Several small ovens were recovered in association with Unit II-1, although none of the larger, heavily-burned ovens or possible kilns which were so abundant in Late Formative times were discovered. It may be, therefore, that pottery making and maguey cooking were either no longer practiced or at least were not practiced on the scale of the Late Formative Period. The implications of such a shift are that the proposed community specialization of the Late Formative may have begun to decline in favor of a return to more generalized activities by Terminal Formative times.

Craft and Exchange Activities

It appears that the Terminal Formative community at Tomaltepec participated to a very limited extent in exchange of non-local goods. We know that in Terminal Formative times imported obsidian was still reaching the Valley of Oaxaca in reasonable quantities. At Tomaltepec, however, no excavated Monte Albán II feature contained any obsidian, and only a few tiny pieces were recovered from the Structure 14 area. Since the latter seems to have been a temple, this obsidian may be fragments from blades used in ritual bloodletting (Marcus, 1978).

No marine or freshwater shell was recovered from any Monte Albán II provenience, in contrast to the 13 whole or partial shells found in Monte Albán Ic deposits. In comparison with the preceding Late Formative Period, then, it seems clear that non-local goods reached the Terminal Formative community at Tomaltepec in much reduced quantities. This evidence, taken together with the decline in community specialization suggested in the preceding section, further suggests that the interaction sphere (or effective social environment) of the Terminal Formative community at Tomaltepec may have been considerably simplified from its Late Formative apogee.

Summary and Discussion of the Terminal Formative Evidence

The Terminal Formative community at Tomaltepec (ca. 100 B.C.–A.D.100) can be described as a small agricultural community centered around a temple on the same mound that had been the hub of the community since Early Formative times. The exact size of the community is not known, but it appears to have declined from the preceding period. The only Monte Albán II household unit excavated was in a locality which had served as a house site throughout virtually the entire prehistoric sequence at Tomaltepec. It was suggested that the community more closely resembled its Middle than its Late Formative predecessors in physical structure, consisting, that is, of a single large structure surrounded by simpler dwellings. Maize farming, hunting, and consumption of domestic dog sustained the community. Other details of Terminal Formative subsistence are very poorly known. Likewise, little is known of trade and exchange at this time. A simplification of external relations has been suggested.

With reference to the criteria of social complexity discussed earlier in this study, the Tomaltepec community structure certainly seems to have become less complex in many ways during the Terminal Formative. The structure of authority in the community, as represented by the extent of development of the central portion of the site, seems to have become considerably simpler, with suggested implications for the complexity of social differentiation within the community. Also, there is some tentative indication that the degree of administrative specialization among the upper elements of society declined. There is also some indication that the hypothesized level of specialization of the community itself declined appreciably. Finally, the paucity of imported items suggests that Tomaltepec was no longer in the mainstream of interregional exchange, resulting in circumscription to some degree of the effective social environment of the community.

At some point (perhaps late) in the Monte Albán II phase, the community at Tomaltepec was abandoned, never to be significantly reoccupied. This abandonment also coincides with the gradual decline of Dainzú, the secondary level center to which, it has been postulated, Tomaltepec was tied. At the same time, a large, new Classic Period center was established quite nearby at Tlalixtac, very possibly absorbing the population of Tomaltepec.

At this point, we have arrived at the end of the Formative Period developmental sequence at Tomaltepec. The factors contributing to the Formative/Classic transition most probably involved regional politics rather than small community mechanics, and so are somewhat beyond the reach of the Tomaltepec data.

The final chapter of this study concerns itself with the extension of the Tomaltepec data to consideration of Formative developments on the regional (i.e., Valley of Oaxaca) level.

Chapter VIII

Formative Period Development Within the Valley of Oaxaca: A Regional Perspective

Foregoing chapters have considered evolutionary processes within a single Formative community in the Valley of Oaxaca. It is the object of this concluding chapter to consider the place of the Tomaltepec community in a developing regional framework. Each major division of the Formative is briefly considered below.

The Early Formative

Available survey and excavation data suggest that variation in form and function between contemporary Early Formative communities was minimal. The Tomaltepec community and nearly all of its contemporaries, in other words, seem to have been small, general purpose residential villages characterized by generally low levels of economic and social specialization. The single exception to this generalization is San José Mogote, a community which appears to have been developing both special functions and at least some partly specialized personnel in the Early Formative. The degree of influence of San José Mogote on contemporary small communities is not entirely clear. One of the reasons for choosing the Tomaltepec comunity for intensive excavations was its distance from San José Mogote. Since all previously excavated Early Formative communities had been in the immediate vicinity of San José Mogote, it was hoped that more distant sites would have features (public buildings, for instance) which were absent at communities nearer the large center. Such discoveries would then indicate a relatively greater degree of autonomy for communities outside the immediate vicinity of San José Mogote, effectively delimiting the sphere of domination of that center.

It will be recalled that a higher status residential platform (Structure 11) was found at Tomaltepec. A similar house platform (Structure 16) is known from residential area A at San José Mogote (Flannery and Marcus, personal communication). Clearly, there are considerable social-organizational implications in the existence or non-existence of such structures at other sites in the valley. For example, they have not been found at sites like Tierras Largas and Abasolo, nor have those sites produced any evidence of Early Formative public buildings. However, there are many unexcavated sites in various parts of the valley where such platforms might occur.

The Middle Formative

It has been suggested in Chapter 1 that by the Middle Formative period both the absolute numbers of sites and the numbers of different kinds of sites had begun to increase in the Valley of Oaxaca. Two examples of small Middle Formative communities located in the piedmont zone of the Valley of Oaxaca (Tomaltepec and Fábrica San José) have now been investigated, together with two small, excavated valley floor hamlets (Abasolo and Tierras Largas) and two riverside ceremonial-civic centers (Huitzo and San José Mogote, where work is still in progress).

A major difference between Tomaltepec and sites like Fábrica San José or Tierras Largas is the presence of a substantial public building (Structure 13) at the former community and the apparent absence of any such structure at the latter sites. Drennan (1976) suggests that the absence of such structures at Fábrica San José implies a certain degree of ceremonial reliance on San José Mogote, and he also raises the qustion as to whether other contemporary communities were similarly dependent.

If we were to establish a hierarchy of relative complexity among known communities during the Rosario phase of the Middle Formative in Oaxaca, it might be arranged in three levels, read from most complex downward as follows: (1) San José Mogote, (2) Huitzo and Tomaltepec, and (3) Fábrica San José, Abasolo, and Tierras Largas. San José Mogote, as previously noted, was a large center of over 40 ha with at least two large, stone-faced platforms (Structures 14 and 19) over 3 m high and more than 20 m on a side (Flannery and Marcus, 1976a).

A second level of ceremonial/civic activity would seem to be represented by sites such as Huitzo and Tomaltepec. Platform 2 at Huitzo was a sizable Rosario phase platform with earthen fill and retaining walls of adobe brick (Flannery et al. 1970:36). The platform was oriented to the cardinal points, although its exact size and shape are unclear. As previously mentioned, the skeleton of an adult male was found beneath one of the retaining walls. The Tomaltepec Rosario phase platform is also of unknown size and shape. It is estimated that the platform was perhaps 15 m on a side and some 3 m high; human burials were also found within it.

It is interesting to observe that the Tomaltepec Rosario phase structure, while certainly less impressive than Structure 19 at San José Mogote, is nevertheless similar in some respects to that structure. The Tomaltepec platform appears to have been founded on slabs of stone reminiscent of those used in the San José Mogote structure. Construction of the same order of magnitude was clearly not involved, as the Tomaltepec slabs weigh only 50 kilos or so, as opposed to the half-ton limestone blocks from San José Mogote (Flannery and Marcus 1976a). It may be, however, that some widespread concepts about the design of public buildings existed in the Valley of Oaxaca by Rosario times.

A third type of Rosario community is represented by sites without any evidence of public buildings. Fábrica San José (Drennan 1975) is a good example, Tierras Largas (Winter 1972) may well be another, and Abasolo (Flannery et al., 1970) may be a third.

Winter (1972:121) suggests that a substantial Guadalupe phase structure may have been present at Tierras Largas, although it is not clear whether this structure (assuming it existed) was residential or public. Drennan (1975) argues that if a Guadalupe phase public building did exist at Tierras Largas, a different sort of relation between that community and San José Mogote is implied. Both authors note, however, that the evidence for such a structure at Tierras Largas is tentative and still requires further substantiation. It is quite clear, however, that no Middle Formative structures comparable to those of Huitzo and Tomaltepec existed at Fábrica San José or Tierras Largas.

There are also some evident differences in status differentiation among contemporary communities during the Rosario phase. The Tomaltepec excavations unfortunately produced no sample of burials which could be compared with Drennan's (1976) Rosario phase burial population from Fábrica San José. It is illuminating, however, to compare the two communities on the basis of architecture. Aside from the already-discussed public building at Tomaltepec, both communities had residences with long, narrow, well-made stone foundations, each built near the end of the piedmont spur on which the village was located. Similar residences occur at San José Mogote, where they are regarded as the houses of families of no more than average status (Flannery and Marcus, personal communication); families of much higher status resided in large adobe compounds atop Mound 1 at this latter site, and had tombs as elaborate as those of Monte Albán I (Ibid).

As a tentative generalization, then, it may be suggested that the extent of San José Mogote's control over contemporary small communities was probably limited to the Etla subvalley during all of the time periods thus far considered, although certainly all these Formative villages were in contact. The relationship between San José Mogote and a distant community like Tomaltepec might be described as influential, rather than involving any direct form of control.

With the founding of Monte Albán, San José Mogote, Huitzo, and Fábrica San José were wholly or partially depopulated, with their occupants perhaps participating in the founding of the former center. Tomaltepec, on the other hand, grew during Period Ia. Clearly, therefore, relations between Tomaltepec and Monte Albán were somewhat different from the relations shown by the Etla area sites.

The Late Formative

By Late Formative times in the Valley of Oaxaca, we can suggest that differentiation of form and function between contemporary communities was amplified as never before. Tombs and elaborate burials such as those described at Tomaltepec (Chapter 6) and Abasolo (Flannery et al. 1970) attest to a high level of status differentiation within communities, although the data are not complete enough to adequately characterize status differences between individuals and groups at different kinds of communities. Given the structure we have postulated for Late Formative society in the Valley of Oaxaca, it is evident that social integration would have to be effected by more powerful means than ever before, although it is not necessary to conclude that such integration was achieved by identical means everywhere in the Valley of Oaxaca. Nor is it clear yet what Monte Albán's role was in the Tlacolula region.

The Terminal Formative

In form, the Tomaltepec Terminal Formative community seems to have come to resemble more closely the community structure of the Early and Middle Formative periods: a single public building (a Monte Albán II temple) with ordinary residences arranged around it. Fábrica San José may have been similar in Period II, with a small mounded building (suspected by Flannery to be another small two-room temple, judging by its size and the slope of the mound) and several interesting tombs found by Drennan (1976).

On the other hand, during Period II San José Mogote saw considerable expansion and elaboration becoming a major ceremonial center for the Etla region (Flannery and Marcus 1976a).

In general, the Monte Albán II phase in the Valley of Oaxaca was one of considerable development, although the end of the phase saw abandonment or reduction of a number of communities. Flannery (personal communication) notes that the phase saw considerable development of such communities as Teotitlán, Macuilxóchitl, Dainzú, and Abasolo, all Tlacolula sub-valley communities less than 10 km from Tomaltepec. Pressures leading to the eventual abandonment of the Tomaltepec village, then, could have come from within the Tlacolula sub-valley as easily as from the more distant center of Monte Albán.

Concluding Remarks

In sum, this study has been concerned with evolutionary development within a single small community in the Valley of Oaxaca during the Formative period. This final chapter has also attempted to summarize the position of that community in regional interaction and development. It is clear that as the Formative period progressed, both community and regional organization grew more encompassing, more intricate, and more specialized. Throughout this study, attention has focused on the definition of some of the processes of social, political, environmental, and economic change observable during the Formative.

The question of why such changes come about is, of course, the more complicated one, which must ultimately be faced if we are ever to achieve archaeology's ultimate goal of explaining prehistoric change. It is also clear, however, that as the Formative advanced, more and more and more of the pressures to which the Tomaltepec community responded were extra-community ones, sources of which are most probably not readily apparent at any small community in the area. The most extreme example of this is the Terminal Formative decline and abandonment of the Tomaltepec settlement, largely attributable, it was suggested, to regional changes in socio-political organization which mark the Formative-to-Classic transition in Oaxaca. To search entirely within the confines of the Tomaltepec community for the sources of many of the changes which took place there would, it is felt, be extremely unrewarding, attesting to the necessity of well-developed regional perspective in dealing with cultural-evolutionary questions. This study is intended to contribute to refinement of such a perspective. Only after we arrive at an in-depth understanding of how regional cultural systems operated, it is maintained, will we be in a position to adequately specify why they changed their structures.

APPENDIX I
PROVENIENCE DESCRIPTIONS

The features and structures described in the following tables include all of those excavated in the 1969, 1972, and 1974 field seasons at Tomaltepec. Features 1 through 8 were originally described by Wright and Lees (in Flannery et al. 1970), and Features 9 through 27 were originally described by Wright (n.d.). Features 30 through 117 were excavated in the course of the 1974 field season. All house and structure numbers were assigned in the 1974 season, although several of these were originally given feature numbers by Wright in 1972.

The feature, structure, and house descriptions given in Tables 8 and 9 include the field number of each feature, the general period or date of each as determined from ceramic refuse, the area of the site in which each was found (refer to Fig. 4, for the location of each area), and a brief characterization of each feature or structure.

All features, structures, and houses mentioned in the text of this monograph are referred to by the field numbers given in Tables 8 and 9.

Table 8: Feature Descriptions

Field Number	Period	Area	Description
1	M.A.V	B	Stone house foundation
2	M.A.V	B	Medium-sized rocky pit
3	M.A.II	B	Large oven
4	M.A.I?	B	Disturbed burial
5	?	B	Oven
6	M.A.Ic	B	Small rocky pit
7	Tierras Largas	B	Large bell-shaped pit
8	M.A.V	D	Rocky pit
9	?	D	Small rocky pit
10	M.A.Ic/II	D	Plastered floor
11	M.A.Ia	D	Medium-sized rocky pit
12	M.A.Ia	D	Burial 2
13	M.A.II?	D	Burial 90
14	?	D	Small pit
15–17	M.A.Ia	D	House floors (Houses 2/3)
18	M.A.II?	B	Shallow pit
19	M.A.II	D	Medium-sized pit
20	M.A.II	D	Oven
21	M.A.Ia	D	Burial 1
22	M.A.Ic	B	Small pit
23	San José	D	Very small pit
24	Middle Formative	D	Medium-sized rocky pit
25	San José	B	House 4
26	M.A.II	B/D	Oven, in road between B/D
27	M.A.I	B	Rocky pit
30	M.A.Ia	E (T.2)	Pile of puppy bones
31	M.A.Ic?	D	Small stone wall; association uncertain
32	M.A.Ic	D	Large trash midden
33	Rosario	D	West wall of House 5
34	M.A.Ic/II	B	Large trash midden
35	Rosario	B	Small pit
36	M.A.Ic	D	West wall of Structure 9
37	M.A.Ic	D	Rubble fill of Structure 9
38	M.A.Ic/II?	D	Fragment of stone wall
39	M.A.Ic/II?	D	Fragment of adobe brick wall
40	M.A.Ia	F	Small rocky pit
41	?	F (T.4)	Large burned pit
42	M.A.Ia?	D	Small ashy pit
43	Rosario	B	West wall of House 7
44a	Rosario	B	Large roasting pit
44b	M.A.Ic	B	Small, slightly bell-shaped pit
45	M.A.Ic	D	Rubble fill of Structure 9
46	M.A.Ic	D	Small burned pit
47	M.A.Ic	D	Large, burned rocky pit
48	M.A.Ic	D	Small hearth
49	M.A.V	F	Large, oblong oven
50	Rosario	F	Large bell-shaped pit
51	M.A.Ic	D	Large adobe-walled fire pit

Table 8: continued

Field Number	Period	Area	Description
52	?	F (T.21)	Small hearth
53	M.A.Ic	E	Large adobe-walled fire pit
54	M.A.Ic	E	Very large roasting pit
55	M.A.Ic	D	North wall of Structure 10
56	M.A.II	B	Large trash midden
57	San José	B	Tiny cluster of rocks
59	M.A.V	F	Section of irrigation canal
61	M.A.Ic	E	Large adobe-walled fire pit
62	San José	E	Very small trash lens
64	M.A.Ic	E	Small hearth
65	San José	E	Shallow rocky pit or lens
66	M.A.Ic	E	Thin trash and rock layer
67	M.A.Ic	F	Very small trash pile
68	M.A.Ic	E	Large burned pit
69	M.A.Ia	F	Large trash midden
70	San José	H(T.26)	Two whole vessels; cache?
72	San José	E	Shallow rocky pit or lens
73	M.A.Ic	E	Large roasting pit or oven
74	Middle Formative	I	Large, deep pit with rock fill
75	M.A.Ic	E	Large adobe-walled fire pit
76	M.A.Ic	E	Medium-sized burned pit
77	M.A.Ia	F	Small hearth
78	M.A.Ic	E	Large burned pit; rock fill
79	M.A.Ia	E	Medium-sized bell-shaped pit
80	?	E	Part of large fire pit
82	M.A.Ia	F	Shallow trash midden
84	M.A.Ic	J	North wall, main mound terrace (Structure 13)
85	M.A.Ic	J	Adobe wall associated with terrace, Structure 13
86	Middle Formative	J	Stone footing of Structure 12
87	M.A.V	F	Medium-sized burned pit
88	M.A.Ia	F	Small pit
89	M.A.V	B	Cluster of large stones
90	M.A.II/V	B	Dark trash layer
90b	?	B	Shallow pit under Feature 90
91	M.A.Ia	B	Shallow pit or midden
92	M.A.Ia	B	Small bell-shaped pit
94	?	F	Shallow pit or lens
95	M.A.Ia	B	Small, cylindrical pit
96	Middle Formative	J	Small hearth atop mound
97	M.A.Ia?V?	B	Small stone wall fragment
98	M.A.V	B	Medium-sized burned pit
99	M.A.V	B	Medium-sized burned pit.
100	?	F	Small rock cluster
101	San José	B	Very small pit
102	Tierras Largas	B	Small, rubble-filled, bell-shaped pit
103	San José	B	Very small pit
104	M.A.Ia	F	Rock and rubble cluster
105	M.A.Ic?	J	Small, burned, rocky pit
106a	M.A.Ia?	B	Small hearth
106b	M.A.Ia	B	Large cylindrical pit
107	M.A.Ia?	F	Small hearth
108	Tierras Largas	J	Large oblong pit with trash fill; not burned
109	San José	J	Large bell-shaped pit
110	M.A.Ia?	F	Small hearth
111	San José	J	Small shallow pit
112	San José	I	Large cylindrical pit
117	San José	J	Trash midden underlying Structure 11

APPENDIX I

Table 9: House and Structure Descriptions

Field Number	Period	Area	Description
House 1	M.A.V	B	Foundation of large stones; no floor left.
House 2/3	M.A.Ia	D	Two superimposed earth and adobe structures.
House 4	San José	B	Nearly complete floor of wattle and daub house
House 5	Rosario	B	Stone foundation of long narrow structure; floor not excavated.
House 6	M.A.II	B	Remnant of stone foundation and floor.
House 7	Rosario	B	Stone foundation of long narrow structure.
House 8	San José	J	Badly preserved floor of a wattle and daub house.
Structure 9	M.A.Ic	D	Stone house platform with plastered floor.
Structure 10	M.A.Ic	D	Stone house platform with plastered floor.
Structure 11	San José	J	Stone and adobe house platform.
Structure 12	Middle Formative	J	Small public building with stone footing.
Structure 13	M.A.Ic	J	Medium-sized public building with cut stone and adobe terraces.
Structure 14	M.A.Ic/II	J	Surface and structure added to top of Structure 13.

APPENDIX II

EARLY FORMATIVE CERAMICS AND THE EARLY SAN JOSÉ OCCUPATIONAL SEQUENCE AT TOMALTEPEC

The study of Early Formative ceramics from the Valley of Oaxaca was begun between 1966 and 1969. The Early Formative period itself was defined by Flannery and his colleagues (Flannery et al. 1970) during that time, and the period was subdivided into the San José and Tierras Largas phases. The San José phase ceramic assemblage was initially characterized during the 1966-67 excavations at San José Mogote, while the Tierras Largas phase assemblage was characterized during the 1969 excavations at San José Mogote and Tierras Largas (Flannery et al. 1970).

The early Tierras Largas assemblage is characterized by jar and hemispherical bowl vessel forms. In the latter part of the phase, some new vessel forms appear, these being flat-bottomed bowls, bottles, and *tecomates* or neckless jars.

Decoration during the Tierras Largas phase frequently includes red striping or red slipping on hemispherical bowls, and less frequently includes plastic decoration (such as dentate rocker stamping) on tecomates. Tierras Largas ceramic wares include burnished, unpainted cooking jars (Tierras Largas Burnished Plain), two varieties of red on buff (Clementina and Avelina), and an orange ware (Matadamas Orange).

In the succeeding San José phase, there was a considerable increase in ceramic variety. Vessel forms included jars, hemispherical bowls, flat-bottomed, outleaned-wall bowls, tecomates or neckless jars, cylinders, bottles, and effigy vessels, especially those representing squashes. Red wash becomes more common, especially on the upper parts of Fidencio Coarse vessels. Plastic decoration included incising, excising, punctate designs, and rocker stamping. Excised designs are frequently found on cylinders and outleaned-wall bowls. Common motifs in these cases were the St. Andrew's Cross, the 'U' motif, a stylized Fire-Serpent, and a stylized Were-Jaguar. These last are Olmecoid motifs, as discussed in Chapter IV. It is in the early San José phase that these designs first appear on Oaxacan pottery.

San José ceramics may be gray (Leandro Gray and Delfina Fine Gray), off-white slipped (Atoyac Yellow-white), red on white (San José Red-on-white), red (San José Specular Red), and fire-clouded white (San José Black-on-white). Orange ware (Matadamas Orange) is also occasionally present. Heavy cooking wares are Lupita Heavy Plain and Fidencio Coarse.

The Tomaltepec ceramic assemblage contains all of these San José phase types. The Tomaltepec sample seems to date from the earliest part of the phase, however. Hemispherical bowls are very common, especially among the cemetery offerings, where they outnumber outleaned-wall bowls by more than 4:1. Throughout the site, the ratio of red painted to plain jars is low, plastic decoration on any type of vessel is quite rare, and the ratio of Leandro Gray to Atoyac Yellow-white is as much as 7:1.

The Tomaltepec assemblage also suggests that our excavations did not recover any proveniences of the late San José phase. The tabulations described below are clearly lacking the later San José phase characteristics which in the Etla region gave rise to the succeeding Guadalupe assemblage; especially scarce is the Atoyac Yellow-white outleaned-wall, flat-bottomed bowls with "double-line-break" elements incised around the rims. Table 10 shows the frequency and distribution of each ware for each feature of the San José phase. Table 11 shows the distribution and frequency of decorative techniques, and Table 12 shows the distribution and frequency of vessel forms.

APPENDIX II

Table 10: Distribution and Frequency of Early Formative Wares

Ware	ESJ-1		STR 11		ESJ-2	ESJ-3			ESJ-4		TL-1		TL-2
	F.109	F.117	Cell	U.L.*	H.4	F.72	T.2	F.62	F.112	Cemetery	F.7	F.102	F.108
Fidencio Coarse	51	47	102	74	55	36	55	8	21	8			
%	52.8%	54.1%	51.0%	44.3%	57.9%	49.9%	68.7%	66.8%	87.5%	10.0%			
Leandro Gray	18	18	53	41	12	5	2	0	1	3			
%	18.9%	20.8%	26.5%	24.5%	12.6%	6.9%	2.5%	—	4.2%	3.8%			
Atoyac Y/W	7	6	8	6	6	15	12	2	0	24			
%	7.4%	6.9%	4.0%	3.5%	6.3%	20.9%	15.0%	16.6%	—	30.0%			
Lupita H. Plain	5	4	14	18	6	11	2	0	2	0			
%	5.7%	4.6%	7.0%	10.7%	6.3%	15.4%	2.5%	—	8.3%	—			
S.J. Red-on-White	14	3	21	27	10	5	0	2	0	0			
%	14.8%	3.3%	10.5%	16.1%	10.5%	6.9%	—	16.7%	—	—			
M. Orange	0	9	2	0	0	0	0	0	0	42			
%	—	10.3%	1.0%	—	—	—	—	—	—	52.5%			
Atoyac Y/W and M. Orange on same vessel	0	0	0	0	3	0	4	0	0	2			
%	—	—	—	—	3.2%	—	5.0%	—	—	2.5%			
T.L. Burn. Pln.	0	0	0	1	0	0	0	0	0	1	17	10	9
%	—	—	—	0.5%	—	—	—	—	—	1.3%	41.4%	76.9%	90.0%
A. Red-on-Buff	0	0	0	0	3	0	5	0	0	0	24	3	1
%	—	—	—	—	3.2%	—	6.3%	—	—	—	58.5%	23.1%	10.0%
%	100.0%	100.0%	100.0%	100.0%	100.0%	100.0%	100.0%	100.0%	100.0%	100.0%	100.0%	100.0%	100.0%
Total # Diag. Sherds	95	87	200	167	100	72	80	12	24	80 Vessels	41	13	10

*U.L. = The upper levels of San José phase trash covering Structure 11.

Table 11: Distribution and Frequency of Early Formative Decorative Techniques

Technique	F.109	F.117	Cell	U.L.	H.4	F.72	T.2	F.62	F.112	Cemetery
F. Coarse Ratio Pln./Red Wash	36/9 4.0	29/14 2.1	41/48 0.9	34/21 1.6	21/25 0.8	12/23 0.5	13/42 0.3	1/3 0.3	5/12 0.4	1/14 0.1
F. Coarse Plastic Decoration	6 6.3%	4 4.6%	13 6.3%	18 10.4%	5 4.7%	1 1.4%	0 —	4 33.3%	4 14.3%	0 —
Leandro Gray Plastic Dec.	2 2.1%	6 6.9%	11 5.3%	11 6.3%	6 5.7%	2 2.7%	1 1.4%	0 —	0 —	2 2.5%
Atoyac Y/W Plastic Dec.	1 1.0%	0 —	1 0.5%	0 —	1 0.9%	3 3.5%	1 1.4%	0 —	0 —	3 3.8%
All Plastic Dec.	11 11.6%	11 12.6%	37 17.8%	39 22.5%	5 4.7%	15 20.8%	3 4.1%	4 33.3%	4 14.3%	6 7.5%

Table 12: Distribution and Frequency of Early Formative Vessel Forms

Vessel	F.109	F.117	Cell	U.L.	H.4	F.72	T.2	F.62	F.112	Cemetery
Hemispherical Bowl	14 16.8%	11 15.1%	34 19.6%	12 11.3%	20 27.7%	9 15.7%	10 14.6%	1 12.5%	2 12.5%	35 42.2%
Outleaned Wall Bowl	22 26.5%	26 34.6%	54 31.2%	37 34.9%	5 6.9%	17 29.9%	11 15.9%	3 37.5%	5 31.3%	8 9.6%
Jar	35 42.2%	25 34.2%	68 39.3%	41 38.6%	29 40.2%	25 43.8%	42 60.8%	3 37.5%	6 37.5%	17 20.4%
Tecomate	2 2.4%	2 2.7%	2 1.2%	4 3.8%	1 1.3%	1 1.8%	1 1.4%	0 —	0 —	8 9.6%
Cylinder	10 12.1%	10 13.8%	15 8.7%	12 11.4%	17 23.5%	5 8.8%	5 7.6%	1 12.5%	2 12.5%	15 18.2%

PLATE 44. Vessels of the San José phase, I. Top, large jar. Bottom, small jars. (Scale in cm.)

APPENDIX II

PLATE 45. Vessels of the San José phase, II. Top, bottles. Bottom, hemispherical bowls.

PLATE 46. Vessels of the San José phase, III. Top, outleaned-wall bowls. Bottom, tecomates.

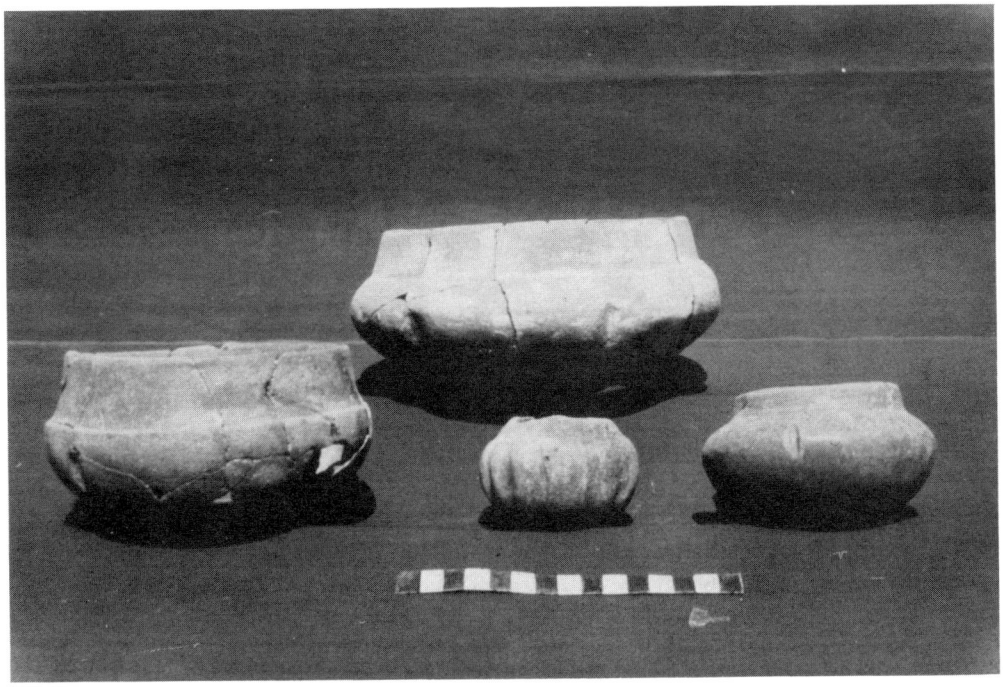

PLATE 47. Vessels of the San José phase, IV. Squash effigy vessels.

APPENDIX III

HUMAN BURIALS FROM TOMALTEPEC

Summarized below are several major classes of data for the many human burials recovered at Tomaltepec. Burials 1 and 2 were excavated by Wright and associates in 1972 (Wright, n.d.) and the remainder were recovered during the 1974 field season.

Burials are arranged by chronological phase and by field excavation number within each phase. Field numbers do not reflect the locations of the burials, so that consecutively numbered burials are not necessarily spatially associated. Information about each burial is given under five headings, labeled A–E, to be read as follows:

A. Sex and age. These identifications were made in Oaxaca by Richard Wilkinson of the State University of New York at Albany. Wilkinson has identified all human skeletal material recovered by the Oaxaca Human Ecology Project. "Sex (?)" indicates that sex could not be determined. "Male (?)" or "Female (?)" indicates probable sex in less clear cases.

B. Position and orientation. The position designations are largely self-explanatory. In the early San José phase cemetery, however, a "flexed" burial is one bundled into a squatting position (knees against the chest, arms folded) and laid on its face. This is the normal prone position, but with knees drawn up agains the chest. Orientation refers to the position of the head of the corpse with respect to magnetic north. A corpse extended east-west, with head to the east, would be recorded as 90°. Unless otherwise specified, burial is in a simple pit grave.

C. Burial offerings. These include all vessels (denoted V.1 . . . n) and other objects (Obj. 1 . . . n) evidently intentionally buried with the corpse as offerings. The locations of these within the grave are also given. If no offerings were present, it is noted whether this is likely to have been the original condition or whether the burial was too badly disturbed to be certain about presence or absence of offerings.

D. Other associated burials. Most of the burials described under this heading are secondary burials associated with primary interments in the early San José phase cemetery. Primary burials are occasionally clearly associated in a single burial event and this is also noted here. One corpse buried in its own grave without secondary human accompaniments is designated as "alone".

E. Location of the burial. Most burials could be clearly associated with particular household units, the number of which is given here. The early San José phase cemetery burials cannot be characterized in these terms, however. Instead, a diagram of the cemetery is provided (Figure 13) together with the number of the one meter square in which the head of the corpse was located. For example, "558/491" should be read as square number 558 North, 491 West. Square 500N, 500W is near the main mound. Other pertinent remarks are included here as well. Selected burials and burial offerings are illustrated for each phase.

APPENDIX III

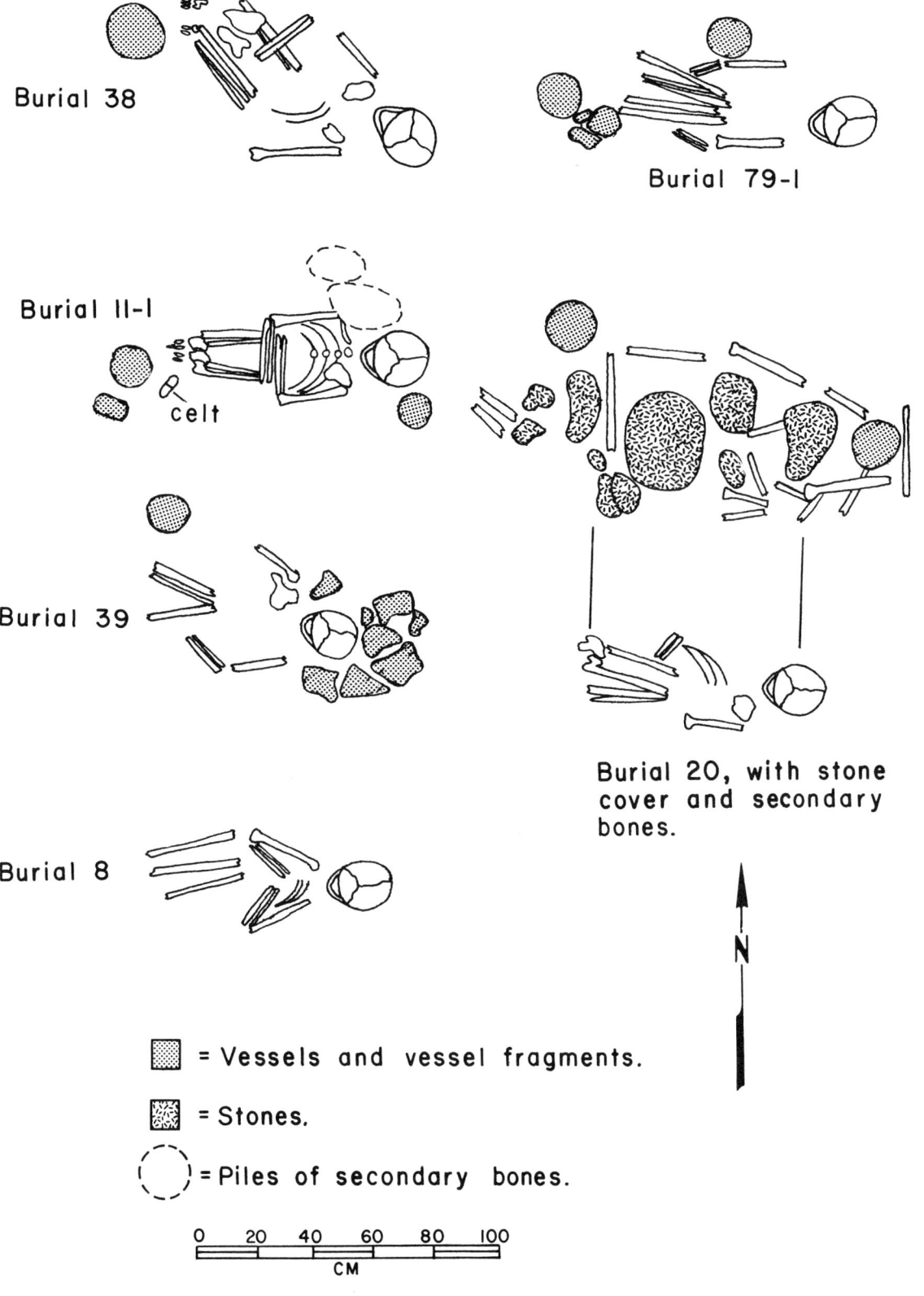

FIGURE 31. Flexed burials from the San José phase cemetery.

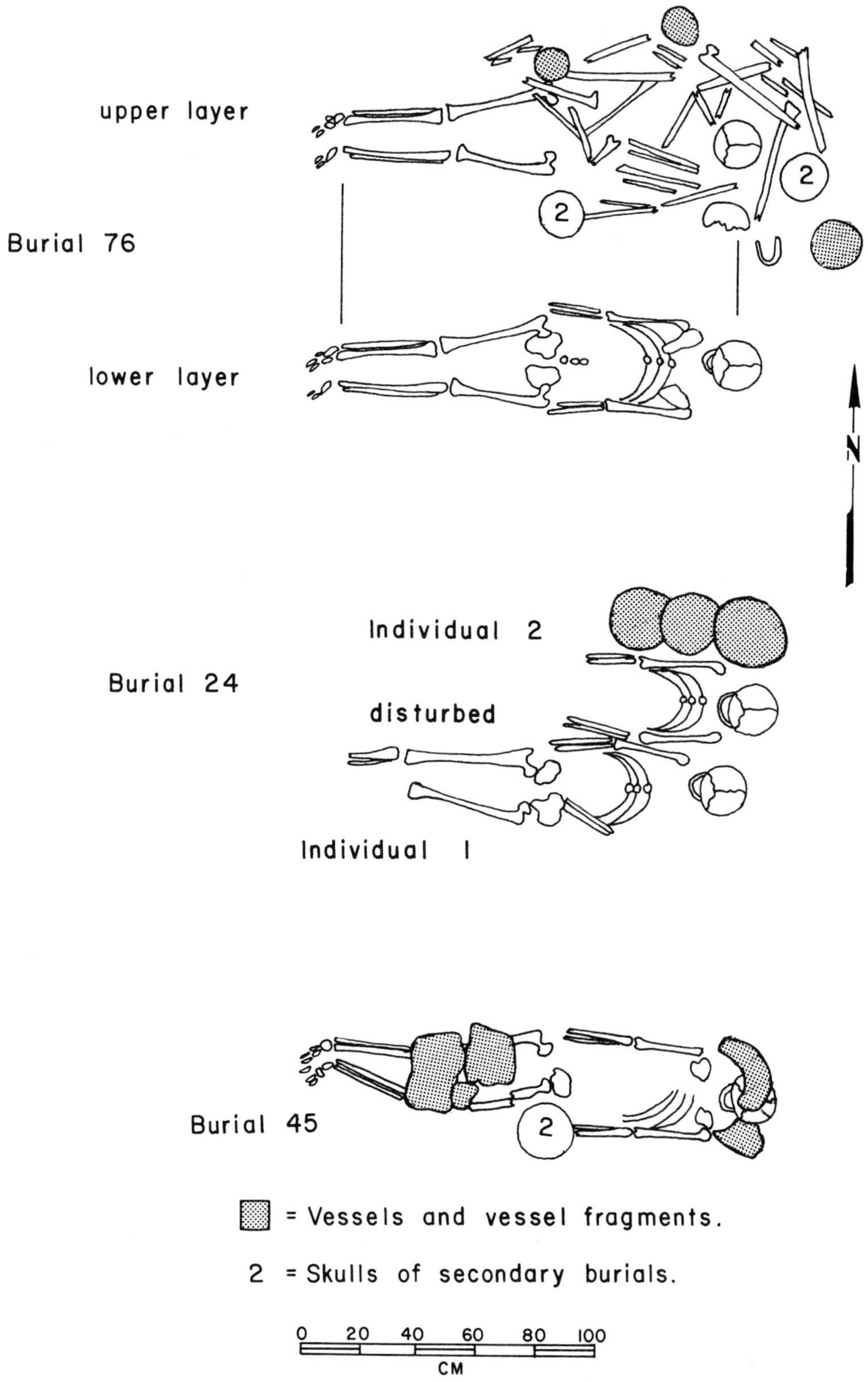

FIGURE 32. Extended burials from the San José phase cemetery, I.

APPENDIX III

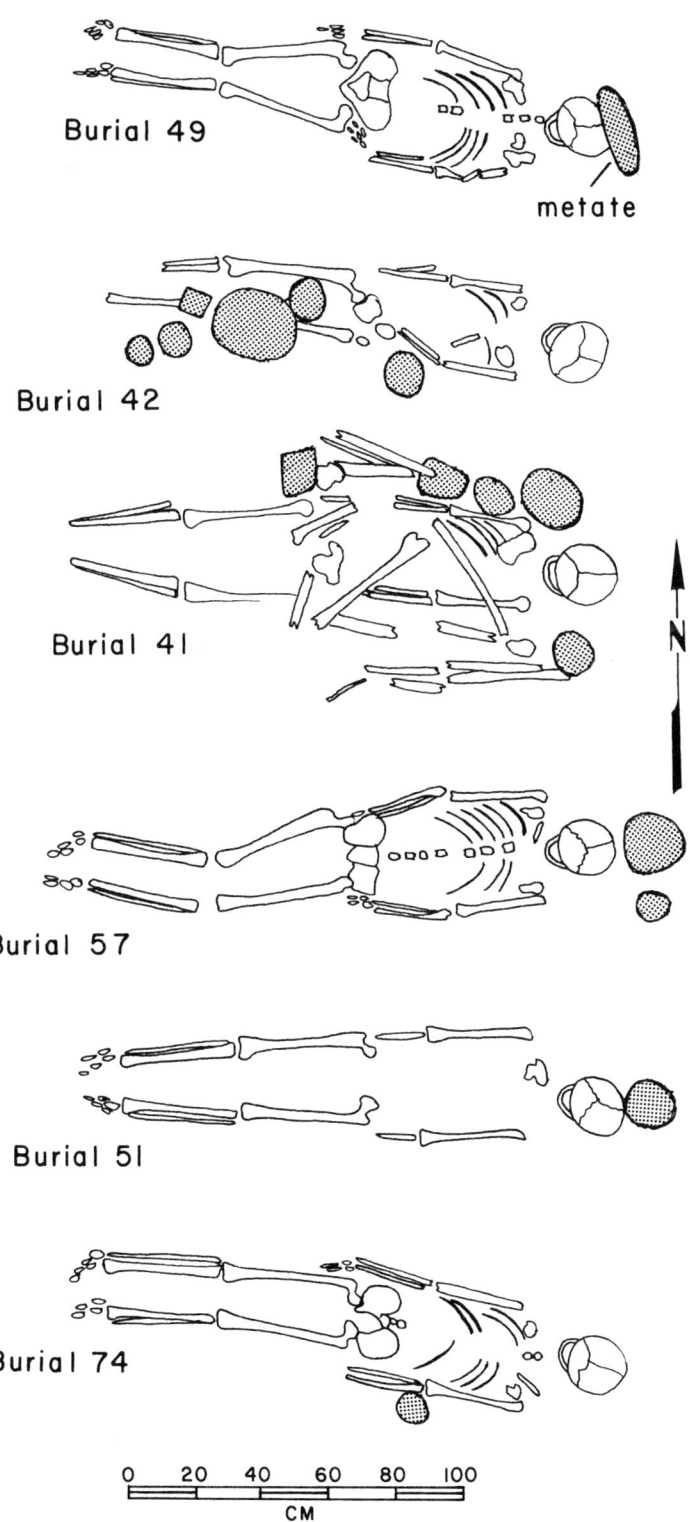

FIGURE 33. Extended burials from the San José phase cemetery, II.

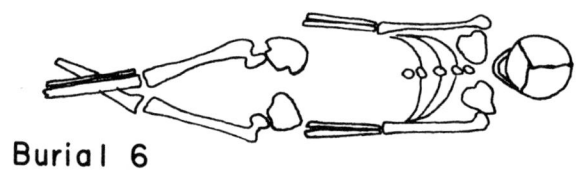

Burial 6

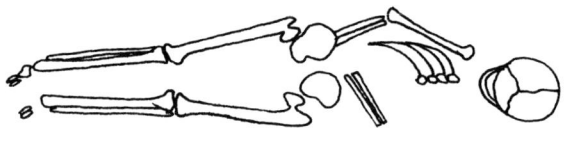

Burial 44-3

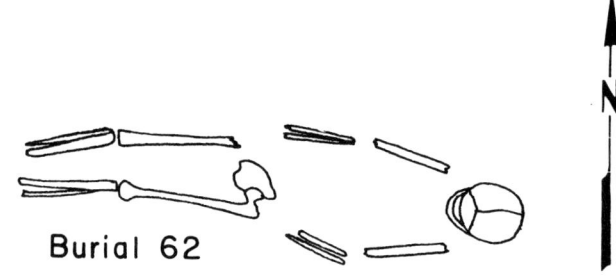

Burial 62

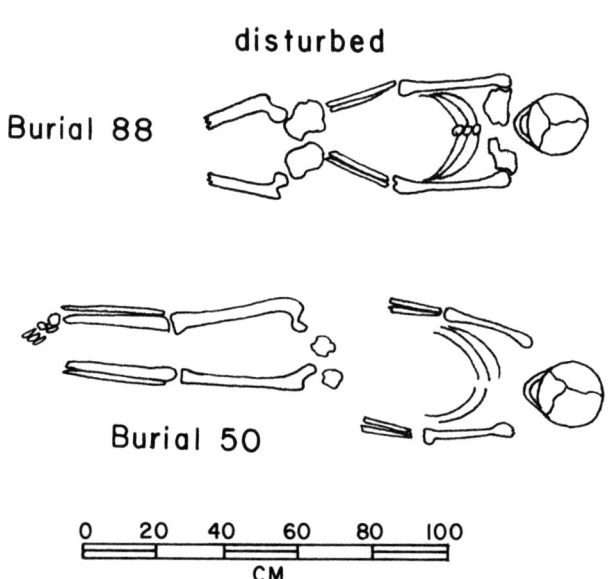

FIGURE 34. Extended burials from the San José phase cemetery, III.

APPENDIX III

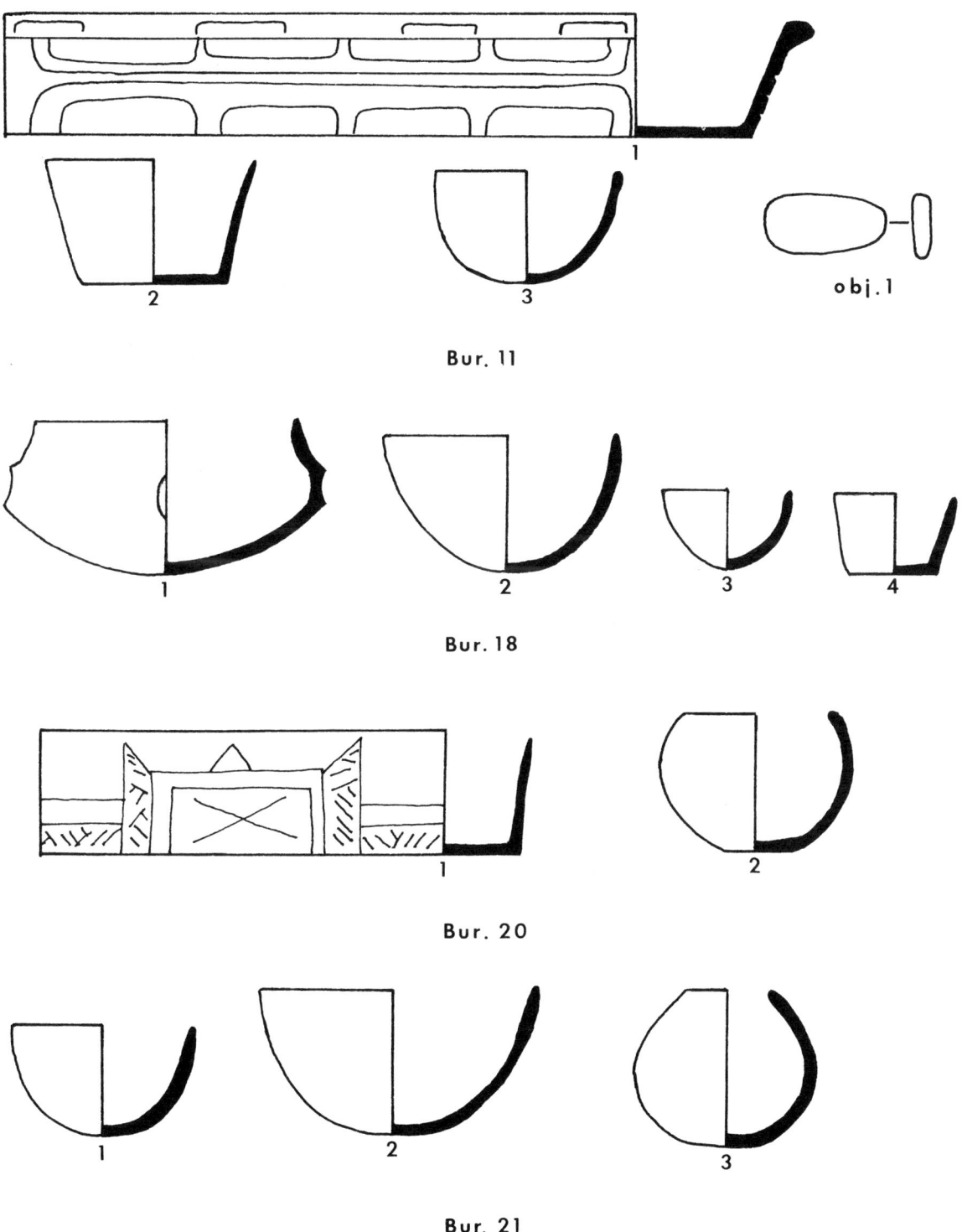

FIGURE 35. Burial goods from the San José phase cemetery, I. Rim diameter of Vessel 2 from Burial 21, 18 cm.

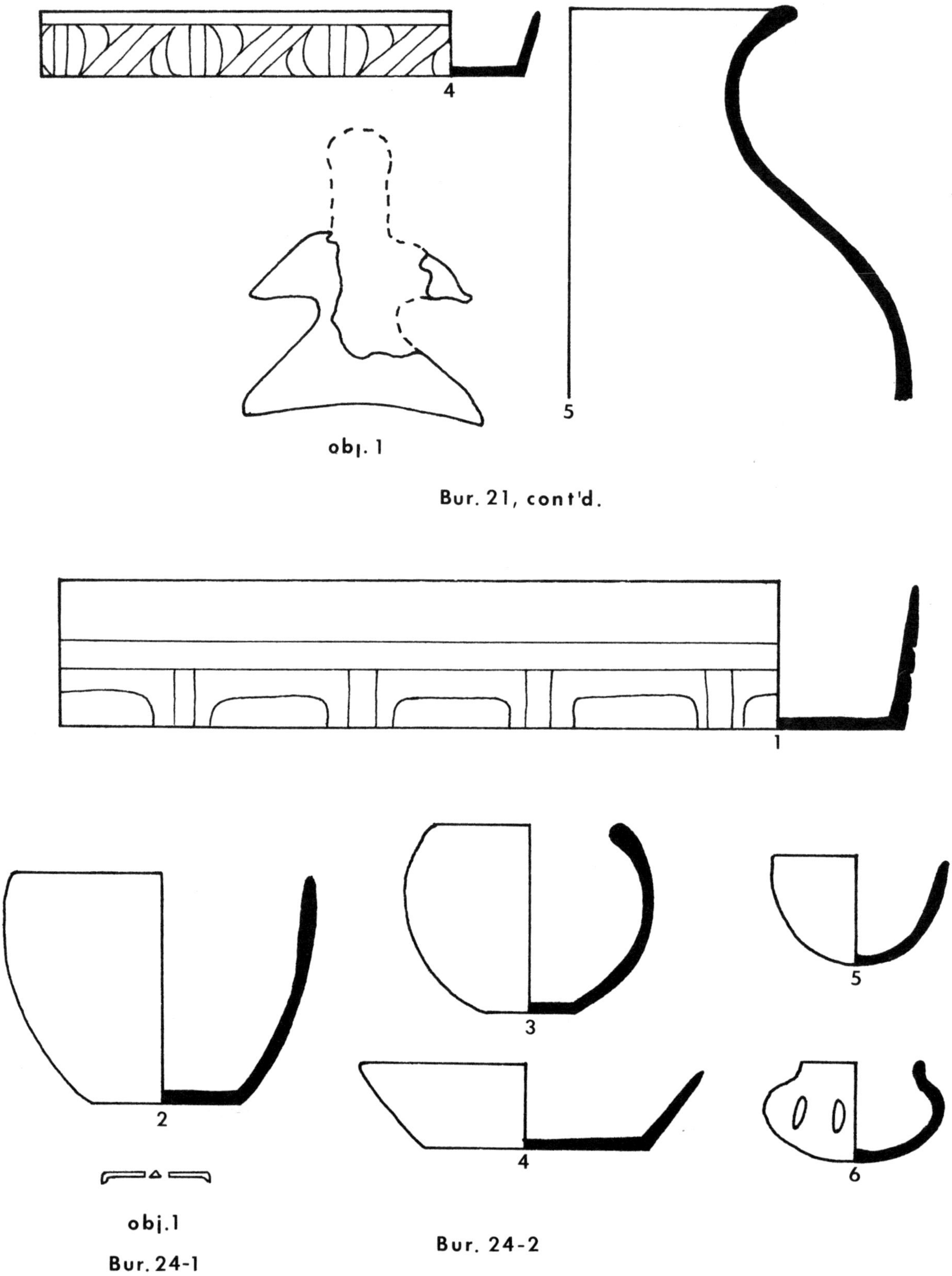

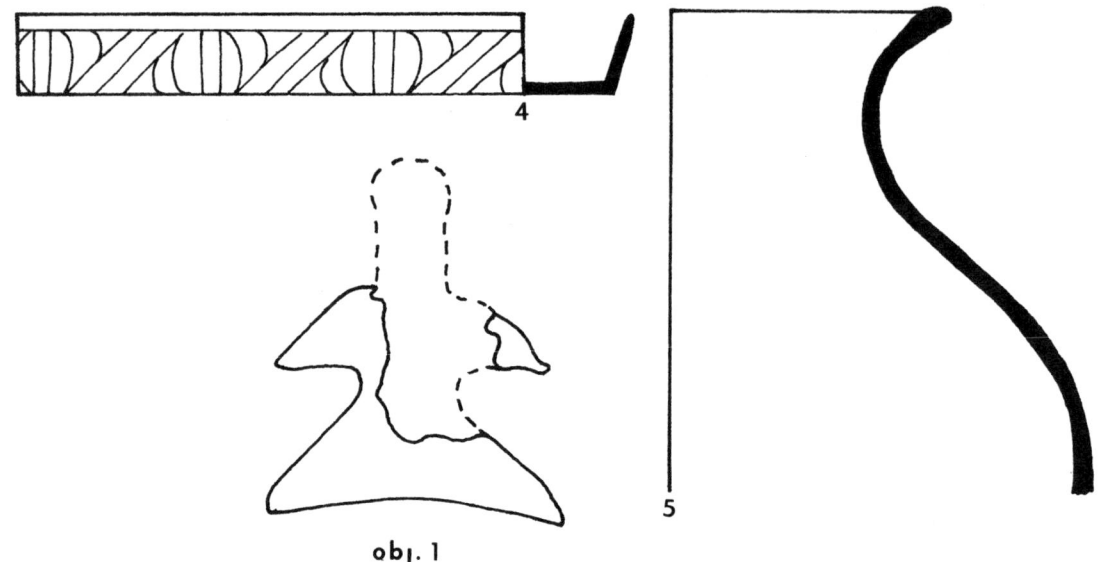

FIGURE 36. Burial goods from the San José phase cemetery, II. Rim diameter of Vessel 4 from Burial 24-2, 23 cm.

APPENDIX III

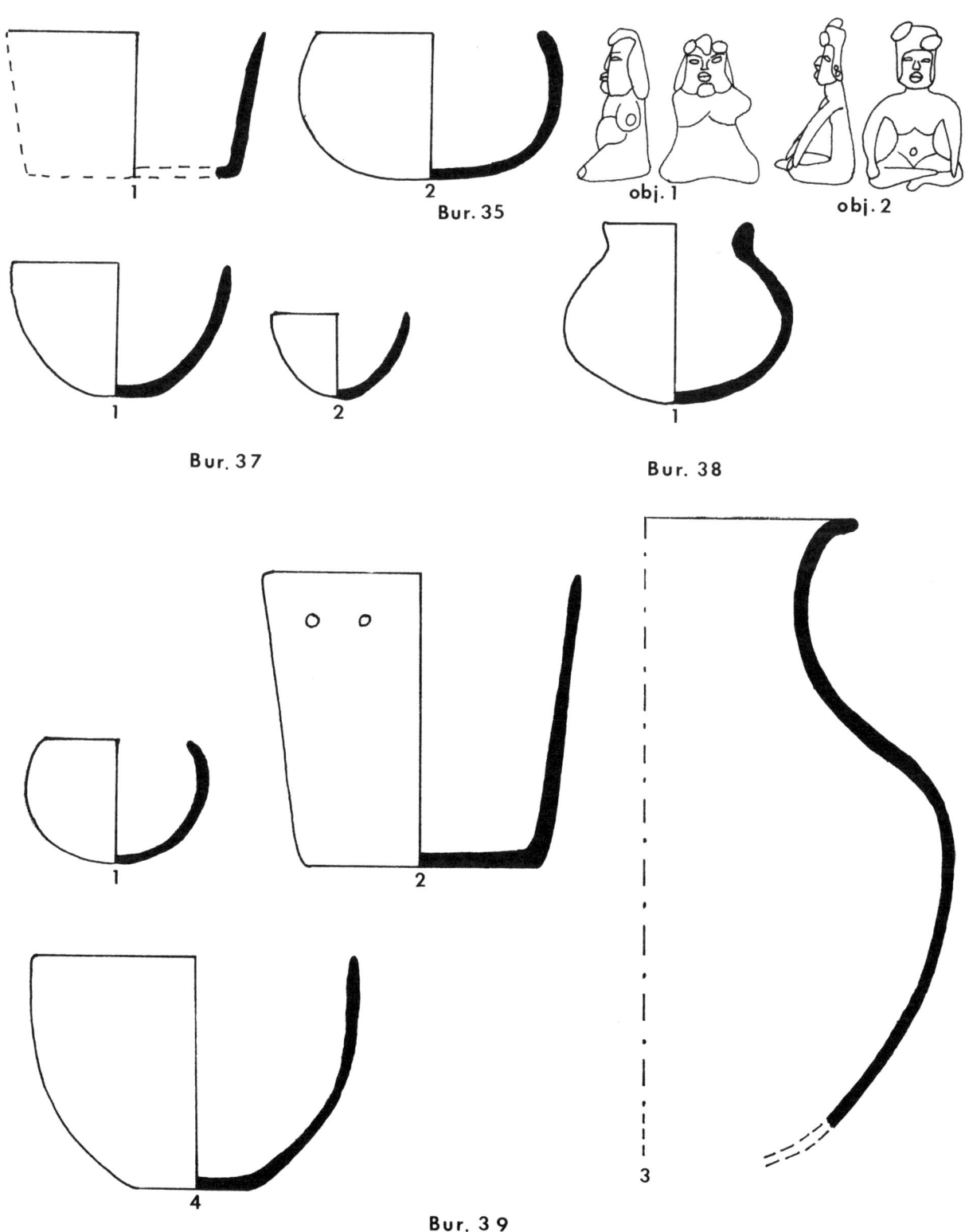

FIGURE 37. Burial goods from the San José phase cemetery, III. Rim diameter of Vessel 4 from Burial 39, 22 cm.

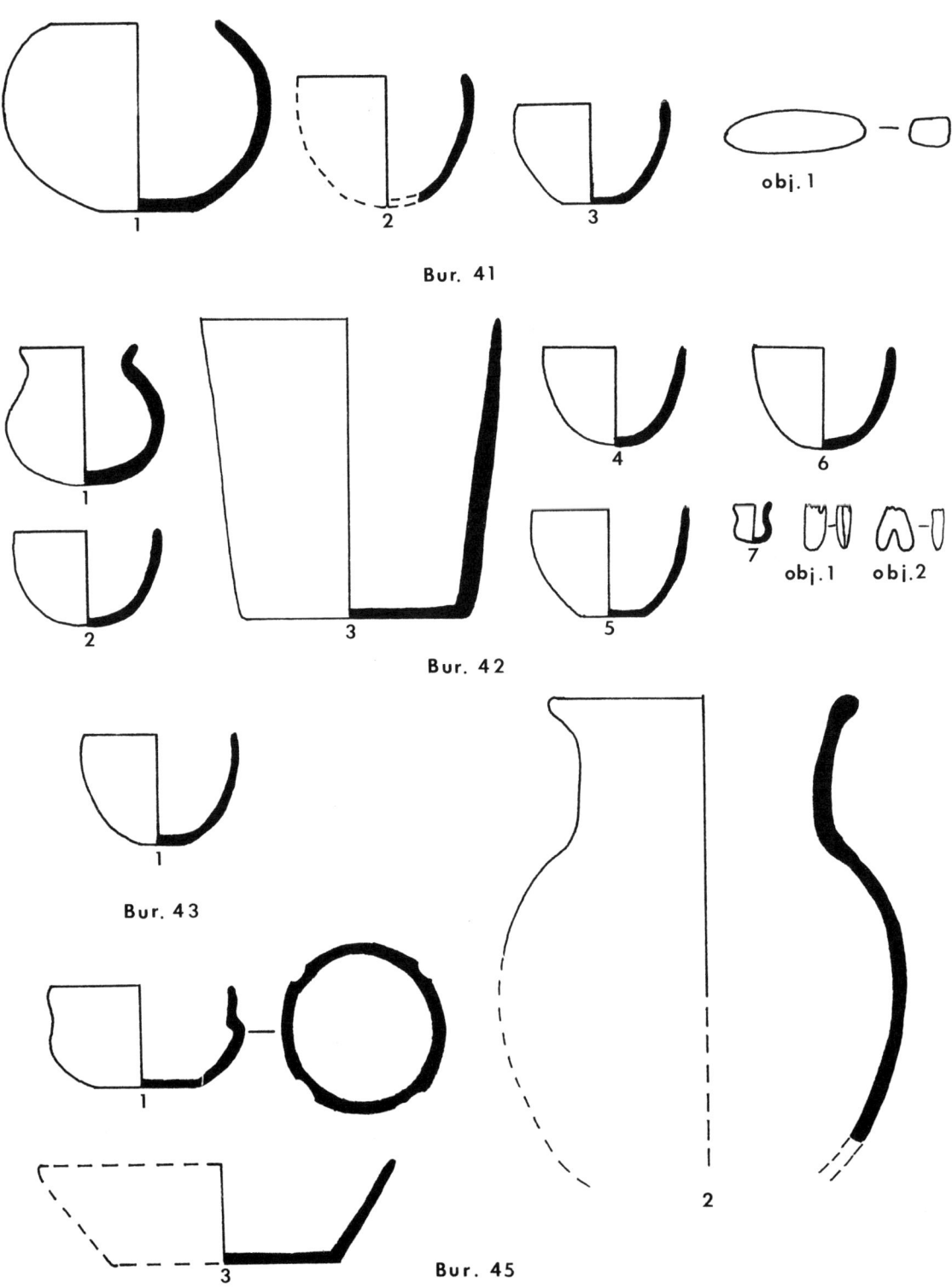

FIGURE 38. Burial goods from the San José phase cemetery, IV. Rim diameter of Vessel 3 from Burial 42, 21 cm.

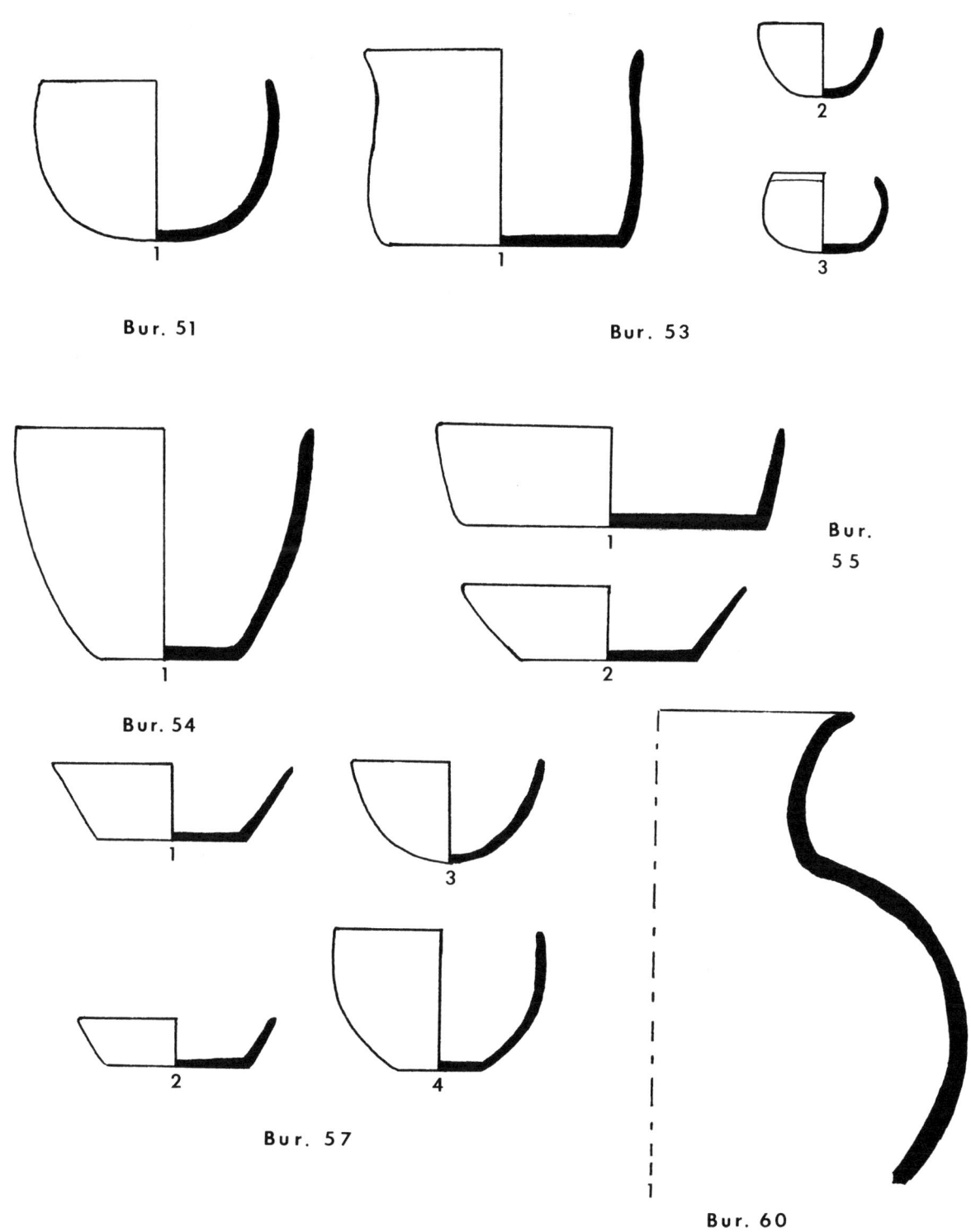

FIGURE 39. Burial goods from the San José phase cemetery, V. Rim diameter of Vessel 1 from Burial 55, 24 cm.

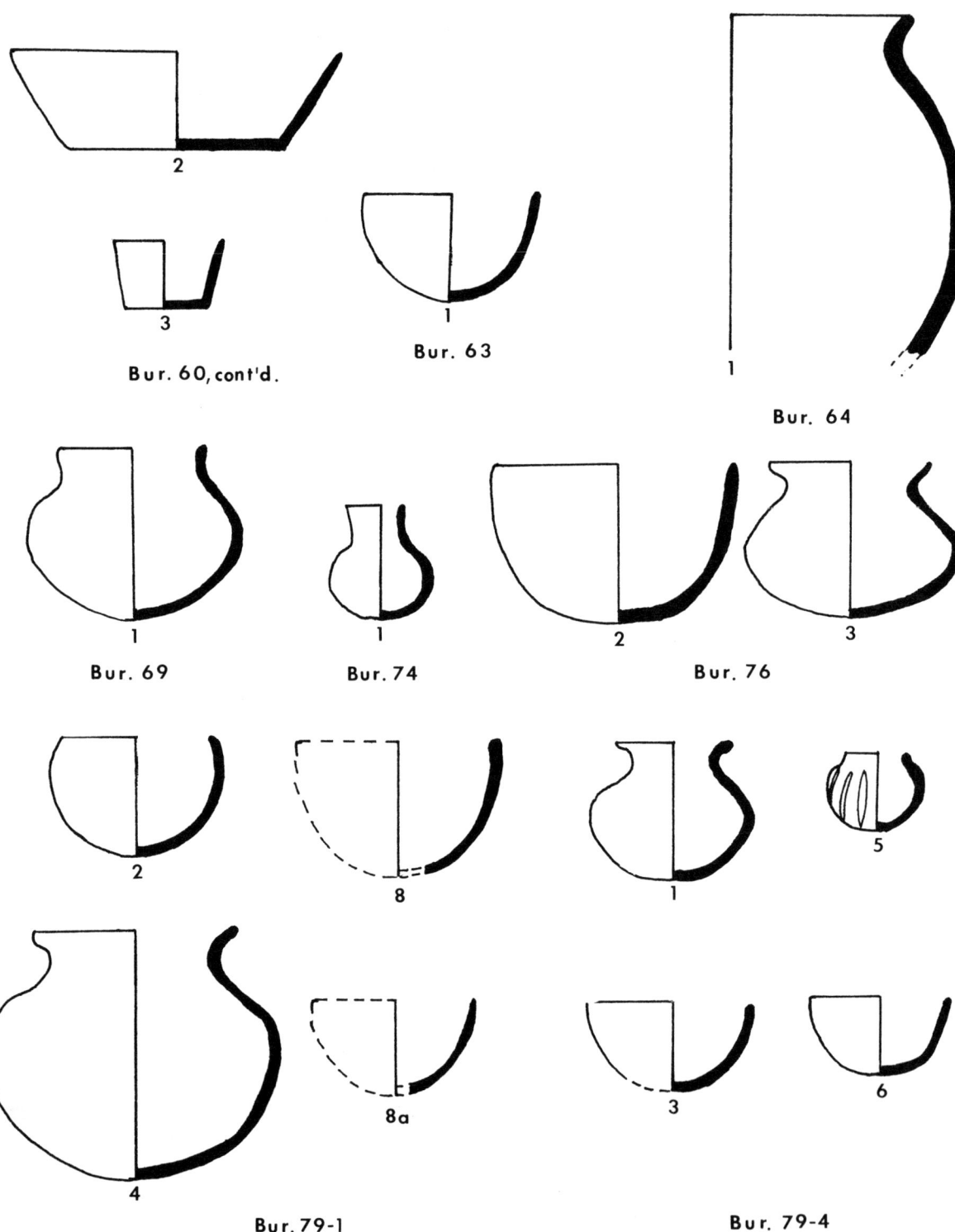

FIGURE 40. Burial goods from the San José phase cemetery, VI. Rim diameter of Vessel 2 from Burial 60, 23 cm.

APPENDIX III

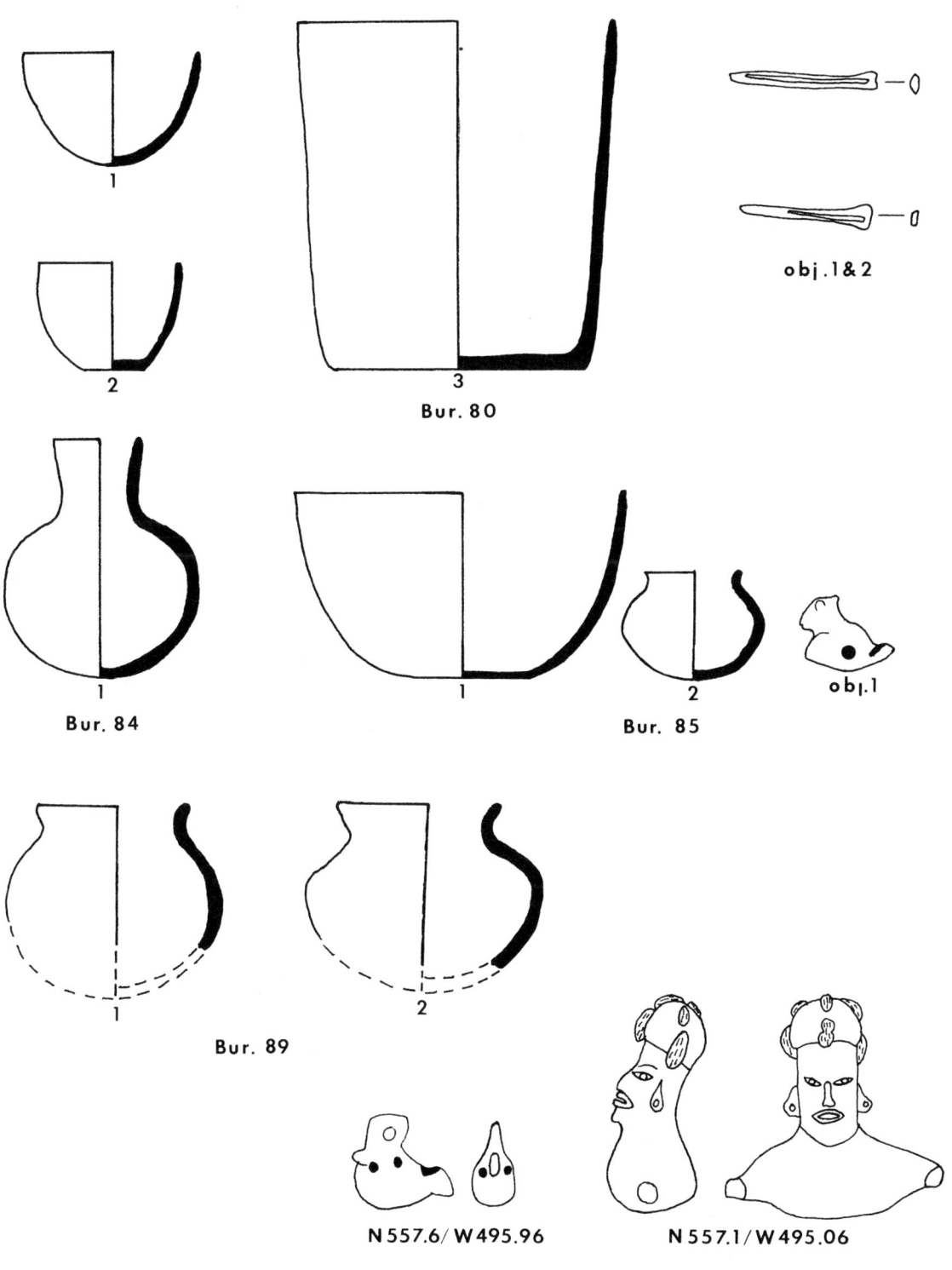

FIGURE 41. Burial goods from the San José phase cemetery, VII. Rim diameter of Vessel 3 from Burial 80, 22 cm.

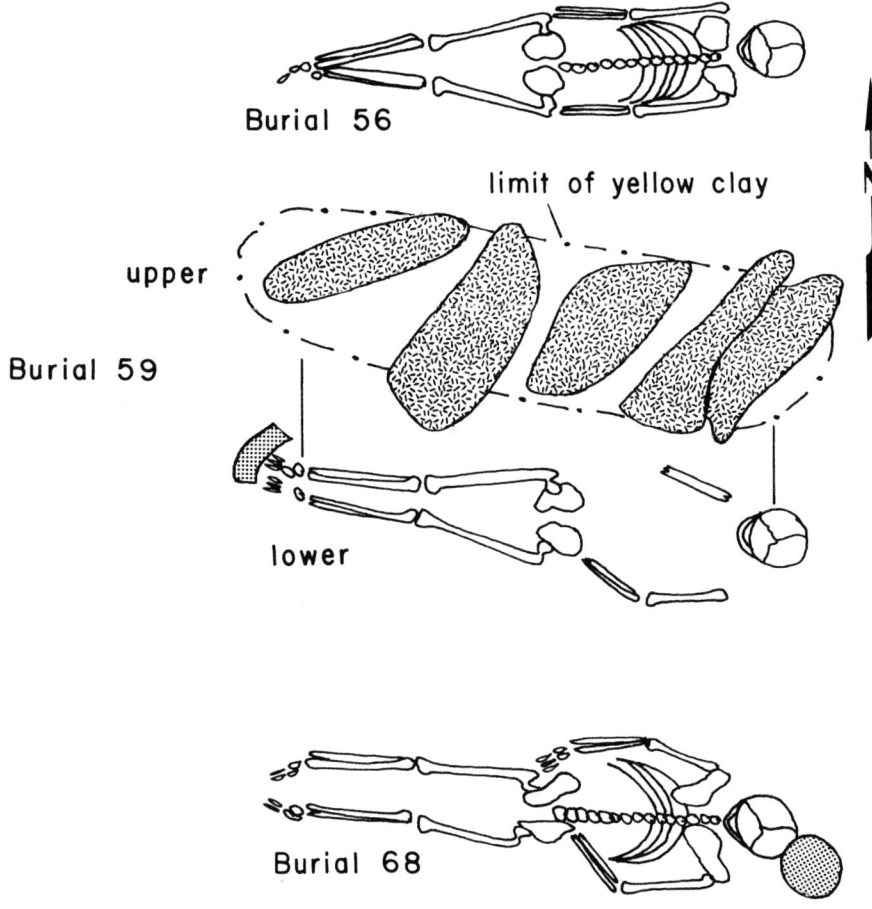

FIGURE 42. Burials with Guadalupe phase affiliations, all located atop Structure 12.

APPENDIX III 137

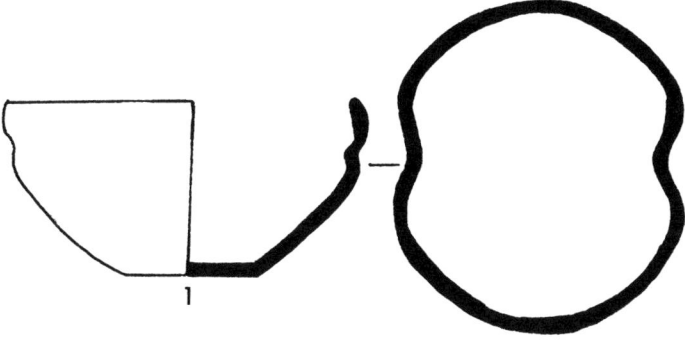

Bur. 47

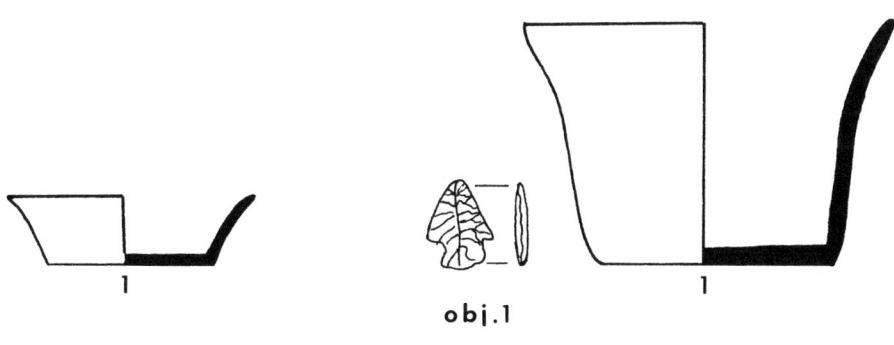

Bur. 59 Bur. 68

FIGURE 43. Burial goods from burials with Guadalupe phase affiliations.

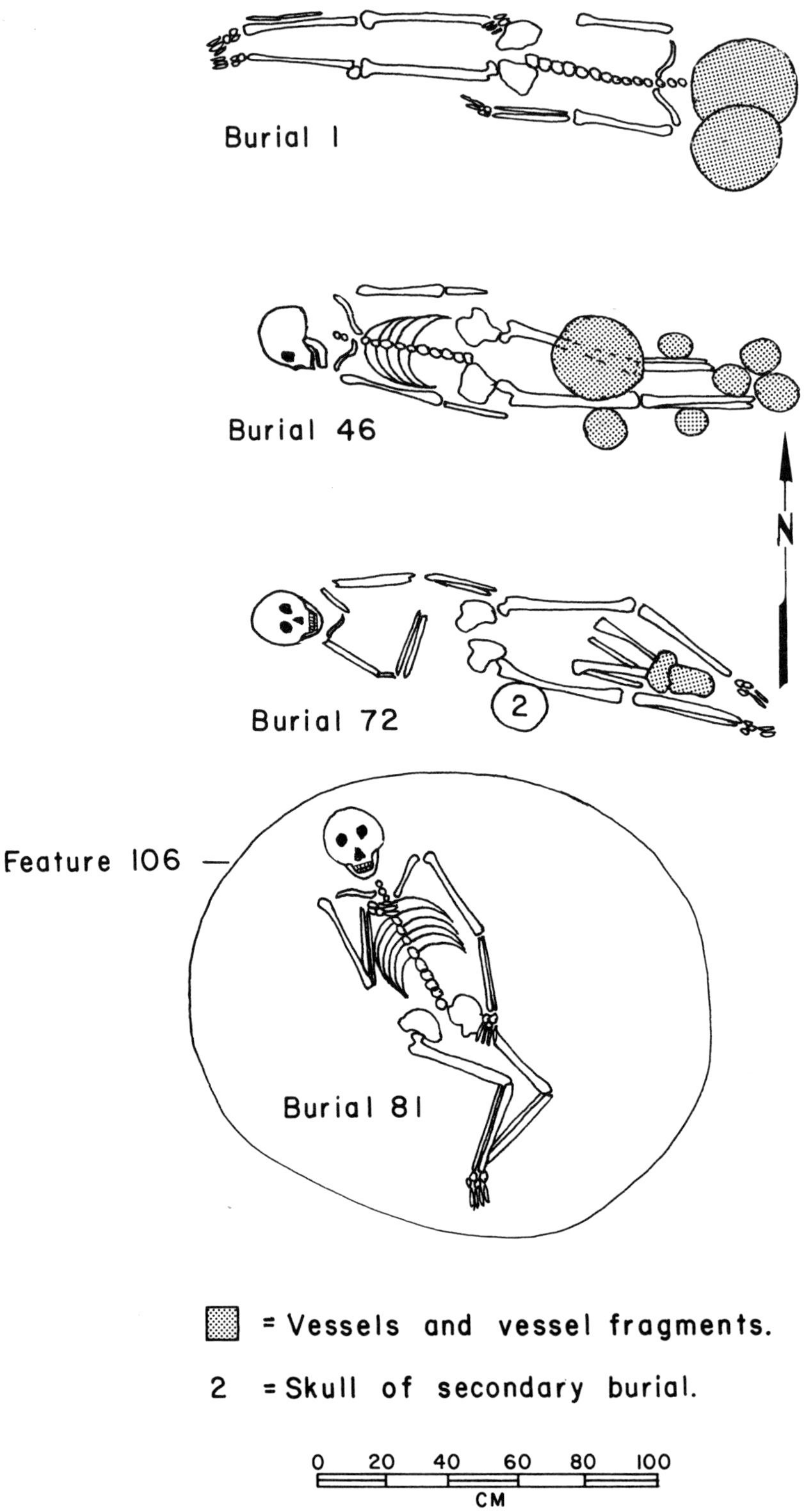

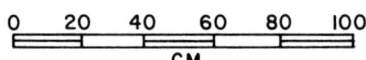

FIGURE 44. Monte Albán Ia burials. Feature 106 is a large cylindrical pit associated with Household Unit Ia-1.

APPENDIX III

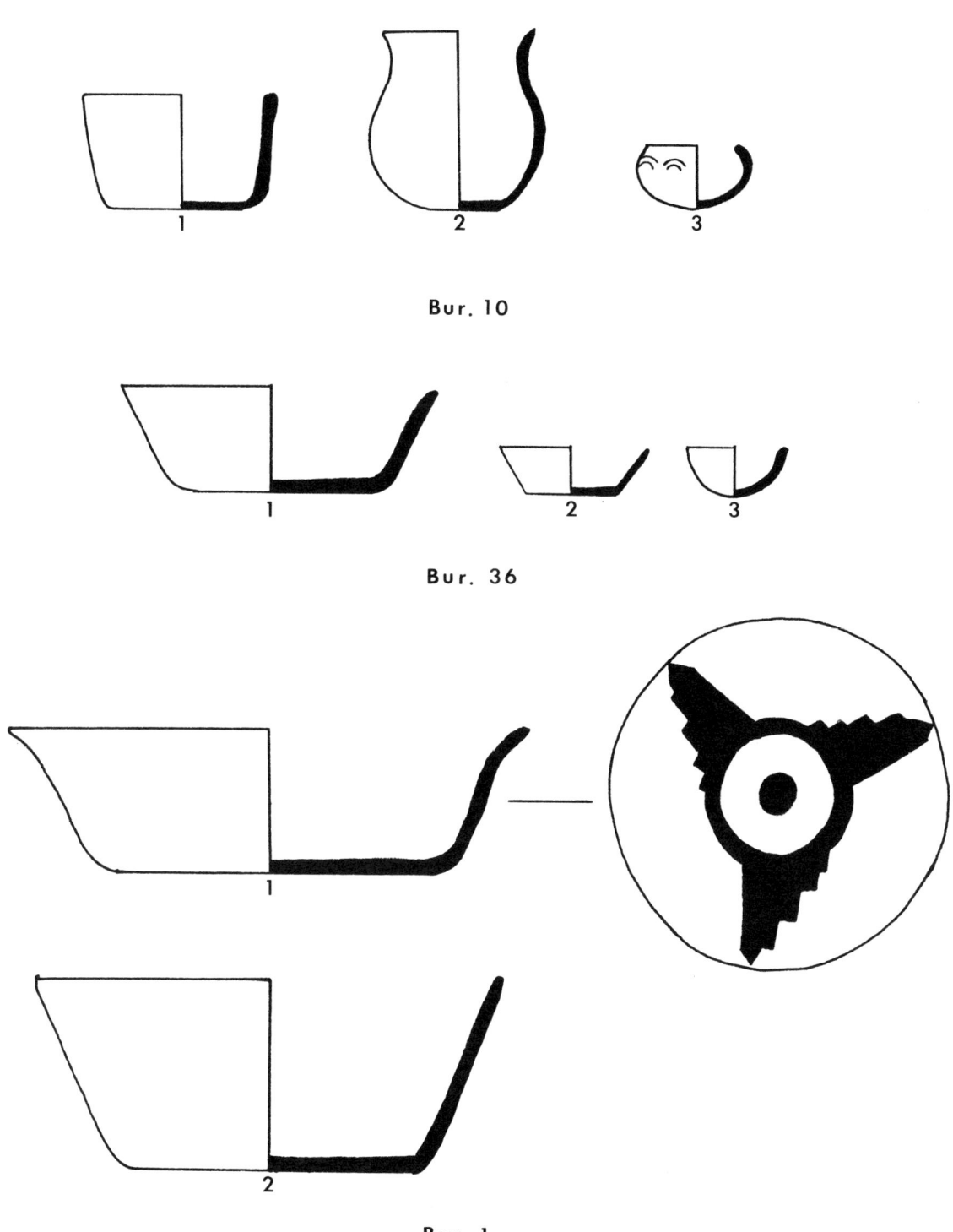

FIGURE 45. Rosario phase and Monte Albán Ia burial goods, I. Rim diameter of Vessel 2 from Burial 1, 30 cm.

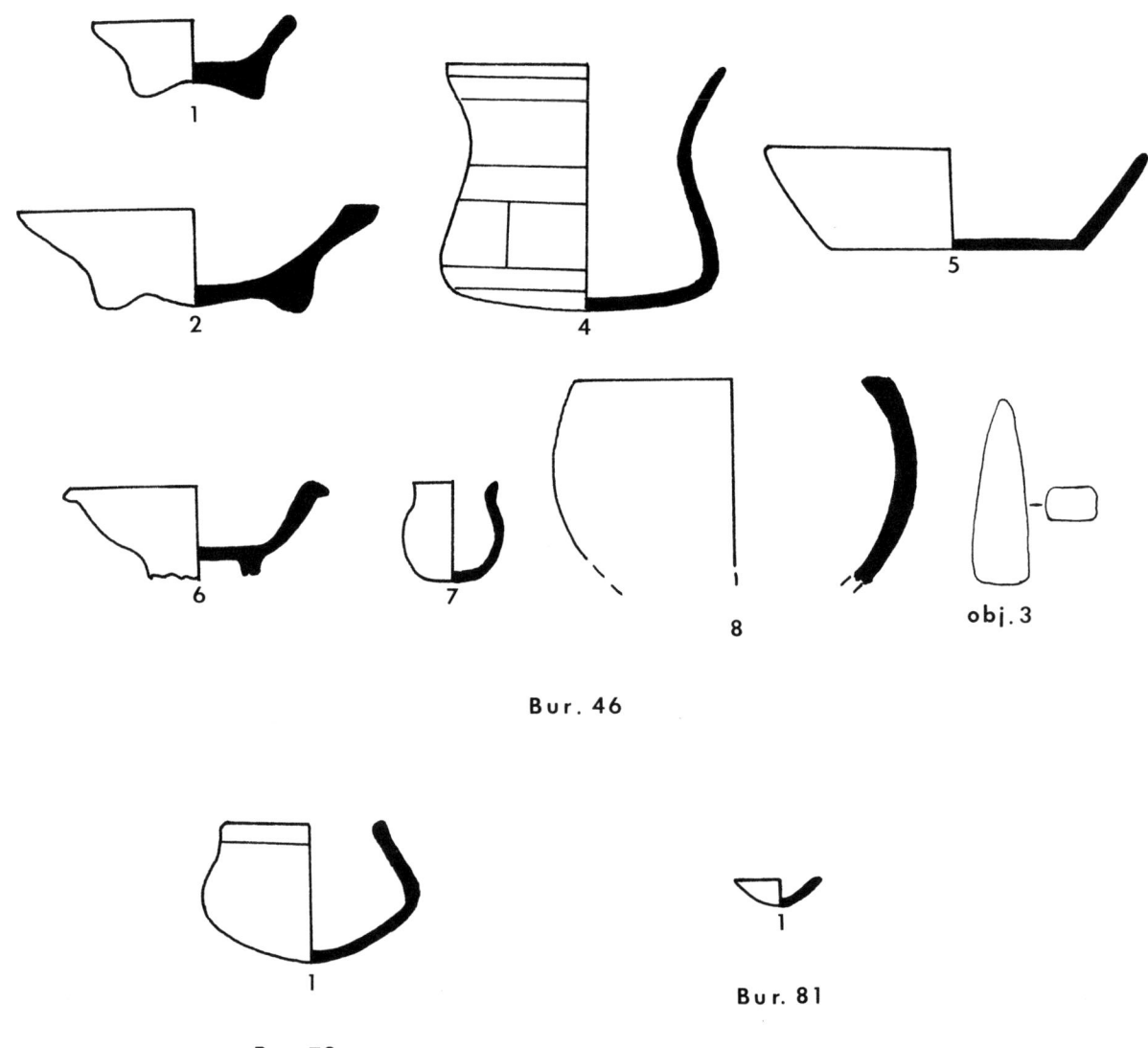

FIGURE 46. Rosario phase and Monte Albán Ia burial goods, II. Rim diameter of Vessel 5 from Burial 46, 23 cm.

APPENDIX III

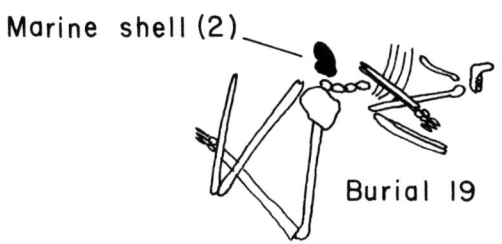

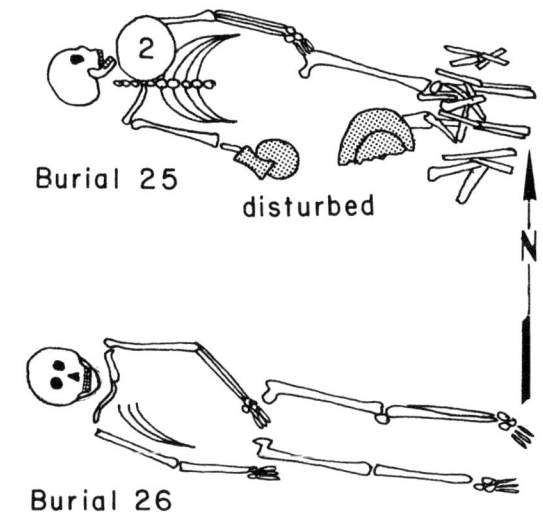

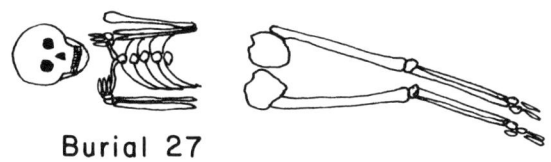

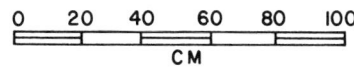

FIGURE 47. Monte Albán Ic burials.

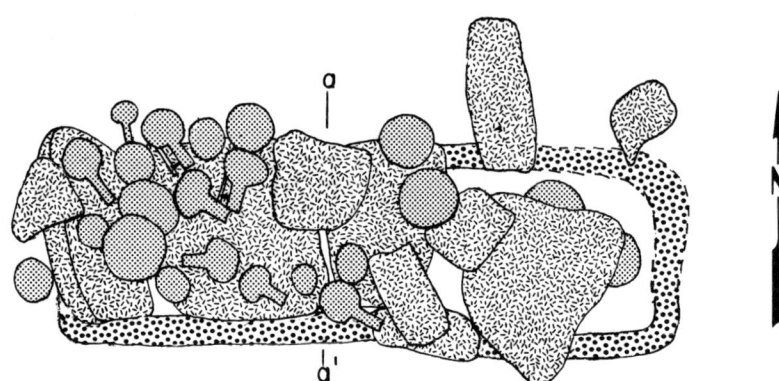

a. Plan of the tomb, showing covering slabs and ceramic offerings.

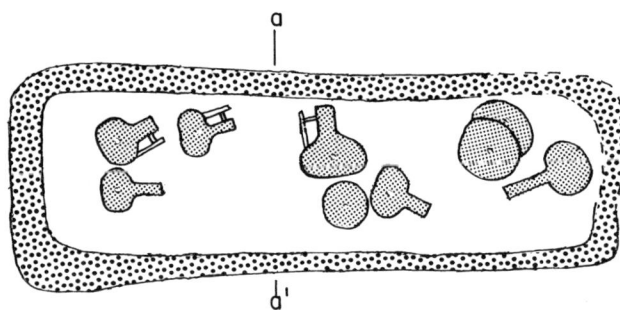

b. Plan of the tomb, with covering slabs and upper ceramic offerings removed. Vessels found inside the tomb are shown here.

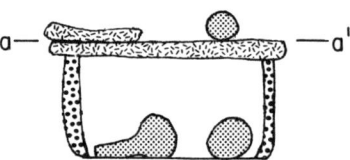

c. Section of the tomb, showing covering slab and interior dimensions.

▨ = Vessels.

▨ = Stone covering slabs.

▨ = Adobe walls.

FIGURE 48. Details of tomb associated with Burial 5, a Monte Albán Ic interment found inside Structure 9 of Household Unit Ic-1.

APPENDIX III

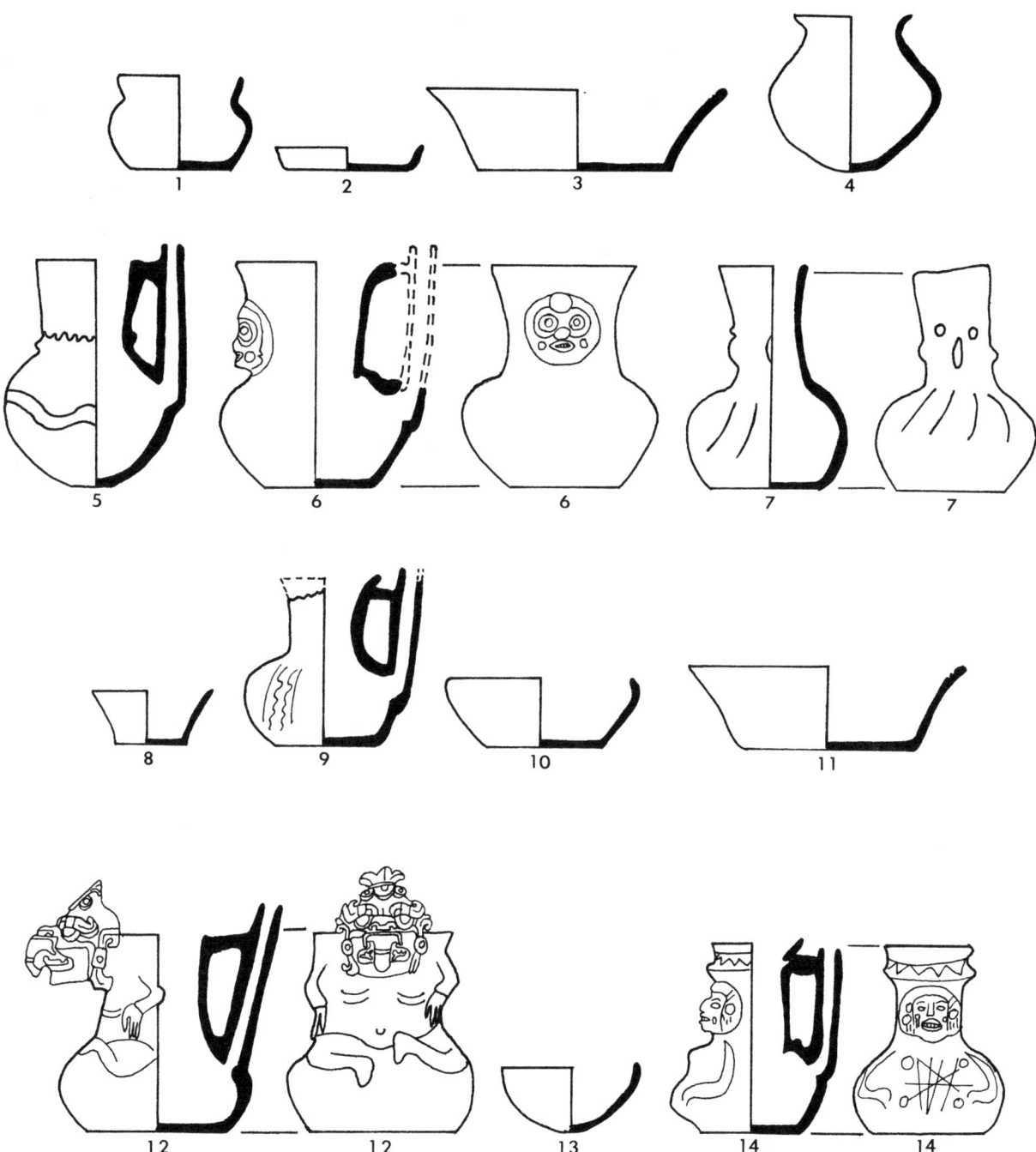

FIGURE 49. Vessels accompanying Burial 5, I.

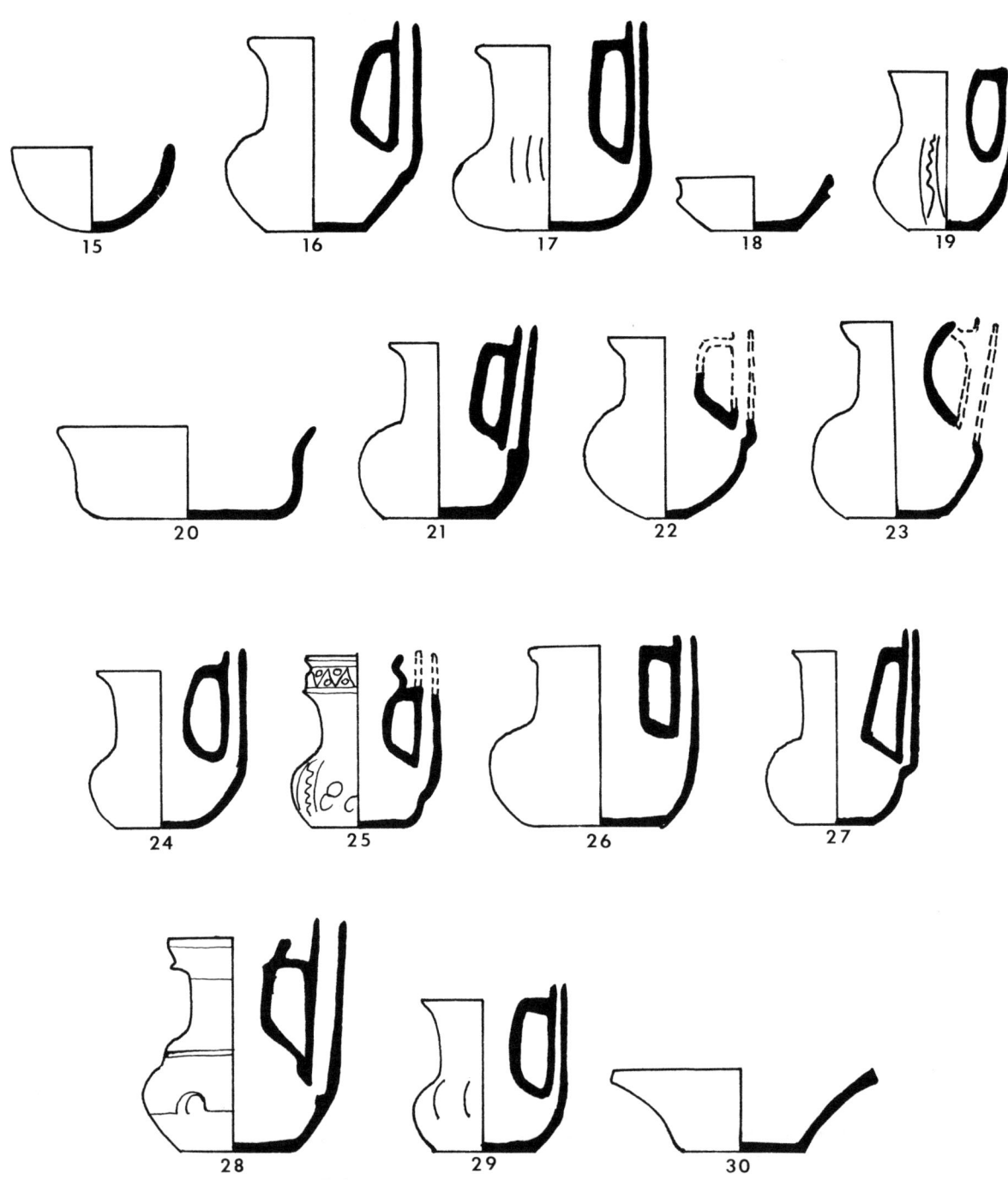

FIGURE 50. Vessels accompanying Burial 5, II.

APPENDIX III

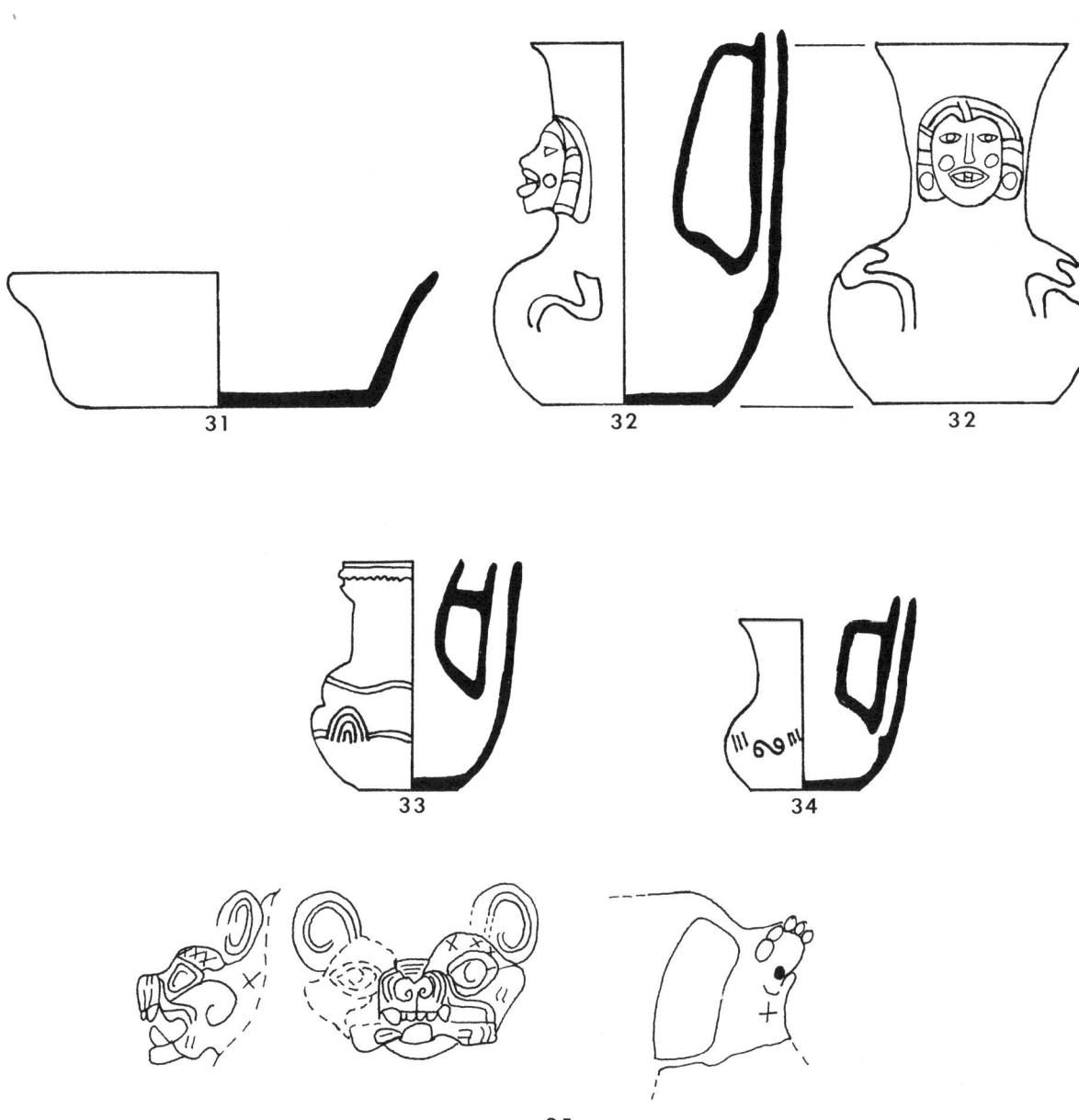

FIGURE 51. Vessels accompanying Burial 5, III.

FIGURE 52. Vessel 12 from Burial 5, an elaborate Monte Albán Ic bridge-spout jar.

APPENDIX III

Early San José Burials

Burial 6
- A. Male, 30–40
- B. Prone, extended, 95°
- C. No offerings
- D. Alone
- E. Cemetery. 558/491

Burial 8
- A. Male, ca. 20
- B. Prone, flexed, 270°
- C. No offerings
- D. Alone
- E. Cemetery. 558/494. Somewhat disturbed

Burial 9
- A. Female, 20–25
- B. Prone, extended, 90°
- C. No offerings
- D. Alone
- E. Cemetery. 558/493. Lower body disturbed by Burial 8

Burial 11-1
- A. Male, 30–40
- B. Prone, flexed, 95°
- C. V.1: Medium outleaned wall bowl. Raspada Olmecoid were-jaguar motif. At feet
  V.2: Small plain yellow-white cylinder. At feet
  V.3: Small orange hemispherical bowl. At head
  Obj. 1: Small plain greenstone celt. At feet
  Obj. 2: Necklace of 15 greenstone beads. Around neck
  Obj. 3: Single greenstone bead. In mouth
- D. Accompanied by two badly preserved secondary burials (11-2; 11-3). Both piled over left shoulder and near left side of skull of 11-1. 11-2 is an adult of unknown sex. 11-3 is a female (?) of 40+
- E. Cemetery. 557/493

Burial 12
- A. Male (?), 30–40
- B. No position data
- C. Unknown (?)
- D. Alone
- E. Cemetery. 557/495. Disturbed

Burial 16
- A. Male (?), adult
- B. prone, extended ca. 90°
- C. Unknown
- D. Alone
- E. Cemetery. 555/496. Disturbed

Burial 17
- A. Female(?), 30+
- B. Prone, extended, ca. 90°
- C. Unknown
- D. Alone
- E. Cemetery. 555/496. Disturbed

Burial 18
- A. Female, ca. 30
- B. Prone, extended, 110°
- C. V.1: Yellow-white squash effigy bowl. At feet
  V.2: Yellow-white exterior, Matadamas Orange interior hemispherical bowl. At feet.
  V.3: Small San José Black-on-white hemispherical bowl. Inside V.1
  V.4: Small S.J. Black-on-white cylinder. Inside V.1
- D. Alone
- E. Cemetery. 555/494

Burial 20-1
- A. Male, ca. 30
- B. Prone, flexed, 90°
- C. V.1: Small Black-on-white cylinder with raspada design. Just to N. of feet
  V.2: Small Black-on-white hemispherical bowl. At head
- D. Accompanied by one secondary burial, 20-2, which is female, ca. 20. Skull of 20-2 is at feet of 20-1, long bones of 20-2 scattered over back of 20-1.
- E. Cemetery. 557/492. Burial 20-1 was also covered by four flat stones, largest of which is ca. 40 x 40 x 2 cm

Burial 21
- A. Female, 20–25
- B. Prone, extended 80°
- C. V.1. Small orange hemispherical bowl
  V.2.: Larger orange hemispherical bowl
  V.3: Large yellow-white tecomate
  V.4: Small vertical walled yellow-white bowl with incised designs and red paint
  V.5: ½ of a full-sized jar
  Obj. 1: Large, hollow, seated figurine
  Offerings under and around knees
- D. Alone
- E. Cemetery. 556/497

Burial 24-1
- A. Female, ca. 25
- B. Prone, extended, 90°
- C. Obj.1: Thin, 3-piece magnetite line-break motif (probably an inlay) under chest
  Obj. 2: Greenstone beads in mouth
- D. Associated with Burial 24-2. The two were buried together in the same grave. Both primary burials.
- E. Cemetery. 555/492.

Burial 24-2
- A. Male, ca. 25
- B. Prone, extended, 95°
- C. V.1: Large Leandro Gray cylinder with raspada were-jaguar motif
  V.2: Large orange hemispherical bowl
  V.3: Large yellow-white hemispherical bowl/tecomate
  V.4: Large orange outleaned wall bowl
  V.5: Small orange hemispherical bowl
  V.6: Small squash effigy bowl
  All vessels piled along left humerus
  Obj.1: Small, crude obsidian blade
  Left lower arm
- D. Buried together with Burial 24-1, as above. Both primary
- E. Cemetery. 555/492

Burial 29
- A. Male(?), adult
- B. Prone, extended, ca. 90°
- C. Unknown
- D. Alone
- E. Cemetery. 557/496. Disturbed by later intrusion. Only legs remain

Burial 30
- A. Female(?), 40+

	B.	No data
	C.	Unknown
	D.	Alone(?)
	E.	Cemetery. 556/495. Badly disturbed and mixed. Only loose bones remain
Burial 31	A.	Female, ca. 20
	B.	Prone, extended, ca. 90°
	C.	Unknown
	D.	Alone(?)
	E.	Cemetery. 556/494. Badly disturbed. Only upper body remains
Burial 32	A.	Sex(?), child
	B.	No position data
	C.	Unknown
	D.	Alone(?)
	E.	Cemetery. 657/495. Badly disturbed. Only loose bones remain
Burial 33	A.	Female, 30+
	B.	Prone, extended, ca. 90°
	C.	No offerings
	D.	Alone
	E.	Cemetery. 555/495. Poor bone preservation
Burial 34	A.	Male, adult
	B.	Prone, extended, ca. 280°
	C.	No offerings
	D.	Alone
	E.	Cemetery. 557/498. Unusual orientation. Absence of offerings makes dating questionable. Could be Ia as easily as Early San José. Lower legs missing
Burial 35	A.	Female, adult
	B.	Prone, extended, 88°
	C.	V.1: Medium yellow-white cylinder fragment. Over neck V.2: Large yellow-white hemispherical bowl. Under knees Obj. 1, 2: Small, solid figurines in Olmec style, Obj. 1 at right femur, Obj. 2 inside V.2
	D.	Alone
	E.	Cemetery. 557/497
Burial 37	A.	Sex(?), ca. 14
	B.	Prone, extended, 100°
	C.	V.1: Large yellow-white hemispherical bowl. At head V.2: Small orange hemispherical bowl. At left hip
	D.	Alone
	E.	Pit grave
	F.	Cemetery. 557/498. Slightly disturbed by later intrusion. Poor bone preservation
Burial 38	A.	Sex(?), ca. 20
	B.	Prone, flexed, 115°
	C.	V.1: Small sooted Fidencio Coarse jar. At feet
	D.	Alone
	E.	Cemetery. 555/449
Burial 39	A.	Male(?), early 20's
	B.	Prone, possibly flexed, 111°
	C.	V.1: Small orange hemispherical bowl, ca. 20 cm to N of feet. Association slightly questionable V.2: Large orange cylinder with pairs of small holes spaced around rim. At head V.3: Half of a full-sized Fidencio Coarse jar. At head V.4: Large orange hemispherical bowl. At head
	D.	Alone
	E.	Cemetery. 554/499. Slightly disturbed. From area with many closely packed burials. Skull and fragments of limbs remain
Burial 40	A.	Male, adult
	B.	Disarticulated burial
	C.	See Burial 41
	D.	Secondary accompaniment for Burial 41
	E.	Cemetery. 553/500. Skull of Burial 40 rests on feet of Burial 41. Long bones piled over back of Burial 41. Not clear if this is a real secondary accompaniment or a primary burial disturbed by Burial 41
Burial 41	A.	Female, ca. 25
	B.	Prone, extended, 99°
	C.	V.1: Large yellow-white tecomate. At left side of head V.2: Small orange hemispherical bowl. At left shoulder V.3: Same as V.2. At right side of head V.4: Large orange hemispherical bowl. Fragments at left hip. Not restorable V.5: Medium orange hemispherical bowl. Fragments at left elbow. Not restorable Obj. 1: Small greenstone celt ca. 30 cm from right shoulder, associated with long bones that may belong to Burial 40 *Note:* It seems most likely that V.4, V.5, and Obj.1 were originally associated with Burial 40
	D.	Accompanied by one secondary burial (Burial 40, male, adult)
	E.	Cemetery. 553/499. In area with many closely packed burials. Some associations therefore questionable
Burial 42	A.	Female (?), 20's
	B.	Prone, extended, 92°
	C.	V.1: Small Fidencio Coarse jar. At right elbow V.2. Small, black-on-white hemispherical bowl. Between femurs V.3: Large orange cylinder. Over right knee V.4: Small Leandro Gray(?) hemispherical bowl. Right knee V.5: Small orange hemispherical bowl. Right lower leg V.6: Same as V.5. Right lower leg V.7: Tiny finger-molded jar. Inside V.2 Obj.1: Lower half (legs) of small, solid figurine. Left pelvis

APPENDIX III

          Obj.2: Half of broken ground stone (U motif?) pendant. Inside V.2
    D. Alone
    E. Cemetery. 554/499. Directly under Burial 39 and beside Burial 41, although all three are separate and independent burials

Burial 43
    A. Sex(?), 10–11
    B. Prone, extended, 88°
    C. V.1: Small orange hemispherical bowl at right knee
    D. Alone
    E. Cemetery. 554/499. This is the youngest individual recovered from the cemetery

Burial 44-1
    A. Male, adult
    B. Prone, extended, ca. 110°
    C. Unknown
    D. Alone
    E. Cemetery. 551/489. Disturbed by later feature. Missing from knees up

Burial 44-2
    A. Male, ca. 30
    B. Prone, extended(?), 98°
    C. No offerings
    D. Alone
    E. Cemetery. 551/489. Lower part disturbed by Burial 44-3. Legs displaced

Burial 44-3
    A. Female, 20–25
    B. Prone, extended, 96°
    C. No offerings
    D. Alone
    E. Cemetery. 551/490

Burial 44-4
    A. Male, adult
    B. Supine, extended(?), ca. 270°
    C. Unknown
    D. Alone
    E. Cemetery. 551/490. Underlies Burials 44-1, 2,3. Very badly disturbed. Only ribs, spine, and upper arm left

Burial 45
    A. Male(?), 40+
    B. Prone, extended, 93°
    C. V.1: Small specular red squash effigy bowl. At right hip
       V.2: Large straight-necked jar. Red paint on neck. Over knees
       V.3: Half of a large Orange outleaned wall bowl. Over head
    D. Alone
    E. Cemetery. 553/499

Burial 49
    A. Male, ca. 40
    B. Prone, extended, 107°
    C. Stone metate fragment leaned against top of head.
    D. Alone
    E. Cemetery. 554/497

Burial 50
    A. Sex(?), adult
    B. Prone, extended, 97°
    C. No offerings
    D. Alone
    E. Cemetery. 555/498. Undisturbed, but poor bone condition

Burial 51
    A. Male(?), adult
    B. Prone, extended, 93°
    C. V.1: Large orange hemispherical bowl
    D. Alone
    E. Cemetery. 557/497. Undisturbed but poor bone preservation

Burial 52
    A. Sex(?), adult
    B. Prone, extended, 95°
    C. No offerings
    D. Alone
    E. Cemetery. 556/498. Undisturbed, but very poor bone preservation

Burial 53
    A. Sex(?), sub-adult
    B. Disarticulated. Skull only
    C. V.1: Large yellow-white cylinder
       V.1a: Small orange hemispherical bowl inside V.1
       V.2: Small orange tecomate with thin line incised around rim
    D. Unknown
    E. Cemetery. 556/497. Very badly disturbed. Skull and vessels clustered in one small area, covered with piece of stone metate. Other small stone slabs also scattered in area

Burial 54
    A. Female(?), 20–40
    B. Prone, extended, 97°
    C. V.1: Tall, yellow-white cylinder. Mouth twice as wide as base. At right shoulder
    D. Alone
    E. Cemetery. 554/494

Burial 55
    A. Sex(?), young adult
    B. Prone, extended, 94°
    C. V.1: Large yellow-white outleaned wall bowl. Along left side
       V.2: Medium orange outleaned wall bowl. Along left side
    D. Alone
    E. Cemetery. 559/497. Undisturbed, but poor bone preservation

Burial 57
    A. Female, ca. 40
    B. Prone, extended, 90°
    C. V.1: Small yellow-white outleaned wall bowl. At head
       V.2: Small orange outleaned wall bowl. Inside V.1
       V.3: Small orange hemispherical bowl
       V.4: Medium orange hemispherical bowl At head
    D. Alone
    E. Cemetery. 560/492

Burial 58
    A. Male, 30's
    B. Prone, extended(?), 103°
    C. Unknown
    D. Alone
    E. Cemetery. 559/492. Very badly disturbed and poor bone preservation

Burial 60
    A. Female, ca. 20
    B. Prone, extended, 95°
    C. V.1: Half of a full-sized Fidencio Coarse jar Left side of head
       V.2: Medium orange outleaned wall bowl. At top of head

V.3: Small Leandro Gray cylinder. Left side of head
D. Alone
E. Cemetery. 559/494

Burial 61
A. Female(?), 25–29
B. Prone, extended, 97°
C. No offerings
D. Alone
E. Cemetery. 559/494. Lower legs missing

Burial 62
A. Male, 35–40
B. Prone, extended, 102°
C. No offerings
D. Alone
E. Cemetery. 560/493

Burial 63
A. Sex(?), adult
B. Prone, extended, ca. 93°
C. V.1: Small yellow-white exterior, orange interior, hemispherical bowl. Right hip
D. Alone
E. Cemetery. 557/495. Badly disturbed. Only legs left

Burial 64
A. Female, ca. 60
B. prone, extended, 276°
C. V.1: Large piece of Fidencio Coarse(?) jar. Under right lower leg
D. Alone
E. Cemetery. 559/493. This burial *may* not be early San José. Its dating is questionable. If it is early San José, orientation is odd. It might also be Monte Albán Ia.

Burial 65
A. Female(?), 40+
B. Prone, extended, 108°
C. No offerings(?)
D. Alone
E. Cemetery. 554/497. Only skull, left arm, femurs are present

Burial 66
A. Sex(?), adult
B. Disarticulated
C. Unknown
D. Unknown
E. Cemetery. 559/496. Badly disturbed. Only a heap of loose bone

Burial 67
A. Sex(?), adult
B. Prone, extended, ca. 90°
C. Unknown
D. Alone(?)
E. Cemetery. 559/496. Badly disturbed and poorly preserved. Only fragments of legs and one arm left

Burial 69
A. Sex(?), adult
B. Disarticulated
C. V.1: Small Fidencio Coarse jar
D. Alone(?)
E. Cemetery. 560/496. Badly disturbed. Only a heap of disjointed long bones and V.1

Burial 70-1
A. Female, 35+
B. Disarticulated
C. Unknown
D. Unclear if originally associated with 70-2.
E. Cemetery. 553/498. Either badly disturbed and reburied or a secondary burial. Remains of 70-1 and 70-2 in the same heap

Burial 70-2
A. Sex(?), 12–13
B. Disarticulated
C. Unknown
D. Unclear if originally associated with 70-1
E. Cemetery. 553/498. See Burial 70-1

Burial 74
A. Female, 20–25
B. Prone, extended, 102°
C. V.1: Small, tall-necked, black-on-white bottle. At left elbow
D. Alone. Distinct from 70-1, 2
E. Cemetery. 553/496

Burial 75
A. Male(?), adult
B. Prone, flexed, 98°
C. No offerings
D. Alone
E. Cemetery, 552/500

Burial 76
A. Male, 25–30
B. Prone, extended, 95°
C. V.1: Miniature Fidencio Coarse(?) jar. At left hip. Not restorable
V.2: Medium orange hemispherical bowl. At left shoulder
V.3: Small Leandro Gray(?) jar. At top of head
D. Accompanied by four secondary burial skulls placed along right side. Long bones from these secondary burials are laid over back of Burial 76. Ages and sexes of these secondary burials are: 76-2=sex(?), 40+; 76-3=M(?), 30–40; 76-4=sex(?), adult; 76-5=sex(?), adult.
E. Cemetery. 552/499. Bone preservation is not good here

Burial 77
A. Sex(?), less than 6 months
B. On right side, folded at waist; ca. 0°
C. No offerings
D. Alone
E. Probably associated with House 9. Seems to have been buried in trash heap associated with that house. *Not a cemetery burial*

Burial 78
A. Female(?), adult
B. Prone, extended(?), 98°
C. No offerings(?)
D. Alone
E. Cemetery. 552/498. Badly disturbed. Only skull and arms left

Burial 79-1
A. Male, 40+
B. Prone, flexed, 94°
C. V.2: Small orange hemispherical bowl. At feet
V.4: Small Fidencio Coarse jar. At left elbow
These two vessels are definitely associated with 79-1
V.8: Fragment of medium orange hemispherical bowl
V.8a: Fragment of small orange hemispherical bowl

APPENDIX III

These two fragments are questionably associated with 79-1
D. Accompanied by secondary burial 79-2, an adult of unknown sex
E. Cemetery. 551/499. Burial is also covered with small stone slabs

Burial 79-3
A. Sex(?), ca. 15
B. Disarticulated
C. Unknown
D. Unknown association
E. Cemetery. 551/498. Skull only. Body seems to have been disturbed by Burial 79-1. *May* have been associated with Burial 79-4

Burial 79-4
A. Male(?), adult
B. Disarticulated, was prone, ca. 90°
C. V.1: Small orange jar
V.3: Small orange hemispherical bowl
V.5: Small black-on-white squash effigy bowl
V.6.: Small orange hemispherical bowl
All vessels along left side
D. Possibly accompanied by Burial 79-3, of unknown sex, ca. 15. Association is unclear
E. Cemetery. 551/498. Skull only. Body seems to have been badly disturbed by Burial 79-1. Only skull and a few long bones remain

Burial 79-5
A. Sex(?), old adult
B. Prone, extended, 98°
C. V.7: Large orange hemispherical bowl. Under left femur
D. Alone(?)
E. Cemetery. 551/498. *May* have been a double burial with 79-4, but this is unclear. This burial is the lowermost of an area with many close-packed, overlapping burials

Burial 80-1
A. Female, adult
B. Prone, extended, 100°
C. V.1: Small orange hemispherical bowl
V.2: Same as V.1.
V.3: Large orange cylinder with three pairs of holes around rim
V.4: Small black-on-white hemispherical bowl or tecomate. Not restorable
Obj. 1 and 2: Two deer bone awls, 9 and 10 cm long, found inside V.1
V.1 and V.2 at head. V.3 and V.4 over and around pelvis
D. Accompanied by secondary burials 80-2, of unknown sex, ca. 30-35; and 80-3, an adult of unknown sex. Skull of 80-2 by pelvis of 80-1. Long bones of 80-2 and 80-3 piled over back and legs of 80-1
E. Cemetery. 550/499. Burials 80-2 and 80-3 are intermixed and seem to represent a male and a female adult

Burial 82
A. Sex(?), 20-40
B. Prone, extended, ca. 90°
C. V.1: Yellow-white cylinder with raspada Olmecoid fire-serpent motif. Not restorable
D. Alone
E. Cemetery. 560/497. Very poor bone preservation

Burial 84
A. Female(?), 20-30
B. Prone, extended, ca. 90°
C. V.1: Round-bodied, high-necked specular red(?) bottle. At head
V.2: Medium yellow-white cylinder. At head. Not restorable
D. Alone
E. Cemetery, 559/498. Very poor bone preservation

Burial 85
A. Sex(?), 15-20
B. Prone, extended, ca. 90°
C. V.1: Large orange hemispherical bowl
V.2: Miniature jar
Obj. 1: Ceramic bird-effigy whistle
D. Alone
E. Cemetery. 560/490. Poor bone preservation

Burial 86
A. Sex(?), adult
B. Prone extended, ca. 90°
C. V.1: Medium Fidencio Coarse jar
V.2: Large cylinder. Badly eroded and unrestorable
V.3: Large bowl or jar bottom
V.4: Large bowl(?)
V.5: Small red(?) hemispherical bowl.
All vessels very badly disturbed and very badly eroded. None restorable
D. Alone
E. Cemetery. 560/495. Badly disturbed and poor bone preservation

Burial 87
A. Sex(?), adult
B. Prone, extended, ca. 90°
C. V.1: Small specular red hemispherical bowl. At right elbow. Not restorable
D. Alone
E. Cemetery. 560/499. Very poor bone preservation. Skull missing

Burial 88
A. Male, 30-40
B. Prone, extended, 90°
C. No offerings
D. Alone
E. Cemetery. 551/495. Later intrusion destroyed legs from mid-femur

Burial 89
A. Sex(?), 20-25
B. Position unclear. Very possibly flexed; ca. 90°
C. V.1: Small jar
V.2: Same as V.1
V.3: Medium jar, not restorable
V.4: Medium bowl, not restorable
V.5: Same as V.4
All vessels are very badly eroded.
D. Alone(?)
E. Cemetery. 561/497. Badly disturbed. Also poor bone preservation

Burial 90
A. Sex(?), adult
B. Prone, flexed, ca. 100°
C. Unclear may be one plain gray cylinder
D. unclear

Burial 91
- A. Sex(?), adult
- B. Prone, flexed. Orientation unclear
- C. V.1: Black/white hemispherical bowl
  V.2: Black/white tecomate
- D. unknown
- E. Cemetery 556/496. Badly disturbed

Burial 92
- A. Sex(?), adult
- B. Prone, extended, ca. 90°
- C. unclear
- D. unclear
- E. Cemetery 557/496. Badly disturbed.

Late Guadalupe Burials

Burial 47
- A. Female(?), ca. 14
- B. Prone, extended, 89°
- C. V.1: Buff (misfired gray?) eccentric rim bowl ("acorn bowl"). Covering feet
  Obj. 1: Stone bead against left mandible
- D. Alone
- E. Buried atop Structure 12. Seems to have been just under upper floor level

Burial 56
- A. Male, 40+
- B. Prone, extended, 106°
- C. Obj. 1, 2: Small marine shell discs in chest area (under body)
  Obj. 3: Bone awl or flaker among ribs (probably under body)
- D. Alone
- E. Buried atop Structure 12. Seems to have been just under upper floor level. Very near and slightly below Burial 47

Bural 59
- A. Female, ca. 30
- B. prone, extended, 102°
- C. V.1: Small gray outleaned wall bowl at feet
- D. Alone
- E. Buried atop Structure 12. Seems to have been just under upper floor level. Just below Burials 47 and 56. Pit grave with cover of five stone slabs (ca. 75 x 40 x 5 cm). Body evidently wrapped in coarsely woven *petate* and covered with yellowish clay

Burial 68
- A. Female, ca. 40
- B. Prone, extended, 97°
- C. V.1: Medium yellow-white wide-mouthed cylinder at head
  Obj. 1: Chert projectile point under (in?) chest
  Obj. 2-5: Several greenstone beads in chest/neck area and in mouth
- D. Alone
- E. Buried atop Structure 12. Seems to have been just under upper floor level. Same general area as preceding three burials

Rosario Burials (not illustrated)

Burial 10
- A. Sex(?), ca.2
- B. Supine, extended, 290°
- C. V.1: Plain gray cylinder
  V.2: Small plain gray wide-mouth jar
  V.3: Small gray hemispherical bowl with incised double crescent motifs on rim
  All arranged along right femur
- D. Alone
- E. Buried in patio of Household Unit R-1.

Burial 36
- A. Sex(?), less than 1
- B. Prone, extended, 188°
- C. V.1: Large gray outleaned wall bowl. Plain
  V.2: Small gray outleaned wall bowl. Plain
  V.3: Small hemispherical bowl. Red paint inside and out
  V.1. inverted over head. V.2 and V.3 at left shoulder
- D. Alone
- E. Buried in patio of Household Unit R-1

Monte Albán Ia Burials

Burial 1
- A. Female(?), ca. 20
- B. Supine, extended, 90°
- C. V.1: Outleaned wall bowl. Cream slip, red painted design on bottom
  V.2: Hemispherical bowl. Plain brown. Both inverted over face
  Obj. 1: Shell disc bead covered with red ochre at right elbow
- D. Alone
- E. Household Unit Ia-1

Burial 26
- A. Male, adult
- B. Prone, extended, 287°
- C. Obj. 1: Stone bead with skull fragments
- D. Alone
- E. Household Unit Ia-2

Burial 46
- A. Sex(?), adult
- B. Supine, extended, 272°
- C. V.1: Small red tripod plate
  V.2: Large red tripod plate
  V.3: Gray flat bottomed jar(?). Not restorable
  V.4: Same as V.3, with incised decoration
  V.5: Gray outleaned wall bowl. Undecorated
  V.6: Small gray bowl, fluted rim, annular base
  V.7: Small red wide-mouth jar
  V.8: Large red bowl
  Vessels over and under knees
  Obj. 1, 2: Quartz beads under skull
  Obj. 3: Small stone pestle under V.2
- D. Alone
- E. Household Unit Ia-2

Burial 72-1
- A. Male(?), ca. 40
- B. Supine, extended, 90°
- C. V.1: Yellow-white incised wide-mouthed jar between legs
- D. Accompanied by one secondary burial (72-2). Skull by right ilium of 72-1; long bones between lower legs of 72-1. 72-2 is an adult of unknown sex
- E. Household Unit Ia-2

Burial 81
- A. Male, 30-40
- B. Supine, extended (legs slightly bent), 90°.

APPENDIX III

Buried in refuse area in reused circular pit (Feature 106)
- C. V.1: Miniature bowl. Poorly finished. Among ribs
  Obj. 1: Tiny, crude figurine. On left shoulder. Questionable offering
- D. Alone
- E. Near Household Unit Ia-1

Monte Albán Ic Burials

Burial 4
- A. Sex(?), 4–6
- B. Supine, extended, 280°
- C. V.1: G–12-type gray outleaned wall bowl
  V.2: Flat-bottomed gray hemispherical bowl
  V.3: Same as V.2
  All vessels along left arm
- D. Alone
- E. Household Unit Ic-1

Burial 5-1
- A. Sex(?), 40 ± 10
- B. Disturbed; no positive data. Buried in tomb which is oriented east–west
- C. V.1: Miniature wide-mouthed jar. Plain
  V.2: Small dish. Gray. Plain
  V.3: Gray outleaned wall bowl (G–12 in Caso, Bernal, and Acosta [1967] typology)
  V.4: Small gray jar. Plain
  V.5: Gray spouted jar. Incised decoration. Composite silhouette
  V.6: Gray spouted jar with appliqué monkey face
  V.7: Gray high-necked bottle. Decorated with crude pinched face and incised lines
  V.8: Miniature G–12-style vessel. No combing
  V.9: Gray spouted jar. Incised decoration
  V.10: Gray hemispherical bowl
  V.11: Gray outleaned wall bowl (G–12)
  V.12: Gray spouted jar. Appliqué face and moulded limbs
  V.13: Small red-brown hemispherical bowl
  V.14: Gray spouted jar. Appliqué face. Incised limbs. Composite rim
  V.15: Red-brown hemispherical bowl
  V.16: Gray spouted jar
  V.17: Gray spouted jar. Incised decoration
  V.18: Small gray dish with basal flange
  V.19: Gray spouted jar. Incised decoration
  V.20: Brown vertical-walled bowl
  V.21: Gray spouted jar
  V.22: Gray spouted jar
  V.23: Gray spouted jar
  V.24: Gray spouted jar
  V.25: Gray spouted jar. Incised decoration. Composite silhouette neck
  V.26: Gray spouted jar
  V.27: Gray spouted jar
  V.28: Gray composite silhouette and rim, spouted. Incised decoration
  V.29: Gray spouted jar. Incised decoration
  V.30: Gray outleaned wall bowl
  V.31: Large G–12 outleaned wall bowl
  V.32: Large gray spouted jar. Appliqué face. Incised Lines
  V.33: Gray spouted composite silhouette body *and* rim. Incised decoration.
  V.34: Gray spouted vessel. Incised decoration
  V.35: Gray effigy vessel. Tiger mask, tiger paw spout (whistle inside). Unrestorable
  Obj. 1 & 2: Greenstone beads. Loose in tomb fill. Were probably more before tomb was opened and looted
- D. Burial 5-2 and 5-3 also occupy the tomb; unclear whether all buried at once
- E. Household Unit Ic-1. Adobe-walled tomb with roof of flat stone slabs. Tomb is built into the fill of one of the house platforms there. Bones seem to have been badly disturbed when tomb was reopened, looted, and closed again

Burial 5-2
- A. Female, 35–40
- B. Disturbed; no position data. Tomb
- C. See list of Burial 5 offerings
- D. As above
- E. As above

Burial 5-3
- A. Male(?), ca. 12
- B. No position data. Tomb
- C. See list of Burial 5 offerings
- D. As above
- E. As above

Burial 13
- A. Sex(?), less than 6
- B. Supine, extended, 0°. Buried in trash fill of large oven (Feature 54)
- C. No offerings
- D. Alone
- E. Household Unit Ic-3

Burial 14-1
- A. Sex(?), newborn or fetal
- B. Supine, extended 179°
- C. Large sherd covering face. No offerings
- D. 14-2 possibly buried at same time
- E. Household Unit Ic-1. Buried in front of steps of one platform. Probably a late Ic burial. Seems to post-date use of platform. Seems to be buried with 14-2

Burial 14-2
- A. Sex(?), newborn or fetal
- B. Supine, extended, 25°
- C. No offerings
- D. Burial 14-1 possibly buried at the same time
- E. As above. Lower body missing from later intrusion

Burial 19
- A. Male, 35+
- B. On left side with arms and legs partially drawn up, ca. 90°
- C. Obj.1,2: Two unmatched marine shells; one bivalve (cf. *Megapitaria aurantiaca*), pierced for hanging at valve; one similarly shaped piece cut from unidentified marine gastropod shell
- D. Alone
- E. Household Unit Ic-3. Buried among, but not in, the many ovens there

Burial 25-1
- A. Male, 40+

B. Supine, extended, 265°
C. V.1: G-12-type gray outleaned wall bowl
V.2: Gray spouted bottle
V.3: Buff hemispherical bowl
All vessels along right femur. Not illustrated
Obj. 1: cup or hemispherical bowl made from human skull. On chest of 25-1
D. Accompanied by secondary burial 25-2, a male of about 40. Skull of 25-2 is on chest of 25-1, long bones of 25-2 piled around legs and feet of 25-1.
E. Household Unit Ic-3. Buried among, but not in, the many ovens there

Burial 27
A. Female(?), ca. 40
B. Supine, extended, 278°
C. No offerings
D. Alone
E. Household Unit Ic-4. Dating of this burial somewhat uncertain. It is possibly Ia, probably Ic

Burial 26
A. Sex(?), adult
B. Supine(?), extended, ca. 278°
C. Unknown
D. Alone
E. Same as Burial 27, above. Disturbed and poor bone preservation. Possibly Ia, probably Ic

Burial 71
A. Sex(?), less than 1 year
B. Supine, extended, ca. 270°
C. No offerings
D. Alone
E. Buried in rubbish heap at foot of outer wall of Structure 13

Burial 73
A. Sex(?), fetal or newborn
B. No position data
C. Bones covered by fragment of a black, straight-sided, circular bowl. Not illustrated
D. Alone
E. Buried in rubbish heap at foot of outer wall of Structure 13

Monte Albán V Burials

Burial 48
A. Female, 15-16
B. Seated in circular pit. Facing 295°
C. V.1: Large, coarse basin (*apaxtle*) covering grave
D. Alone
E. Near remains of Monte Alban V house located over ruins of Household Unit Ic-2. Upper incisors of this burial have had notches filed into them

APPENDIX IV

FORMATIVE FIGURINES FROM TOMALTEPEC

Compared to other excavated Formative communities in the area, relatively few figurines were recovered from Tomaltepec. This is especially true of the Early Formative period. Animal figurines are first found in the Middle Formative deposits at Tomaltepec, and they evidently increased in numbers throughout the Late Formative. Abdominal and back cavities on human and animal figurines respectively also seem to make their initial appearance in Late Formative deposits, and the single complete specimen recovered suggests that these cavities were covered by thin clay domes for possible use as whistles.

All figurines and figurine fragments recovered at Tomaltepec are described in terms of the several variables identified in Table 13. Table 14 contains coded descriptions of each figurine and figurine fragment, as well as the household unit and/or other specific provenience of each.

Plates 48–51 contain illustrations of a number of these figurines.

Table 13: Variables Used in Figurine Descriptions

Variable	Variable Name	Variable States	Variable	Variable Name	Variable States
I	Figure represented	0 = undetermined 1 = human 2 = animal 3 = bird 4 = fantastic			4 = helmet 5 = tattoos or body paint 6 = headband 7 = loin cloth 8 = sandals 9 = "combed" hair 10 = nothing
II	Position of the figure	0 = undetermined 1 = standing 2 = lying 3 = seated	V	Sex	0 = undetermined 1 = male 2 = female 3 = pregnant female 4 = sexless
III	Part present	0 = undetermined 1 = arm 2 = leg 3 = head 4 = body 5 = head + body 6 = whole	VI	Clay paste	0 = no data 1 = cream 2 = gray 3 = dark brown
IV	Ornamentation and dress depicted	0 = undetermined 1 = necklace 2 = earspools 3 = deformed head	VII	Size	Maximum dimension in cm

Table 14: Attributes of Formative Figurines Recovered at Tomaltepec

	Provenience	I	II	III	IV	V	VI	VII	Comments (+ = not illustrated)
					EARLY FORMATIVE				
1	Fea. 7 in TL-1	1	0	1	0	1	1	3.2	
2	Fea. 102 in TL-1	1	0	3	0	1	2	2.6	
3	Fea. 109 in ESJ-1	1	0	3	4	2	2	4.1	
4	House 4 in ESJ-2	1	4	4	0	0	2	3.1	Floors D to E
5	House 4 in ESJ-2	0	0	1	0	0	2	4.4	+Floors D to E
6	House 4 in ESJ-2	1	4	4	0	4	2	2.5	+Just below Floor E (last floor)
7	House 4 in ESJ-2	1	0	2	0	0	2	3.9	+Just below Floor E (last floor)
8	Fea. 72 in ESJ-3	1	1	4	1	2	2	3.8	Claw necklace
9	Fea. 72 in ESJ-3	1	0	3	10?	0	2	2.6	+Very poorly preserved
10	Fea. 72 in ESJ-3	1	0	1	0	0	2	2.5	+
11	Fea. 72 in ESJ-3	1	0	1	0	0	2	3.7	+
12	Fea. 112 in ESJ-4	1	4	4	10	2	2	5.1	+
13	Cemetery burial	1	1	6	1,4	4	2	11.2	Olmecoid appearance
14	Cemetery burial	1	3	6	3,4	4	2	12.5	Olmecoid appearance
15	Cemetery burial	1	*	6	2,3,4	0	2	16.3	*A bust in non-Olmecoid style
16	Str. 11 Upper	1	1	4	*	0	2	7.5	*May be necklace or hair (?)
17	Str. 11 refuse	1	1	2	10	0	2	8.6	
18	Str. 11 layer	1	0	3	*	0	2	3.7	*May be helmet or combed hair (?)
19	Str. 11 layer	1	0	1	10	0	2	3.6	
					MIDDLE FORMATIVE				
20	House 5	2	1	5	10	0	2	5.0	
21	House 5	1	0	3	0	0	3	4.8	Yellow-white slip
22	House 5	1	0	3	2,9	0	3	2.8	+
23	House 7	4	0	3	10	0	3	3.0	*Ia midden in Rosario House
24	House 7	1	0	3	2,6	0	3	3.5	*Adorno*: has rim fragment attached
25	House 7	1	0	3	2,4	0	3	4.8	
26	Fea. 50 in R-2	1	0	3	10	0	3	4.0	One slit eye, one round eye.
27	Fea. 50 in R-2	1	0	3	2	0	3	5.0	Wedge-shaped face; common at Tomaltepec
28	Fea. 11 in Ia-1	1	4	4	10	4	2	3.7	
29	Fea. 69 in Ia-2	1	3	4	10	4	3	2.8	
30	Fea. 69 in Ia-2	1	3	4	10	3	3	3.7	2 parallel slashes on each flank
31	Fea. 82 in Ia-2	1	0	3	6	0	3	2.8	+Very crude
32	Fea. 82 in Ia-2	1	4	4	0	2	3	4.5	Slit from genitals across stomach
33	Fea. 74 in Ia-3	1?	0	3	*	0	3	7.7	*Conical "clown's hat"
34	Fea. 74 in Ia-3	1	4	4	10	2	2	3.2	+
35	Fea. 74 in Ia-3	1	4	4	10	2	2	3.2	+
36	Fea. 74 in Ia-3	1	3	4	10	0	2	4.7	+Very crude
37	Fea. 74 in Ia-3	–	–	–	–	–	3	5.1	Clay stamp with incised design; flat with pinched handle on back; see photo
38	Mid. Form. layers Area B	0	0	4	0	0	0	2.3	+
39	Mid. Form. layers Area B	1	0	4	1	0	3	3.6	Claw necklace
40	Mid. Form. layers Area B	1	1	4	0	0	0	4.5	
41	Mid. Form. layers Area B	1	1	4	0	0	0	5.3	+
42	Mid. Form. layers Area B	1	1	4	10	2	3	7.1	Nude female
43	Mid. Form. layers Area B	1	3	4	1?	1	3	4.7	
44	Mid. Form. layers Area D	1	0	5	1	0	1	6.9	
45	Mid. Form. layers Area F	1	0	3	2	0	3	5.9	
46	Mid. Form. layers Area F	1	0	5	0	0	3	5.3	
47	Mid. Form. layers Area F	1	0	5	0	0	3	4.8	
48	Mid. Form. layers Area F	1	0	3	2	0	3	5.2	Wedge-shaped face
49	Mid. Form. layers Area F	1	0	4	1*	2	1	2.4	*Necklace? Collar?
50	Mid. Form. layers Area F	1	1	4	10	3	3	5.0	
51	Mid. Form. layers Area F	1	0	3	0	0	3	4.6	Wedge-shaped face
52	Mid. Form. layers Area F	1	1	4	10	0	0	3.3	
53	Mid. Form. layers Area J	1	1	4	10	0	3	4.9	*Vicinity of Structure 12
54	Mid. Form. layers Area J	1	1	2	10	0	1	8.2	
55	Mid. Form. layers Area J	1	0	2	10	0	1	4.6	
					LATE AND TERMINAL FORMATIVE				
56	Fea. 45 in Ic-1	1	1	4	10	4	2	5.7	+
57	Fea. 45 in Ic-1	1	1	4	7	0	3	4.5	+Possibly painted red
58	Fea. 45 in Ic-1	1	2	0	10	0	3	5.2	+Appliqué fragment (?)

APPENDIX IV

Table 14: continued

	Provenience	I	II	III	IV	V	VI	VII	Comments (+ = not illustrated)
59	Fea.46 in Ic-1	1	1	4	10	2	3	7.5	+Entirely painted red
60	Fea.47 in Ic-1	1	1	4	10	0	2	5.4	
61	Fea.47 in Ic-1	1	1	7	1	0	2	6.5	Abdominal cavity
62	Fea.51 in Ic-1	4	1	6	10	4	2	9.0	+
63	Fea.51 in Ic-1	1	1	4	7	4	2	4.5	+
64	Fea.51 in Ic-1	1	0	3	2,3,4	0	2	4.7	+
65	Fea.51 in Ic-1	1	0	1	10	0	1	5.0	+
66	Fea.51 in Ic-1	2	0	3	10	0	2	6.2	
67	Fea.51 in Ic-1	1	0	2	8	0	2	5.0	+
68	Fea.51 in Ic-1	1	1	4	8	4	2	4.0	Long slit up abdomen
69	Fea.51 in Ic-1	1	4	4	10	4	2	3.8	+Abdominal cavity
70	Fea.51 in Ic-1	1	0	3	5	0	2	3.5	+Appliqué fragment (?)
71	Fea.51 in Ic-1	1	0	1or2	10	0	2	4.5	+
72	Fea.51 in Ic-1	1	0	1or2	10	0	2	2.6	+
73	Fea.51 in Ic-1	1	1	6	10	4	2	8.5	Abdominal cativity
74	Fea.55 in Ic-1	1	1	4	1	4	2	8.0	+
75	Fea.32 in Ic-2	1	1	4	10	4	2	3.8	Abdominal cavity
76	Fea.32 in Ic-2	1	1	4	10	4	2	3.2	Abdominal cavity
77	Fea.32 in Ic-2	1	1	4	10	4	2	5.0	+
78	Fea.32 in Ic-2	1	0	1	10	0	2	4.5	+
79	Fea.32 in Ic-2	3	0	3	10	0	2	3.8	Polished rim adornment
80	Fea.32 in Ic-2	1	1	4	10	2?	2	6.0	
81	Fea.32 in Ic-2	2	2	5	10	0	2	5.0	Back cavity
82	Fea.32 in Ic-2	1	1	4	10	2	2	5.5	+
83	Fea.32 in Ic-2	1	3	4	10	3	2	6.5	
84	Fea.32 in Ic-2	1	1	4	10	3	3	5.1	Abdominal cavity
85	Fea.34 in Ic-2	2	1	4	10	0	2	6.3	
86	Fea.44b in Ic-2	1	1	4	10	2	1	6.1	+Polished
87	Fea.44b in Ic-2	1	0	3	10	0	2	3.9	
88	Fea.44b in Ic-2	1	1	4	10	4	2	5.0	+
89	Fea.53 in Ic-3	1	0	3	5	0	2	4.0	
90	Fea.53 in Ic-3	1	1	4	*	4	2	5.5	*Incised line where legs join body
91	Fea.53 in Ic-3	1	1	5	1,2	2	2	7.5	+
92	Fea.53 in Ic-3	1	1	4	10	0	3	5.0	Slit from navel up
93	Fea.54 in Ic-3	2	2	4	10	0	2	4.5	Back cavity
94	Fea.54 in Ic-3	1	1?	2	8	0	2	3.7	
95	Fea.61 in Ic-3	1	0	3	4	0	2	5.0	Appliqué fragment
96	Fea.66 in Ic-3	1	1	4	*	4	2	4.8	*Large collar or small cape
97	Fea.68 in Ic-3	1	1	6	3or4?	4	2	4.3	
98	Fea.78 in Ic-3	2	2	6	10	0	2	7.5	Back cavity
99	Late Form. Deposits Area B	2	2	6	0	0	2	6.4	
100	Late Form. Deposits Area B	1	1	4	1	0	2	5.8	
101	Late Form. Deposits Area B	1	0	4,2	*	0	2	5.3	*Cavity in one leg; thin clay dome cover
102	Late Form. Deposits Area B	1	1	4	0	4	2	4.2	+
103	Late Form. Deposits Area B	1	1	4	1	0	2	5.6	Abdominal cavity covered by clay dome
104	Late Form. Deposits Area B	1	1	4	1	2?	2	5.3	
105	Late Form. Deposits Area B	1?	0	3	0	0	3	3.0	
106	Late Form. Deposits Area B	1	0	5	0	0	3	5.3	
107	Late Form. Deposits Area B	2	2	4	10	0	3	5.4	
108	Late Form. Deposits Area B	1?	1	4	10	4	0	6.1	+
109	Late Form. Deposits Area B	1	1	4	0	0	3	3.8	
110	Late Form. Deposits Area B	1	1	4	10?	2	0	6.0	+
111	Late Form. Deposits Area B	1	0	3	10	0	3	4.3	
112	Late Form. Deposits Area B	1	1	4,2	10	0	2	4.1	+
113	Late Form. Deposits Area B	1	1	4	*	0	2	3.1	*Large collar or cape
114	Late Form. Deposits Area B	1	0	3	2,4	0	3	4.7	
115	Late Form. Deposits Area B	1	1	2	8	0	2	2.0	
116	Late Form. Deposits Area B	1	1	5	2,4	0	3	3.1	
117	Late Form. Deposits Area B	1	0	4	10	0	2	4.6	
118	Late Form. Deposits Area B	1	1	2	8	0	2	6.2	
119	Late Form. Deposits Area B	1	1	4,2	*	0	2	5.8	+*Groove where leg joins body; loincloth?
120	Late Form. Deposits Area B	1	0	1?	10	0	0	4.9	+
121	Late Form. Deposits Area B	3	0	5	10	0	2	5.3	
122	Late Form. Deposits Area B	1	1	4,2	*	0	2	6.0	*Same kind of groove as #119

Table 14: continued

	Provenience	I	II	III	Variable IV	V	VI	VII	Comments (+ = not illustrated)
123	Late Form. Deposits Area D	1	1	4	7	0	2	3.9	
124	Late Form. Deposits Area D	1	0	*	8	0	2	4.6	*Foot of large hollow figurine
125	Late Form. Deposits Area D	1	1	4,2	10	0	0	4.3	+
126	Late Form. Deposits Area D	1	0	*	1?	2?	2	4.0	*Possibly had movable head; see photo
127	Late Form. Deposits Area D	1	0	2	10	0	0	4.5	+
128	Late Form. Deposits Area D	1	1	4	*	0	3	6.3	*Wide collar or cape
129	Late Form. Deposits Area D	2	3	5	10	0	2	4.9	Handle or adornment
130	Late Form. Deposits Area D	1	1	4,2	10	0	2	5.0	Abdominal cavity
131	Late Form. Deposits Area D	2	3	5	*	0	2	6.3	*Incised & dotted band across back; back cavity
132	Late Form. Deposits Area D	1	1	4,2	10	0	0	4.8	+
133	Late Form. Deposits Area D	1	1?	5	10	2?	2	5.2	
134	Late Form. Deposits Area D	1	1	2	8	0	0	3.1	+
135	Late Form. Deposits Area E	1	0	3	10	0	2	5.3	
136	Late Form. Deposits Area E	1	1	4,2	10	0	0	4.2	+
137	Late Form. Deposits Area E	1	0	4	*	2	2	5.0	*Necklace or collar on shoulders
138	Late Form. Deposits Area E	1	1	4	10	0	0	4.0	+
139	Late Form. Deposits Area E	1	1	4	1	0	2	4.1	
140	Late Form. Deposits Area J	1	1	4	1	0	0	3.2	+
141	Late Form. Deposits Area J	2	0	3	10	0	0	5.0	+
142	Late Form. Deposits Area J	1	0	3	4	0	0	4.1	+
143	Late Form. Deposits Area J	1	1	4	*	2	2	8.0	*Child (?) on back
144	Fea.19 in II-1	1	0	3	4,5,6	0	2	4.1	
145	Fea.56 in II-1	1	1	4	4	2	2	4.0	

APPENDIX IV

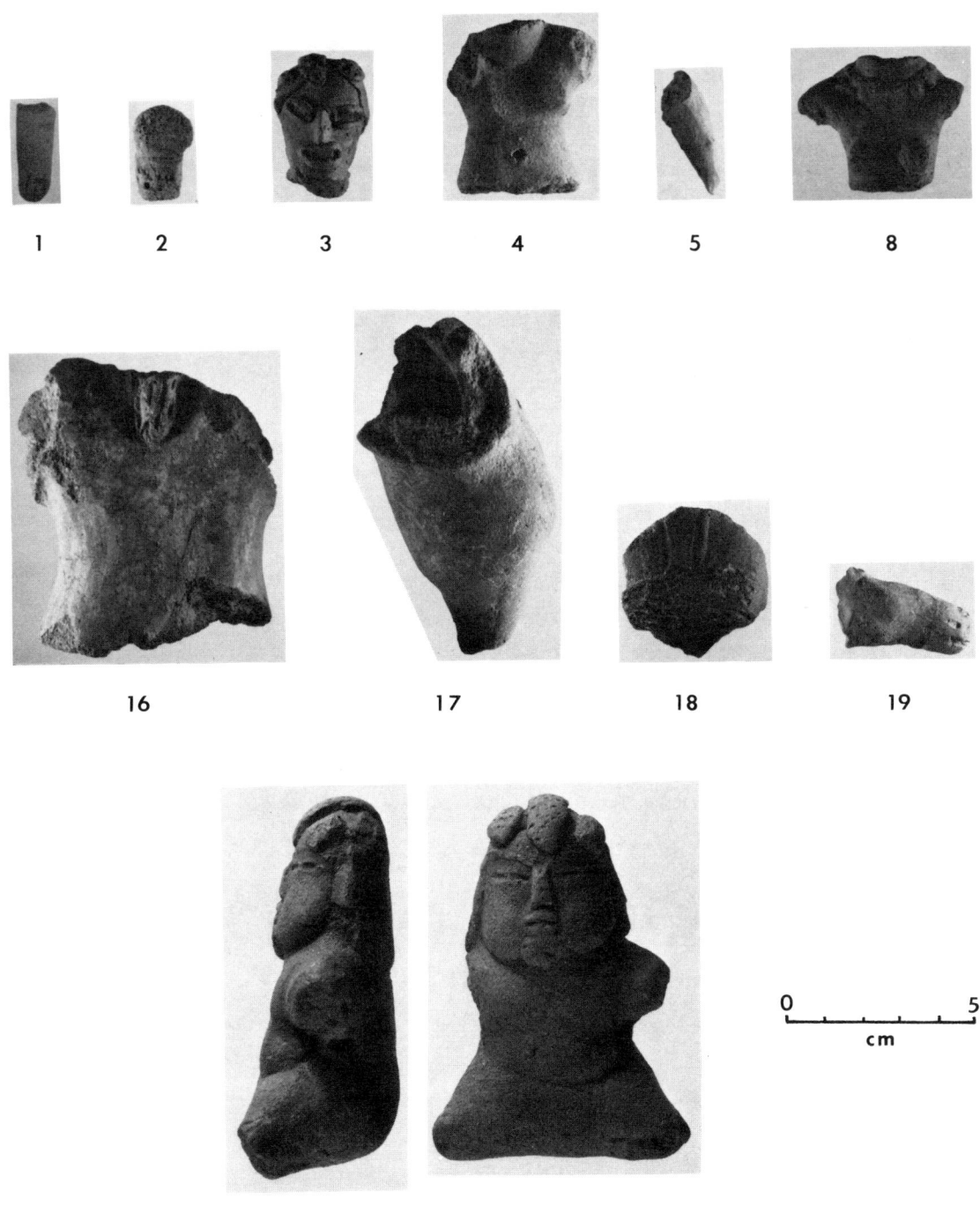

PLATE 48. Figurines from Early Formative proveniences at Tomaltepec, I. Numbers refer to items in Table 14.

14

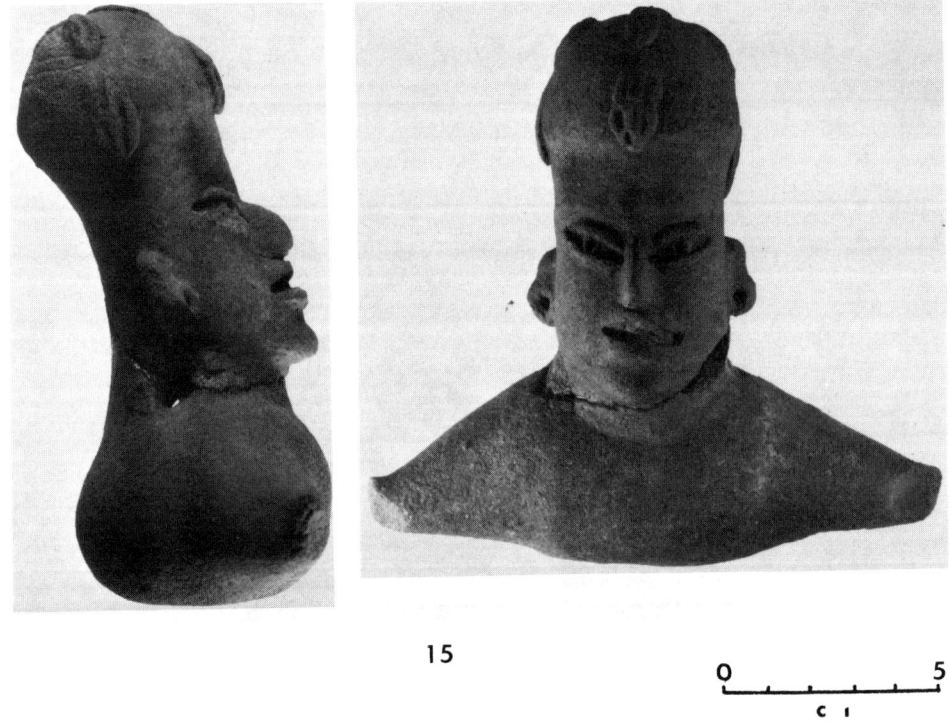

15

PLATE 49. Figurines from Early Formative proveniences at Tomaltepec, II. Numbers refer to items in Table 14.

APPENDIX IV

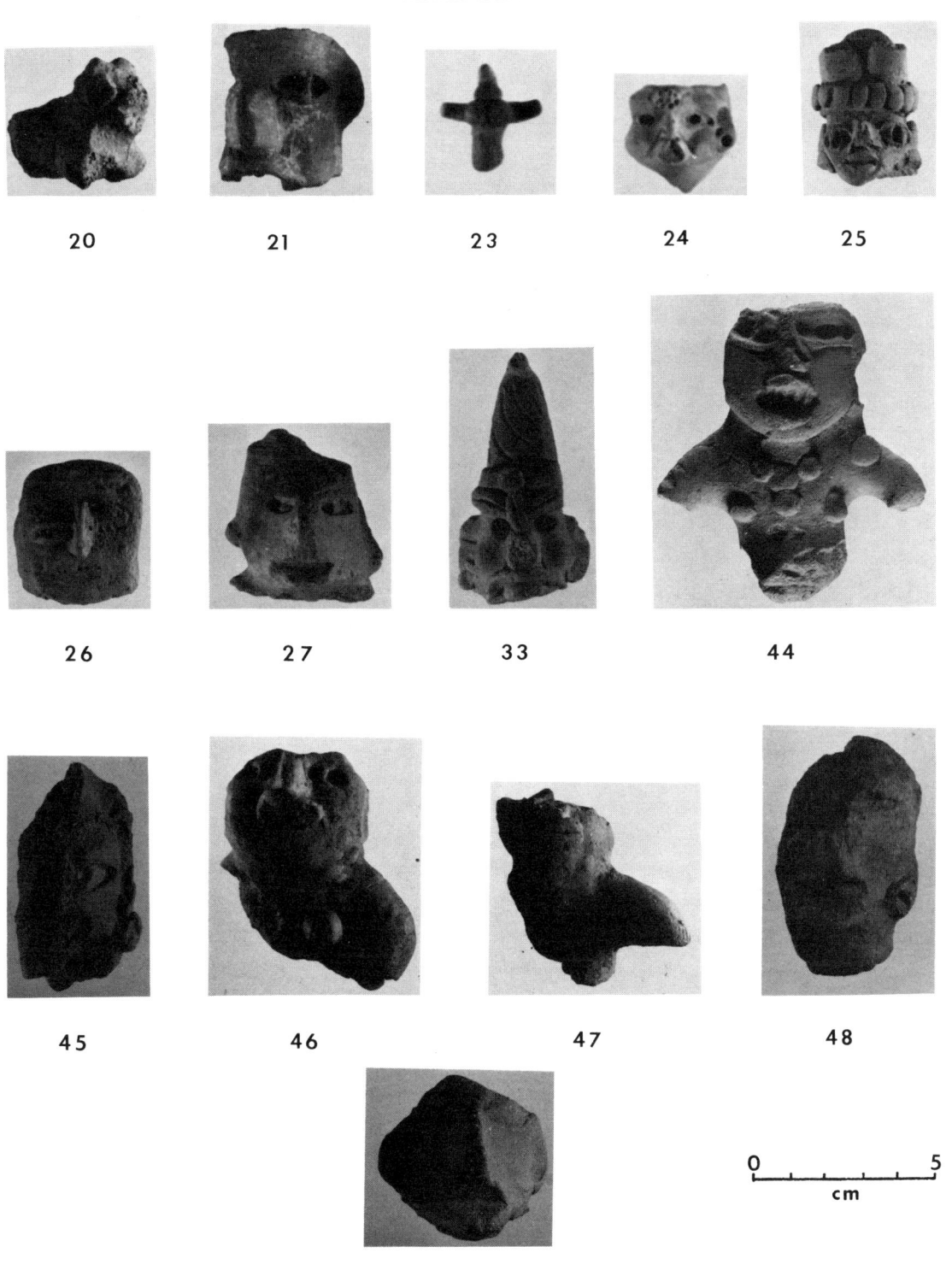

PLATE 50. Figurines from Middle Formative proveniences at Tomaltepec, I. Numbers refer to items in Table 14.

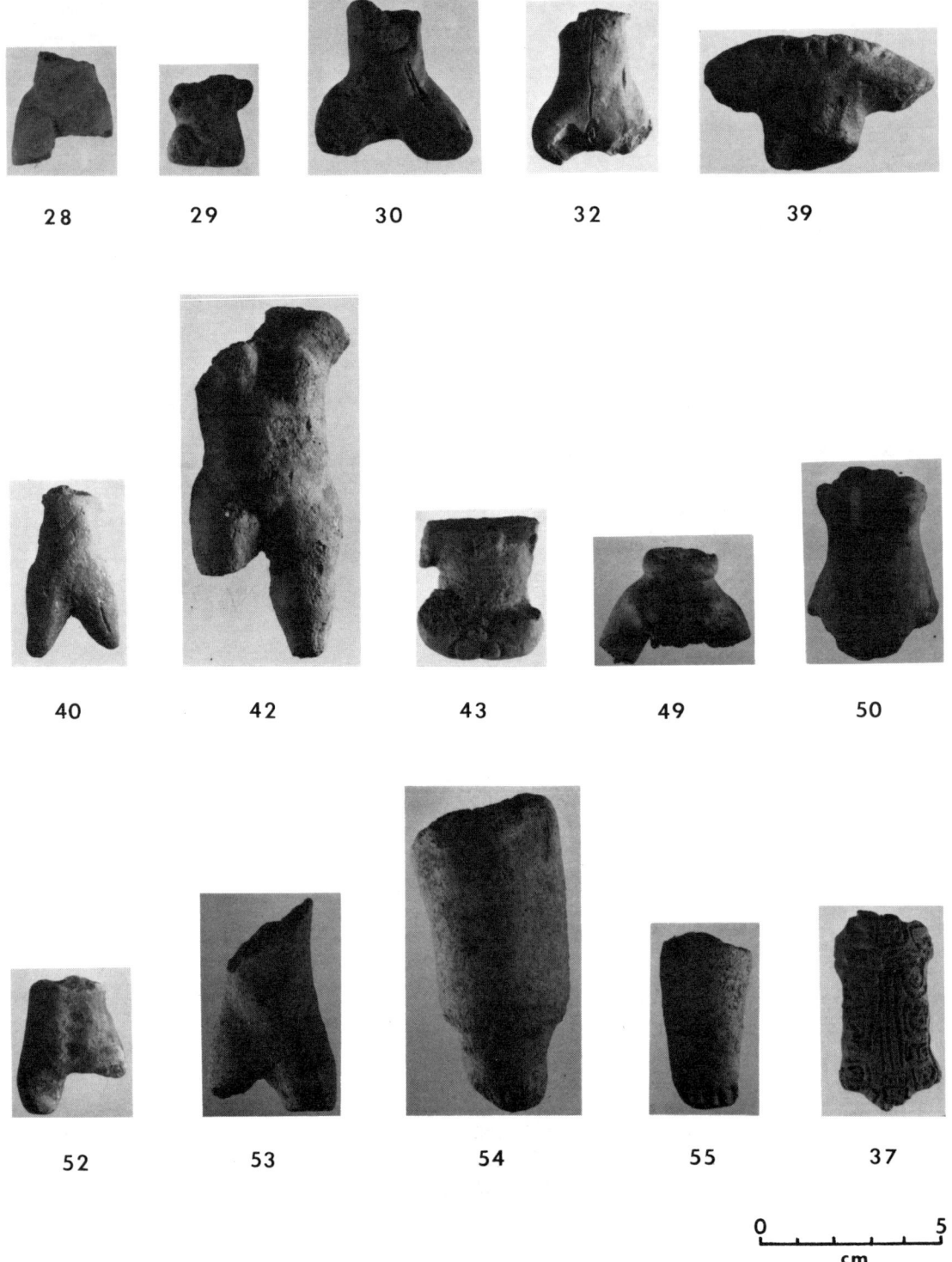

PLATE 51. Figurines from Middle Formative proveniences at Tomaltepec, II. Numbers refer to items in Table 14.

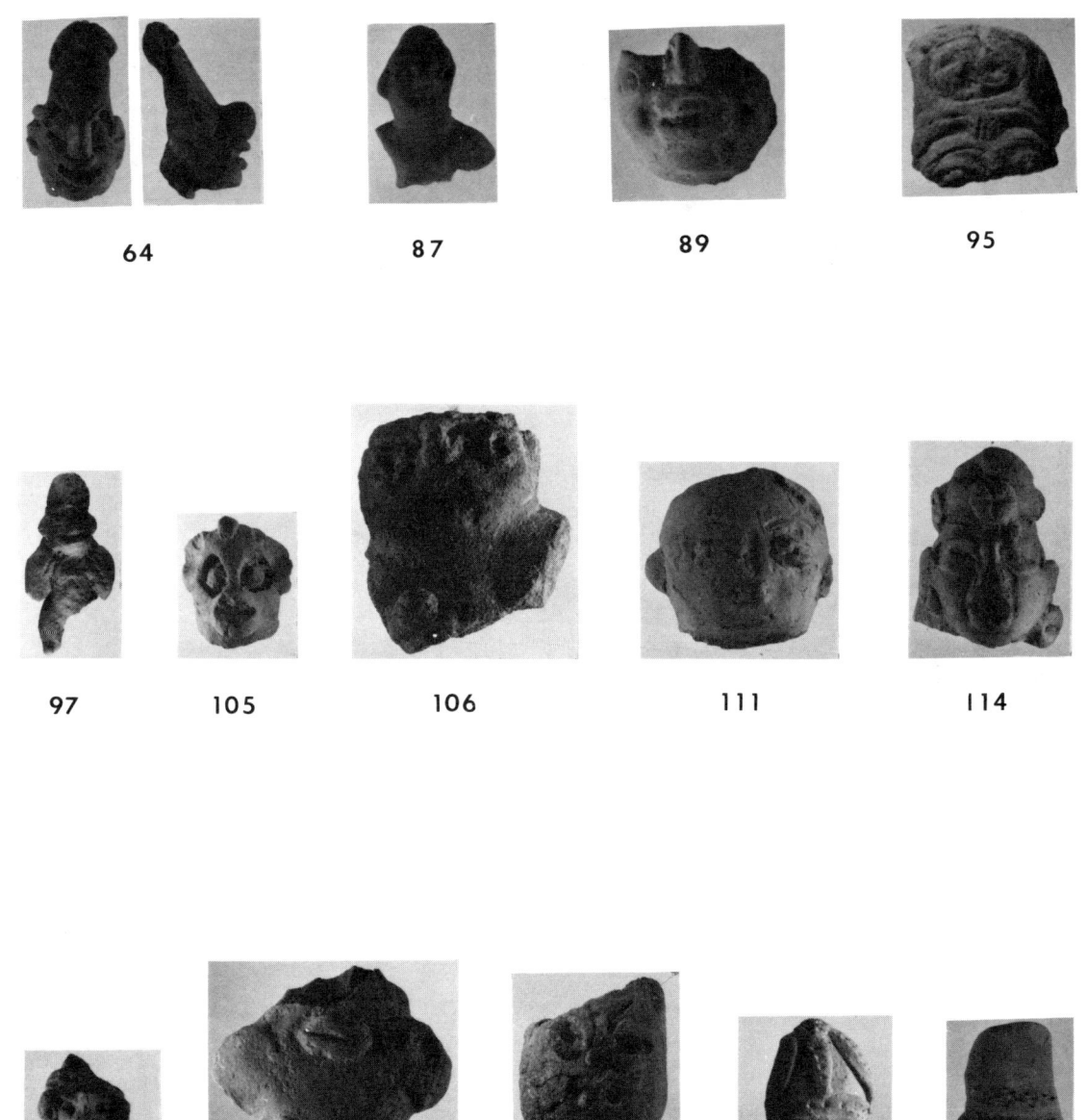

PLATE 52. Figurines from Late Formative proveniences at Tomaltepec, I. Numbers refer to items in Table 14.

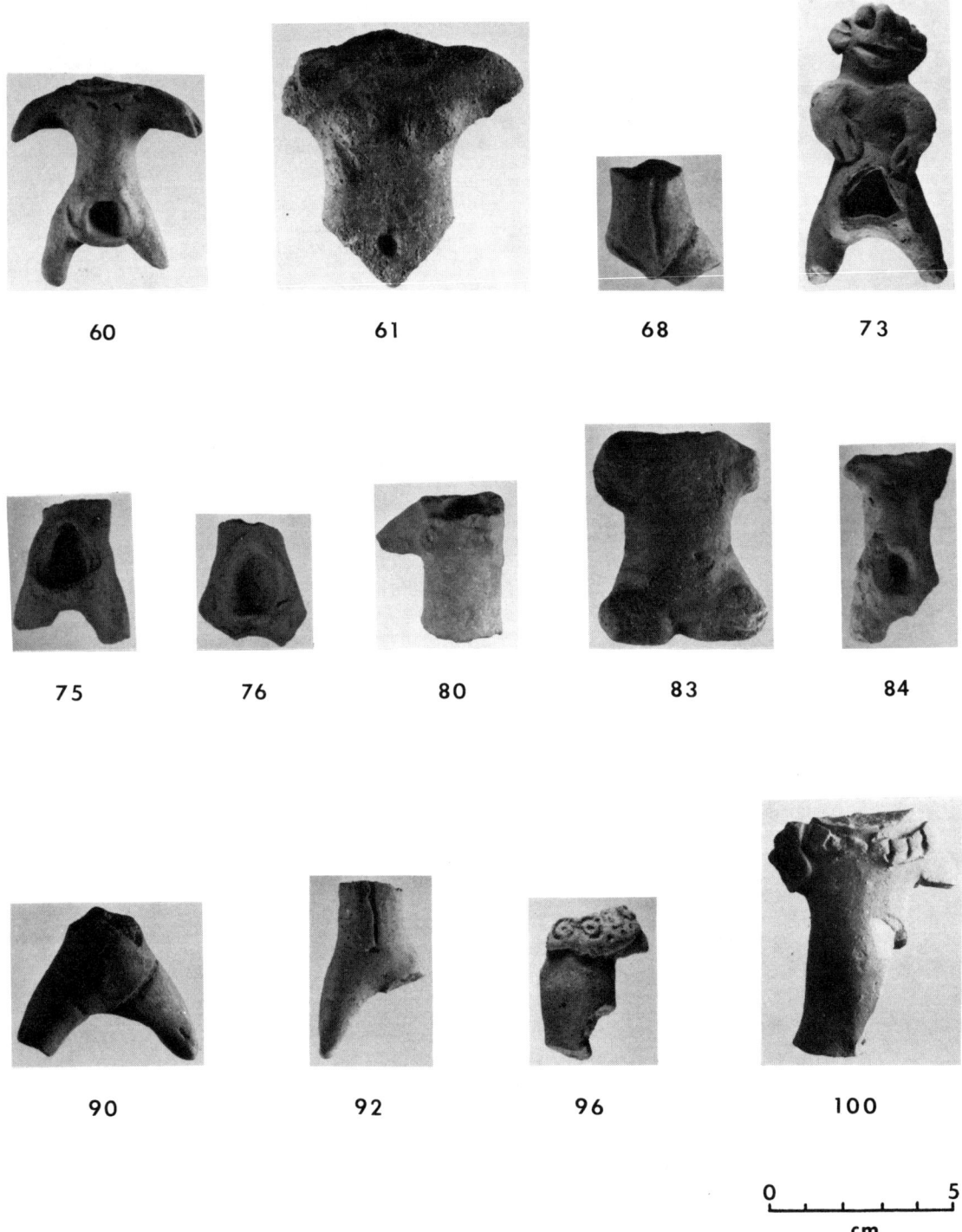

PLATE 53. Figurines from Late Formative proveniences at Tomaltepec, II. Numbers refer to items in Table 14.

APPENDIX IV

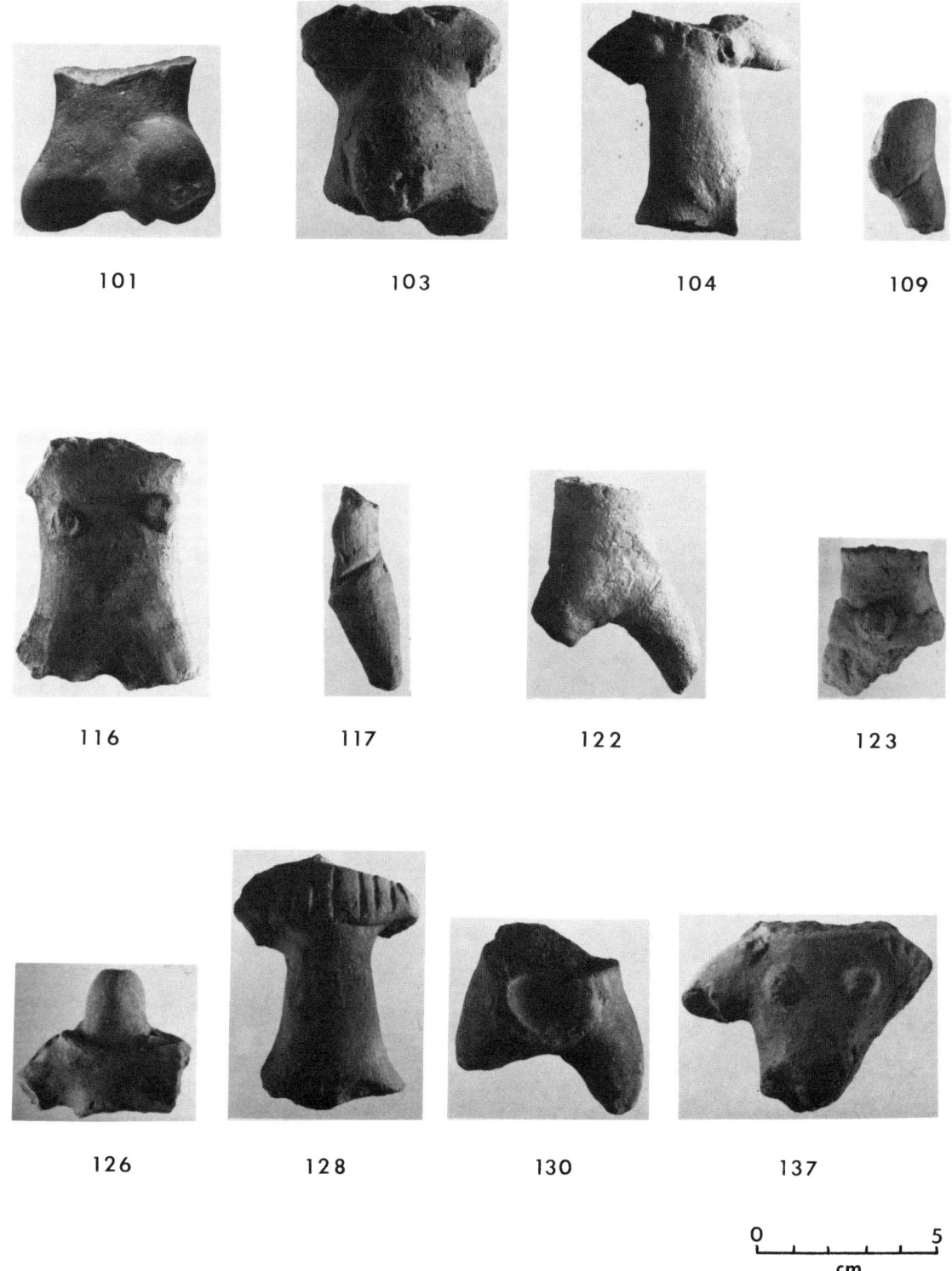

PLATE 54. Figurines from Late Formative proveniences at Tomaltepec, III. Numbers refer to items in Table 14.

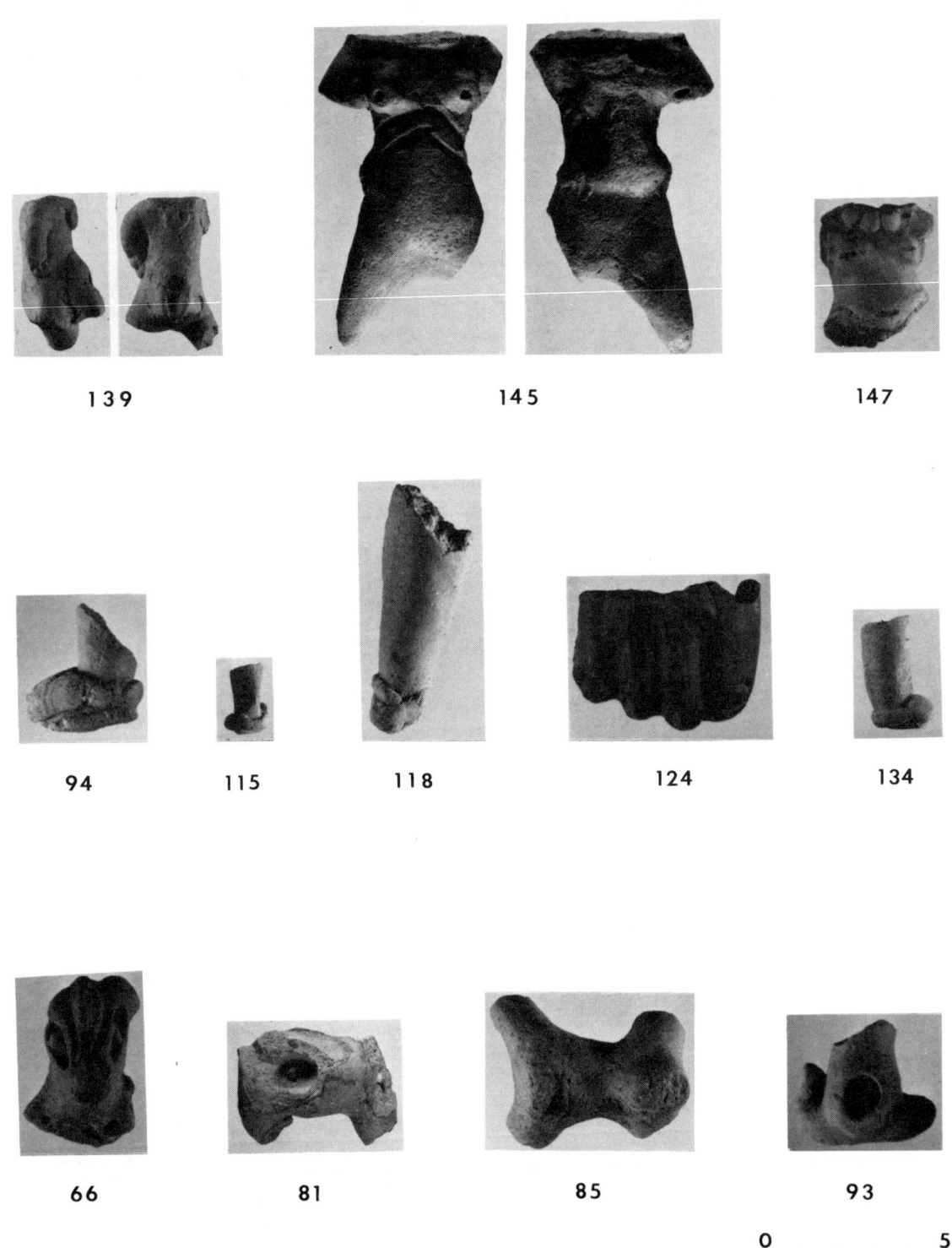

PLATE 55. Figurines from Late Formative proveniences at Tomaltepec, IV. Numbers refer to items in Table 14.

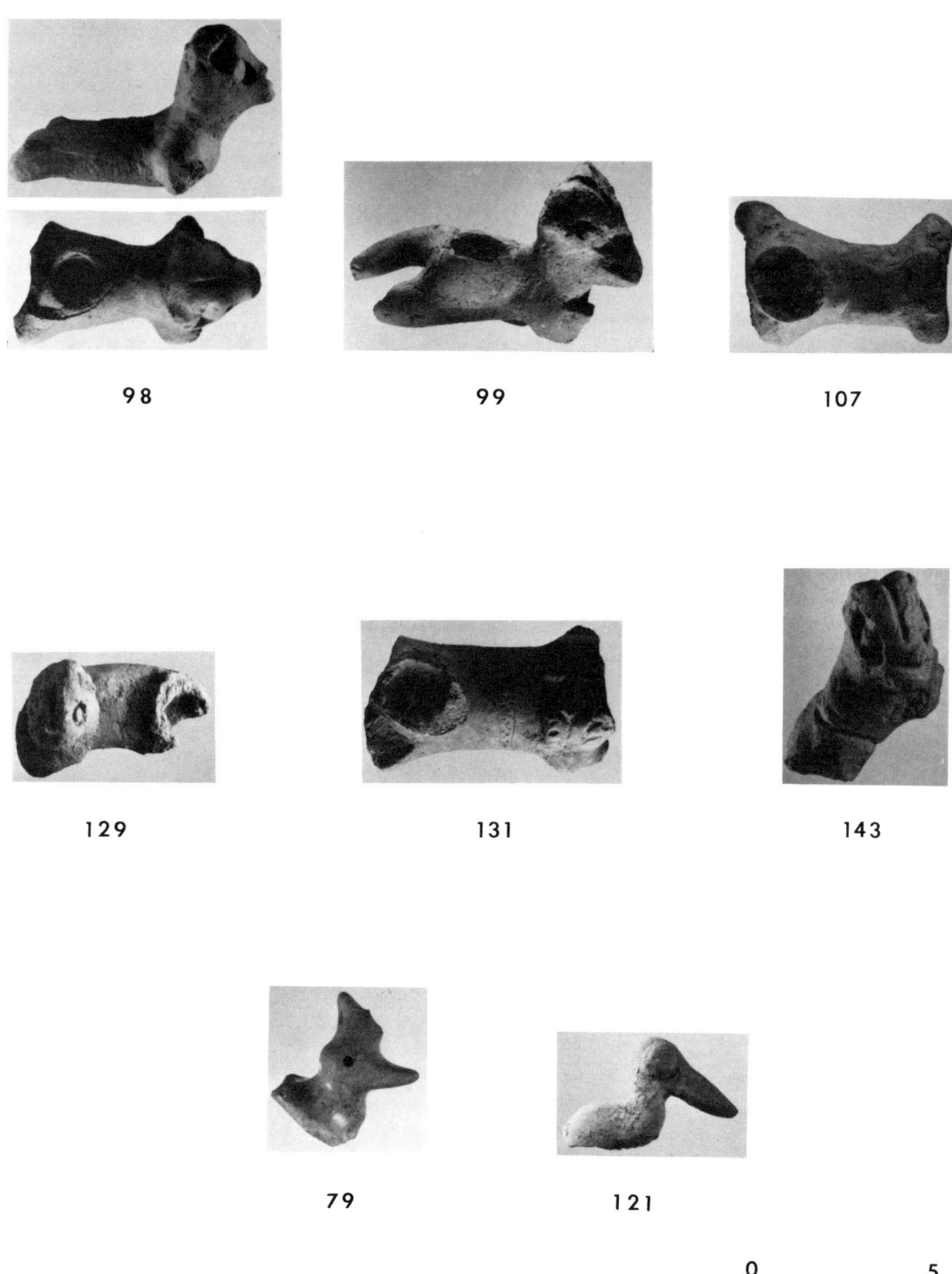

PLATE 56. Figurines from Late Formative proveniences at Tomaltepec, V. Numbers refer to items in Table 14.

APPENDIX V

MODIFIED AND UNMODIFIED BONE

The following tables provide a species by species summary of all bone recovered from Formative features at Tomaltepec, including bone tools and other cut, drilled, or otherwise modified specimens. Proveniences without bone have not been included in these tables. All identifications were made by Kent Flannery of the University of Michigan Museum of Anthropology. The following species abbreviations have been used:

Bufo:	*Bufo marinus*: toad. Apparently intrusive in all features.
Sylvil.f.:	*Sylvilagus floridanus*: Eastern cottontail rabbit
Sylvil.c.:	*Sylvilagus cunicularius*: Mexican cottontail rabbit
Sylvil.sp.:	*Sylvilagus* of indeterminate species
Odoco.:	*Odocoileus virginianus*: white tailed deer
Canis:	*Canis familiaris*: domestic dog
Dicotyl:	*Dicotyles tajacu*: collared peccary
Orthog.:	*Orthogeomys grandis*: pocket gopher
Didel.:	*Didelphis marsupialis*: opossum
Kinost.:	*Kinosternon integrum*: mud turtle
Dermat:	*Dermatemys mawii*: lowland turtle. (The only specimen is a fragment of a turtle shell drum.)
Bird:	The only specimen is *Buteo jamaicensis*, the red-tailed hawk.
Cut:	Bones with butchering marks. Also included in species counts.
Worked:	Bones with cut edges or other modification into any unnatural shape. Also included in species counts.
Awl:	Awls or punches made from splinters of (usually) deer limb bones. Wear on tip indicates use with a pushing/twisting motion.
Needle:	A smaller, sharper implement than an awl or punch.

Table 15: Bone from Early Formative Proveniences

Provenience		Bufo	Sylvil.f.	Sylvil.c.	Sylvil.sp.	Odoco.	Canis	Dicotyl.	Orthog.	Didel.	Dermat.	Kinost.	Bird	Unident.*	Burned	Cut	Worked	Used	Awl	Needle
TL-1	F.7	10		6		8		2					1							
	F.102		1	1	5									2					1	
TL-2	F.108		2			1			3					7						
Tierras Largas Total		10	3	7	5	9	0	2	3	0	0	1	0	9	0	0	0	0	1	0
ESJ-1	F.109		1	7		61		2					1	15			1			
	F.117	1		5		97		1	2					11		1			2	
STR-11	Cell		1	3	2	120	1	1	3	1				13					2	
	Upper Lev.			1		30		1						4					1	
	H.4,Flr-E					2				1				25						
ESJ-2	H.4, on E					1								19						
	H.4, SubE			1		10								28					2	
ESJ-3	F.72			2		66				1				9		1				
	F.81/65						2													
ESJ-4	F.112					18	1													
	F.111		1	1																
Cemetery Burial 80																			2	
Early San José Total		1	3	20	2	405	4	3	7	3	0	0	1	124	0	2	1	0	9	0
Early Formative Total		11	6	27	7	414	4	5	10	3	0	1	1	133	0	2	1	0	10	0

*Mostly deer, some rabbit, peccary.

Table 16: Bone from Middle Formative Proveniences

Provenience		Bufo	Sylvil.f.	Sylvil.c.	Sylvil.sp.	Odoco.	Canis	Dicotyl.	Orthog.	Didel.	Dermat.	Bird	Unident.	Burned	Cut	Worked	Used	Awl	Needle
R-1	H.4a,Sub-floor 1												1			1			
	Fea. 35	1				1													
R-2	Fea. 50					13	2		2		1								
Rosario Total		1	0	0	0	14	2	0	2	0	1	0	0	0	0	1	0	0	0
Ia-1	Fea. 11		2			11	1												
	Fea. 11a					1													
	Fea. 92a												1						
	Fea. 92b				1	1							1						
	Fea. 95												2						
	Fea. 106	2		1		5		1					10						
	Ia-1 Total	2	2	1	1	18	1	1	0	0	0	0	14	0	0	0	0	0	0
Ia-2	Fea. 40						6												1
	Fea. 69					5	1												
	Fea. 77												2						
	Fea. 82/93					1	3	1											
	Ia-2 Total	0	0	0	0	6	10	1	0	0	0	0	2	0	0	0	0	0	1
Ia-3	Fea. 79					6													
	Fea. 30						100												
Ia Total		2	2	1	1	30	111	2	0	0	0	0	16	0	0	0	0	0	1
Middle Formative Total		3	2	1	1	44	113	2	2	0	1	0	16	0	0	0	0	0	1

Table 17: Bone from Late Formative Proveniences

Provenience	Bufo	Sylvil.f.	Sylvil.c.	Sylvil.sp.	Odoco.	Canis	Dicotyl.	Orthog.	Didel.	Dermat.	Bird	Unident.	Burned	Cut	Worked	Used	Awl	Needle
Structure 13, Upper Floor																		
Ic-1 Feature 51						1						2						
Feature 55					1	1						2		1				
Ic-1 Total	0	0	0	0	1	1	1	0	0	0	0	4	0	1	0	0	0	0
Ic-2 Midden, Layer II, III					20	9						2						
Feature 32					2												1	
Feature 34					7	9						2						
Ic-2 Total	0	0	0	0	29	18	0	0	0	0	0	4	0	0	0	0	1	0
Ic-3 Feature 53					3	2						2						
Feature 54					5							1						
Feature 61			1									1						
Feature 68												1						
Feature 73					1													
Ic-3 Total	0	0	1	0	9	2	0	0	0	0	0	5	0	0	0	0	0	0
Late Formative Total	0	0	1	0	48	21	1	0	0	0	0	13	0	1	0	0	1	0

Table 18: Bone from Terminal Formative Proveniences

Provenience	Bufo	Sylvil.f.	Sylvil.c.	Sylvil.sp.	Odoco.	Canis	Dicotyl.	Orthog.	Didel.	Dermat.	Bird	Unident.	Burned	Cut	Worked	Used	Awl	Needle
Structure 14						1												
II-1 House 6, to Floor 1						1												
Fea. 56					1			1				10						
Fea. 19												2						
Fea. 3	1											1						
Total II-1	1	0	0	0	1	1	0	1	0	0	0	13	0	0	0	0	0	0
Terminal Formative Total	1	0	0	0	1	2	0	1	0	0	0	13	0	0	0	0	0	0

APPENDIX VI

SHELL AND MARINE OBJECTS

The following tables describe and provide proveniences for all of the shell found at Tomaltepec. Shell was not found at Tomaltepec in great quantity, although a partially drilled shell disk from an Early Formative provenience (Structure 11) attests to at least some production of shell ornaments. Shell identifications were done by Lawrence H. Feldman, of the University of Missouri Museum of Anthropology.

Also present in the deposits overlying the San José House 8 was a 1.5 cm fragment of the fin spine of a marine Grunt (family *Pomadasyidae*). These fish are available in the shallow waters along the Pacific Coast of Oaxaca. There is some evidence for the use of fish spines in ritual bloodletting in Oaxaca, and the spine described above may have served such a purpose. It should also be noted that the spine was found in the high status area of the community.

Table 19: Shell from Tomaltepec

Item Number	Provenience	Comments
	EARLY FORMATIVE	
1	Unit TL-2, Fea.108	*Freshwater clam (?) fragment; cut
2	Burial 69, Obj.1 San José cemetery	Magnetite mirror holder (?) carved from thick piece of marine gastropod shell
3	ESJ Structure 11 Cell fill	Freshwater clam (?) fragment; incompletely drilled
4	Unit ESJ-1, Fea.109	Freshwater clam (?) fragment; hole near valve hinge for suspension
5	Unit ESJ-1, Fea.109	Freshwater clam (?) fragment; cut
6	Unit ESJ-1, Fea.109	Freshwater clam (?) fragment; cut
	MIDDLE FORMATIVE	
7	Unit Ia-1 vicinity. Misc. Mid. Form. deposits.	Fragment of *Oliva* sp.
8	Unit Ia-1 vicinity. Misc. deposits.	Unident. Molluscan frag.; cut to elongated rectangle
9	Unit Ia-1 vicinity. Misc. deposits.	Freshwater clam fragment
10	Unit Ia-1 vicinity. Misc. Mid. Form. deposits.	Fragment of *Fissurella gemmata*; Pacific coast
11	Unit Ia-1 vicinity. Misc. Mid. Form. deposits.	Freshwater clam (?) fragment; cut
12	Unit Ia-1, Burial 1, Obj.1	Freshwater clam (?) fragment; disk, drilled center hole
	LATE FORMATIVE	
13	Unit Ic-3, Fea.73	Unmodified *Chione subrugosa*; Pacific coast
14	Area Ic-2. Misc. Late Form. deposits.	*Turritella leucostoma*; Atlantic or Pacific estuary; unmodified
15	Area Ic-2. Misc. Late Form. deposits.	*Mitrella dorma*; Pacific; top cut off for stringing (?)
16	Area Ic-2. Misc. Late Form. deposits.	Freshwater clam (?); long pin w/ hole at one end
17	Unit Ic-3 vicinity. Misc. Late Form. deposits.	Freshwater clam (?) fragment; seems to be cut
18	Unit Ic-3 vicinity. Misc. Late Form. deposits.	Molluscan fragment, cf. *Pinctada* sp. or freshwater clam; cut
19	Unit Ic-1 vicinity. Misc. Late Form. deposits.	*Neocyrena ordinaria*; ground & drilled at hinge; Pacific
20	Unit Ic-1 vicinity. Misc. Late Form. deposits.	*Fissurella gemmata*; top cut off; Pacific coast
21	Structure 13 area, surface find	Unmodified *Chione subrugosa*; Pacific coast
22	Unit Ic-3, Burial 19, Obj.1	cf. *Megapitaria aurantiaca*; pierced at hinge
23	Unit Ic-1 vicinity. Misc. Late Form. deposits.	Same identification as above; cut into rectangular ornament w/ hole at each end
24	Unit Ic-3, Burial 19, Obj.1	Dome-shaped piece cut from unident. marine gastropod
25	Unit Ic-1 vicinity. Misc. Late Form. deposits.	Molluscan fragment, cf. *Pinctada* sp. or freshwater clam (?); cut into long pin with hole at top

*Some of the shells identified as 'freshwater clam(?)' may also be *Pinctada* sp., the Pacific Coast pearl oyster.

PLATE 57. Shell objects from Formative proveniences at Tomaltepec, I. Numbers refer to items in Table 21. Length of item 8, 25.3 mm.

PLATE 58. Shell objects from Formative proveniences at Tomaltepec, II. Numbers refer to items in Table 21. Length of item 16, 39.3 mm.

APPENDIX VII
GROUND STONE ARTIFACTS

The tables which follow very briefly characterize the ground stone artifacts from all Formative Period features at Tomaltepec. The artifacts are grouped into the categories described below:

Manos:

type 1: large, fairly heavy grinding stones up to 30 cm. long, used with two hands in a push-pull motion. These may be roughly triangular, ovoid, or lenticular in cross section and roughly cigar shaped in plan view. They may be worn only on one side, or both sides, or on three sides in the case of triangluar specimens. Ends of all shapes frequently show traces of battering or pounding. (Plate 59)

type 2: small, fairly light grinding stones of about 10 cm. maximum dimension, used with one hand in a circular or rotary motion. These may be flat, ovoid, or subrectangular in cross section and oval in plan view. They may be worn on one or both sides. These stones also were sometimes used for pounding, but less frequently or less heavily than the large manos. (Plate 60)

Pestles:

These are also grinding stones, but the end rather than the side is utilized. Pestles are roughly conical in plan view, with a hemispherical end which usually shows heavy wear. They seem to have been used with a type 3 metate (below) and were carefully pecked and then ground to shape. (Plate 61)

Metates:

These are the grinding surfaces upon which manos and pestles were used. Three types were noted:

type 1: stones with a flat or very slightly basin shaped grinding surface. This type probably starts nearly flat and becomes more basin shaped with long use. (Plate 62)

type 2: trough shaped stones made with distinct, parallel, near vertical sides. Most suitable for use with a type 1 metate. This type is quite rare. (Plate 63)

type 3: circular stones with deep round basins in their centers. Grinding here can only be done with a rotary motion, using a one-hand metate or a pestle. (Plate 64)

There are doubtless functional distinctions between type 1, 2 and 3 metates, although these are not well understood. Type 1 and 2 metates seem most useful for larger, harder or coarser grinding, while type 3 seems to be better for smaller, softer, and/or finer materials.

Axes:

Ground stone axe heads range from 5-10 cm. miniatures (termed 'celts' and denoted by 'C' in the tabulations) to 20 cm. tools with heavily worn and battered edges. All axes are cigar shaped, with a bit at one end and a blunt, hammer-like opposing end. They were most probably hafted, although they do not have hafting grooves, and used for heavy chopping and pounding. An unfinished example shows that they were made from elongated river cobbles of appropriate sizes. (Plate 65)

Stone Balls:

These small, carefully ground stone balls are 2 to 3 cm. in diameter and are found only occasionally in Early San José features. Their function is entirely unclear, although they might possibly be sling stones. They do *not* seem to have been hammer stones. (Refer to Plate 14)

Hammer Stones:

These egg sized and shaped stones are not strictly classifiable as ground stone, as they seem to have been used in their natural condition. They probably served every function from food preparation to stone tool making.

In general terms, it should be noted that many of the Tomaltepec ground stone tools, especially Early Formative manos and metates, show minimal modification from their natural forms. Appropriately-sized river cobbles seem to have been used frequently as manos, for instance. The backs of metates also show very little modification, the cortex of the stone generally remaining in place. No feet were found on any Early Formative metate. Following are ground stone tabulations by period and provenience.

Table 20: Ground Stone from Formative Proveniences

Provenience		Mano type 1	Mano type 2	Pestle	Metate type 1	Metate type 2	Metate type 3	Celt	Axe	Stone Ball	Hammer Stone
				EARLY FORMATIVE							
TL-1	Fea. 7	4	1					1			
	Fea. 102	2		1							
Tierras Largas phase Total		6	1	0	1	0	0	1	0	0	0
ESJ-1	Fea. 109	1	1							2	
	Fea. 117	1	2								
STR.11	Cell fill			1					1		
	Upper levels	1		1							
ESJ-2	House 4				1						
	Cemetery						1*	1*			
San José phase Total		3	3	2	1	0	1	1	1	2	0
Early Formative Total		9	4	2	2	0	1	2	1	2	0
				MIDDLE FORMATIVE							
	Fea. 44a	2	3								1
	House 7	2	1								
Rosario phase total		4	4	0	0	0	0	0	0	0	1
Ia-1	Fea. 11										1
	Fea. 92								1		
Ia-2	Burial 46			1							
	Fea. 40								1		
	Fea. 69									1	
	Fea. 82/93				1						
	Fea. 74	2			1						1
	Fea. 79									1	
Monte Albán Ia phase Total		3	0	1	2	0	0	0	2	2	2
Middle Formative Total		7	4	1	2	0	0	0	2	2	3
				LATE FORMATIVE							
Structure 13					1						
Ic-1	Fea. 45		1								
	Fea. 47	1	1								
	Fea. 51		1								
Ic-2	Fea. 32	3									1
	Fea. 44B	1					1				
Ic-3	Fea. 61	2									
	Fea. 68	3	2								
Late Formative Total		10	5	0	1	0	1	0	**	0	1

*Metate accompanies Burial 49. Celt accompanies Burial 11.
**Three axes were recovered in association with M.A. Ic sherds in test pit layers not assignable to any of the above Household Units.

PLATE 59. Type 1 manos. Top, view of upper surface. Bottom, side view.

APPENDIX VII

PLATE 60. Type 2 manos. Top, view of widest surface. Bottom, side view.

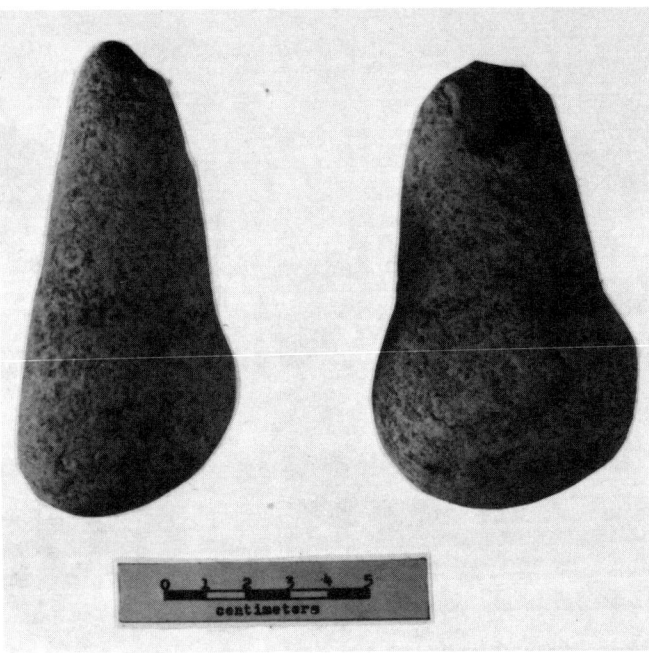

PLATE 61. Pestle (two views of same artifact).

PLATE 62. Type 1 metate.

APPENDIX VII

PLATE 63. Type 2 metate.

PLATE 64. Type 3 metate.

PLATE 65. Ground stone axes. (The middle row represents a side view of the same axes shown in the top row.)

APPENDIX VIII

EARLY FORMATIVE CHIPPED STONE TOOLS FROM TOMALTEPEC

by
John W. Rick

General Characterization

The Early Formative stone tool assemblage from Tomaltepec is best described as the product of a flake and core industry. The technique of manufacture, in other words, largely involved hard hammer percussion, largely lacked soft hammer percussion, and almost completely lacked pressure retouch. Hard hammer percussion flakes and the cores from which they were removed thus constitute the bulk of utilized material, while retouched tools of any sort are quite rare.

Good single platform polyhedral cores are found at Tomaltepec, demonstrating that core preparation techniques had been developed for use on better quality raw materials. Interestingly enough, however, most of these cores were not exhausted and nearly all have been used as heavy choppers or scrapers. There is not a particularly high utilization rate for flakes, and flake production may have been incidental much of the time to chopper/scraper production.

Retouched tools are restricted to core tools, notched spokeshaves, scrapers, bifaces, and denticulates. Most gravers, drills, reamers, and borers are on pieces already of appropriate shape after departure of the initial flake, or shattering of the initial debitage, and are not retouched. The remainder of identified tools—mostly scrapers or choppers—are simply utilized edges of non-retouched materials.

There is a noticeable emphasis on scraping and light chopping tools with concave utilized edge outlines. The size range of these tools is extreme, extending from small notches of 2-3 mm in diameter to concave scrapers having an arc belonging to a circle of up to 12 cm in diameter. The number of samples is small, but there is at least tentative indication of bimodality in the notch diameters represented, with one peak of size around 5-10 cm and another at 7-15 mm in diameter. Some of these tools may well have been used for making projectile shafts or other small diameter dowels. Some of the smallest notches may also have been used to make awls or needles in wood or bone. As noted earlier, a relatively large number of these sorts of bone tools were found in Early Formative refuse. The largest of these concave-edge scrapers would probably have been used for stripping, or trimming, pole-sized branches.

Much of the Early Formative stone tool industry at Tomaltepec, in fact, appears to have a strong woodworking bent. There is, for example, extensive damage, but with little of the polish or wear characteristic of use on soft materials. Structure 11 deviates noticeably from this pattern, as will be discussed presently.

Raw Materials Utilized

Four basic raw material classes are represented in the Tomaltepec remains. The most common material is a locally available silicified siltstone of a dark gray to black color. Fracture in this material can be highly irregular due both to the bedding planes and natural fracture planes in the stone. This siltstone is somewhat softer than most Valley of Oaxaca chert—perhaps around 6.0 on the Mohs scale. The fracture strength of the stone is certainly less than chert, bordering on the fragility of obsidian.

A great deal of angular debitage of local siltstone was recovered at Tomaltepec, and this is entirely consistent with the highly variable quality of the stone. It seems likely that much of the breakdown of the siltstone was by simply smashing one block against another. In general, it seems that little effort was expended in production of flake tools from the local siltstone, and wear on these suggests that they were used for short periods and discarded.

Chert is the next most common material used at Tomaltepec. Most specimens are fine grained, with sub-waxy luster and a fine conchoidal fracture. Hardness is about 6.5-6.9 on the Mohs scale. Very few of the pieces had any cortex, making it likely that users traveled to non-local sources and did much of the rough chipping there. A survey and initial characterization of chert sources in the Valley of Oaxaca (Whalen, n.d.) revealed several chert sources of reasonable quality in the Tlacolula Valley, although no sources are known from the immediate vicinity of Tomaltepec. The range of colors of the Tomaltepec chert suggests that it comes from the local Tlacolula sub-valley and surrounding mountains rather than from the Etla sub-valley or any more distant source examined in the course of the chert survey.

Chert tools are both tougher and of better quality than those of local siltstone, and chert tools at Tomaltepec show more wear marks and reflect longer use than those of any other raw material category. It was observed in an earlier chapter, in fact, that higher status households at Tomaltepec contained more chert and less siltstone than those of lower status. It should be emphasized, however, that chert never composed a high percentage of utilized stone at Tomaltepec.

Obsidian occurred sporadically in all investigated Early Formative proveniences. Translucent green obsidian was quite rare, most specimens being black to translucent gray. Green obsidian became fairly common at Tomaltepec during the Late Formative. Prismatic blades do not appear in the Early Formative obsidian tool kit, and most pieces recovered were thin flakes or angular debitage.

Pure white macrocrystalline quartz with a crude, irregular fracture was occasionally used at Early Formative Tomaltepec. The nature of the stone produces blocky surfaces and quite dull edges. A number of fragments of this quartzite do show intentional fracture, although it occurs very rarely relative to any other type of lithic raw material.

Tools from Early Formative Proveniences

The tables below contain several classes of information on tools identified from each Early Formative provenience at Tomaltepec. Tools were identified by visible wear: edge retouch, edge damage, and/or edge polish or scratching. The first two columns of the following tables are self-explanatory. The "Material" column refers to the type of stone: S = local silicified siltstone; C = chert; O = obsidian. The "Duration" column indicates the term of use of the tool, when such could be determined: S = short term use; L = long term use. Form categories include angular debitage (A), flakes (F) flakes, and cores (C). The "Remarks" column includes comments on the probable use to which the tool was put.

Comparison of Several Early Formative Proveniences

Three Early Formative proveniences at Tomaltepec are especially interesting in terms of their stone tool assemblages. These are Feature 7 (a Tierras Largas bell-shaped pit), House 4, floors D and E (early San José), and Structure 11 (early San José). House 4 and Structure 11 are approximately contemporary. The three proveniences differ significantly in form and type of tools and debitage, as well as in raw materials utilized.

Feature 7 is notable in that it contains a sizable quantity of large angular debitage and cores, much of which has been used for heavy chopping. Also present are exceptionally large numbers of small flakes, evidently representing preparation of core tool edges. Most of the heavy tools are made of the local silicified siltstone and have been used for a short time only. Included are a number of heavy concave-edge scrapers and choppers appropriate for use on cylindrical surfaces. This, combined with wear suggestive of woodworking, leads to the conclusion that cutting, chopping, and scraping of large wooden branches or limbs was done by the tools later deposited in this feature. The presence of the other large angular debitage in local material suggests that most of these tools were made, used, and deposited over a very short period of time, so that the debitage and tools were never spatially separated. In general, the tool kit recovered from Feature 7 is one that might well have been used in construction of a wooden structure, such as the pole framework of a wattle-and-daub house. It might also represent a more generalized woodworking kit, of course.

House 4, floors D and E, yielded a more

APPENDIX VIII

Table 21: Stone Tools from Early Formative Proveniences

Tool	Description	Material	Duration	Form	Remarks
			Feature 7*		
			Tierras Largas Phase		
78	Concave chopper	S	S	A	Heavy duty use on wood
79	Small endscraper	S		F	Wood, bone
80	Chopper-shaver	S		C	Wood
81	Concave chopper	S		C	Wood
82	Concave scraper	S		C	Heavy duty use on wood
83	Plane scraper	S		A	Heavy duty use on wood
84	Scraper	S	S	A	Wood
85	Scraper	S	L	A	Light duty—hides
86	Scraper	S		F	Heavy duty—wood, bone
87	Scraper-chopper	S		A	Wood
88	Chopper	S		C	Heavy duty—wood
89	Chopper	S		A	Heavy duty—wood
90	Scraper	S		A	Heavy duty—wood
91	Chopper-cutter	S	S	A	Light duty
92	Denticulate	S		A	Fiber
93	Scraper (fragment)	S		A	Heavy duty
94	Scraper (fragment)	C		A	Heavy duty—wood
95	Chopper	S	L	A	Heavy duty—wood
96	Chopper	S	S	C	Light duty—wood
97	Scraper	C	L	C	Heavy duty—wood
			Feature 102		
			Tierras Largas Phase		
98	Chopper	S	S	A	Light duty—wood
99	Chopper	C	S	C	
			Feature 109**		
100	Chopper	S	L	A	Heavy duty—wood
101	Chopper	S	L	A	Heavy duty—wood
102	Chopper	S	S	A	Light duty
103	Small spokeshave	C		A	Bone, wood, fiber
104	Spokeshave	S	L	F	
105	Chopper	S		C	Wood
106	Chopper	S	S	A	Wood, bone
107	Scraper	C		A	Wood, bone, hides; steep edge angle
			Feature 117†		
135	Knife fragment	S		F	Light duty—meat
136	Knife fragment	S		F	Light duty—meat
137	Knife fragment	S		F	Light duty—meat
138	Saw—rasp	C		F	Light duty—meat, fiber
139	Spokeshave	C	L	F	Heavy duty—wood, bone
140	Biface fragment	C			Unfinished
			Structure 11—Cell Fill‡		
108	Scraper—knife	C		F	Light duty—wood, hide
109	Scraper	S		F	Light duty—hide
124	Chopper	C		A	Light duty—wood
125	Chopper	C		A	Heavy duty—wood
126	Multiple notch spokeshave	C		A	Hide, wood
127	Spokeshave	C		A	Bone, wood
128	Small spokeshave	C		A	Wood, bone, fiber
129	Denticulate frag.	C		A	
130	Knife fragment	C		F	Meat, tendons
131	Chopper fragment	S		F	Heavy duty—wood
132	Scraper	S	L	F	Heavy duty
133	Knife	C		F	Light duty—meat
134	Knife	C		F	Meat, soft material
153	Scraper fragment	O		A	Light duty—wood
154	Knife	O		A	Light duty—meat, hides
155	Biface fragment	O		F	Hard material cutting (?)
156	Knife	O	S	F	Light duty—general purpose
158	Scraper	O	L	F	Wood, bone

Table 21: continued

Tool	Description	Material	Duration	Form	Remarks
		Structure 11—Upper Levels§			
110	Knife/saw	S		A	Soft material
111	Spokeshave	C		A	
112	Chopper fragment	C		A	Heavy duty—hard material
113	Endscraper	C		A	Light duty
114	Spokeshave	C		F	
115	Chopper	S	S	C	Heavy duty—wood
116	Retouched sidescraper	C		A	Light duty—meat, hide
117	Sidescraper	C		A	
118	Knife	C	L	F	Light duty—meat
119	Scraper fragment	C		F	
120	Thumbnail scraper	C		F	Light duty—hides, tendons
121	Scraper fragment	C	L	F	Heavy duty—wood, bone
122	Sidescraper/knife	C	L	F	Light duty—meat, tendons
123	Projectile point fragment	C			
		House 4, Floor D–E			
1	Spokeshave	C		F	
2	Spokeshave	S		A	
3	Tiny core scraper	C		A	
4	Groover	C		A	
5	Grooving scraper	S	S	A	
6	Steep-edged knife	C	L	F	Heavy duty
7	Small core scraper	C	L	C	Extensive wear, wood, hides
8	Flake scraper	S	S	F	
9	Concave scraper	S		A	
10	Flake knife	S	L	F	
11	Spokeshave	S		F	
12	Scraper-reamer	S	L	A	
13	Scraper	S	L	F	Heavy duty
14	Concave scraper/ spokeshave	S		A	
15	Endscraper	S		A	
16	Chopper	S		A	
17	Small endscraper	S	S	F	
18	Plane scraper	S	S	A	
19	Flake knife	S	S	F	
20	Spokeshave	S		C	
21	Multipurpose tool	S	S	A	
22	Possible awl	S	S	A	
23	Scraper	C		A	Steep edge
24	Flake knife	C		F	Light duty
150	Microlith(?)	O		F	Light duty—hides
		House 4, Floor E, Surface			
141	Knife fragment	C		F	Light duty—soft material
142	Chopper	S	S	C	Light duty
143	Spokeshave, small	S	S	C	
144	Scraper	S	S	A	Heavy duty, hard material
145	Scraper	S		F	Light duty—hides(?)
		House 4, Sub-Floor E			
25	Denticulate (?)	C		A	
26	Borer, small	C		F	
27	Borer, small	S		A	
28	Multipurpose scraping, boring tool	S	S	A	
29	Borer, small	S	S	F	
30	Light endscraper/denticulate sidescraper	S	S/L	F	Light duty/heavy duty
31	Scraper, knife	S		F	Light duty
32	Endscraper	C	L	F	Heavy duty—steep edge
33	Endscraper	C	L	A	Heavy duty—steep edge
34	Flake knife	S	S	F	
35	Graver	S	S	A	

Table 21: continued

Tool	Description	Material	Duration	Form	Remarks
36	Microlith (?)	S	S	F	
37	Pounder/pecker	S		C	
38	Knife	S	S	A	
39	Scraper	S	L	A	Heavy duty
40	Chopper	S	L	A	Heavy duty—60° edge
41	Saw	S	L	A	Heavy duty
42	Endscraper	C	L	F	Heavy duty—heat treated
43	Scraper	C	L	F	Heavy duty
151	Prismatic blade	O	L	PB	Light duty—planing or scraping

*Local stone = 90%; chert = 10%; obsidian = 0%.
**Local stone = 75%; chert = 25%; obsidian = 0%.
†Local stone = 50%; chert = 50%; obsidian = 0%.
‡Local stone = 16.8%; chert = 55.5%; obsidian = 27.7%.
§Local stone = 14.3%; chert = 85.7%; obsidian = 0%.

generalized group of tools such as heavy duty sidescrapers, spoke-shaves, drills, gravers, and occasional knives. Most heavy duty tools are in chert, while many of the local material tools seem to have had relatively short use periods on light duty tasks. Much of the chert found, both in tool and debitage form, is angular, a surprise in terms of the value of the material. Surprisingly lacking is the presence of low edge angle tools such as knives or light scrapers in chert, something this material would be quite appropriate for.

Structure 11 contained a markedly different tool assemblage. here, the percentage of chert found is much higher than in House 4 or Feature 7. Unlike House 4, most of the chert tools are fine-edge flake tools, scrapers, or flake knives, all evidently used in low stress situations and for extensive lengths of time. Meat or tendon cutting is a very likely possible use. Tools in the local materials are of a more general nature, with a selection of most functions represented. Very heavy choppers occur in nowhere near the concentration found in Feature 7. Bifaces make their only significant appearance in Structure 11, represented by a roughout, a projectile point fragment, and some biface retouch flakes. It may be suggested that many of the tools found in House 4 and Structure 11 served the same functions, although the latter residential unit probably was processing larger quantities of meat and other animal products. Most significant are the raw material differences, with obsidian and chert occurring in much higher proportions in Structure 11. In fact, the presence of angular chert in the lower status House 4 may represent scavenging of chert waste from higher status residence areas. Feature 7, on the other hand, represents only tools for limited and short term use, and represents an activity focus instead of a broad-range adaptation suitable for general subsistence activities.

APPENDIX IX

FORMATIVE BOTANICAL REMAINS AT TOMALTEPEC

by Judith E. Smith

Introduction

The recovery and analysis of plant remains at Tomaltepec was directed by questions and ideas regarding Formative subsistence and land use in the Valley of Oaxaca. While dependence on rainfall horticulture was assumed, botanical analysis was expected to provide more information on 1) the range of plants under cultivation, previously known to be rather limited in number in Formative Oaxaca; 2) the relative importance of domesticates versus wild plants and annuals growing in the fields; and 3) changes in the productivity of cultivation through time. Additionally, it was hoped that specific relationships between human populations and plant resources of different ecological zones could be demonstrated and that a clearer understanding could be obtained regarding the organization of subsistence activities in terms of the utilization of space both within the community and within the household.

With these goals in mind, every effort was made to maximize the recovery of plant remains in the excavation of the site. Macroscopic pieces of charcoal, corn cobs, and large seeds were collected throughout the excavation when seen. Samples of the soil contents of hearths, bell-shaped storage pits, roasting pits, middens, and other features of indefinite function were taken and the plant remains were later separated by water flotation in the laboratory. As quantifiable data on the distribution of wood and other plant remains within houses were desired, flotation samples of uniform size were taken from each quarter of a square meter of house floors.

The botanical separation procedure consisted of floating all soil at least twice, first passing the liquid fraction through loose-weave cloth to insure recovery of very small particles. In the second float, which released any carbonized material trapped in the silt during initial separation, fine mesh (0.75 mm) carburetor screen was used.

All plant remains were sorted from the samples in the laboratory in Oaxaca, and charcoal was classified by types representing unknown genera or species. Samples of each charcoal type, plus all seed and corn remains, were later identified by the author at the University of Michigan Ethnobotanical Laboratory utilizing its comparative collections of carbonized plant material from Mexico. Twenty pieces of charcoal were identified generically from each level of each feature except in cases where the quantity was insufficient to obtain twenty identifiable pieces. Charcoal identifications appear in Table 23; the feature levels have been combined in the tabulation and thus larger features generally received more identifications than smaller ones. In the house floor samples, charcoal was present only in very small quantities of minute fragments and thus was weighed but not identified (see Spencer, Appendix X, for quantitative charcoal distribution in House 4). Species identification was attempted for other plant remains from all samples and these are recorded in Tables 24 and 25.

Data in this report also include botanical specimens recovered in Wright's 1972 excavations of parts of three Early Formative features at Tomaltepec. These specimens were identified by Joel Elias and Richard I. Ford of the University of Michigan Ethnobotanical Laboratory.

Early Formative

The two Early Formative phases at Tomaltepec, Tierras Largas and San José, yielded the greatest quantity of plant remains, particularly domesticates and species associated with the cultivated fields.

APPENDIX IX

Table 22: Charcoal Identifications*

Phase and Provenience		Total weight of charcoal (grams)	*Pinus* spp. (pine)	*Quercus* spp. (oak)	*Prosopis* (mesquite)	Tree Legume	*Populus* or *Salix*	*Arctostaphylos*	*Byrsonima*	Unknown
Tierras Largas										
TL-1	Fea. 7	33	16	15	32					1
	Fea. 102	72	20	15	9					4
TL-2	Fea. 108	117	6	19	16	1				4
Early San José										
ESK-1	Fea. 109	206	39	18	58	3				2
Str. 11	Cell	150	25	55	24	5	1			1
	Upper levels	38	2	4	10	2				2
ESJ-2	Fea. 90B	>1	2	4						
ESJ-3	Fea. 65	5		10		1				1
Rosario										
R-1	Fea. 44A	310	4	46	6	4				3
R-2	Fea. 50	110	2	5		56	11			17 (inc. 14 of 1 sp.)
MA Ia										
Ia-1	Fea. 28	>1				9				
	Fea. 92A	5	1		21					
	Fea. 92B	15	10	7	43				12	1
	Fea. 95	>1	1	1	3					
	Fea. 106	37	25	21	18					6
Ia-2	Fea. 40	2	3	1	8					
	Fea. 77	3	2	13						
	Fea. 82	13	16	11	10					
	Fea. 69	8	2	12	4	2				
Ia-3	Fea. 79	20	47		49					4
MA Ic										
Ic-1	Fea. 46	5	12	7	2					
	Fea. 47	>1	1	2	3					
	Fea. 48	246	5	25+						8 (1 sp.)
	Fea. 51	67		39	40	2		1		
Ic-2	Fea. 44B	3	3	15	2					
Ic-3	Fea. 53	256	3	168	7					6
	Fea. 54	23	9	35	3					2
	Fea. 61	34		61		7		2		1
	Fea. 64	13	1	24						5 (1 sp.)
	Fea. 66	6		20						
	Fea. 67	91	6	12				8		
	Fea. 68	344		23				19		3
	Fea. 73	15	2	15	5					
	Fea. 75	159		25						
	Fea. 76	14		10	9					
	Fea. 78	126		61	7					
Str. 13	Fea. 84	1.5		3						
	Fea. 105	12		20						
MA II										
II-1	Fea. 56	8	12	15	1					
MA V										
	Fea. 50A	840	2	55		5			1	2
	Fea. 59	16	5	6	23		1		1	15
	Fea. 87	2	17							3
Misc.										
	Fea. 90	6	4	6	5					3
	Bur. 73	1	16	2						1

*First column is grams. All other figures are number of pieces of charcoal identified.

Table 23: **Percentages of Charcoal Species by Phase**

Phase	Sample size (no. of pieces)	*Pinus* spp.	*Quercus* spp.	*Prosopis*	Tree Legume	Other or Unknown
Tierras Largas	199	21%	45%	29%	—	5%
Early San José	269	25%	34%	34%	4%	3%
Rosario	154	4%	33%	4%	39%	20%
MA Ia	363	30%	18%	43%	3%	6%
MA Ic	749	6%	76%	10%	1%	7%
MA II	28	42%	54%	4%	—	—
MA V	136	17%	45%	17%	4%	17%

Corn (*Zea mays*) was undoubtedly of major dietary importance by the Early Formative, and a good sample of carbonized cupules and small globular kernels was recovered from Tierras Largas and early San José phase features, particularly bell-shaped storage pits. In addition, as indicated in Table 3, these same pits contained the largest quantity of prehistoric teosinte (*Zea mexicana*) yet reported for Mesoamerica. The carbonized fragments of teosinte caryopses and a number of entire grains are representative of a type

Table 24: **Carbonized *Zea* Remains**

Phase and Provenience		*Zea mexicana* teosinte			*Zea mays* corn						
		No. of carysopses and fragments	Mean length mm	Mean width mm	No. of kernels and fragments	No. of cupules and fragments	Mean width of cupules mm	No. of cob pieces	Row number	Width of cupule pairs	Teosinte introgression
Tierras Largas											
TL-1	Fea. 7	106	3.61	2.87	21	31	2.70	6			
	Fea. 102	1			16	136	3.73				
TL-2	Fea. 108	33	3.61	2.84	71	21	3.80				
Early San José											
ESJ-1	Fea. 109	11			968	347					
	House 9	2	3.70	2.70	51	121	3.82				
Str. 11	Cell				49	51	3.46				
Str. 11	Upper levels				7	12					
ESJ-2	House 4 (Fl. E)	1	3.60	2.40	6	28					
ESJ-3	Fea. 65					1					
Rosario											
Str. 12	Fea. 96				3	1			14	5.8	no
R-1	Fea. 44A				20	20			14?	5.7	no
R-2	Fea. 50				7	12	3.76	6	14	5.1	no
									12	5.5	no
									14	4.7	no
									12?	5.4	no
MA Ia											
Ia-1	Fea. 92B					2					
	Fea. 106				4	15					
Ia-2	Fea. 82					17	4.45				
Ia-3	Fea. 79					6					
MA Ic											
Ic-1	Fea. 46				3	1					
Ic-2	Fea. 44B					5					
Ic-3	Fea. 53					4					
	Fea. 54				8						
	Fea. 68					3					
MA II											
II-1	Fea. 56				1	47	4.18	1	12?		no
MA V											
	Fea. 59					10	4.05				
	Fea. 87				1	3					
	Fea. 98					3					
	Fea. 99					9	4.60				

Table 25. Counts of Carbonized Seeds

Phase and Provenience	Persea americana	Phaseolus acutifolius	Phaseolus vulgaris	Phaseolus spp.	Dalea	Unknown legume	Chenopodium	Amaranthus	Cenopodium or Amaranthus	Portulaca	Argemone mexicana	Mollugo	Opuntia	Organ cactus	Unknown
Tierras Largas															
TL-1 Fea. 7	2	6	1	5		2	110	3	26	11				1	25 (very fragmentary)
Fea. 102						1	2								
TL-2 Fea. 108	1	2		13			22		3	1			2		5
Early San José															
ESJ-1 Fea. 109	1	2	1			2	23	9							38 (very fragmentary)
House 9					2		4	1	1		1				5
ESJ-2 House 4 (Floor E)					1			1							
Structure 11 (Cell)	2						2				3				4
Rosario															
R-1 Fea. 44A							136					1			5
R-2 Fea. 50	2		1			1				2					4
MA Ia															
Ia-2 Fea. 82						1									
Ia-3 Fea. 79															2
MA Ic															
Ic-1 Fea. 46															1
Ic-2 Fea. 44B							1								
Ic-3 Fea. 53															1
Fea. 54									2						1
Fea. 64															1
Burial 5	1														

with small triangular seeds. A few of the caryopses show maize introgression. No maize cobs were found in Early Formative deposits but maize-teosinte introgression would be expected. The teosinte probably grew in the maize fields to be collected and preserved archaeologically with the corn, and teosinte was undoubtedly utilized as food, as were other weedy species left to grow on the cultivated land. A similar pattern of utilization of corn, teosinte, and corn-teosinte hybrids was found in Middle Formative phases at Fábrica San José, a village in a comparable ecological setting in the Etla arm of the Valley of Oaxaca (Ford, 1976).

The Early Formative storage pits at Tomaltepec also contained at least one other domesticate, the bean, as 10 examples of *Phaseolus acutifolius* and two of *Phaseolus vulgaris* indicate. These two beans were apparently under cultivation in the Tehuacán Valley in Early Formative times as well (Kaplan, 1967).

It is not clear as to whether the five avocado seeds (*Persea americana*) recovered from the Early Formative bell-shaped pits and other features represent fruits collected from wild or purposefully planted trees. All of the seeds are considerably smaller than any domesticated avocado seed known from Oaxaca, even when carbonization is taken into account (c.f. Merrill n.d.). Whether from wild or domestic trees, the avocado was already part of the menu by Early Formative, its oily fruits potentially supplying an important non-meat source of fat in the diet.

A number of carbonized seeds of plants likely to have been growing in cultivated fields were recovered. Some of these "weeds" may not have been considered edible, such as *Argemone mexicana* (Mexican prickle poppy) and *Dalea* (a small seeded herbaceous legume), and in fact these were recovered in very small quantities from associations other than the bell-shaped pits. In the storage

PLATE 66. Sample of teosinte caryopses from Feature 7, a Tierras Largas phase bell-shaped pit. (Scale in mm.)

APPENDIX IX

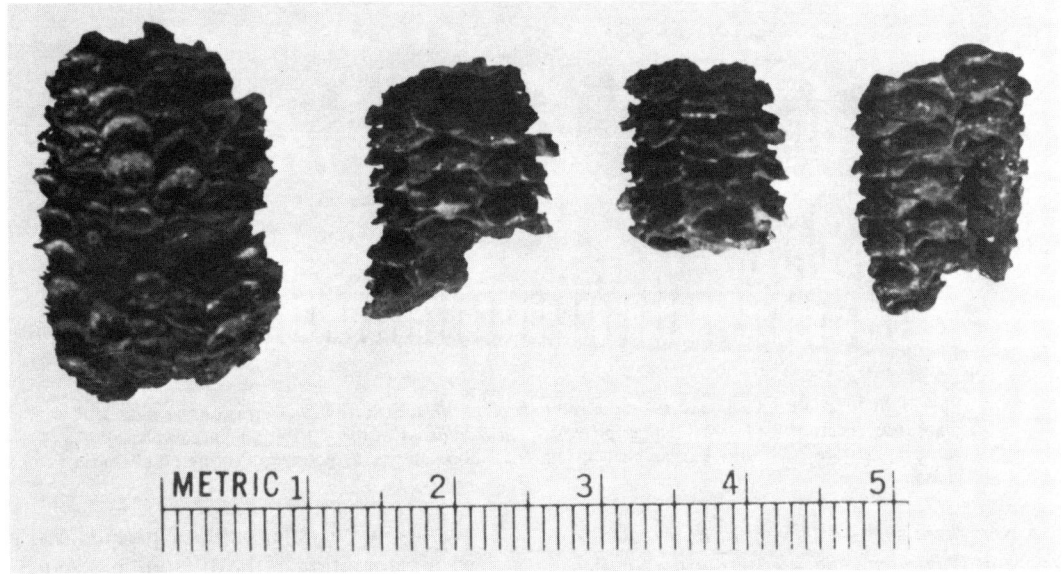

PLATE 67. Middle Formative corn cob fragments showing no introgression with teosinte (from Feature 50, a Rosario phase roasting pit).

PLATE 68. Carbonized avocado seeds. *Top row*, all Early Formative. Left to right: Feature 7 (Tierras Largas phase); Feature 108 (Tierras Largas phase); Feature 109 (early San José phase); two fragments from interior cell of Structure 11 (early San José phase). *Bottom row*, left to right: Feature 50 (Rosario phase, Middle Formative); two halves of same seed, Feature 50 (Rosario phase); Burial 5 (Late Formative, Monte Albán Ic); modern cultivated "criollo" variety, Valley of Oaxaca.

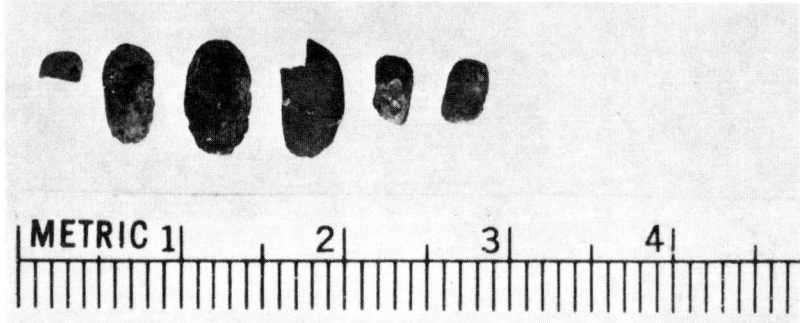

PLATE 69. Carbonized *Phaseolus*. Left to right: *P. acutifolius*, Feature 108 (Tierras Largas phase); *P. acutifolius*, Feature 7 (Tierras Largas phase); *P. acutifolius*, Feature 7 (Tierras Largas phase); *P. vulgaris*, Feature 7 (Tierras Largas phase); two cotyledons of one *P. vulgaris*, Feature 50 (Rosario phase).

pits, however, were seeds of *Chenopodium, Amaranthus*, and *Portulaca*, species that grow in the cultivated fields in Oaxaca today whose greens are consumed at an immature stage (Messer, 1975:186). At Tomaltepec, quantities seem to indicate that the seeds were utilized as food as well, particularly those of *Chenopodium*. It is of interest to note that in present day Oaxaca, field plants gathered at the immature stage for greens are selectively collected—some plants are left to seed because of cultural restrictions on their collection in certain areas, with plants growing within the *milpa* with the corn much preferred over those of field borders and roadsides (Messer, 1975:187-188).

Non-woody species from environmental zones other than the agricultural fields are poorly represented. Two *Opuntia* and one organ cactus seed found in features with maize and other food plants may mean fruit collection from cacti growing in the piedmont. These are the only preserved examples of the collection of edible parts of wild, non-weedy species unless the avocado was not yet domesticated.

While the leguminous-grasslands, piedmont slopes, and mountains were minor plant food resource areas, these zones provided wood for construction and fuel. Charcoal identification indicated that the number of tree genera used for fuel during the Early Formative was small. Oak (*Quercus* spp.), the most common fuel, and pine (*Pinus* spp.) were collected from the mountains, and the piedmont and valley floor provided mesquite wood (*Prosopis*). Only about 5 percent of the total Early Formative charcoal was from other genera. Although other trees were available in the vicinity of the site, cultural preferences, probably with recognition of the different burning properties of different woods, favored oak and to a lesser extent pine and mesquite.

Middle Formative

Although the total quantity of plant remains from Middle Formative levels is less than that of the Early Formative, corn, beans and avocado were all recovered. No teosinte was found in Middle Formative proveniences even though other weedy species from agricultural fields are still present. Six cob pieces from a Rosario phase roasting pit show no teosinte introgression. Thus, by the Middle Formative the practice of weeding teosinte out of the fields apparently had begun. At Fábrica San José, Ford postulates the elimination of teosinte from the *milpas* slightly later—sometime after the end of the Rosario phase at about 500 BC (Ford 1976: 267). As Ford points out, increased maize yields would result.

The avocado seeds from a Rosario bell-shaped pit are both larger than any of the Early Formative examples and one, measuring 2.3 cm in length and 1.58 cm in width, is within the range of modern cultivated avocado seeds collected in Oaxaca by Merrill* (Merrill n.d.; c.f. Ford, 1976:266). It is thus probable that selection for larger fruit size was under way by this time and that avocado trees were intentionally planted. The same bell-shaped pit yielded the single Middle Formative bean, a small

---

*Minimum length of modern specimens after carbonization was 2.1 cm; minimum width was 1.5 cm.

type of *Phaseolus vulgaris*. Unfortunately, carbonization destroys the color of the bean seed coat, but small black beans of similar size are a staple in Oaxaca today.

Even though the villagers were eliminating teosinte from their fields by the Middle Formative, the weeding process was a selective one. *Chenopodium* and *Portulaca*, two of the "weeds" with edible leaves and seeds, were still left in the fields; the greatest quantity of carbonized *Chenopodium* seeds at the site was from a Rosario phase bell-shaped pit. Additionally, a seed of carpetweed (*Molluga*), another field plant, was found, but it probably does not represent a human food source.

The relative importance of oak as firewood declined during the Middle Formative. More use was made of *Prosopis* and other leguminous trees from the high alluvium and lower piedmont. Also, small amounts of *Populus* or *Salix* and *Byrsonima*, species of water areas, indicate the wood was now collected from the alluvial plain close to the river. Possibly the increased collection of wood from the alluvial valley floor was due to the clearance of large areas of these zones for cultivation at this time. Thus, a substantial increase in food production, through more extensive land clearance and planting and larger maize yields resulting from the removal of teosinte from the fields, may be postulated for the Middle Formative at Tomaltepec.

Late Formative

It is clear in Tables 24 and 25 that the quantity of food plant remains recovered from Late Formative features is much smaller than that of previous periods. It is likely that this is because the Late Formative excavated areas were located around what by then had become the central plaza area of the village. In line with Whalen's suggestion of the development of a more formalized utilization of community space by Late Formative times, we would expect subsistence activities to be located outside of the central plaza area, and the small quantity of food plants found here substantiates such a reconstruction.

Small quantities of corn were found in some Late Formative features. Two of these features also contained *Chenopodium/Amaranthus* seeds, implying that these plants remained at home in the *milpas*. The only other datum on Late Formative cultivation at Tomaltepec is one avocado seed from Burial 5; the seed, although incomplete, is clearly as large as or larger than the Rosario phase example which fell within the size range of modern cultivated specimens.

The Late Formative witnessed another change in the distribution of firewood collection over environmental zones. Oak regains and actually far exceeds its former popularity as a fuel, and *Arctostaphylos*, another mountain tree, is represented for the first time. Trees from the wetter lands of the river alluvium are now absent, probably due to the clearance of primary growth in this area for cultivation. Wood of the leguminous trees is present, but in smaller quantities than ever before, possibly also indicating a decrease in the availability of these woods due to the expansion of agriculture on the valley floor and even a shortening of the fallow period in old fields.

The overwhelming dominance of oak in the botanical record may be a reflection of function as well. A number of Late Formative features appeared to be large ovens or pottery kilns. Four of these large pits were bisected by adobe walls (Features 51, 53, 61, and 75) and four were not (Features 54, 68, 73, and 78). Of these eight pits, only three contained any plant remains except wood charcoal, and then in very small quantities. The preferred fuel in these pits was clearly oak, which composed a minimum of half of the total charcoal in two pits and almost all of the fuel in the others. Oak was probably selected over other woods still available in the higher elevations (e.g., *Pinus*) because of its higher heat value. The lack of other plant remains and the high heat intensity of the burning oak wood in these pits suggests that they represent some specializd activity unrelated to food processing; they would be well-suited, as Whalen proposes, to pottery firing.

Summary and Conclusions

Cultivated species and annuals growing in the cultivated fields clearly made up the bulk of the non-meat portion of the villagers' diet throughout the Formative. Corn, avocados, and two types of beans are the only crops for which we have evidence at Tomaltepec (or elsewhere in the Valley of Oaxaca, for that matter). Squash remains are conspicuously absent at Tomaltepec as they were at Fábrica San José (Ford 1976:268). We do know that the seeds of a number of plants growing spontaneously in the fields were utilized as food in addition to the domesticates themselves and really formed a separate category of resource exploitation that may prove to have been a significant contributor to the prehistoric diet. These plants here include *Chenopodium*, probably *Amaranthus* and *Portulaca*, and, in the Early Formative only, teosinte. Such seeds may have been prepared by grinding, parching, boiling, or in the case of teosinte, popping. Wild plants, like the cactus fruits for which we have evidence, must have been a menu supplement at least seasonally but they seem to have been a very minor food source.

An increase in productivity of the cultivated plants is seen in the trends toward increased size of avocado seeds and corn cupules through time (see Tables 24 and 26). In the case of the avocado, tree planting and selection for larger fruits probably began sometime during the Formative, since our small sample of Middle and Late Formative seeds included examples as large as the small cultivated "*criollo*" varieties grown in Oaxaca today. It is likely that corn productivity increased when teosinte was eliminated from fields in the Middle Formative. It was also suggested on the basis of the charcoal data that it was at this time that the amount of land cleared of primary growth and brought under cultivation was significantly expanded. This interpretation is consistent with the decrease in hunting after the early San José phase, as postulated by Whalen.

With the increase in cultivation, the character of the landscape around Tomaltepec was changing and the ways in which people made use of their surroundings changed as well. It is assumed that advantage was taken of the ready firewood produced by the clearance of land for agriculture—thus the greater quantities of valley floor species charcoal in the Middle Formative. By the Late Formative, the decreased availability of valley floor species is shown by the substantial drop-off in use of the leguminous trees and those of the wetter areas. The upper slopes of the mountains were the primary suppliers of wood in the Late Formative as they had been in the Early Formative.

The attempt to determine the organization of subsistence activities within the household and the community was partially successful. Quantitative distribution of charcoal within at least one level of House 4, the least disturbed and most extensively excavated house, proved significant (see Spencer, Appendix X). However, very few food plant remains were recovered from undisturbed house floors. Regarding intra-community organization, subsistence activities moved away from the central area of the site by the Late Formative when a much more formalized utilization of space within the community is evident.

Table 26: Measurements of Avocado Seeds and Beans*

Phase and Provenience	Avocado Seeds	*Phaseolus acutifolius*	*Phaseolus vulgaris*
Tierras Largas			
TL-1 Fea. 7	l.=11.0 w.=inc.	l.=4.1 w.=2.6	l.=7.2 w.=4.1
	l.=inc. w.=inc.	l.=3.9 w.=2.5	
		l.=7.3 w.=4.0	
		plus 3 fragments	
TL-2 Fea. 108	l.=inc. (14.0+)	l.=4.2 w.=2.4	
	w.=10.9	plus fragment	
Early San José			
ESJ-1 Fea. 109	fragmentary	l.=inc. w.=4.5	l.=inc. w.=inc.
		plus fragment	
Str. 11 Cell	fragmentary		
Rosario			
R-1 Fea. 44a	l.=18.3 w.=12.0		l.=6.1 w.=3.2
	l.=23.0 w.=15.8		
MA Ic			
Burial 5	l.=inc. (18.8+)		
	w.=inc. (13.6+)		

*Length and width in mm

APPENDIX X

SPATIAL ORGANIZATION OF AN EARLY FORMATIVE HOUSEHOLD

by Charles S. Spencer

The work in Area B at Santo Domingo Tomaltepec resulted in the exposure of a nearly complete early San José phase domestic structure. Designated House 4, the remains consisted of some 42 postholes and two packed earth occupation surfaces, representing two successive floorings of the house. Although an intrusive Late Formative (Monte Albán Ic) pit destroyed the northwest corner of the rectangular structure, three of the walls and approximately 75 percent of the floor area were undisturbed, making House 4 one of the more complete examples of an Early Formative wattle-and-daub house so far discovered in Mesoamerica. It thus presents an unusual opportunity for conducting a spatial analysis of artifact distributions within the house. The goal of such an analysis is, of course, a reconstruction of the activities that occurred therein, with an eye toward elucidating the nature of household-level socioeconomic organization.

A total of five floors were encountered in excavating House 4. Only the bottom-most two (Floors D and E), however, date to the Early Formative period. Floors A and B have a Middle Formative date and have been interpreted as the outside work area or patio associated with House 4-A, a Middle Formative (Rosario phase) residence, which was also uncovered in Area B. Floor C probably represents the interim ground surface between the Early and Middle Formative occupations.

The Early Formative levels associated with House 4 first came to light in 1972 when Henry T. Wright of the University of Michigan directed a brief but very productive excavation at the site of Tomaltepec. He uncovered approximately three sq m of what eventually turned out to be the outside ground surface immediately to the south of House 4. Large-scale work began on the upper-most levels of House 4 in the 1974 season. The floors were excavated in 50 cm by 50 cm units, and all artifacts and other objects were collected by sifting each unit through a ¼ in mesh screen. Floors A through D were excavated in this manner. Upon arriving at Floor E, however, we decided to alter the strategy somewhat by plotting two-dimensionally each object discovered on the occupation surface. In order for an item to be plotted, it had to be 1) visible, and 2) impressed into the surface. Objects impressed into the floor, we surmised, got there by being trodden in after they were broken and/or dropped. Consequently, most of the plotted items were quite small. Plate 70 shows house floor E, partially gridded for artifact plotting.

Loose items "on" or above the floor would be more subject to what Ascher (1968) has termed post-depositional "smearing" and would be less likely to remain near the point of dropping. A further complication would be introduced by the laying down of Floor D. In order to create a packed-earth floor, dirt must obviously be gathered from somewhere and spread upon the surface to be covered, and it is likely that this soil was collected close by the house. It also seems reasonable that a certain amount of outside debris would be scraped along with the soil, and would thus be laid down on top of Floor E in the process of creating Floor D. Even if some of the loose items on or above Floor E were the debris of domestic activity occurring on this bottom level, it would be extremely difficult to develop a set of criteria for separating the loose items on this basis, especially during the course of excavation. Therefore, we decided that in addition to the usual recording by quadrant of those objects present between Floors D and E, we would plot two-dimensionally those items both visible on, and impressed into, Floor E. Such two-dimensional plotting is extremely time-

PLATE 70. Floor E of House 4, gridded for artifact plotting.

consuming, but it permits nearest-neighbor analysis (Whallon 1974) of the artifact distributions on Floor E.

The basic assumption of such an analysis is, of course, that the spatial relationships among items in the archaeological record reflect their associations in the functioning system. A corollary is that items which are functionally related will tend to spatially co-occur. In analyzing occupation surfaces, the procedure is used to demonstrate the existence of "activity areas," defined by the spatial co-occurrence of functionally related items.

As Schiffer (1972) has pointed out, these fundamental assumptions are not always easy to justify. Many factors may contribute to the final composition of the archaeological record. Certainly not all items are left where they fall, and while archaeologists would like to attribute careless housekeeping to prehistoric housekeepers, there is little real basis for doing so. All evidence from present-day rural households in Oaxaca indicates that houses are kept relatively clean. Only very small items could be expected to escape the broom and be trodden into the dirt floor. By plotting only such small and impressed items, we hoped to minimize the effects of smearing.

The following categories of objects were systematically sought and plotted on Floor E: 1) Potsherds; 2) Chipped stone; 3) Bone fragments; 4) Charcoal fragments; 5) Daub fragments; and 6) Shell and other exotic items. After plotting all the visible and impressed items, the floor itself was taken up and saved by quadrant. It was later subjected to water flotation to recover floral remains.

Of the plotted items, only the potsherds, chipped stone, bone, and charcoal yielded samples large enough for further analysis. The sherds were analyzed by the authors, ninety tiny sherds in all being plotted. These were described according to the attributes of form, paste, surface finish, and decoration. This resulted in the definition of two major categories of sherds: those from burnished jars and those from burnished bowls. These two categories account for about 70 percent of the sherds found on Floor E. The remaining sherds comprised categories that were either too small in number or too loosely defined to justify their use in a rigorous analysis. The functions tentatively assigned to the two useful categories were 1) Burnished jars—Short-term storage or food preparation; and 2) Burnished bowls—Food serving or consumption.

The chipped stone debris was analyzed by John Rick (see Appendix VIII of this study). Stone was subdivided into the major categories of 1) Angular debitage; 2) Small flakes (flakes less than 2.5 cm maximum dimension); 4) Cores; and 5) Various categories of tools (see Appendix VIII). Unfortunately, only the angular debitage and small flakes had sample sizes large enough to justify their use in further analysis. Of these two, the smaller flakes had the less ambiguous functional implication of tool maintenance and the finer stages of tool manufacture.

The plotted bone fragments were mostly too small for positive identification. However, it is tentatively suggested that the bone fragments are largely the remains of food preparation activities.

The plotted charcoal fragments were also too small for clear wood identification. The charcoal collected from the flotation procedures on Floor E, however, has been identified primarily as pine (see Appendix IX). The pine forest of the sierra zone is but a half-hour's hike from the archaeological site, and the ancient inhabitants of Tomaltepec could have gathered firewood in much the same manner as do their present-day counterparts. It seems clear that a functional correlate of charcoal is cooking, which would fall under the general rubric of food preparation.

In sum, then, we have five categories of items to use for spatial analysis that satisfy the two criteria of sufficiently large sample size and relatively unambiguous functional significance. These are 1) Charcoal fragments; 2) Bone fragments; 3) Burnished jar sherds; 4) Burnished bowl sherds; and 5) Small flakes. Figures 33 through 46 present the distributions of the above categories on Floor E. All maps employed in this analysis were generated using the Plot Description System of the University of Michigan Computing Center (Fronczak, 1971).

The excellent preservation of the postholes associated with House 4 allowed us to distinguish between the inside and outside of the house. This will permit a spatial analysis of those activities that occurred within the house without the complications introduced by deposition from outside activities. It was also possible to infer various features of the house from the posthole patterns alone. Figure 11 (Ch. 3) is a drawing of House 4 labeled with the field interpretations of several distinctive features. Along the south wall of the house is a 1.25 m gap in the posthole alignment that we interpreted as the major door to the house. Running parallel to and approximately 0.5 m south of the doorway is a line of smaller postholes that would seem to be a windbreak, sheltering the entrance and providing privacy. Some wattle-and-daub houses in the Oaxaca Valley today have this feature. The absence of artifacts in the vicinity of the proposed doorway lends credence to this interpretation.

The odd circular pattern of postholes in the eastern part of the house was tentatively identified as the remains of a firestand for cooking. There is also some ethnographic basis for this interpretation. Similar features have been noted by the author in wattle-and-daub houses in the town of Xaaga in the Valley of Oaxaca, and in the town of Huamelulpan in the neighboring Mixteca Alta area of the State of Oaxaca. These firestands are constructed by sinking posts into the dirt floor upon which a box, often filled with dirt or sand, is mounted. Fires are then lit inside the box. Occasionally small braziers are placed on the stand as well. The curving line of postholes to the north of the house was given the field interpretation of a small auxiliary structure, perhaps a storage area.

The flotation of Floor E itself yielded a substantial amount of charcoal. Weights by grid unit were then obtained and used as input for the Geog:Contur program, a computer routine of the Michigan Terminal Service which draws the best fitting contour map based on a lattice of density

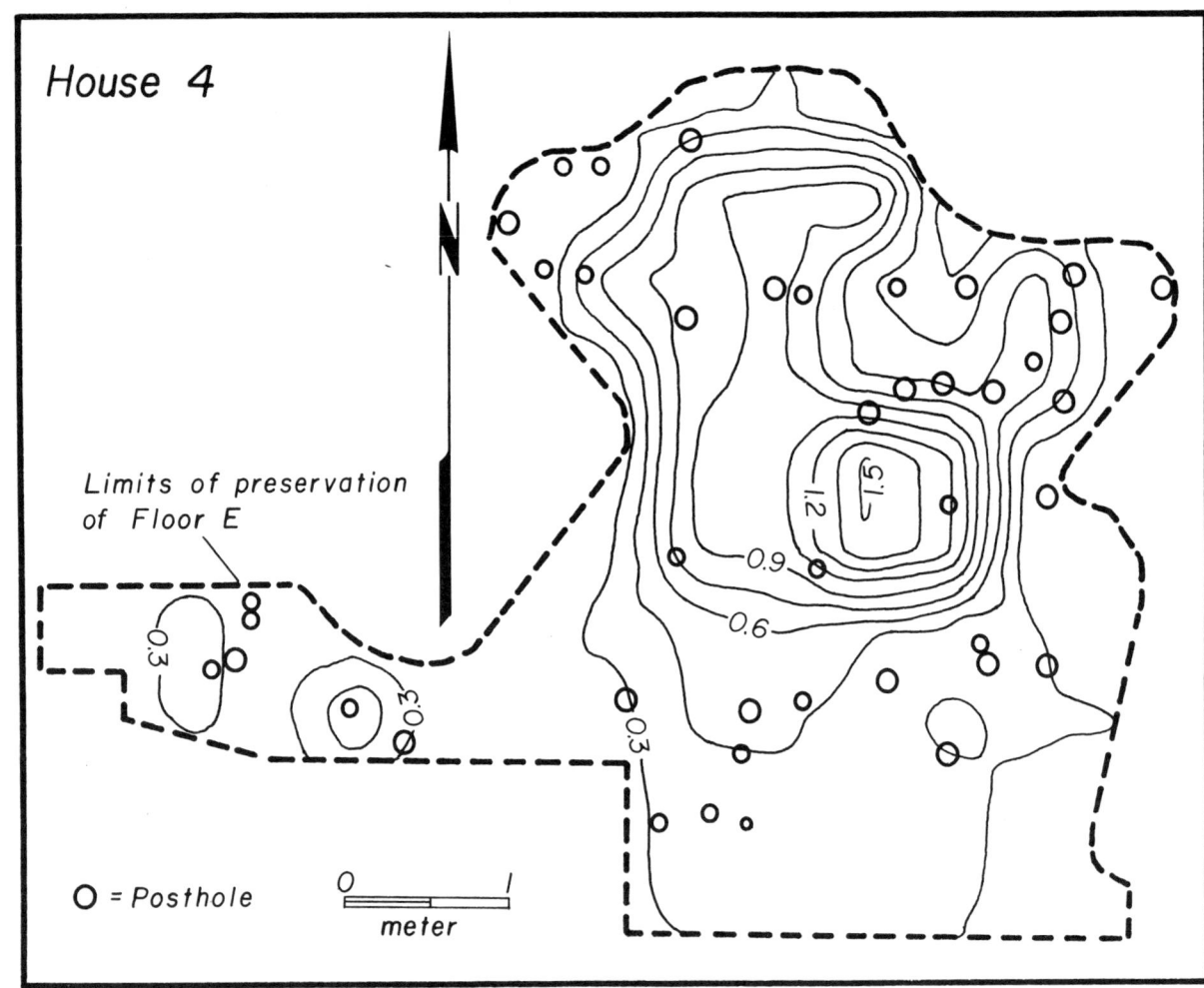

FIGURE 53. House 4, Floor E, contour map of charcoal density. Contour interval, 0.15 gm. per square meter. Highest contour level, 1.50 gm. per square meter. Lowest contour level, 0.15 gm. per square meter.

values. (Dept. of Geography, University of Michigan 1974). The map generated by this program is shown in Fig. 53. If the base map of the house floor with postholes is examined in conjuction with this contour map, it can be clearly seen that the area of highest charcoal density is highly associated spatially with the above-mentioned circular pattern of postholes. The field interpretation of a firestand is evidently substantiated.

Having demonstrated the probable location of cooking in the household on the basis of posthole patterns and charcoal density, we should see if the distributional patterns of the plotted items inside the house manifest any sort of non-random clustering, and whether the objects related to food preparation are spatially associated with the inferred locus of cooking. The subsequent analysis consists of four steps: 1) Determining if there exist any tendencies toward non-random spatial clustering for each category of plotted items; 2) Examining the patterns of mutual spatial association among these categories; 3) Using the results of the first two steps to postulate the existence of activity loci; and 4) Examining the spatial relationships between the plotted items and the locus of cooking as inferred from the posthole pattern and charcoal density.

A nearest-neighbor analysis was carried out for

APPENDIX X

each of the five categories of plotted items. Following Whallon (1974), the statistic used was:

$$R = \frac{\bar{r}_o}{\bar{r}_e}$$

where $\bar{r}_o$ = the observed average nearest-neighbor distance
and $\bar{r}_e$ = the expected average nearest-neighbor distance, which is computed as follows:

$$\bar{r}_e = \frac{1}{2\sqrt{d}}, \text{ where } d = \text{the density of the category, i.e.,}$$

$$d = \frac{\text{no. of items}}{\text{area}}$$

The following within-category nearest-neighbor indices resulted:

Charcoal fragments	R = 0.66073
Bone fragments	R = 0.75092
Burnished jars	R = 0.83143
Burnished bowls	R = 1.01389
Small flakes	R = 1.06597

R values less than 1.0 indicate tendencies toward non-random clustering; values near 1.0 suggest that the spacing is random; values larger than 1.0 indicate tendencies toward non-random regular spacing, approaching R = 2.1491 as an upper limit for perfect hexagonal spacing.

Based on the R values alone, it can be seen that non-random clustering tends to characterize the distributional patterns of charcoal, bone, and burnished jars. The R values of the burnished bowls and the small flakes suggest randomness.

A level of significance can also be attached to this statistic. It is calculated (under the assumption of a normal distribution of nearest-neighbor distances) by using the standard normal variate:

$$Z = \frac{\bar{r}_o - \bar{r}_e}{\bar{r}_e}, \text{ where } \bar{r}_e = \frac{0.26136}{Nd}$$

$$N = \text{no. of items}$$
$$d = \text{density}$$

A level of significance may then be read from any table of areas under a normal curve. Thus the following significance levels can be assigned to the within-category nearest-neighbor indices:

Charcoal Fragments	0.08 level of significance
Bone fragments	0.09 level of significance
Burnished jars	0.10 level of significance
Burnished bowls	0.80 level of significance
Small flakes	0.60 level of significance

If we take the 0.10 level as our cut-off point, the distributions of charcoal, bone, and jars emerge as significantly clustered, while the bowls and small flakes exhibit non-significant or random distributions.

Having determined which items manifest intra-category non-random clustering, we should proceed to examine the patterns of spatial association among categories. As Whallon discusses in his 1974 article, there is as yet no standardized way of assessing strength of association among categories of plotted items. He proposes a couple of alternative methods, one of which involves drawing a series of circles for each category using the location of every object as an origin and making the radii equal to the average observed nearest-neighbor distance plus 1.65 standard deviations, the object being a kind of 95 percent confidence limit for the distribution of each item. He then suggests that the circumscribed areas be overlaid and the regions of overlap calculated. A numerical index of spatial association between any two categories can be calculated by dividing the area of overlap by the sum of the area of overlap plus the areas of non-overlap for the two categories. The resulting indices can then be ordered in a matrix.

This method was attempted with the House 4 data, but the results were not satisfactory. There seemed to be no logically consistent way to measure the associations between the items that exhibited clustering with those that were randomly distributed. Drawing circles with radii equal to $\bar{r}_o$ plus 1.65 standard deviations around the locations of the burnished bowls and small flakes yielded circles that covered nearly the entire area of Floor E. The resulting matrix seemed inconclusive and somewhat spurious.

A different method was therefore decided upon. Average nearest-neighbor distances between categories were calculated by measuring the distance from each item to its nearest neighbor in the opposite category. This yielded a matrix of distance coefficients in which the patterns of mutual association among categories are more clearly visible.

	Charcoal	Bone	Jars	Bowls	Small Flakes
Charcoal	0.0				
Bone	0.76875	0.0			
Jars	0.83010	0.65708	0.0		
Bowls	1.36914	1.37217	0.92832	0.0	
Small Flakes	1.86136	1.23013	1.78330	1.14584	0.0

Because the matrix is based on measures of distance, the low values indicate categories that have high degrees of spatial association.

In order to obtain a graphical representation of the pattern of inter-category associations, the above matrix was subjected to an Unconditional Monotone Distance Analysis using the Guttman-Lingoes Non-metric Program SSA-I (Lingoes 1972; 1973). Also known as multi-dimensional scaling, this analysis orders the variables on a matrix of similarity or dissimilarity coefficients through a specified number of dimensions so that the spatial relationships in the resulting configuration reflect the patterns of association denoted by the matrix. In this case, a two-dimenstional plot was generated with a Guttman-Lingoes Coefficient of Alienation of 0.0, and a Kruskal's Stress of 0.0, both measures indicating perfect fit between the matrix and the configuration. Figure 54 shows the resulting configuration. By assigning the postulated functional correlates of each category to the points on the plot, it can be easily seen that the items pertaining to food preparation, namely the charcoal, bone, and jars, exhibit a marked degee of inter-category clustering relative to burnished bowls (food serving, consumption) and small flakes (tool maintenance). The configuration demonstrates that the three functionally similar items tend to be spatially associated. The fact that these items also exhibited intra-category non-random clustering leads us to posit the existence of an activity area pertaining to food preparation, defined solely on the basis of artifact distribution.

After carrying out this stage of the analysis, it seemed possible that the average nearest-neighbor distances between categories might be partially dependent upon variations in density between each pair of categories. To test this possibility, a linear regression analysis was carried out using the total density for each pair of categories as the independent variable and the average nearest-neighbor distance between categories as the dependent variable. The results of the regression analysis are presented in Table 27. It can easily be seen that the regression is not very significant (S = .2554). The correlation coefficient is likewise not large (-.397). The R-Sqr value indicates that only 15.79 percent of the variation in the average nearest-neighbor distances between categories is explained by a simple linear regression model using density as the independent variable.

Nevertheless, the residuals from this regression were computed and utilized as an input matrix in the SSA-I Guttman-Lingoes Non-metric Program. A two-dimensional plot was generated with a Coefficient of Alienation of 0.00109 and a Stress of 0.00065. As can be seen in Figure 55, this configuration does not differ significantly from that generated by using the matrix of unadjusted average nearest-neighbor distances between categories. Charcoal, bone, and jars continue to be associated while bowls and small flakes do not. This suggests that the associational patterns are relatively independent of the variation in density.

The next step in the analysis consists of relating the distribution of artifacts to the already-discussed patterning in the density of charcoal fragments in the floor itself. To this end, the distributional maps of the various artifact categories were laid over the charcoal density contour map (shown in Figure 53). The distances from the epicenter of the charcoal density contour map to each item of every category were measured, and simple arithmetic means of these distances were computed (Table 28). An inter-category distance matrix was then constructed by computing the absolute values of the differences between average epicenter-to-item distances between all category pairs.

	Charcoal	Bone	Jars	Bowls	Small Flakes
Charcoal	0.0				
Bone	0.48	0.0			
Jars	0.66	0.19	0.0		
Bowls	1.89	1.41	1.23	0.0	
Small Flakes	2.37	1.90	1.71	0.49	0.0

This matrix was also analyzed using the Guttman-Lingoes SSA-I program. The resulting two-dimensional configuration (with a Coefficient of Alienation of 0.0 and Stress of 0.0) is shown in Figure 56.

The above procedure suggests that the five artifact categories can be combined into two groups based on similar patterning in epicenter-to-item distances. One group consists of charcoal, bone and jars. These artifact categories have low average epicenter-to-item distances and tend to

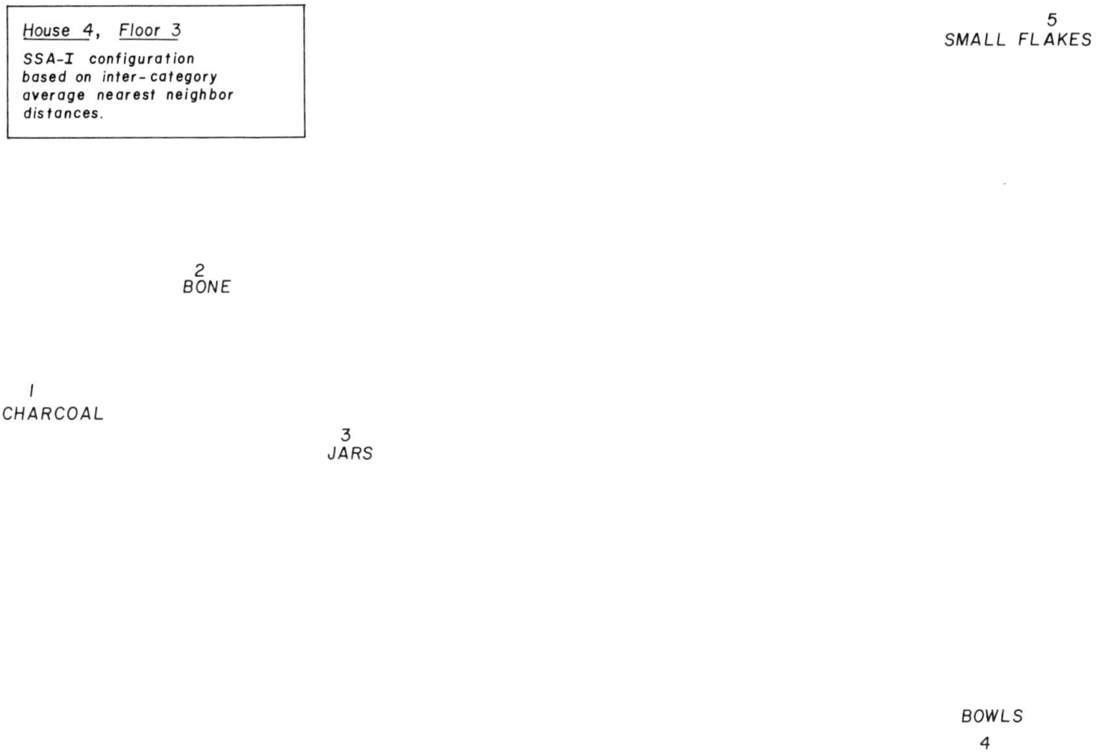

APPENDIX X

```
House 4, Floor 3
SSA-I configuration
based on inter-category
average nearest neighbor
distances.
```

                                                            5
                                                      SMALL FLAKES

                    2
                   BONE

    1
  CHARCOAL
                              3
                             JARS

                                                            BOWLS
                                                              4

FIGURE 54. House 4, Floor E, SSA–I configuration based on inter-category average nearest neighbor distances.

Table 27: Least Squares Regression Analysis of Variance of Inter-Category Average Nearest-Neighbor Distance

Source	DF	Sum of Sqrs	Mean Sqr	F-Stat	Signif
Regression	1	.24180	.24180	1.5007	.2554
Error	8	1.2890	.16113		
Total	9	1.5308			

Multiple	R = .39744		R-Sqr. = .15796	SE = .40141	
Variable	Partial	Coeffic	Std Error	T-Stat	Signif
Constant		1.6869	.42143	4.0028	.0039
Density	−.39744	−.67163	.54826	−1.2250	.2554

occur equidistant from the charcoal density epicenter. These three categories, all assigned functional correlates of food preparation and cooking, were also shown to be characterized by intra-category non-random clustering as well as inter-category spatial association. The conjunction of these several lines of evidence strongly supports the hypothesis that a food preparation and cooking locus existed in the eastern half of the house, probably focused on the inferred firestand.

The other group of artifact categories derived from the matrix based on epicenter-to-item distances is comprised of burnished bowls and small flakes. These two categories have high average epicenter-to-item distances and tend to occur equidistant from the charcoal density epicenter, although these categories evince rather more variability on this last point than do the categories in the first group. This means that although the burnished bowls and small flakes exhibit neither intra-category clustering nor inter-category spatial association (as determined by our previous nearest-neighbor analyses), they do manifest associational tendencies based on the variable of distance from the charcoal density epicenter. They tend to occur equidistant from the locus of food preparation activities. Clearly, the intra-category randomness of distribution for bowls and small flakes should not be taken to mean that their distributions are not "significant". The other three categories of plotted items manifest non-random intra-category spatial clustering. If the bowl and retouch flake distributions were random because of post-depositional smearing, one would expect all the categories to be similarly distributed. The only reasonable conclusion is that the activities which resulted in the deposition of bowls and

```
5
SMALL FLAKES                                    ┌─────────────────────────┐
                                                │ House 4,  Floor 3       │
                                                │ SSA-I configuration     │
                                                │ based on residualized matrix. │
                                                └─────────────────────────┘


                                                                  BONE
                                                                   2
                                                                   |
                                                                CHARCOAL




                                                                   JARS
                                                                    3




  BOWLS
    4
```

FIGURE 55. House 4, Floor E, SSA-I configuration based on residualized matrix.

Table 28: Descriptive Measures of Epicenter-To-Item Distances

Artifact Category	Mean	Standard Deviation
Charcoal fragments	1.06 m	0.52 m
Bone fragments	1.54 m	0.60 m
Plain burnished jar sherds	1.73 m	0.92 m
Burnished bowl sherds	2.95 m	1.82 m
Small flakes	3.44 m	2.34 m

retouch flakes were themselves not clustered in a non-random manner. It seems that there were no well-defined loci within this household where food consumption and tool maintenance took place. However, these activities manifest spatial structuring with respect to the locus of food preparation, in that they tend to occur equidistant from this locus.

In sum, the spatial organization of activities in House 4 is characterized by a dichotomous structure: a "core" area of food preparation activities on the one hand, with a zone of non-food preparation activities on the other. While the zone itself is relatively distinct, activities seem to have occurred within it in a less structured, *ad hoc* fashion.

If we can assume that food preparation was essentially a female activity, and that tool maintenance was primarily a male one (a not unreasonable assumption on the basis of ethnographic activity patterns), it becomes possible to infer certain features of household-level socio-economic organization. Perhaps the most distinctive quality of the patterning of activities in House 4 is a well-defined locus of female activities. The patterns gleaned from the above analysis also suggest that males were doing very little in the household itself. It must be emphasized that some 20 percent of the west side of the house was destroyed by a later intrusion. By the same token, however, if 20 percent of the eastern (food preparation) end of the house was similarly removed, considerable evidence of those activities would still remain.

This pattern becomes especially interesting in light of what Flannery (1972a:45) has reported from the sites of Tierras Largas and San José Mogote in the Etla branch of the Oaxaca Valley.

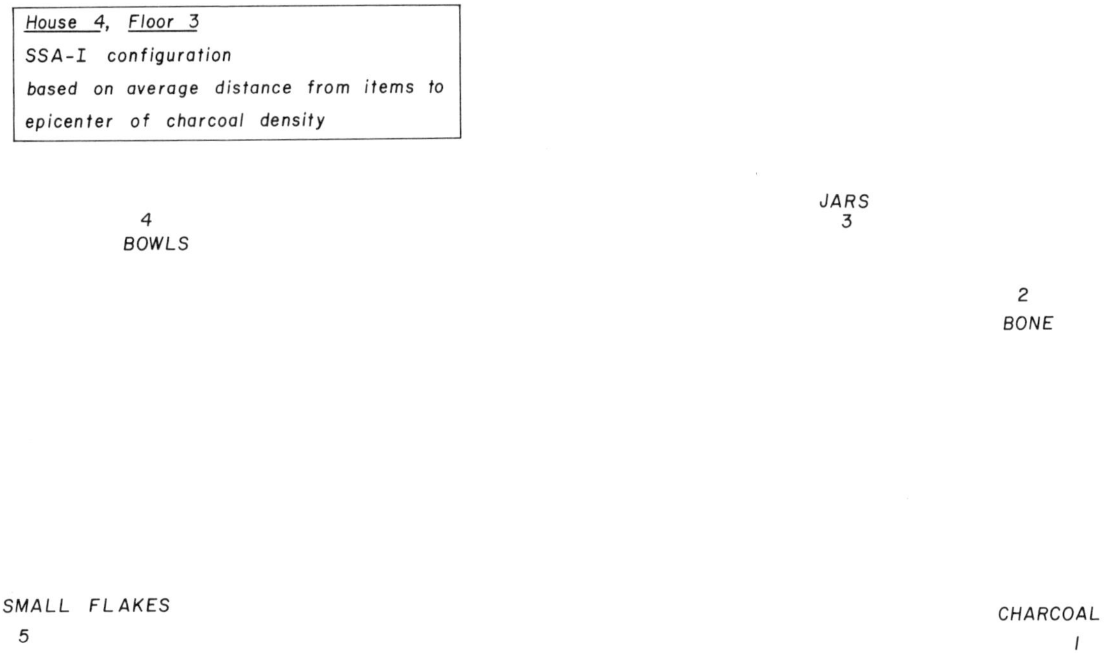

APPENDIX X

House 4, Floor 3
SSA-I configuration
based on average distance from items to
epicenter of charcoal density

```
              4                                              JARS
           BOWLS                                              3

                                                              2
                                                            BONE




SMALL FLAKES                                               CHARCOAL
     5                                                         I
```

FIGURE 56. House 4, Floor E, SSA–I configuration based on average distance from items to epicenter of charcoal density.

Table 29: Least Squares Regression, House 4: Analysis of Variance of Inter-Category Average Nearest-Neighbor Distance

Source	DF	Sum of Sqrs	Mean Sqr	F-Stat	Signif
Regression	1	.24180	.24180	1.5007	.2554
Error	8	1.2890	.16113		
Total	9	1.5308			

Multiple R = .39744   R-Sqr. = .15796   SE = .40141

Variable	Partial	Coeffic	Std Error	T-Stat	Signif
Constant		1.6869	.42143	4.0028	.0039
Density	−.39744	−.67163	.54826	−1.2250	.2554

He finds that households at these sites are characterized by distinct male and female activity areas, defined on the basis of artifact concentrations.

> In every case where extensive floor scatters could be mapped, "women's tools" ... were in the northern half (to the right as one entered the door). To the south (on the left as one entered the door) ... were the flint-chipping areas with cores, scrapers, knives, burins, drills, and presumed "men's tools."

> (These) ... tool scatters which could be plotted on the house floors suggest that houses were "conceptually divided" into men's and womens's work areas, as are present-day Indian households in highland Chiapas.

The analysis of House 4 at Tomaltepec certainly does not contradict this suggestion, although it may suggest that in this case the locus of female-related activities was the better defined one. Clearly, more Early Formative houses must be excavated and quantitatively analyzed to clarify our understanding of the use of household space. This appendix has attempted to explore some of the necessary methodological and analytical techniques.

APPENDIX XI

EXCAVATION AND ANALYSIS OF STRUCTURE 14

by Jane Katherine Sallade

Introduction

The Monte Albán II occupation of Tomaltepec has already been described by Whalen in Chapter VII. This appendix describes the excavation and analysis of Structure 14, a Monte Albán II building which represents the final construction atop Mound 1. All that remained of Structure 14 was a remnant of heavy stucco floor and the traces of an adobe wall which divided it into two rooms: an eastern room with evidence of burning and smoke-staining, and a western room without such burning. On the basis of their recent excavation of similar structures at San José Mogote, Kent Flannery and Joyce Marcus (1976a, 1976b, and personal communication) believe Structure 14 to be the remnant of a standard Monte Albán II two-room temple.

Excavation of Structure 14

One-meter grids for the (main mound) excavations were established using a cartesian coordinate system. The zero-zero point lay in a field to the southeast of the site, such that all possible extensions of the site would be in the northwest quadrant of the coordinate system. A baulk, running east-west through squares 501 North, was left for future reference.

Excavation began in the area with the greatest marginal exposure of the floor, to the south of the baulk and east of an old looters' trench, running southwest-northeast across the mound. The dark brown silt, from 0-5 cm above the cement floor, was carefully screened (using a .5 cm screen) to retrieve any small plaster fragments, rocks, sherds, and other materials. Recovery of material from peripheral squares, which did not have five cm of fill above the semi-exposed floor, was selective. These latter materials were not used in the later analyses because of the possibility of disturbance and contamination. Temporally diagnostic pottery sherds from the eastern squares appeared to date to Late Monte Albán I or Monte Albán II. Plate 8 (Chapter I) shows the excavated eastern portion of the stucco floor, with large rocks and fragments of a metate still in place. The crack in square 500 North 499 West became a hole during the course of the excavation, through the activities of villagers who visited the site in the evenings. When the edges of the stucco floor had been cleaned and reinforced with stones and cement, the hole was enlarged, explored, and sealed with cement in the hope of dissuading villagers from digging on their own.

Initial work on the western area of the floor, separated from the east by the previously mentioned trench, isolated a wall running through the eastern squares of the western area of the floor. Foundation stones, which were smooth faced on the western side, supported remnants of an adobe brick superstructure. The stucco of the lower, western floor curved upward where it met the wall. Sherds from the western squares were clearly Monte Albán II.

During excavation of the eastern floor, it was noted that sherds and other cultural debris, while present from 0 to 5 cm above the floor, could not be ascertained to lie directly on the floor. Therefore, it appeared that the soil above the eastern portion of the floor might have been disturbed sometime after abandonment and/or building collapse. However, the very dark brown silt over the western portion of the floor was much more compact and yielded almost twice the amount of material as that recovered from the eastern squares. A large portion of the sherds and other materials recovered from the western area were found on or near the surface of the floor.

The "eastern" and "western" areas of the floor are discussed as separate sections of the excavation. The eastern floor extends into that portion of the excavation which is west of the looters' trench. However, it is still convenient to discuss the two floors as "eastern" and "western", since the area of the eastern floor to the west of the looters' trench was either too exposed or too eroded to be a part of the analysis.

Data Integration and Analysis

Laboratory Procedures

After washing and sorting of gross categories of materials in the lab, a typology was established, which defined 18 categories of material present in sufficient sample sizes for statistical manipulations. Table 30 lists these 18 categories.

Table 30. Eighteen Categories of Material from Structure 14, Tomaltepec

Variable	Category	Computer Code Name
1	Thin gray jar	THGRJR
2	Thin jar, other	THOJR
3	Medium gray jar	MGRJR
4	Medium jar, other	MOJR
5	Thick jar, other	TKOJR
6	Thin gray bowl	THGRBL
7	Thin bowl, other	THOBL
8	Medium gray bowl	MGBL
9	Medium bowl, other	MOBL
10	Plaster fragment	PLFRAG
11	Plaster fragment with smooth face	PLFACE
12	Cracked rock	CRKRK
13	Pebble	PEBS
14	Rough flakes	RFLK
15	Flakes	FLK
16	Fragment of adobe	ADOBE
17	Fragment of animal bone	BONE
18	Chert fragment	CHERT

The pottery was divided into two basic classes called "bowls" and "jars". These labels refer to those vessels which are burnished or not burnished on the interior, respectively. The labels may, or may not, refer to their actual reconstructions. Bowl and jar categories were separated into thin, medium, and thick classes, based on the distribution of wall widths in a non-random sample of sherds. Thin sherds are those with walls of less than .5 cm in thickness. Thick sherds are those with walls greater than 1 cm thick. Each of these classes was subdivided further into Monte Albán gray and "other", based on the prevalent ware types. In this manner, twelve pottery categories were established. However, no thick gray jar sherds were present, and the samples of two thick gray bowl sherds and ten thick other bowl sherds were too small for inclusion in the analysis.

The other established categories were plaster fragments, plaster fragments with a smooth face, cracked rock, pebbles, rough flakes, flakes, adobe, bone, and chert. Such small samples of obsidian, shell, and cane-impressed daub were present that they were excluded from statistical analysis. (The sample sizes of these latter materials were, respectively: ten pieces, weighing a total of less than six gm; two fragments, weighing a total of less than one gm; and six pieces, weighing a total of less than 52 gm.)

Counts and weights were recorded, by square, for all materials larger than one cubic cm. Materials which passed through a one cm screen were sorted into five categories: plaster, pebbles, rock, sherd, and adobe. These latter materials were weighed, but not counted, and the information was tabulated separately, by square. Densities were calculated for all materials, by square, since the excavated areas of all squares were not equal. Standardized densities were calculated for each category, by square, as weights per 1/20th cubic meter. These densities are presented in Tables 31 and 32.

Data Analysis
ANALYSIS NO. 1 OF MACRO-MATERIAL

Correlation analyses were run first on materials from the east and west floors, treating the two as a single unit. Pearson's r and Spearman's *rho* values were calculated for the resulting eighteen squares, using as variables the densities of occurrence of the eighteen material categories. The resulting correlation matrices were ordered to help define sets of inter-related variables. The ordered matrices (not shown) were not highly informative. Some positive correlations appeared to result from arbitrary typological divisions, such as between medium jars other than gray and thick jars other than gray; or between flakes and rough flakes. Other strong positive correlations were not expected and were less easily explained, such as those between adobe and thin jars other than gray; thick jars other than gray and bone; and medium jars other than gray and cracked rock. Some were much lower than expected, such as among the various categories of building materials: adobe, plaster fragments, plaster faces, and pebbles.

Table 31: Materials Larger Than One Cubic Centimeter and Variable Labels: Densities per 1/20th Cubic Meter

Squares	Square Number	Level	1	2	3	4	5	6	7	8	9	10	11	12	Variable
1	498N 499W	2	11	61	48	322	64	19	19	35	34	1434	1	2629	1 THGRJR
2	498N 500W	2	24	35	13	93	72	15	9	26	35	1076	65	1206	2 THOJR
3	498N 501W	2	23	20	28	110	30	13	13	1	69	269	15	1090	3 MGRJR
4	499N 499W	2	44	56	60	260	42	6	8	32	78	790	1	2140	4 MOJR
5	499N 500W	2	34	4	8	300	130	1	1	1	82	118	1	1630	5 TKOJR
6	499N 501W	2	10	28	18	296	57	8	1	1	79	122	1	1198	6 THGRBL
7	500N 499W	2	70	48	16	832	134	8	1	1	180	280	124	3758	7 THOBL
8	500N 500W	2	53	80	22	544	147	1	1	38	35	71	422	4144	8 MGBL
9	500N 501W	2	186	264	50	1000	50	1	21	1	171	1871	3550	8936	9 MOBL
10	500N 504W	2	8	23	8	287	351	1	13	1	42	549	100	2000	10 PLFRAG
11	502N 503WE	2	18	26	1	118	1	1	1	1	1	279	65	1044	11 PLFACE
12	502N 502WW	2	40	1	1	347	173	1	1	1	1	4533	2933	4600	12 CRKRK
13	502N 504W	2	82	86	10	900	170	8	14	1	78	1320	2110	3336	13 PEBS
14	502N 505W	2	42	234	34	610	260	2	22	16	210	1560	10	1466	14 RFLK
15	503N 503WE	2	1	1	80	173	93	33	1	1	33	1500	800	2033	15 FLK
16	503N 503WW	2	52	26	1	322	69	1	1	1	1	78	609	2848	16 ADOBE
17	503N 504W	2	16	36	1	1342	392	1	1	1	38	416	22	7044	17 BONE
18	503N 505W	2	79	265	98	796	265	1	6	1	31	653	153	6414	18 CHERT
19	504N 504W	2	47	220	87	1313	106	47	1	567	133	1920	80	6667	
20	504N 505W	2	22	433	100	1389	833	1	55	122	33	1222	111	9667	

Table 32: Materials Smaller Than One Cubic Centimeter and Variable Labels: Densities per 1/20th Cubic Meter

Squares	Square Number	Level	1	2	3	4	5	Variable
1	498N 499W	2	60	1	61	11	1	1 PLASTER
2	498N 500W	2	535	10	634	42	4	2 PEBBLES
3	489N 501W	2	13	1	10	23	1	3 ROCK
4	499N 499W	2	82	12	234	33	1	4 SHERD
5	499N 500W	2	1	1	11	1	1	5 ADOBE
6	499N 501W	2	28	1	119	15	1	
7	500N 499W	2	113	30	740	455	1	
8	500N 500W	2	2	1	8	2	1	
9	500N 501W	2	71	29	254	132	1	
10	500N 504W	2	67	12	1168	34	40	
11	502N 503WE	2	362	9	2116	28	20	
12	502N 503WW	2	3333	40	3720	30	1	
13	502N 504W	2	1310	28	2680	112	7	
14	502N 505W	2	2080	91	1127	200	24	
15	503N 503WE	2	1300	20	3333	40	1	
16	503N 503WW	2	928	25	2236	76	27	
17	503N 504W	2	3497	1333	9667	410	123	
18	503N 505W	2	1173	27	3184	139	23	
19	504N 504W	2	2780	67	3533	200	93	
20	504N 505W	2	2053	79	6158	311	132	

APPENDIX XI

ANALYSIS NO. 2 OF MACRO-MATERIALS

For further analysis, the eastern and western floors were divided into separate units. Correlation analyses were run separately on materials from the two areas. The division was undertaken for several reasons. First, the two rooms involved, separated by a wall, could have had different functions. Second, the soil color and compactness, as well as the depth of deposit of artifacts, were noted to be quite dissimilar between the two areas during the course of excavation. These differences suggested several types of distinction between the two rooms. If there were functional (or other) distinctions between these two rooms, which might be masked by analyzing them as a unit, these might be uncovered by analyzing them separately.

Matrix ordering for Pearson's r values, using only nine cases (admittedly dangerous) and 18 variables, revealed five sets of interrelated variables for the western floor. One set consisted of thin bowls other than gray, thick jars other than gray, and chert. The second consisted of cracked rock and medium jars other than gray. The third set of interrelated materials consisted of plaster fragments, plaster faces, and flakes. The fourth set consisted of thin jars other than gray and medium gray jars. The fifth set consisted of medium gray bowls and thin gray bowls. This last grouping may suggest that our distinction between "thin" and "medium" may be of little significance. The ordered matrix is presented in Table 33.

The matrix ordering of Pearson's r values for the eastern floor suggested two sets of interrelated variables. The major set consisted of building materials (including plaster faces, adobe, cracked rock, plaster fragments, and, by visual inspection, daub) and sherds of thin gray jars, thin jars other than gray, and medium jars other than gray. Medium bowls other than gray partially associate with this set, as do thin bowls other than gray. Medium gray bowls and pebbles constitute a separate set of related variables. The ordered matrix is presented in Table 34.

Categories of small sample sizes (and those which did not relate to any set of interrelated variables at a statistically significant level) were then excluded from further consideration. Spearman's rho matrices using the remaining variables were next ordered and examined.

Examination of the ordered rank-correlation values for the western floor indicated a strong pattern of interrelation among cracked rock, chert, and medium jars other than gray. Building materials do not associate positively with each other on the western floor (Table 35).

Examination of the ordered rank-correlation for the eastern floor did not reveal the same pattern of interrelationships observed for the western floor. The matrix is dominated by two overlapping sets of related variables: 1) cracked rock, thin gray jars, and plaster face fragments; and 2) cracked rock, medium jars other than gray, and thin jars other than gray. Medium bowls other than gray correlated in part with medium jars other than gray, but otherwise was distributed independently of the above five variables (see Table 36). The variation of cracked rock and medium jars other than gray was further examined by constructing two residualized variables. These two residualized variables did not correlate with any other variables (matrices not shown).

Interpretation of Breakage Patterns

Sherds of thin jars other than gray were found to have consistently greater weights than thin gray jar sherds. Such sherds, on the average, weigh 3.06 gm more per sherd than do thin gray jar sherds. However, there would also seem to have been a greater breakage rate for medium (and thin) jars other than gray when compared with thin gray jars. The former may have been subjected to activities which resulted in greater stress, and subsequently more frequent breakage, than the latter. This greater breakage rate for medium (and thin) jars other than gray, is indicated by a 8.02:1 ratio of sherd *counts* of the former to thin gray jars. (The effects of differences in vessel size among the three ceramic categories on the breakage rate cannot be evaluated here with the present data.)

Analysis and Interpretation of Micro-Materials

A rank-correlation analysis of densities of small materials (those which passed through a 1 cm screen), gave somewhat different results on both the western and eastern floors than did the macro-material analyses (Tables 37 and 38). In general, both floors exhibit a pattern of correlation among micro-materials used together in building con-

Table 33: Western Floor—Seriation of Correlations (Nine Cases, Eighteen Variables)

REL	REL 0	1	11	15	10	14	9	13	7	5	18	2	3	12	4	8	6	16	17
1	0	350	44	39	-10	87	-33	-25	-51	-32	85	196	-12	-6	-1	144	-1	-58	
11	350	0	856	720	272	-32	-49	-24	-35	-26	-46	-45	-20	-36	-26	-14	-36	-33	
15	44	856	0	912	537	-26	-19	-23	-23	-22	-38	-36	-11	-39	-19	-16	-34	-27	
10	39	720	912	0	554	25	-2	-9	-16	-8	-11	-7	22	-16	152	159	-26	-24	
14	-10	272	537	554	0	469	538	-4	-14	-28	-13	-32	-38	-28	-26	-24	31	-32	
9	87	-32	-26	25	469	0	556	130	-14	-16	327	198	-30	189	372	418	284	-3	
13	-33	-49	-19	-2	538	556	0	460	364	354	532	278	94	214	103	-6	114	-23	
7	-25	-24	-23	-9	-4	130	460	0	857	853	749	460	360	340	-5	-24	-33	43	
5	-51	-35	-23	-16	-14	-14	364	857	0	899	622	413	608	482	-11	-34	-6	146	
18	-32	-26	-22	-8	-28	-16	354	853	899	0	732	563	760	617	158	-7	-11	-6	
2	85	-46	-38	-11	-13	327	532	749	622	732	0	904	578	574	347	166	-1	-18	
3	196	-45	-36	-7	-32	198	278	460	413	563	904	0	647	555	533	384	54	-10	
12	-12	-20	-11	22	-38	-30	94	360	608	760	578	647	0	804	374	202	315	-24	
4	-6	-26	-39	-16	-28	189	214	340	482	617	574	555	804	0	516	426	643	-23	
8	-1	-26	-19	152	-26	372	103	-5	-11	158	347	533	374	516	0	960	234	105	
6	144	-14	-16	159	-24	418	-6	-24	-34	-7	166	384	202	426	960	0	294	84	
16	-1	-36	-34	-26	31	284	114	-33	-6	-11	-1	54	315	643	234	294	0	-23	
17	-58	-33	-27	-24	-32	-3	-23	43	146	-6	-18	-10	-24	-23	105	84	-23	0	

Table 34: Eastern Floor—Seriation of Correlations (Nine Cases, Eighteen Variables)

REL	REL 0	6	15	8	13	3	7	10	2	16	11	12	1	4	9	17	5	14	18
6	0	578	255	234	80	412	262	-37	-45	-45	-49	-56	-53	-24	0	-44	-32	-28	
15	578	0	420	219	114	305	124	-22	-31	-32	-19	-43	-21	-24	-12	58	265	-22	
8	255	420	0	706	361	36	205	-7	-22	-26	-11	-29	-27	-57	-31	79	342	-32	
13	234	219	706	0	79	-28	26	-23	-40	-40	-13	-23	1	-12	403	422	207	24	
3	80	114	361	79	0	641	653	529	383	390	407	351	182	209	-27	-59	-40	-76	
7	412	305	36	-28	641	0	781	520	491	494	356	342	47	172	-34	-70	-36	-63	
10	262	124	205	26	653	781	0	705	639	637	564	524	291	308	-22	-48	-52	-44	
2	-37	-22	-7	-23	529	520	705	0	971	971	957	929	758	540	-9	-19	-24	-45	
16	-45	-31	-22	-40	383	491	639	971	0	998	922	939	710	509	-15	-18	-21	-30	
11	-45	-32	-26	-40	390	494	637	971	998	0	928	950	733	559	-11	-18	-24	-30	
12	-49	-19	-11	-13	407	356	564	957	922	928	0	953	897	645	118	69	-9	-32	
1	-56	-43	-29	-23	351	342	524	929	939	950	953	0	848	687	134	-1	-19	-21	
4	-53	-21	-27	-1	182	47	291	758	710	733	897	848	0	818	495	323	-8	-13	
9	-24	-24	-57	-12	209	172	308	540	509	559	645	687	818	0	648	35	-49	-6	
17	0	-12	-31	403	-27	-34	-22	-9	-15	-11	118	134	495	648	0	453	-11	189	
5	-44	58	79	422	-59	-70	-48	-19	-18	-18	69	-1	323	35	453	0	670	610	
14	-32	265	342	207	-40	-36	-52	-24	-21	-24	-9	-19	-8	-49	-11	670	0	226	
18	-28	-22	-32	24	-76	-63	-44	-45	-30	-30	-32	-21	-13	-6	189	610	226	0	

Table 35: Western Floor—Seriation of Rank Orders (Nine Cases, Eleven Selected Variables)

REL	REL 0	2	1	3	10	8	9	6	7	5	4	11		
2	0	433	117	-58	0	-27	-29	-40	-37	-65	-64		1 THGRJR
1	433	0	150	209	-13	17	-19	183	-67	-33	-58		2 PLFACE
3	117	150	0	-3	17	133	-14	117	-22	83	-29		3 PLFRAG
10	-58	209	-3	0	444	670	562	502	92	368	110		4 PEBS
8	0	-13	17	444	0	833	865	367	400	250	135		5 TKOJR
9	-27	17	133	670	833	0	865	633	383	433	143		6 CHERT
6	-28	-19	-14	562	865	865	0	593	559	203	436		7 THOJR
7	-40	183	117	502	367	633	593	0	417	383	185		8 CRKRK
5	-37	-67	-22	92	400	383	559	417	0	267	311		9 MOJR
4	-65	-33	83	368	250	433	203	383	267	0	269		10 ADOBE
11	-64	-58	-29	110	135	143	436	185	311	269	0		11 BONE

Note—change in variable labels for this table only.

APPENDIX XI

Table 36: Eastern Floor—Seriation of Rank Orders (Nine Cases, Eleven Selected Variables)

REL	REL 0	11	10	9	4	6	5	7	3	8	2	1	
	11	0	316	627	−13	17	−20	−19	−53	−11	−46	−88	1 MGRJR
	10	316	0	504	97	17	−10	−18	−29	−51	−60	−47	2 PLFRAG
	9	627	504	0	279	283	417	400	100	25	−42	−63	3 THOJR
	4	−13	97	279	0	731	601	505	548	18	148	44	4 PLFACE
	6	17	17	283	731	0	783	633	533	293	133	150	5 CRKRK
	5	−20	−10	417	601	783	0	867	850	427	267	317	6 THGRJR
	7	−19	−18	400	505	633	867	0	617	686	100	167	7 MOJR
	3	−53	−29	100	548	533	850	617	0	167	467	633	8 MOBL
	8	−11	−51	25	18	293	427	686	167	0	385	92	9 TKOJR
	2	−46	−60	−42	148	133	267	100	467	385	0	483	10 RFLK
	1	−88	−47	−63	44	150	317	167	633	92	483	0	11 CHERT

Note—change in variable labels for this table only.

Table 37: Western Floor—Seriation of Rank Orders (Nine Cases, Five Variables)

REL	REL 0	5	4	2	1	3
	5	0	695	367	100	367
	4	695	0	787	460	444
	2	367	787	0	850	500
	1	100	460	850	0	650
	3	367	444	500	650	0

Table 38: Eastern Floor—Seriation of Rank Orders (Nine Cases, Five Variables)

REL	REL 0	2	4	3	1	5
	2	0	895	858	785	150
	4	895	0	850	850	274
	3	858	850	0	900	411
	1	785	850	900	0	548
	5	150	274	411	548	0

struction. Chunks of plaster found on the western floor, for example, also contained many pebbles. The reasons for the distribution of adobe and rock on the two floors are not clear.

The correlation of different categories of building materials at the micro-material level, but not at the macro-material level, is noteworthy. Two alternative explanations for this discrepancy may be proposed. First, the extreme generality of the micro-material typology may have masked the more complex effects observed when using the macro-material typology. Secondly, the results may indicate that the different size ranges of debris were affected by different depositional processes. That is, if both the large and small debris fragments were produced by a single kind of depositional event, the correlation analyses of density values in both size ranges should have produced similar results. This assumption perhaps could be checked ethnographically and, if supported, could be used to detect different depositional processes which may have operated on occupational surfaces.

General Interpretation

Any interpretation of the debris patterns seen in Structure 14 must take into account what is known ethnohistorically about Zapotec temples. According to Marcus (1978), the *bigaña* or minor priests frequently lived in the temple and are described by some Spanish accounts as "hardly ever leaving it." If this is the case, one might expect them to have taken some meals in the temple, possibly served in thin gray bowls or jars.

On the other hand, it is hard to imagine that debris or broken pottery were allowed to accumulate in the temple. Marcus and Flannery (personal communication) report finding dumps of ritual debris, including bowls, jars, and incense burners, on the slopes below some temples at San José Mogote, indicating the structures were periodically swept out. They also report extensive areas of burning on the plaster floors of the temples, presumably from the large incense burners (*braseros*) which were set on the floor by the Zapotec priests.

There are thus several possible sources for the items found on the floors of Structure 14:

1) Some vessels, such as thin gray bowls and jars, might have contained meals for the resident priests.
2) Some items, including sherds, might have been included in the adobes of the temple walls, and eroded out later.
3) Some items might represent debris thrown into the temple after abandonment.
4) Some items in the outer room might represent material swept from the inner room.

Strong correlations seen in some of the Structure 14 materials suggest both alternatives 1 and 4 above, although Flannery (personal communication) holds out the possibility that most of the material recovered by our excavation postdates the occupation of the temple (alternatives 2 and 3, above).

Based on similar Monte Albán II temples at San José Mogote, the eastern floor of Structure 14 can be interpreted as belonging to the innermost or "more sacred" of the two rooms (Marcus 1978). This is indicated by the burned condition of the floor surface, and the low density of debris. Whether the ceramic fragments found in the eastern room were from vessels used by the minor priests (who may have taken some meals in the temple), whether these sherds were included in the adobes used in construction of the temple, or whether they represent debris thrown in later is difficult to determine. The low density of artifactual materials deposited over the eastern floor may indicate that the room was kept relatively clean, and that debris accumulated for only a short interval, perhaps following abandonment.

The more compact, dark deposits on the western floor may mean that this outer, "less sacred" room contained some debris swept from the floor of the eastern room. The relative lack of patterning in the relationships among debris categories on the western floor, when compared to the eastern floor, is consistent with this interpretation. It also appears that when the wall separating the western and eastern rooms collapsed (or was pulled down so that some of its adobes could be used elsewhere) it probably fell to the west. This is indicated by the greater density of building materials above the western floor, and the more disturbed condition of the overburden on the eastern floor. The lower levels of correlation among building material categories on the western floor, which occur despite the higher densities of such materials there, may result only from the greater thickness of other deposits also present on this floor (in the analyzed zone of from 0 to 5 cm above the surface of the floor).

The above interpretation, of course, must be viewed not only against the analytical results but also against the methods of field recovery, measurement, and statistical analysis, and the interpretive assumptions employed. Problems encountered in the use of these methods and assumptions, during the present study, offer several lessons for future studies.

First, it was difficult in this experiment to distinguish empirically among the effects, on the arrangement and condition of artifactual debris on the floors, of *in situ* disposal behavior, post-abandonment disposal behavior, and post-abandonment disturbance and weathering. The necessity for using a 5 cm zone of potentially disturbed deposit, without first being able to examine the distribution of different materials within a sealed deposit above the plaster floor, contributed to this difficulty. The difficulty perhaps could have been avoided if a better-preserved surface had been available for study. On Mound 1, for example, it would have been more productive to examine one of the floors sealed beneath Structure 14. The distinctions among the several possible sources of deposition and disturbance would have been easier to make in such a sealed deposit. And the information yielded from such a deposit might have been of more interpretive and applied value, in relation to the man-hour, monetary and other costs of the methods and techniques employed.

Second, archaeologists often assume that the effects of normal patterns of activities (e.g., manufacture, use, storage, and discard) on the location of materials can be readily distinguished from the effects of building collapse and other post-abandonment disruptive activities, for example, using micro-stratigraphy. While this may be true in some cases, the logical tools for distinguishing among the wide ranges of potential effects of such activities are in fact not yet well-developed. As a result, considerable ambiguity will exist in any interpretation of an occupational surface. Some of this ambiguity could be alleviated by ethnoarchaeological research on traditional, sedentary communities. For example, it would be useful to know if regularities exist in the relationships among several variables of traditional building construction, use, and abandonment, or in the spatial organization of domestic activities. That is, it would be helpful to develop and test our analytical assumptions using "real", systematically collected behavioral information, and to use the results to increase the reliability of our archaeological interpretations. Future work on the spatial analysis of architecturally-bound occupational surfaces would benefit greatly from this suggested line of research.

APPENDIX XII

POSTCLASSIC OCCUPATION AT TOMALTEPEC

As noted in the text of this monograph, the culture history of Prehispanic Tomaltepec effectively ends with the Formative Period. There was, however, a light reoccupation of part of the site in Postclassic (Monte Albán V) times, description of which is the object of this appendix.

It appears that one house, or at most only a few houses, composed the Monte Albán V occupation, and there is no evidence of use of any of the Formative public buildings at this time. There is good evidence of canal irrigation at Tomaltepec in Postclassic times. Remnants of irrigation canals were found on two separate parts of the site. One of the canals (Feature 59) measured some 70 m deep by 50 m wide. The other canal segment, observed in a road-cut to the southeast of the main area of the Formative site, seems to have been of a similar size.

One Monte Albán household unit was defined, and is designated Unit V-1. This household unit is located in the same small area that contained Household Units TL-1, ESJ-2, R-1, Ia-2, and Area Ic-2. This same area, in other words, was discontinuously used as a household site from 1400 B.C. to somewhere around the middle of the second millennium A.D., a period of almost 3,000 years.

Unit V-1 is composed of a cut-stone house foundation (House 1) oriented about 98°-278°, (Plate 71) four small features (Features 8, 89, 98, and 99), and one human burial (Burial 48). Very little cultural material was recovered from this household unit. Sufficient pottery was recovered to date the features to early Monte Albán V, although the exact functions of the features remain ambiguous, Features 8, 98, and 99 appear to be medium-sized roasting pits or ovens (Plate 72), and Feature 89 is simply a pile of stones and trash on top of the Burial 48 grave. Burial 48, the seated skeleton of a 14-15 year old girl with notches filed in her upper incisor teeth, was found in a small cylindrical pit a few meters to the northeast of House 1. The corpse was covered with a large, coarse, inverted *apaxtle*, or basin. No other offerings of any sort were recovered (Plate 73).

Figure 57 shows what is known of the Monte Albán V occupation at Tomaltepec, and Figure 58 shows the layout of Household Unit V-1.

APPENDIX XII

PLATE 71. Stone foundation of House 1, Household Unit Monte Albán V-1.

PLATE 72. Large roasting pits associated with Unit V-1 (photograph taken after heavy spring rain).

APPENDIX XII

PLATE 73. Two views of Burial 48, a 14–15 yr. old girl associated with Unit V-1. Top, large apaxtle inverted over skeleton. Bottom, skeleton with apaxtle removed.

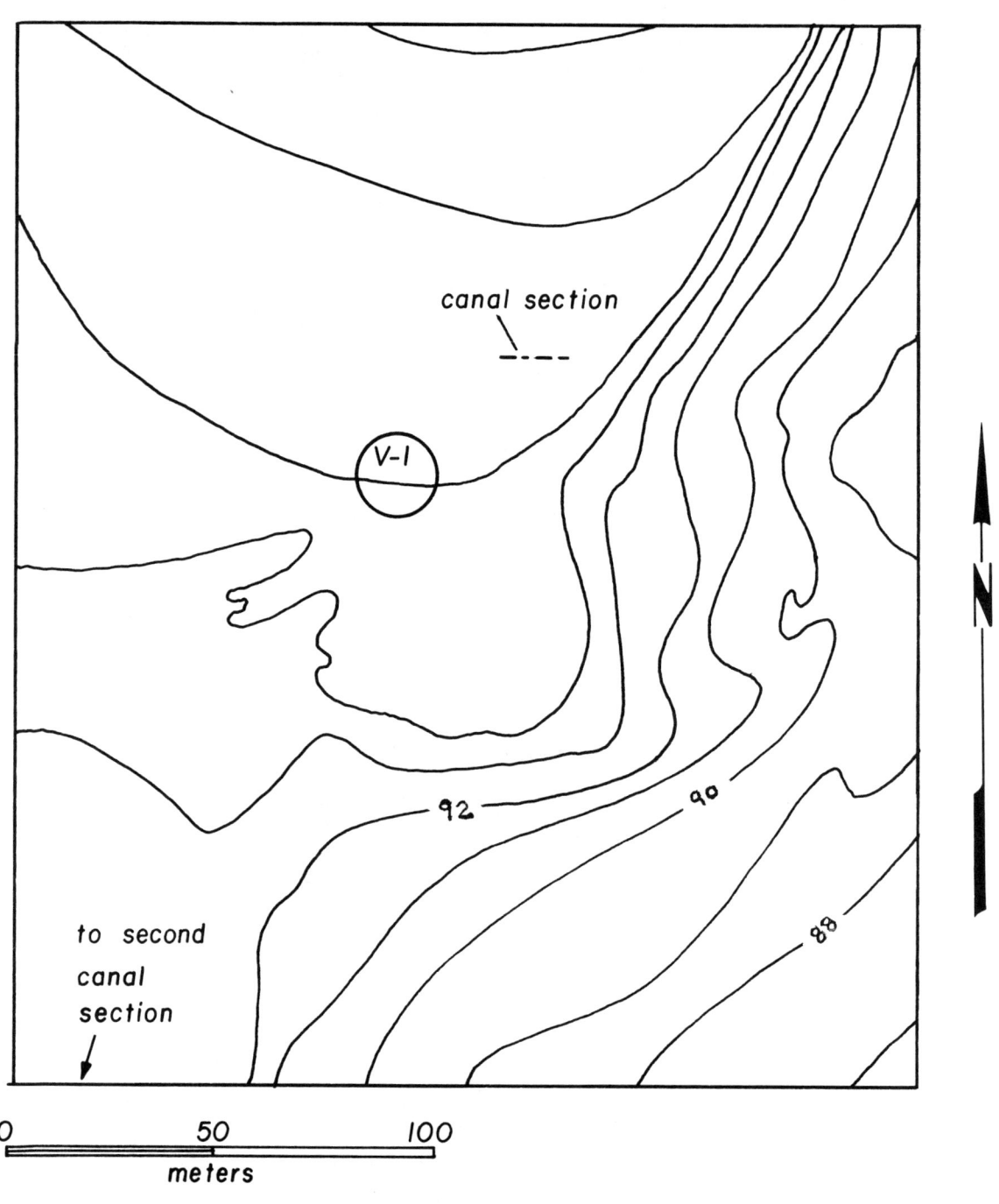

FIGURE 57. Monte Albán V occupation at Tomaltepec.

APPENDIX XII

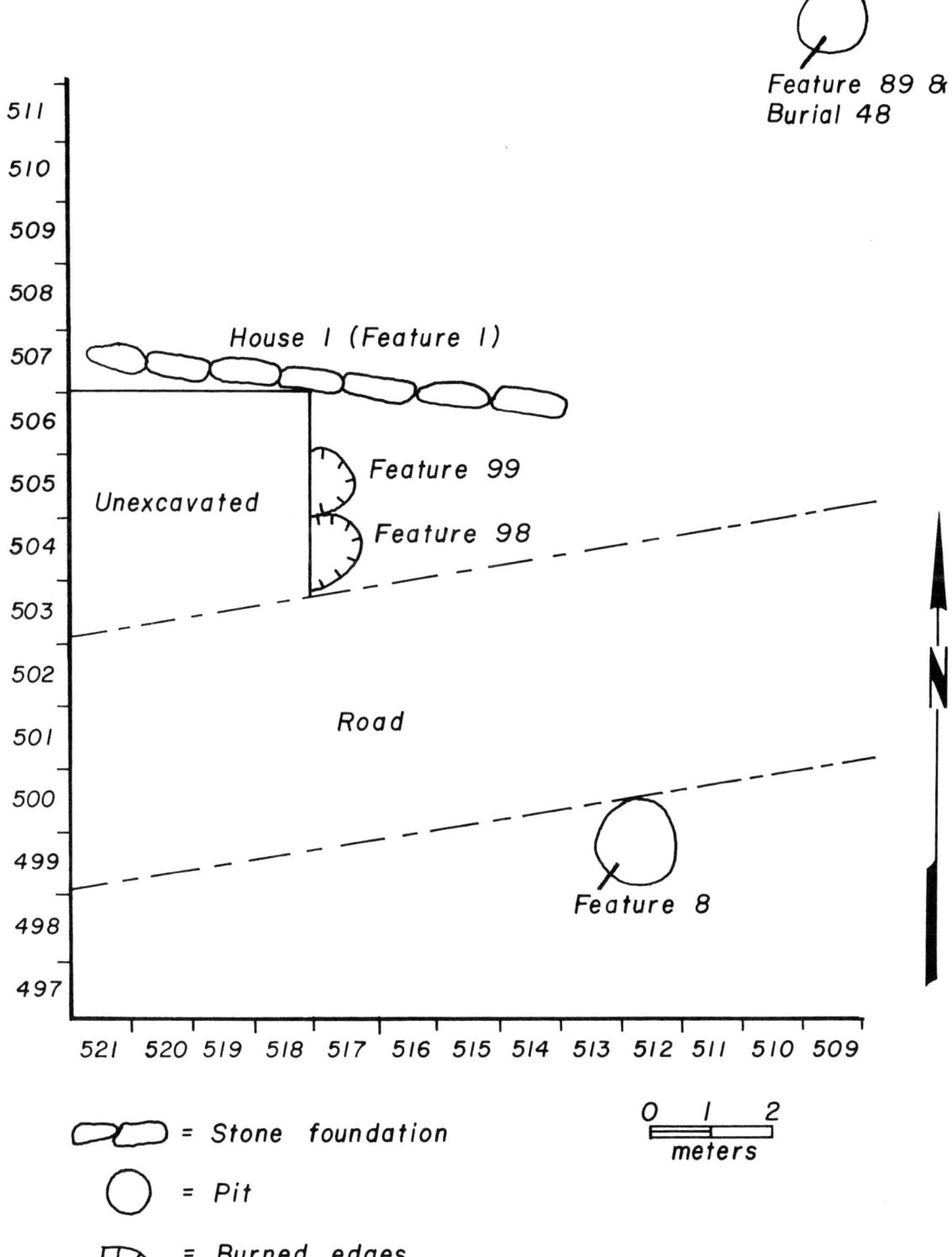

FIGURE 58. Components of Household Unit V-1.

REFERENCES

Ascher, Robert
    1968   Time's Arrow and the Archaeology of a Contemporary Community. In *Settlement Archaeology*. K. C. Chang, ed. pp. 43–52. National Press Books, Palo Alto.

Bernal, Ignacio
    1965   Archaeological Synthesis of Oaxaca. In *Handbook of Middle American Indians*. Gordon R. Willey, ed. Vol. 3, Part 2, pp. 788-813. University of Texas Press. Austin.

Binford, Lewis R.
    1971   Mortuary Practices: Their Study and Their Potential. In Approaches to the Social Dimensions of Mortuary Practices, James Brown, ed., *Society for American Archaeology Memoir* No. 25, pp. 6-29.

Blanton, Richard E.
    1976   The Origins of Monte Albán. In *Cultural Continuity and Change*. Charles Cleland, ed., pp. 223-232. Academic Press. New York.
    1978   Monte Albán: Settlement Patterns at the Ancient Zapotec Capital. New York, Academic Press.

Buckley, Walter W.
    1968   Society as a Complex Adaptive System. In *Modern Systems Research for the Behavioral Scientist*. Walter Buckley, ed. pp. 490-513. Aldine. Chicago.

Caso, Alfonso
    1965   Zapotec Writing and Calendar. In *Handbook of Middle American Indians*, Vol. 3, Part 2, pp. 931-947. Gordon R. Willey, ed. University of Texas Press. Austin.

Caso, Alfonso, Ignacio Bernal, and Jorge Acosta
    1967   La Cerámica de Monte Albán. *Memorias del Instituto Nacional de Antropologia e Historia*, XIII. Mexico, D.F.

Chadwick, Robert
    1966   Tombs of Monte Albán I Style at Yagul. In *Ancient Oaxaca*. John Paddock, ed. pp. 245-255. Stanford University Press. Stanford.

Clarke, David L.
    1968   *Analytical Archaeology*. Methuen and Co., Ltd. London.

Coe, Michael D.
    1961   La Victoria: An Early Site on the Pacific Coast of Guatemala. *Papers of the Peabody Museum of Archaeology and Ethnology*, Vol. LIII. Harvard University. Cambridge.
    1962   *Mexico*. Praeger. New York.
    1965a   Archaeological Synthesis of Southern Veracruz and Tabasco. In *Handbook of Middle American Indians*, Vol. 3. Gordon Willey and R. Wauchope, eds. pp. 679-715. University of Texas Press. Austin.
    1965b   *The Jaguar's Children: Pre-classic Central Mexico*. Museum of Primitive Art. New York.
    1968   San Lorenzo and the Olmec Civilization. In *Dumbarton Oaks Conference on the Olmec*. E. P. Benson, ed. pp. 41-78. Dumbarton Oaks. Washington, D.C.
    1970   The Archaeological Sequence at San Lorenzo Tenochtitlán, Veracruz. *Contributions of the University of California Archaeological Research Facility*, No. 8 pp. 21-34. Berkeley.

Coe, Michael D., Richard A. Diehl and Minze Stuiver
    1967   Olmec Civilization, Veracruz, Mexico: Dating of the San Lorenzo Phase. *Science* 155:1399-1401.

Coe, Michael D. and Kent V. Flannery
    1967   Early Cultures and Human Ecology in South Coastal Guatemala. *Smithsonian Contributions to Anthropology*, Vol. 3. Washington, D.C.

Covarrubias, Miguel
    1957   *Indian Art of Mexico and Central America*. Knopf. New York.

Department of Geography, University of Michigan
    1974   Interactive contouring program. *Cartographic Laboratory Report* No. 7. Ann Arbor.

Deutsch, Karl
    1968   Toward a Cybernetic Model of Man and Society. In *Modern Systems Research for the Behavioral Scientist*. Walter Buckley, ed. pp. 387-400. Aldine. Chicago.

Drennan, Robert D.
    1976   Fábrica San José and Middle Formative Society in the Valley of Oaxaca, Mexico. *Prehistory and Human Ecology of the Valley of Oaxaca*. Vol. 4. Memoirs, No. 8, Museum of Anthropology, University of Michigan. Ann Arbor.

Drucker, Philip
    1943   Ceramic Stratigraphy at Cerro de las Mesas, Veracruz, Mexico. Smithsonian Institution. *Bureau of American Ethnology Bulletin* 141. Washington, D.C.

Ekholm, Susanna M.
    1969   Mound 30A and the Early Pre-classic Sequence at Izapa, Chiapas, Mexico. *New World Archaeological Foundation Paper* No. 25. Brigham Young University. Provo.

Flannery, Kent V.
    1966   The Postglacial "Readaptation" as Viewed from Mesoamerica. *American Antiquity* 31:800-805.
    1968a   The Olmec and the Valley of Oaxaca: A Model for Interregional Interaction in Formative Times. *Dumbarton Oaks Conference on the Olmec*. Elizabeth P. Benson, ed. pp. 79-110. Dumbarton Oaks. Washington, D.C.
    1968b   Archaeological Systems Theory and Early Mesoamerica. In *Anthropological Archaeology in the Americas*. B. J. Meggers, ed. pp. 67-87. The Anthropological Society of Washington. Washington, D.C.
    1972a   The Origins of the Village as a Settlement Type in Mesoamerica and the Near East: A Comparative Study. In *Man, Settlement, and Urbanism*, P. J. Ucko, R. Tringham, and G. W. Dimbleby, eds. pp. 23-53. Gerald Duckworth and Co., Ltd. London.

1972b		Evolutionary Trends in Social Exchange and Interaction. *In* Social Exchange and Interaction . Edwin N. Wilmsen, ed. *Anthropological Papers* No. 46. pp. 129-135. University of Michigan Museum of Anthropology. Ann Arbor.
1972c		The Cultural Evolution of Civilizations. *Annual Review of Ecology and Systematics*, 3:399-426.
1973		The Origins of Agriculture. *Annual Review of Anthropology*, 2:271-310.
1976		The Early Mesoamerican House. In *The Early Mesoamerican Village*. Kent V. Flannery, ed., pp. 16-24. Academic Press. New York.

Flannery, Kent V.
    in press   The Tierras Largas phase and the analytical units of the early Oaxacan village. In *The Cloud People: Evolution of the Zapotec and Mixtec Civilizations of Oaxaca, Mexico*. Kent V. Flannery and Joyce Marcus, eds. University of New Mexico Press, Albuquerque.

Flannery, Kent V. (editor)
    1976   *The Early Mesoamerican Village*. Academic Press. New York.

Flannery, Kent V., Anne V. T. Kirkby, Michael J. Kirkby and Aubrey W. Williams, Jr.
    1967   Farming Systems and Political Growth in Ancient Oaxaca. *Science* 158: 445-454.

Flannery, Kent V. and Joyce Marcus
    1976a   Evolution of the public building in Formative Oaxaca. In *Cultural change and continuity: essays in honor of James Bennett Griffin*, edited by Charles Cleland, pp. 205-221. Academic Press. New York
    1976b   Formative Oaxaca and the Zapotec Cosmos. *American Scientist* 64: 374-83.

Flannery, Kent V. and Joyce Marcus (editors)
    in press   *The Cloud People: Evolution of the Zapotec and Mixtec Civilizations of Oaxaca, Mexico*. University of New Mexico Press, Albuquerque.

Flannery, Kent V. and James Schoenwetter
    1970   Climate and Man in Formative Oaxaca. *Archaeology* 23:144-152.

Flannery, Kent V., Marcus Winter, Susan Lees, James Neely, James Schoenwetter, Suzanne Kitchen, and Jane C. Wheeler
    1970   Preliminary Archaeological Investigations in the Valley of Oaxaca, Mexico, 1966-1969: A Report to the National Science Foundation and the Instituto Nacional de Antropología e Historia. Mimeographed. University of Michigan Museum of Anthropology. Ann Arbor.

Ford, James A.
    1969   A Comparison of Formative Cultures in the Americas. *Smithsonian Contributions to Anthropology*, Vol. 11. Smithsonian Institution. Washington, D.C.

Ford, Richard I.
    1976   Carbonized Plant Remains. Appendix XIII in *Prehistory and Human Ecology of the Valley of Oaxaca*, Vol. 4. *Memoirs* 8, pp. 261-268, Museum of Anthropology, University of Michigan, Ann Arbor.

Fried, Morton H.
    1967   *The Evolution of Political Society: An Essay in Political Anthropology*. Random House. New York.

Fronczak, Edward J.
    1971   *The Michigan Terminal System*, Vol. 11, Plot Description System, 3rd edition. The University of Michigan Computing Center, Ann Arbor.

Green, Dee F. and Gareth W. Lowe
    1967   Altamira and Padre Piedra, Early Pre-classic Sites in Chiapas, Mexico. *New World Archaeological Foundation Paper* No. 20. Brigham Young University. Provo.

Grove, David C.
    1970   The San Pablo Panteón Mound: A Middle Pre-classic Site in Morelos, Mexico. *American Antiquity* 35:62-73.

Hall, A.D. and R.E. Fagan
    1968   Definition of System. In *Modern Systems Research for the Behavioral Scientist*. Walter Buckley, ed. pp. 81-92. Aldine. Chicago.

Heizer, Robert F.
    1961   Inferences on the Nature of Olmec Society Based Upon Data from the La Venta Site. *Kroeber Anthropological Society Papers* XXV:43-57.

Joralemon, Peter D.
    1971   A Study of Olmec Iconography. *Studies in Pre-Columbian Art and Archaeology*, No. 7. Dumbarton Oaks. Washington, D.C.

Kaplan, Lawrence
    1967   Archaeological *Phaseolus* from Tehuacán *In* The Prehistory of the Tehuacán Valley, Vol. 1: Environment and Subsistence. Douglas S. Byers, ed. University of Texas Press, Austin.

Kidder, Alfred V.
    1924   *An Introduction to Southwestern Archaeology*. Yale University Press. New Haven.

Kirkby, Anne V. T.
    1973   The Use of Land and Water Resources in the Past and Present Valley of Oaxaca, Mexico. *Prehistory and Human Ecology of the Valley of Oaxaca*, Vol. 1. Memoir 5, Museum of Anthropology, University of Michigan. Ann Arbor.

Kowalewski, Stephen A.
    1974   Ancient Settlement Patterns in the Central Valley of Oaxaca, Mexico. Paper presented at the 73rd Annual Meeting of the American Anthropological Association. Mexico, D. F.
    1976   Prehistoric Settlement Patterns in the Central Part of the Valley of Oaxaca, Mexico. Ph.D. Dissertation, Department of Anthropology, University of Arizona, Tucson.

Kowalewski, Stephen A. and D. M. Varner
    1975   Early Classic Economic Formations in the Valley of Oaxaca, Mexico. Paper presented at the 74th Annual Meeting of the American Anthropological Association. San Francisco.

Lees, Susan H.
  1970   Test Excavations at Santo Domingo Tomaltepec (B-176). In *Preliminary Archaeological Investigations in the Valley of Oaxaca, Mexico, 1966-69*. A Report to the National Science Foundation and the Instituto Nacional de Antropología e Historia, by K. V. Flannery, *et al.*, pp. 80-82.
Lingoes, James C.
  1972   A General Survey of the Guttman-Lingoes Nonmetric Program Series. In *Multi-dimensional Scaling:Theory and Applications in the Behavioral Sciences*, Vol. 1. Romney, Shepard, and Nerlove, eds. Seminar Press, New York.
  1973   *The Guttman-Lingoes Nonmetric Program Series*. Mathesis Press, Ann Arbor.
Lowe, Gareth W. and Pierre Agrinier
  1960   Mound 1, Chiapa de Corzo, Chiapas, Mexico. *New World Archaeological Foundation* Paper No. 8. Brigham Young University. Provo.
MacNeish, Richard S.
  1964   The Origins of New World Civilization. *Scientific American*, vol. 211, no. 5, pp. 29-37.
MacNeish, Richard S., Frederick A. Peterson, and Kent V. Flannery
  1970   *The Prehistory of the Tehuacán Valley, Vol. 3: Ceramics*. University of Texas Press. Austin.
MacNeish, Richard S., Melvin L. Fowler, Angel García Cook, Frederick A. Peterson, Antoinette Nelken-Terner, and James A. Neely
  1972   *Prehistory of the Tehuacán Valley, Vol. 5: Excavations and Reconnaissance*. University of Texas Press. Austin.
Marcus, Joyce
  1974   The Iconography of Power Among the Classic Maya. *World Archaeology* 6:83-94.
  1976a The Size of the Early Mesoamerican Village. In *The Early Mesoamerican Village*. Kent V. Flannery, ed., pp. 79-90. Academic Press. New York.
  1976b The Iconography of Militarism at Monte Albán and Neighboring Sites in the Valley of Oaxaca. In *The Origins of Religious Art and Iconography in Preclassic Mesoamerica*. Henry B. Nicholson, ed. pp. 123-139. Latin American Research Center. University of California at Los Angeles.
  1978   Archaeology and religion: A comparison of the Zapotec and Maya. *World Archaeology*, vol. 10, no. 2, pp. 172-91.
Marquina, Ignacio
  1951   Arquitectura Prehispánica. *Memorias del Instituto Nacional de Antropología e Historia*, No. 1. México, D. F.
Maruyama, Magoroh
  1963   The Second Cybernetics: Deviation-Amplifying Mutual Causal Processes. *American Scientist* 51:164-179.
Meggitt, Mervyn J.
  1965   *The Lineage System of the Mae Enga of New Guinea*. Oliver and Boyd. Edinburgh.
Merrill, William
  n.d.   Avocados in the Valley of Oaxaca. Mimeographed.
Messer, Ellen
  1975   Zapotec Plant Knowledge: Classification, Uses, and Communication about Plants in Mitla, Oaxaca, Mexico. Ph.D. Dissertation. University of Michigan Department of Anthropology, Ann Arbor.
Miller, James G.
  1965a Living Systems—Basic Concepts. *Behavioral Science* 10(3):193-237.
  1965b Living Systems—Structure and Process. *Behavioral Science* 10(4):337-79.
Millon, René
  1967   Teotihuacán. *Scientific American* 216:38-48.
Morgan, Lewis H.
  1877   *Ancient Society*. World Publishing Co. New York.
Neely, James A.
  1967   Organización Hidráulica y Sistemas de Irrigacíon Prehistóricos en el Valle de Oaxaca *Boletin* No. 27:15-17. Institutio Nacional de Antropología e Historia. México, D. F.
Parsons, Jeffrey R.
  1971a Prehistoric Settlement Patterns in the Texcoco Region, Mexico. *Memoirs of the Museum of Anthropology*, No. 3. University of Michigan, Ann Arbor.
  1971b Prehispanic Settlement Patterns in the Chalco Region, Mexico: 1969 Season. Mimeographed report submitted to Departamento de Monumentos Prehispánicos. Instituto Nacional de Antropología e Historia. México, D. F.
Peebles, Christopher
  1971   Moundville and Surrounding Sites: Some Considerations of Mortuary Practies II. *In* Approaches to the Social Dimensions of Mortuary Practices, James Brown, ed. *Society for American Archaeology*. Memoir No. 25:68-91.
Pires-Ferreira, Jane W.
  1975   Formative Mesoamerican Exchange Networks with Special Reference to the Valley of Oaxaca. *Prehistory and Human Ecology of the Valley of Oaxaca*, Vol. 3. Memoir 7 of the Museum of Anthropology. University of Michigan. Ann Arbor.
  1976   Shell and Iron-Ore Mirror Exchange in Formative Mesoamerica, with Comments on Other Communities. In *The Early Mesoamerican Village*. Kent V. Flannery, ed. pp. 311-326. Academic Press. New York.
Plog, Stephen
  1976   The Measurement of Prehistoric Interaction Between Communities. In *The Early Mesoamerican Village*. Kent V. Flannery, ed. pp. 255-272. Academic Press. New York.
Pyne, Nanette M.
  1976   The Fire-Serpent and Were-Jaguar in Formative Oaxaca: A Contingency Table Analysis. In *The Early Mesoamerican Village*. Kent V. Flannery, ed., pp. 272-280. Academic Press. New York.
Rappaport, Roy A.
  1971   The Sacred in Human Evolution. *Annual Review of Ecology and Systematics* 2:23-44.
Read, K.E.
  1959   Leadership and Consensus in a New Guinea Society. *American Anthropologist* 61(3):425-436.

Sahlins, Marshall D.
    1960   Political Power and the Economy in Primitive Society. In *Essays in the Science of Culture: Papers in Honor of Leslie White*. G. Dole and R. Carneiro, eds. pp. 390-415 Crowell Publishing Co. New York.
    1961   The Segmentary Lineage: An Organization of the Predatory Expansion.*American Anthropologist* 63:322-45.
    1963   Poor Man, Rich Man, Big Man, Chief: Political Types in Melanesia and Polynesia. *Comparative Studies in Society and History* 5:285-303.
    1968   *Tribesmen*. Prentice-Hall. New York.
    1972   *Stone Age Economics*. Aldine Press. Chicago.

Sallade, Jane K.
    n.d.   Analysis of a Monte Albán II Occupation Floor From the Main Mound of Santo Domingo Tomaltepec (B-176), Oaxaca. Manuscript. University of Michigan Museum of Anthropology. Ann Arbor.

Sanders, William T. and Barbara Price
    1968   *Mesoamerica: The Evolution of a Civilization*. Random House. New York.

Saxe, Arthur A.
    1970   Social Dimensions of Mortuary Practices. Ph.D. Dissertation. Department of Anthropology. University of Michigan. Ann Arbor.
    1971   Social Dimensions of Mortuary Practices in a Mesolithic Population from Wadi Halfa, Sudan. In Approaches to the Social Dimensions of Mortuary Practices. James Brown, ed. pp. 39-57. *Memoir* No. 25, Society for American Archaeology.

Schiffer, Michael B.
    1972   Archaeological Context and Systemic Context. *American Antiquity* 37:2:156-165.

Service, Elman R.
    1962   *Primitive Social Organization: An Evolutionary Perspective*. Random House. New York.

Siegel, Sidney
    1956   *Nonparametric Statistics for the Behavioral Sciences*. International Student Edition. McGraw-Hill Book Company, Inc. New York.

Smith, C. Earle, Jr.
    n.d.   Vegetal Remains from Tomaltepec (B176). Unpublished Manuscript. University of Alabama. Tuscaloosa.

Spengler, Oswald
    1918   *Der Untergang des Abendlandes*. C. H. Beck'sche Verlagsbuchhandlung, München. Reprinted by A. A. Knopf. 1926, as *The Decline of the West*.

Taylor, William
    1972   *Landlord and Peasant in Colonial Oaxaca*. Stanford Press. Stanford.

Tolstoy, Paul and Louise I. Paradis
    1970   Early and Middle Preclassic Culture in the Basin of Mexico. *Science* 167:344-351.

Ucko, Peter J.
    1969   Ethnography and Archaeological Interpretations of Funerary Remains. *World Archaeology* 1(2):262-279.

Varner, Dudley M.
    1974   Prehispanic Settlement Patterns in the Valley of Oaxaca, Mexico: the Etla arm. Ph.D. Dissertation. Department of Anthropology, University of Arizona, Tucson.

Watson, Patty Jo, Stephen A. Le Blanc, and Charles L. Redman
    1971   *Explanation in Archeology: An Explicitly Scientific Approach*. Columbia University Press. New York.

Weaver, Murial Porter
    1972   *The Aztecs, Mayas, and Their Predecessors*. Seminar Press. New York.

Whalen, Michael E.
    1974   Community Development and Integration During the Formative Period in the Valley of Oaxaca. Mexico. Paper presented at the 73rd Annual Meetings of the American Anthropological Association. Mexico. D.F.
    n.d.   Lithic Resources in the Valley of Oaxaca, Mexico: Report to the Phoenix Memorial Laboratory and the Museum of Anthropology. Manuscript. University of Michigan. Ann Arbor.

Whallon, Robert
    1974   Spatial Analysis of Occupation Floors II: The Application of Nearest Neighbor Analysis. *American Antiquity* 39:1:16-34.

Winter, Marcus C.
    1972   Tierras Largas: A Formative Community in the Valley of Oaxaca. Mexico. Ph.D. Dissertation. Department of Anthropology. University of Arizona, Tucson.
    1974   Residential Patterns at Monte Albán, Oaxaca. Mexico. *Science* 186:981-987.
    1976a   The Archaeological Household Cluster in the Valley of Oaxaca. In *The Early Mesoamerican Village*. Kent V. Flannery, ed., pp. 25-31. Academic Press. New York.
    1976b   Differential Patterns of Community Growth in Oaxaca. In *The Early Mesoamerican Village*. Kent V. Flannery, ed., pp. 227-234. Academic Press. New York.

Winter, Marcus C. and Jane W. Pires-Ferreira
    1976   Distribution of Obsidian Among Households in Two Oaxacan Villages. In *The Early Mesoamerican Village*. Kent V. Flannery, ed., pp. 306-311. Academic Press. New York.

Wittfogel, Karl
    1962   *Oriental Despotism*. Yale University Press. New Haven.

Wright, Henry T.
    1969   Field Report on the 1969 Excavations at Santo Domingo Tomaltepec-B-176. Mimeographed. 3 pages.
    1972   Field Report on the 1972 Excavations at Santo Domingo Tomaltepec-B-176. Mimeographed. 7 pages.
    1977   Toward an Explanation of the Origin of the State. In *Explanation of Prehistoric Change*, James N. Hill, ed., pp. 215-230. University of New Mexico Press. Albuquerque.

Resumen En Español

por *Michael E. Whalen*

El presente estudio fue motivado por un interés en el proceso de desarrollo de sociedades complejas con antecedentes más sencillos. Es decir que la perspectiva del estudio es evolutiva. Cada estudio evolutivo comprende una percepción de (1) cultura y la sociedad humana, y (2) la evolución y los procesos evolutivos. De conformidad con lo anterior, el primer capítulo de este estudio se dedica a una investigación de estos dos temas. El objeto del primer capítulo es establecer la perspectiva teórica del estudio.

En el presente estudio las culturas humanas son vistas como agregados de respuestas adaptativas, por medio de los cuales una sociedad se mantiene en un ambiente particular. Es necesario notar que un ambiente contiene componentes sociales así como físicos.

Acompañando este concepto de la cultura humana existe una dependencia en los conceptos de la Teoría General de Sistemas, y en conceptos asociados tales como la Cibernética. Se ha tenido considerable éxito en la aplicación de modelos sistémicos a los problemas de la biología evolutiva, donde los sistemas vivientes forman un sub-grupo de sistemas generales. Además, como propone un grupo creciente de antropólogos, sería útil organizar las variables en estudios de evolución cultural por medio de la concepción de las culturas humanas como una clase de sistemas vivientes. En consecuencia, se propone que todos los problemas de operación sistémica existen en las culturas humanas así como en los sistemas vivientes. Estos problemas incluyen regulación de relaciones ambientales, mantenimiento de la integración sistémica, transmisión de información, etc.

Un efecto de esta concepción es una definición practicable de complejidad social. Se ha establecido que los sistemas más complejos tienen más partes, mayor especialización de funciones de las partes, y modos más eficientes para la integración de las partes. Mediante el estudio de cambios en el modo de coordinación e integración de los segmentos de una sociedad, se pueden definir cambios en el nivel general de complejidad de la sociedad.

Es necesario acentuar que el cambio no se ve aquí como una característica automática o ubícua de las culturas, que esencialmente son convervadoras. Se propone que las culturas *sí* cambian para adaptarse a cambios en el ambiente físico *o* social. Además, se propone que entre culturas más complejas, los impulsos a cambiar provienen más frecuentemente del ambiente social y político, y no simplemente del ambiente físico. Estos son precisamente los impulsos que son más obscuros al nivel de la comunidad pequeña.

El objeto específico del presente estudio es construir un concepto de la estructura de la comunidad y de los procesos de cambio en la comunidad durante un período crucial en el desarrollo cultural de Mesoamérica. En cada fase del período Formativo (aprox. 1500 a.C.-200 d.C.) el estudio se ocupa con cambios en: (1) el número de partes de la comunidad; (2) niveles de diferenciación entre estas partes; (3) especialización de función de las partes; (4) extensión de integración de las partes; y (5) modos de integración de las partes. La investigación trata sobre cuatro clases de datos arqueológicos: (1) composición de la comunidad; (2) diferenciación social en la comunidad; (3) actividades de subsistencia; y (4) actividades de intercambio.

El objeto del Capítulo II es proporcionar una introducción al ambiente físico y social de la comunidad Formativa de Tomaltepec. El Capítulo II contiene una discusión de cada una de las cuatro divisiones del período Formativo en Mesoamérica: el Formativo Temprano (1600 a.C.-850 a.C.), el Formativo Medio (850 a.C.-300 a.C.), el Formativo Tardío (300 a.C.-100 d.C.), y el Formativo Terminal (100 a.C.-200 d.C.). Cada división del Formativo se considera en términos de los procesos evolutivos que se notan. El Capítulo II además presenta una descripción geográfica y climática del Valle de Oaxaca y del sitio de Tomaltepec. El sitio se encuentra en la orilla del

Valle de Oaxaca, al pie de las montañas circundantes. Se trata sobre la exploración preliminar del sitio en 1969 y 1972, y se presenta la metodología usada en las excavaciones extensivas de 1974, las cuales forman la base del presente estudio.

Con el tercer capítulo empieza la discusión de los datos arqueológicos de Tomaltepec. El Capítulo III trata sobre el Formativo Temprano (*circa* 1600 a.C.-850 a.C.). En el Valle de Oaxaca se divide este período en dos fases: Tierras Largas (1400-1150 a.C.), y San José (1150-850 a.C.). En la fase Tierras Largas evidentemente existía una aldea muy pequeña en Tomaltepec. Fueron excavados restos de dos "unidades domésticas" (*household units*"). No se encontraron restos de casas *in situ*, pero fueron encontrados muchos pedazos de barro quemado que venían de los muros de las casas. Fueron excavados dos pozos grandes, uno de los cuales era del tipo "tronco-cónico" para almacenaje. Los dos pozos contenían mucha basura doméstica. Entendemos muy poco de la forma precisa de la aldea, pero podemos estar seguros que era muy pequeña. Probablemente no había más que tres o cuatro casas o "unidades domésticas". La aldea evidentemente creció durante la fase San José y la cerámica indica que esta ocupación pertenece a la primera parte de la fase. Es evidente que la aldea San José consistía en por lo menos tres zonas distintas: (1) una zona de relativamente baja posición social; (2) una zona de relativamente mayor posición social; y (3) un cementerio totalmente desasociado de las otras partes de la comunidad.

En la zona de menor posición social se excavó el piso casí entero de una casa pequeña (la Casa 4), que debe de representar la mayoría de las casas que formaban la aldea. Era una estructura sencilla de aproximadamente 6 por 3 metros y orientada por su lado más largo hacia el oriente/poniente y el lado más corto hacia el norte/sur. La casa se encontró en medio de un lote de tierra apisonada con una superficie de unos cuarenta metros cuadradros. Los cuatro muros de la casa se definían por cuatro filas de hoyos de postes. Tres pisos delgados de tierra apisonada fueron excavados. El análisis de la distribución de los artefactos del último piso se presenta en un apéndice al presente estudio. Los artefactos encontrados incluyen pedazos de cerámica, pedazos de hueso, herramientas de piedra, y restos de plantas y madera carbonizados. No se encontraron cantidades grandes ni de concha marina ni de obsidiana, las cuales eran importadas y por lo tanto relativamente más caras. Este punto va a ser significativo cuando esta casa se compare con las siguientes estructuras.

En la zona de más elevada posición social fueron descubiertas dos casas superpuestas. La estructura más temprana era una casa ordinaria, acompañada de por lo menos un gran pozo tronco-cónico para almacenaje. Esta casa se identificó como la Casa 8. Restos de barro quemado y marcado por cañas indican que la Caso 8 era una casa semejante a la Casa 4. No obstante, la Casa 8 tenía una cantidad de obsidiana significativamente mayor que la de la Casa 4. Además, se encontraron muchos huesos de venado y conejo, y varios pedazos de concha marina, incluyendo un ornamento de concha aún no terminado. En esta casa parece que no solo había consumo, sino además producción de objetos relativamente más caras.

Construida sobre las ruinas de la Casa 8 estaba una plataforma hecha de piedra y adobe. Esta plataforma evidentement tenía una función primordialmente residencial. Se llegó a esta conclusión tomando en cuenta la enorme cantidad de basura doméstica que se encontró asociada con la plataforma. La plataforma era de 8 metros (norte/sur) por 4 metros (oriente/poniente), y tenía una altura de aproximadamente un metro. En el centro de la plataforma y situada directamente bajo el piso de la casa que estaba situada encima de la plataforma, se encontró una celda o depósito grande, con acabado de lodo. La celda media unos 3 por 5 metros, con una profundidad de 0.6 metros, alcanzando así unos 9 metros cúbicos en volúmen. Esta capacidad es aproximadamente 6 veces más grande que la capacidad de los pozos tronco-cónicos para almacenaje que evidentemente pertenecían a casas comunes. Se debe de añadir que los datos arqueológicos indican que esta plataforma es única en Tomaltepec.

Artefactos asociados con la plataforma incluyen cantidades relativamente grandes de obsidiana, huesos de venado y conejo, y unos pedazos de concha marina. Estos artefactos representan una magnitud de consumo totalmente diferente al consumo relacionado con la Casa 4. Esta zona de mayor posición social no estaba situada en el centro de la comunidad, sino al lado sureste. Puede ser que el plan de la aldea en esta fase no fuera muy formal en este período.

En la orilla noreste de la aldea se descubrió una zona para entierros unicamente. Este cementerio probablemente contenía la mayoría de la población adulta de la comunidad. No se encontró ningún otro entierro adulto aparte de estos del cementerio. Además, no se encontró ningún entierro ni de niño ni de infante en el cementerio. Evidentemente los adultos y adolescentes que ya habían sido iniciados en alguna forma fueron enterrados en esta zona especial. Un entierro de infante se descubrió en un montón de basura fuera del cementerio y en la vecindad de la plataforma.

La uniformidad de posición de los esqueletos del cementerio fue casi absoluta. Casi todos los cadáveres estaban acostados, boca abajo, con la cabeza al oriente. Ofrendas de loza, figuras de barro, cuentas de piedra verde, concha marina, espejos de magnetita, navajas de obsidiana, y agujas de hueso de venado acompañaban algunos de los entierros. Algunas de las vasijas y figuras pertenecían al estilo Olmeca. Estos entierros fueron muy importantes en el estudio de la estructura social de la aldea, y este tema se prosigue en el Capítulo IV.

Los Capítulos V y VI tratan sobre la ocupación del Formativo Mediano (aproximadamente 850 a. de C.-300 a.de C.) en Tomaltepec. El Formativo Mediano se divide en tres fases: Guadalupe (850-700 a.de C.), Rosario (700-500) a.de C.), y Monte Albán Ia (500-300 a.de C.). Debido al hecho que la fase Guadalupe pertenece casi exclusivamente a la zona noroeste del valle (zona de Etla), apareció muy poco material de esa fase en Tomaltepec.

Creció la aldea en la fase Rosario, cuando se construyó una plataforma mucho más grande sobre los restos de la pequeña plataforma San José. Para la base de la nueva plataforma se usaron losas grandes de piedra, las cuales medían unos 100 cm por 50 cm por 30 cm. Se descubrieron cuatro entierros de adultos debajo del piso superior de esta plataforma.

Se excavó también una unidad doméstica contemporánea que consistía en dos casas grandes con cimientos de piedra. Una de las casas estaba orientada al norte/sur y la otra al oriente/poniente, formando así un patio con el ángulo recto que formaban los muros de las casas. En este patio se descubrieron dos entierros de niños, un horno grande, y varios pozos pequeños. Esta unidad doméstica se encontró en la vecindad de la plataforma, y evidentemente esta zona era una de relativamente mayor posición social. Se llegó a esta conclusión tomando en cuenta la construcción elaborada de las casas, además de su proximidad a la plataforma.

Es interesante notar que el cementerio de la fase San José no se usó en ninguna manera en la fase Rosario. Evidentemente enterraban a los cadáveres más cerca de sus casas, no en una sola zona especial usada por toda la comunidad, aunque ésto queda por comprobar. Es casi seguro que había más casas de esta fase en los campos al noroeste de la plataforma, pero el tiempo no alcanzó para investigar bien esta parte de la zona. Se propone que el crecimiento del sitio fuera un reflejo de un crecimiento general de la población del Valle de Oaxaca en esta época.

Evidentemente siguió creciendo la población de Tomaltepec durante la fase Monte Albán Ia. Es muy probable que se amplió la plataforma Rosario y que se usaba como edificio cívico-ceremonial. Respecto a la ocupación ordinaria, se encontraron los restos de una casa con varios entierros. También se descubrieron entierros, pozos para almacenaje, hogares, y otras indicios de ocupación en otros dos lugares distintos. Aparentemente, la unidad doméstica todavía era la base de la organización de la comunidad. Otra observación que se puede hacer es que la zonificación de la Formativo Temprano continuó en la fase Monte Albán Ia. Es decir, la zona de la plataforma siguió como el punto de mayor importancia en la comunidad, y las zonas residenciales también mantuvieron su carácter. El cementerio de la fase San José fue usado como el sitio de una unidad doméstica.

Evidentemente, los cadáveres en el Formativo Medio se enterraban en proximidad a sus casas, y no en una sola zona especial como el cementerio San José, aunque ésto queda por comprobar.

El Capítulo VII trata sobre la ocupación en el Formativo Tardío (300 a.C.-100 a.C.), lo cual fué la fase de desarrollo máximo de Tomaltepec. En esta fase la zona central consistió de cuatro plataformas con un gran patio de estuco entre ellas. Es decir, la zona central era una unidad aparte de los otros componentes de la aldea.

El edificio principal se construyó encima de la plataforma Rosario/Monte Albán Ia. Se sabe poco de la forma de este edificio, pero al menos medía entre 15 y 20 metros oriente/poniente, y unos 10 a 15 metros norte/sur. La altura de la plataforma no era menor de 4 metros. Encima había una estructura con paredes de adobe. Esta estructura no se excavó suficientemente, debido al poco tiempo del que se disponía.

Al pie de la plataforma mayor se excavó una zona de residencias de más elevada posición social. Se encontraron dos plataformas bajas (unos 50 cm de altura) hechas de piedra y tierra. Había muros y escaleras de piedra y pisos de estuco de cal. Las dos plataformas formaban un ángulo recto, con un patio entre ellas. Cada plataforma medía aproximadamente 5 por 5 metros. Una de las plataformas no se encontró intacta, y la otra no se excavó completamente. Asociados con dichas plataformas se descubrieron hornos, pozos, y mucha basura doméstica, lo cual indica una función residencial. Construída dentro de una de las plataformas se descubrió una tumba con muros de adobe y una tapa de losas naturales de piedra. Las losas medían aproximadamente 100 cm por 20 cm por 5 cm. Encima y por debajo de las losas había 38 vasijas, y dentro de la tumba se encontraron los restos de tres personas: una mujer de unos 40 años, uno niño de unos 12 años, y otro adulto (posiblemente de sexo masculino, aunque el sexo no fue determinado con seguridad) de unos 40 ± 10 años. Aparte de unas tumbas del centro ceremonial de Monte Albán, esta tumba es una de las más elaboradas que se han encontrado en el Valle de Oaxaca. Este descubrimiento implica que hasta en las comunidades pequeñas existían familias de considerable importancia.

Al suroeste de montículo mayor se excavó una zona de actividad especial. Parece que dicha zona fué sitio de una unidad doméstica. Implica lo anterior la existencia de familias especializadas en actividades de artesanía. En una área de 8 por 8 metros, se descubrieron 12 pozos grandes, varios de los cuales (según la opinion de Flannery) pueden ser hornos de dos cámaras para hacer cerámica. Además, se encontraron dos entierros de adultos y un entierro de niño an esta área. Todos los entierros fueron contemporáneos (Monte Albán Ic). Había mucha basura doméstica de la misma fase en esta área.

Existen tres montículos más en la comunidad, pero desgraciadamente se sabe muy poco de ellos. Por los cortes pequeños que se hicieron, es evidente que los tres pertenecenal Formativo Tardío; es decir, son contemporáneos con el montículo mayor.

En términos de los conceptos de la Teoría General de Sistemas los cuales fueron introducidos en el Capítulo I, hemos visto la culminación de tres procesos de cambio en esta comunidad Formativa: (1) aumento del número de las partes de la sociedad; (2) aumento del nivel de diferenciación entre las partes; (3) aumento de especialización de función de las partes de la sociedad, especialmente la función administrativa del nivel superior de la comunidad.

El Capítulo VIII contiene una discusión de la decadencia de la comunidad en el Formativo Terminal (fase: Monte Albán II, 100 a.C-200 d.C). Es evidente que la población de la comunidad empezó a disminuir en esta época, y al principio de la fase siguiente (Monte Albán IIIa, al principio de la época Clásica), la comunidad quedó abandonada casi por completo.

No obstante, antes del fin de la fase Monte Albán II, se amplió la plataforma mayor a su tamaño máximo. También se construyó otro edificio encima de la plataforma mayor. Este edificio parece ser un templo de dos cuartos, perteneciendo a un tipo que se ha encontrado en las excavaciones de Monte Albán, Cuilapan, y San José Mogote.

En cuanto a casas ordinarias, se descubrieron los restos de una pequeña parte de una casa. La mayor parte de esta fue destruida, pero quedó suficiente como para distinguir su estructura y dos hornos asociados. Varias muestras arqueo-magnéticas le dan una fecha aproximade de 64 años d. de C., y es probable que esta representa la última ocupación Formativa de la zona. Parece ser que tanto la poblacíon como el nivel de complejidad de organizacioń disminuyeron mucho en esta última fase de ocupación.

El objeto del Capitulo IX es considerar el desarrollo Formativo en el Valle de Oaxaca, utilizando los datos arqueológicos de Tomaltepec y otras comunidades Formativas del Valle. Por cada periodo de la época Formativa en Oaxaca, se consideran los siguientes puntos: (1) variación en forma y función entre comunidades contemporáneas en partes diferentes del Valle de Oaxaca; (2) nivel de diferenciación social entre individuos y grupos de comunidades diferentes, y en partes diferentes del Valle; (3) tipos de relaciones que existían entre comunidades Formativas en distintas partes del Valle. Además, se considera el crecimiento del centro ceremonial-cívico de Monte Albán en términos de la estructura del Valle de Oaxaca en el Formativo Tardío y Terminal. Varios apéndices del estudio presentan aspectos especiales del análisis de los datos arqueológicos de Tomaltepec.